About Island Press

Island Press is the only nonprofit organization in the United States whose principal purpose is the publication of books on environmental issues and natural resource management. We provide solutions-oriented information to professionals, public officials, business and community leaders, and concerned citizens who are shaping responses to environmental problems.

In 2003, Island Press celebrates its nineteenth anniversary as the leading provider of timely and practical books that take a multidisciplinary approach to critical environmental concerns. Our growing list of titles reflects our commitment to bringing the best of an expanding body of literature to the environmental community throughout North America and the world.

Support for Island Press is provided by The Nathan Cummings Foundation, Geraldine R. Dodge Foundation, Doris Duke Charitable Foundation, Educational Foundation of America, The Charles Engelhard Foundation, The Ford Foundation, The George Gund Foundation, The Vira I. Heinz Endowment, The William and Flora Hewlett Foundation, Henry Luce Foundation, The John D. and Catherine T. MacArthur Foundation, The Andrew W. Mellon Foundation, The Moriah Fund, The Curtis and Edith Munson Foundation, National Fish and Wildlife Foundation, The New-Land Foundation, Oak Foundation, The Overbrook Foundation, The David and Lucile Packard Foundation, The Pew Charitable Trusts, The Rockefeller Foundation, The Winslow Foundation, and other generous donors.

The opinions expressed in this book are those of the author(s) and do not necessarily reflect the views of these foundations.

About the Natural Assets Project

The Natural Assets Project, based at the Political Economy Research Institute (PERI) of the University of Massachusetts, Amherst, is a collaborative initiative launched with support from the Ford Foundation. The project aims to promote critical analysis and discussion of the potential for building natural assets—individual and social wealth based on natural resources and ecosystem services—to advance the goals of poverty reduction, environmental protection, and environmental justice.

About the Political Economy Research Institute

The Political Economy Research Institute was founded at the University of Massachusetts, Amherst, in 1998. PERI's mission is to facilitate research, graduate education, and outreach in the area of policy-relevant political economy. To this end, PERI supports research by faculty and graduate students, provides visiting professorships and postdoctoral fellowships, organizes collaborative research projects, and holds workshops and conferences. The institute is committed to conducting and disseminating research to inform policy makers and grassroots activists who are trying to improve living standards and to create a more just, democratic, and ecologically sustainable world.

NATURAL ASSETS

Natural Assets

Democratizing Environmental Ownership

EDITED BY
JAMES K. BOYCE
BARRY G. SHELLEY

FOREWORD BY
MELVIN OLIVER

ISLAND PRESS
Washington • Covelo • London

Library of Congress Cataloging-in-Publication Data
Natural assets : democratizing environmental ownership / edited by James
K. Boyce and Barry G. Shelley (Natural Assets Project, Political Economy
Research Institute, University of Massachusetts, Amherst).
    p. cm.
Includes bibliographical references and index.
   ISBN 1-55963-538-X (alk. paper) — ISBN 1-55963-539-8 (pbk. : alk.
paper)
   1. Environmental justice. 2. Environmental protection. 3.
Conservation of natural resources. I. Boyce, James K. II. Shelley,
Barry G. III. University of Massachusetts at Amherst. Political Economy
Research Institute.
   GE220.N38 2003
   363.7—dc21

                                        2002155547

British Cataloguing-in-Publication Data available

Printed on recycled, acid-free paper

Manufactured in the United States of America
09 08 07 06 05 04 03   10 9 8 7 16 5 4 3 2 1

Contents

List of Figures and Tables

Figures

Tables

Foreword

Melvin Oliver

This book edited by James K. Boyce and Barry G. Shelley is the final volume in a series funded by the Ford Foundation. The series explores the strengths and policy relevance of the asset-building approach to poverty alleviation; at the same time, it points to areas in which the shortcomings of the approach may require further work. In this foreword, I would like to introduce the concepts embodied in the asset-building approach and describe how it is being incorporated into the grant making of the Ford Foundation.

In 1996 the Ford Foundation entered an era of new leadership. Susan Berresford succeeded Franklin Thomas as the foundation's president, and I became the vice president of a newly expanded program to advance the foundation's goal of reducing poverty and injustice. I was given the task of uniting within a single program all of the foundation's work on urban and rural poverty, sexual and reproductive health, and the environment and natural resources. After long consultation and much discussion with the foundation's staff in New York and in our thirteen international offices, we decided to organize our efforts around the theme of asset building. Reflecting on the work in which we had been engaged worldwide, we felt strongly that the most successful work—and the work most needed—is that which empowers the poor to acquire key human, social, financial, and natural assets. So empowered, the poor are better able, in turn, to reduce and prevent injustice.

The focus of the Ford Foundation's Asset Building and Community Development Program is a departure from the conventional wisdom, both within the foundation and in the broader development community, in several ways. Antipoverty policy in the United States and in international development programs worldwide has emphasized efforts to increase income to some predetermined minimum level as the "magic bullet" that will "solve" poverty problems. But that approach builds on the common misconception that poverty is simply a matter of low income or low levels of consumption. This emphasis on income ignores key causes of inequity, overlooks the consequences of low asset accumulation, and fails to address long-term stability and security for individuals, families, and communities.

Nobel laureate Amartya Sen foreshadowed an alternative approach in his 1985 Hennipman Lectures in Economics, and developed it further in his 1999 book *Development as Freedom*. For Sen, poverty is defined not by low income but by "capability deprivation," where capability refers to the whole range of civil and financial abilities or entitlements as well as to human development. Michael Sherraden reached similar conclusions in his pathbreaking 1991 work *Assets and the Poor*. Thomas Shapiro and I provided further support for the importance of asset building for urban poverty alleviation in the United States in our volume *Black Wealth/White Wealth* (1995). And Anthony Bebbington applied the approach to rural areas in his essay *Capitals and Capabilities* (1999).

An "asset" in this paradigm is a special kind of resource that an individual, organization, or entire community can use to reduce or prevent poverty and injustice. An asset is usually a "stock" that can be drawn upon, built upon, or developed, and that can be shared or transferred across generations. Assets are unevenly distributed in all societies, and their distribution is highly related to public policy decisions and cultural traditions that affect the ways in which society structures ownership and investments in assets. These structures often have excluded women and members of racial and ethnic minorities from asset-building activities. As the poor gain access to assets, they become better able to take control of important aspects of their lives, to plan for their future and deal with economic uncertainty, to support their children's educational achievements, and to work to ensure that the lives of the next generations are better than their own.

Over the last six years, the staff of the Ford Foundation's Assets Program has been reexamining its grant-making initiatives and asking hard-hitting questions about how they fit within an asset-building strategy. This evaluation has required careful analysis of the essential attributes of assets, the strategies needed to build them, and the methodology to assess progress in asset accumulation. We have tried to see how best we can support asset-building organizations and bring an assets perspective to the various fields of work we support in nonprofit and nongovernmental organizations.

As our colleagues among practitioners and policy makers have witnessed our struggle to develop the asset-building approach, they have become very enthusiastic about it. This approach, they note, avoids the traditional focus on the "deficits" or "deficiencies" of the poor and disempowered and does not treat them as impassive victims of external forces who are incapable of affecting their own future. It recognizes that injustice is as much a determinant of poverty as the vagaries of individual and community histories. The assets approach builds on the innate ability of all human beings to develop their skills and on the near-universal desire to create a better life for oneself and one's progeny. We found that some researchers are interested in advancing work on specific interventions to build assets, and thought that the paradigm and practice could be advanced further by a broad examination of asset-building concepts and strategies across a range of disciplines.

Bernard Wasow of the Assets Program's Community and Resource Development Unit developed a series of conferences to explore these themes. He sought to bring together researchers who are concerned with various types of asset development, even those who may not have been accustomed to calling it such. He invited them to explore:

- The state of current knowledge about the links between poverty and various kinds of assets;
- The policy implications of an asset-building approach, particularly with respect to improving support for poor people and communities;
- Further related research questions that will assist practitioners and polic makers in developing more effective strategies to reduce poverty and injustice.

The first conference led to the volume *Securing the Future: Investing in Children from Birth to College,* edited by Sheldon Danziger and Jane Waldfogel, published by the Russell Sage Foundation in 2000. Subsequent volumes included *Assets for the Poor: Spreading the Benefits of Asset Ownership,* edited by Thomas M. Shapiro and Edward N. Wolff, which focused on financial assets and poverty alleviation; and *Social Capital and Poor Communities,* edited by Susan Saegert, J. Philip Thompson, and Mark R. Warren, which explored how social capital assets can be used to aid the rebuilding and restoration of poor communities. The papers in the present volume were presented initially at a conference organized by James Boyce and Barry Shelley on building natural assets to reduce poverty, safeguard the environment, and increase environmental justice.

Each of these four conferences brought together some of the nation's most provocative academic thinkers and leading practitioners for what proved to be highly animated discussions of the topics at hand. Each conference provided foundation staff with important new insights into the links between asset building and the foundation's goals. We believe that these insights, as well as the new research themes identified, are now reflected in the work that we support. We hope that the volumes in this series will stimulate scholars, practitioners, and many other institutions worldwide to develop other approaches to reducing poverty and injustice.

This series represents one of many ways in which we at the Ford Foundation are encouraging discussion of the concepts that guide our grant making in the

Assets Program. We congratulate James Boyce and Barry Shelley for the excellent book they have produced. This volume stands out from the others in the way in which scholars and practitioners engage with one another's ideas, leading to a stimulating and provocative analysis of how natural assets can serve as the basis of enduring changes in the status of poor communities and individuals. We welcome further debate and commentary on these themes.

References

Bebbington, Anthony. 1999. *Capitals and Capabilities: A Framework for Analysing Peasant Viability, Rural Livelihoods and Poverty in the Andes.* London: International Institute for Environment and Development.

Danziger, Sheldon, and Jane Waldfogel, eds. 2000. *Securing the Future: Investing in Children from Birth to College.* New York: Russell Sage Foundation Press.

Oliver, Melvin L., and Thomas M. Shapiro. 1995. *Black Wealth/White Wealth: A New Perspective on Racial Inequality.* New York and London: Routledge.

Sen, Amartya K. 1999. *Commodities and Capabilities.* New York and London: Oxford University Press. (Originally published in 1985 as *Commodities and Capabilities: Professor Dr. P. Hennipman Lectures in Economics,* vol. 7 [London: Elsevier Science].)

————. 1999. *Development as Freedom.* New York: Alfred A. Knopf.

Saegert, Susan, J. Phillip Thompson, and Mark R. Warren, eds. 2001. *Social Capital and Poor Communities.* New York: Russell Sage Foundation Press.

Shapiro, Thomas, M., and Edward N. Wolff, eds. 2001. *Assets for the Poor: The Benefits of Spreading Asset Ownership.* New York: Russell Sage Foundation Press.

Sherraden, Michael. 1991. *Assets and the Poor: A New American Welfare Policy.* New York: M. E. Sharpe.

Acknowledgments

This book is an outcome of the Natural Assets Project, a collaborative research initiative based at the Political Economy Research Institute (PERI) of the University of Massachusetts, Amherst.

We are grateful to the Ford Foundation for funding the Natural Assets Project. We owe a special debt of gratitude to Michael Conroy, whose vision and commitment made this project possible.

Most of the essays published here were first presented at a conference in Santa Fe, New Mexico, in January 2000. For thoughtful comments and suggestions, we wish to thank the conference participants, including the late Anil Agarwal, Robert Bullard, Amy Glasmeier, Greg Hicks, Donna House, Owen Lopez, Vernice Miller-Travis, Sunita Narain, Penny Newman, Melvin Oliver, Jeff Olsen, Florence Robinson, Bob Stark, and Steve Viederman.

In preparing the manuscript for publication, we received valuable editorial assistance from Rachel Bouvier, Rob Fetter, Karen Graubart, Susan Harris, and Susan Schacht. We also thank Todd Baldwin at Island Press for his enthusiasm and editorial suggestions.

We thank our partners, Betsy Hartmann and Brenda Wyss, and our families for their constant support and encouragement.

Finally, we want to acknowledge the inspiration provided by the many people, across the country and around the world, who are demonstrating in their work and daily lives that poverty reduction, environmental protection, and environmental justice can and must go together.

J. K. B.
B. G. S.
Amherst, Massachusetts
March 2003

Introduction

This book explores avenues to reduce poverty and protect the environment by building natural assets. These assets include sources of raw materials as well as environmental "sinks" where waste products from the economy are absorbed and decomposed. Drawing on evidence from urban and rural areas across the United States, the contributors to this volume demonstrate that safeguarding the environment and improving the well-being of the poor are mutually reinforcing goals.

This proposition represents a sharp break from the conventional view that these goals are inherently contradictory and that we must trade progress on one front for progress on the other. For example, both advocates and opponents of stronger environmental protection often assume that poverty reduction and environmental protection are at best unrelated objectives and at worst incompatible ones. Poverty reduction requires some combination of economic growth and economic redistribution. The conventional wisdom holds that the former inevitably sacrifices environmental quality, whereas the latter would shift resources to people who are more concerned with day-to-day survival than with safeguarding the environment.

The essays in this book propose a radically different view: that poverty reduction and environmental protection can be advanced simultaneously. Indeed, we believe that both goals not only *can* go together, but *must* go together. One reason is obvious: sustainable advances in human well-being and reductions in poverty are undermined by environmental degradation. The second reason is perhaps less apparent, but no less important: environmental quality is undermined by large disparities of wealth and power.

Assets and Nature

Nature provides the indispensable foundation for the economy as the *source* of our raw materials—food, fiber, water, energy, and minerals—and as the *sink* for wastes generated by production and consumption. In this broad sense, natural assets are the stock of wealth on which human lives and livelihoods ultimately depend. The term *asset* implies not only the existence of wealth, however, but also a set of rules and institutions that govern access to this wealth and the distribution of the benefits derived from it. Resources are things; assets are relationships between things and people.

A variety of rules and institutions govern access to natural assets. These include private property owned by individuals and firms; public property owned by governments; common property held formally or informally by groups; and "open access" in which the resource is, in theory, available to anyone and everyone. These arrangements are not fixed or immutable but change over time, reflecting changes in technologies, preferences, and the distribution of power in our society.

Changes in the amount of assets, their distribution, and the social arrangements that govern access to them are interwoven. The enclosures of common lands in eighteenth-century Britain, for example, involved not only a shift from common property to private ownership but also the redistribution of access rights from poor commoners to wealthy landlords. Similarly, the struggles of low-income communities today to curb pollution from industrial facilities near their homes represent an effort not only to increase the amount of clean air and clean water but also to redistribute rights from the polluters to the people who breathe the air and drink the water.

Building Natural Assets

The essays in this book describe a range of strategies for expanding the quantity and enhancing the quality of natural assets held by low-income individuals and communities and evaluate their potential to reduce poverty and protect the environment. Greater access to natural resources and greater control over environmental sinks can be achieved in two broad ways: by increases in the total stock of society's natural assets and by redistribution of the existing stock so as to increase the share of the poor.

There are two avenues for increasing the total stock of natural assets, or what economists term "investment in natural capital." The first is *ecological restoration,* steps to repair environmental damages inflicted by economic activities in the past. Examples of ecological restoration include reforestation, soil and water conservation, and the cleanup of polluted waterways and contaminated lands. Because such investments simply seek to reverse past depreciation of natural capital, their potential scope is limited by the extent of past environmental degradation.

The second avenue is *coevolution,* whereby human interactions with the environment add to nature's wealth. A prime example is the domestication of plants and animals that began some ten thousand years ago, and the subsequent evolution of the rich agricultural biodiversity on which human sustenance depends today. Coevolution demonstrates that the human impacts on the environment are not always negative, nor are positive impacts necessarily limited to the repair of past damages. Our activities can also enhance nature's long-term capacity to sustain humankind.

Redistribution of access to natural assets also can occur via several avenues. When property rights to natural assets are already intensively defined, redistribution requires reallocations of rights, or of some of the "sticks" in the bundle of rights pertaining to a given asset, from prior owners to new owners. When the poor already manage natural assets, and in doing so can create "positive externalities" for others in the form of ecological services—such as the conservation of crop genetic diversity or watershed management—policies to "internalize" some of these benefits can raise the incomes of the poor and at the same time bolster their incentives to continue providing these services. When natural assets are currently treated as open-access resources, available in principle to all but in practice to those with the power to seize them, the appropriation of these resources on a democratic basis can be an effective way to redistribute their benefits.

The environmental justice movement exemplifies the appropriation route to building natural assets. This grassroots movement has arisen in recent years in response to the disproportionate risks from pollution and other environmental hazards that are often faced by low-income communities in general and by people of color in particular. Its guiding principle is the proposition that all people are endowed with the right to a clean and safe environment. Rather than the parochial slogan, "not in my backyard," the environmental justice movement espouses the broader goal, "not in *anybody's* backyard." Insofar as pollution and hazards cannot be eliminated altogether, the movement demands that their burdens be distributed fairly. In effect, environmental justice seeks the egalitarian appropriation of rights to airsheds and water bodies that were previously treated as open-access environmental sinks.

As this example illustrates, the phrase "natural assets" does not imply that the environment simply can be commodified, or reduced to purely monetary values to be exchanged in markets. Similarly, the phrase "environmental ownership" does not imply unbridled license to use or abuse natural resources. Assets can be owned by communities and the public, as well as by individuals. And ownership entails responsibilities to others as well as rights. The essays in this book do not give a blanket endorsement to any single form of environmental ownership—private property, common property, state property, or open access. Nor do they axiomatically embrace either market-based incentives or government regulation as the best way to protect the environment. Instead the authors propose a variety of institutional arrangements tailored to different circumstances, and they suggest that the quality of the outcomes will depend above all on the degree to which these arrangements are grounded in a democratic distribution of wealth and power.

Plan of the Volume

The book is divided into five parts.

Part 1, "The Wealth of Nature," discusses the importance of natural assets to human well-being and examines the social construction of rights to natural resources and the environment.

Part 2, "Reclaiming Environmental Sinks," examines efforts to curtail the pollution of the air, lands, and water bodies that serve as sinks for the disposal of wastes from production and consumption. Across the United States, struggles for environmental justice are seeking to reclaim environmental resources that have been appropriated and misused by polluters. These creative and dynamic initiatives offer important lessons for natural-asset-building strategies.

Part 3, "Cultivating Natural Capital," challenges the conventional assumption that human economic activities inexorably degrade the natural environment. The essays in this part show that sustainable agricultural practices not only can sustain but also can enhance the stock of natural capital. At the same time, the authors document the formidable threats that are now undermining such practices.

Part 4, "Out of the Woods," documents the range of social benefits that forests provide and explores strategies to expand the rights of forest-dependent communities to public and private forestlands so as to foster sustainable forest management and reduce rural poverty.

Finally, Part 5, "Greening the Cities," considers the prospects for building natural assets in the urban areas where most Americans today live and work. The greening of the cities includes not only the cleanup of environmental sinks, already discussed in Part 2, but also natural-resource-based development strategies that aim to reduce urban poverty and improve environmental quality.

The essays in this volume demonstrate that poverty reduction and environmental protection can indeed go hand in hand, and they suggest that these goals are not only compatible but mutually reinforcing. Yet the authors also make it clear that strategies to build natural assets are still at an early stage, with much scope for further innovation, refinement, and diffusion. We hope that this book will help to stimulate creative thinking and debate about how best to deepen democracy and secure a sustainable future for the generations who will follow us.

PART I

THE WEALTH OF NATURE

The two chapters in Part 1 set the stage for those that follow by discussing how societies transform nature into wealth. The rules and institutions that transform natural resources into natural assets shape a society's answer to the classic economic question of how to allocate scarce resources among competing ends. At the same time, they shape the answer to the central question of political economy: how to allocate resources among competing individuals, groups, and classes.

James Boyce identifies four routes for building natural assets held by the poor. The first route is *investment:* increases in the total stock of natural capital. For example, soil and water conservation projects can enhance the value of farms or forestlands owned by low-income individuals and communities. This route is most feasible when the poor already own some natural assets, the quality or quantity of which can be increased via ecological restoration or coevolution.

The second route is *redistribution:* the transfer of rights to natural assets from others to the poor. Land reform, a central feature of the postwar development strategies in East Asia, is a prime example of this route. In addition to outright transfers of ownership titles, redistribution can involve subsets of rights—such as the right to participate in land-use decisions and the right to share in employment opportunities or other benefits derived from the use of natural resources—making this route feasible in a range of settings.

The third route, *internalization,* arises when the poor own natural assets that generate benefits to others in the form of "positive externalities." Farmers who conserve agricultural biodiversity or forestland owners whose land-use practices regulate waterflows downstream generally receive no compensation for these services. Policies to reward them could improve their well-being and, at the same time, provide incentives for sound ecological stewardship.

The fourth route, *appropriation,* is relevant when nature's wealth is being treated as an open-access resource, as in the case of airsheds and water bodies that serve as environmental sinks. Efforts by citizens to curtail pollution—in effect, transforming the air and water into *their* air and water—seek to appropriate rights to these natural assets. This approach can yield significant benefits not only in the form of better health and environmental amenities but also in the form of income if polluters are required to pay for their use of commonly-owned environmental sinks.

All four routes raise issues of how rights to natural assets are defined and allocated. As Gerald Friedman recounts, American law and jurisprudence have grappled with these issues since the birth of the Republic. Throughout U.S. history, property has been reconfigured in response to competing private claims and interests and changing conceptions of the public good. Further reconfigurations of rights to natural assets to advance the goals of environmental protection and poverty reduction would follow in this democratic tradition.

CHAPTER 1

From Natural Resources to Natural Assets

James K. Boyce

Natural assets are the myriad forms of wealth that nature creates. They include the land on which we live and grow our food and fiber; the water we drink and use to irrigate crops, generate electricity, and dispose of wastes; the atmosphere that envelops our planet; the fish in the ocean, the trees in the forest, and all other animals and plants, wild and domesticated; ores, minerals, and fossil fuels; and the energy of the sun, which powers the biosphere. Human well-being and survival itself ultimately depend on natural assets.

Nature sustains human livelihoods in two fundamental ways. First, it provides the raw materials needed to produce goods and services. Second, it serves as an "environmental sink" for disposal of the wastes our production and consumption generate. Human activities often diminish both kinds of natural assets: we have depleted nature's sources and overfilled nature's sinks.

But humans can also invest in natural assets to increase their quantity and quality. One avenue for such investment is "ecological restoration," which includes such measures as reforestation, the replenishment of fisheries, and the cleanup of polluted land and water. These activities increase natural assets by repairing some of the damage inflicted by past environmental abuses. Another avenue is human engagement in the web of life: the coevolutionary processes that constantly shape and reshape the living world. From the standpoint of human well-being, perhaps the most important example of coevolution is the domestication of rice, wheat, maize, and other crops, which began roughly four hundred human generations ago, and the subsequent development of the many thousands of diverse varieties of these crops that farmers around the world cultivate today.

Natural Assets and Human Well-Being

Although natural resources are the common heritage of humankind, access to them is filtered through human institutions. Resources become assets only when people have rights to them. As with other kinds of assets, some people typically possess more natural assets than others. The resulting imbalances in distribution have long stimulated social struggles, and in recent decades they have fueled popular movements and helped to create public policies for environmental protection and environmental justice. Environmental protection seeks to maintain the quality and quantity of natural assets for present and future generations: it promotes intergenerational equity. Environmental justice promotes equity within the current generation, by demanding that natural assets—in particular, access to clean air and water—be distributed fairly.

Some people hold that these environmental aspirations are at odds with another central social goal: poverty reduction. They claim that the poor face a grim but inescapable choice between higher income and a better environment. This book challenges that belief. We maintain that strategies for increasing the natural assets held by low-income individuals and communities can simultaneously advance the goals of poverty reduction, environmental protection, and environmental justice.

Poverty is not simply a lack of income today but also a lack of assets that will yield income and other benefits tomorrow. This insight is the starting point for the asset-based approach to poverty reduction. Michael Sherraden (1991) and Melvin Oliver and Thomas Shapiro (1995) applied this approach to financial assets and real estate. More recently, it has been applied to "human capital" in the form of health and education and to "social capital" in the form of community organizations and the bonds of trust that underpin cooperation.[1] Natural assets, too, can play an important role in poverty reduction.

Asset-based strategies for reducing poverty have two compelling advantages over conventional income-based strategies. First, income transfers offer only temporary relief from poverty: unless today's income is followed by more tomorrow, the impact of such transfers is transitory. Assets generate income now and in the future, offering a long-term escape from poverty rather than a mere reprieve. Second, assets are a source of leverage, enabling their owners to gain indirect benefits above and beyond those inherent in the asset itself. Examples of indirect benefits include more favorable access to credit markets and greater social standing and power. As Oliver and Shapiro (1995, 32) remark, "Income supplies the necessities of life, while wealth represents a kind of 'surplus' resource available for improving life chances, providing further opportunities, securing prestige, passing status along to one's family, and influencing the political process."

Building natural assets can, and often does, go hand in hand with building other types of assets. For example, Manuel Pastor reports in Chapter 4 that toxic waste facilities in metropolitan Los Angeles are disproportionately located in poor and predominantly minority communities that are experiencing "ethnic churning," with new minorities moving in as others move out. The reason, he suggests, is that stable communities are richer in social capital—informal networks as well as formal community organizations—and hence are better able to resist the siting of hazardous facilities in their midst.

Just as social capital can help to build natural assets, successful efforts to build natural assets can strengthen a community's social capital. A movement to resist the imposition of toxic facilities may set the stage for other community-based campaigns, such as demands for better schools, housing, and public services. In Chelsea, Massachusetts, for example, local efforts to access and restore the riverfront have helped spark the rise of community organizations. Patricia Hynes writes about these efforts in Chapter 15.

Several features distinguish natural assets from financial wealth and real estate. First, the benefits that flow from access to natural assets include not only income but also such crucial non-income benefits as health and environmental quality. Poverty in these dimensions of well-being can be as detrimental as low income. Natural assets share this feature with other types of unconventional assets—including education and community organizations—that also contribute to the non-income dimensions of well-being.

Second, the principle that every person has an equal right to natural assets is widely appealing. Two centuries ago, the revolutionary democrat Thomas Paine (1796) declared that land is "the free gift of the Creator in common to the human race." He proposed that the income from leasing land for individual use should be distributed equitably among all citizens. In a similar vein, many people would agree with the proposition that rights to the air we breathe should be distributed equally. To be sure, public policies in the United States and elsewhere have often granted rights to natural resources and environmental services to the first party that finds a way to seize them. Yet the principle of equal rights to common-heritage resources remains a powerful ideal.

Finally, rights to natural resources are often imprecisely defined. Natural assets are held in a great variety of ways. Individuals or firms own some resources as private property; communities hold some as common property; and governments hold some as public property. In addition, some are open-access resources, owned by no one and available in theory to all, but available in practice only to those with the power to appropriate them. The "bundle of sticks" that constitutes the set of property rights to a given natural asset is often divided among different parties. For example, a farmer may own the surface rights to a tract of land and a coal company may hold rights to the minerals

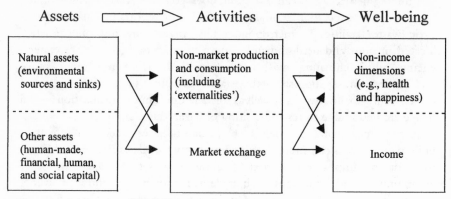

Figure 1.1. Assets and Well-Being.

beneath it, while the air above it is an open-access resource.[2] Many sticks in the property-rights bundle lie somewhere between the polar cases of perfectly defined rights and perfectly unrestricted open access. Do downstream water users, for example, deserve redress if the activities of an upstream landowner decrease the quantity or quality of water available to them? Do government regulations to protect the watershed infringe on the constitutional guarantee that private property shall not be "taken for public use, without just compensation"? The answers to such questions have changed over time, and as rights to natural resources are defined and redefined, the natural assets of the poor can expand—or shrink.

Rethinking the Environment and the Economy

Long before the rise of market economies, people relied on assets for their livelihoods and well-being. Even today, when markets mediate our access to many goods and services, much that is vital to our quality of life remains outside the sphere of market exchange. The nexus linking the various types of assets to the various dimensions of human well-being include non-market activities as well as market exchanges (see Figure 1.1).

Humans versus Nature?

Environmental debates in the United States have often pitted proponents of wilderness preservation against proponents of "rational use." Preservationists typically base their case on the linkages shown in the top half of Figure 1.1. They stress the importance of natural assets, nonmarket activities, and the non-income dimensions of human well-being. The deep-ecology variant of the preservationist school goes further, arguing that the "rights of nature" should trump human well-being as the ethical basis for public policy (Nash 1990). Advocates of rational use typically base their case on the linkages shown in the bottom half of Figure 1.1. They are inclined to see the market as the measure of all things. The libertarian variant of the rational-use school argues not only that free markets maximize well-being but that the individual's "freedom to choose" should be the overriding social goal (Friedman and Friedman 1980).

Notwithstanding their profound and often acrimonious differences, both sides in this debate share certain premises. Both juxtapose nature to humans and the environment to the economy, differing only in which side they favor and think will ultimately prevail. The preservationists believe that in the absence of strict controls, the magnitude of adverse human impacts on the environment will overwhelm nature's capacity to renew resources and assimilate wastes. The proponents of market rationality believe that human ingenuity, guided by price signals, will find a way around environmental constraints. Both sides typically show little concern for the poor. In the preservationist paradigm, the poor are to be fenced out of nature lest they trample upon it; in the greed-as-virtue paradigm, the poor are simply consigned to their free-market fates.

This book offers an alternative vision, one in which humans are not apart from nature but a part of it. Since at least the advent of agriculture, we humans have shaped and reshaped our environment. "Nature," as William Cronon (1995, 25) remarks, "is not nearly so natural as it seems." Human activity does not invariably have a negative impact on the environment. Humans certainly can degrade the environment, but they can also improve it by investing in natural capital. Furthermore, the poor—when they have access to natural resources—often play key roles in making and maintaining such investments.

The acequia communities of the Upper Rio Grande watershed, which Devon Peña describes in Chapter 9, provide a striking example. As long ago as the 1500s, Hispanic farmers constructed gravity-flow irrigation channels (acequias) in what is now northern New Mexico and transformed arid lands into a rich, biologically diverse agricultural ecosystem. Today these acequias are maintained by their descendants, who thereby provide environmental services, including soil conservation, water filtration and retention, preservation of habitats for wild animals and plants, and conservation of crop genetic diversity. Rather than being shortsighted despoilers of nature, humans are, in Peña's words, the "keystone species" of this ecosystem. Human activity produced a new landscape, and continued human engagement is required to sustain it.

Winners versus Losers

The humans-versus-nature dichotomy not only ignores the potential for people to invest in natural assets but also diverts our gaze from the contests *among* people that are crucial to the dynamics of pollution and resource depletion. Environmentally degrading economic activities create winners as well as losers. The winners are those who benefit as producers or consumers by "externalizing" costs; that is, by imposing costs on others from whom they are distanced by time, place, or income. The losers are those who bear the costs of depleted resources and a polluted environment. Without the winners, environmental degradation would not occur. Without the losers, there would be no reason to worry about it from the standpoint of human well-being.

To grasp the causes of environmental degradation—and to understand why it is more prevalent in some times and places than in others—we must ask *why* the winners are able to impose environmental costs on the losers. There are three possible reasons:

- First, the losers may not yet exist: they belong to future generations who are not here to defend themselves. In these cases, the only feasible solution is to nurture an intergenerational ethic of gratitude toward those who preceded us and of responsibility toward those who will follow us.
- Second, the losers may exist but be unaware of their position: they lack information about environmental impacts and hence do not try to defend themselves. These cases underscore the importance of environmental research and education in general and of right-to-know legislation in particular.
- Finally, the losers may exist and know they are losers, but lack the power to prevent the winners from imposing costs upon them. In such cases, the extent of pollution and resource depletion is shaped by the distribution of power: the greater the power of the winners vis-à-vis the losers, the greater the extent of environmental degradation. Hence a solution requires a more equitable distribution of power (Boyce 1994).

Empirical evidence suggests that this third explanation—power disparities between winners and losers—is relevant in many cases. In the United States, the states with greater inequalities of power (as measured by an index derived from data on voter participation, tax fairness, Medicaid access, and the percentage of adults with a high school education) tend to have weaker environmental policies, higher environmental stress, and worse public health (Boyce et al. 1999). Internationally, countries with more equal income distribution, greater political rights and civil liberties, and higher adult literacy—indicators of a more equitable distribution of power—tend to have less air pollution, less water pollution, and wider access to clean drinking water and sanitation facilities (Torras and Boyce 1998).

Links between Asset-Building and Environmental Protection

Strategies that expand the natural asset base of the poor can further the goal of environmental protection in several ways. First, given the correlation between wealth and power, any strategy that increases the assets—natural or otherwise—of the poor will tend to improve their ability to resist having environmental costs imposed on them by others. As Manuel Pastor discusses in Chapter 4 and Nicolaas Bouwes, Steven Hassur, and Marc Shapiro document in Chapter 6, low-income and minority communities in the United States often face disproportionate environmental burdens (see also Bullard 1990, 1994; and Brooks and Sethi 1997). In effect, as Paul Templet observes in Chapter 5, the poor subsidize corporate polluters by allowing them to avoid the costs of pollution control. Strengthening the power of communities to combat these perverse subsidies is one of the ways in which natural-asset building can further the goal of environmental protection.

A second link between asset ownership and environmental protection operates via the effects of asset distribution on the economic valuation of the environment. Research by economists and psychologists has shown that valuations based on people's willingness to *accept* compensation for environmental damage typically exceed those based on their willingness to *pay* to prevent the same damage. For example, when people are asked how much they would have to be paid to agree to breathe dirty air, they typically name a higher price than they do when asked how much they would be willing to pay to breathe clean air. The difference rests on the implicit assignments of property rights. In the first case, the people have the right to clean air; they can impose charges on would-be polluters. In the second case, the polluters have the right to foul the air; the public must bribe them to limit pollution. The resulting valuations differ for two main reasons. First, willingness to pay is constrained by ability to pay, whereas willingness to accept payment is not. Second, ownership of a natural resource often instills a greater sense of moral responsibility to safeguard it.[3] This means that the amount a society is prepared to spend for environmental protection hinges, in part, on the distribution of natural assets and other wealth. Even if social decisions about environmental protection were thoroughly insulated from the effects of power disparities between winners and losers—and were guided instead solely by the "efficiency" criterion of comparing benefits to costs—increasing the natural assets held by the poor would help to protect the environment by raising the economic valuation of the benefits.[4]

A third link results from the impact of asset ownership on what economists term the "real cost of labor." From brownfields redevelopment and urban agriculture to sustainable forest management and the conservation of crop genetic diversity, labor is often a key part of investments in natural capital.[5] The supply of labor tends to be higher—or, put differently, its cost tends to be lower—when people work for themselves rather than for others. One reason is that many people prefer to be their own bosses. Another is that when people work for themselves there is no need to spend money on supervision to make them work harder (Sen 2000). This labor-cost advantage helps to explain why family farming remains widespread in the United States and other industrialized countries and why, worldwide, small farms tend to yield more output per acre than large farms.[6] Likewise, we can expect that more labor will be invested in restoring and building natural assets when these assets are owned by those who provide the labor than when wage labor must be hired for this purpose.

A final connection between asset ownership and environmental protection arises from the importance of local knowledge. The members of local communities often have specialized knowledge about the characteristics and use of natural resources, as illustrated by Devon Peña's description of the acequia farmers of the Upper Rio Grande Valley in Chapter 9, by Stephen Brush's account of the role of small farmers in conserving genetic diversity in Chapter 10, and by Constance Best's discussion of forestry stewardship in Chapter 11. Yet the poor often lack the rights that would enable them to apply this knowledge to managing a sustainable environment. By bridging the gap between rights and knowledge, putting natural assets in the hands of the poor can contribute to environmental quality.

In each of these respects, how we relate to one another has a profound effect on how we relate to the environment. When wealth and power are concentrated in the hands of a few, the ability of the powerful to impose environmental costs on others is greater than when wealth and power are distributed more democratically. Insofar as social decisions are guided by considerations of "efficiency," deep inequalities of wealth and power further undermine environmental protection by reducing the supposed "economic value" of its benefits to the poor. And insofar as the labor and knowledge of the poor are important for investment in natural capital, strategies to expand the rights of the poor to natural assets will foster environmental stewardship.

Building Natural Assets

There are four main routes to increasing the amount and value of natural assets held by the poor: (1) *investment*, creating new natural capital or improving the natural capital to which the poor already have access; (2) *redistribution*, transferring natural capital from the wealthy to the poor; (3) *internalization*, increasing the ability of the poor to capture benefits flowing from natural capital they already own; and (4) *appropriation*, establishing the rights of the poor to environmental sinks and raw materials that previously were treated as open-access resources (see Table 1.1). The first two routes, investment and redistribution, are applicable to many other types of assets; the latter two, internalization and appropriation, are based on special features of certain natural assets.

Table 1.1. Routes to Natural-Asset Building

Route	Definition	Examples
Investment	The creation of new natural capital or the increase of existing natural capital.	Incentives for soil conservation directed to small farmers.
Redistribution	The transfer of natural capital, or some use rights to natural capital, from others.	The granting of the power of eminent domain over vacant lots in inner cities to community organizations.
Internalization	The provision of compensation for previously uncompensated benefits to others that flow from a person's stewardship of natural assets.	Rewarding small farmers for their role in the conservation of crop genetic diversity or small forest owners for their role in watershed management.
Appropriation	The establishment of rights to what previously have been open-access resources.	The mobilization of communities to combat industrial pollution of the air they breathe and the water they drink.

Investment

In recent years, the dismal notion that human activity inexorably depreciates natural capital—our only choice being how rapidly to do so—has been giving way to a more positive vision, founded on the recognition that humans can invest in natural capital (see, for example, Jansson et al. 1994). Such investment offers a route to expand the natural-asset base of the poor. This route is particularly relevant in cases where the poor already own or have access to natural assets whose quantity and quality can be increased.

An example is the case of farmlands owned by poor people. Historically, the soil and water conservation programs of the U.S. Department of Agriculture, which aim to support investments in natural capital, often have discriminated against low-income farmers in general and people of color in particular (Mittal 2000). If this pattern were reversed—if government support were preferentially directed to poor and minority farmers, instead of away from them—such programs could form part of a natural-asset-building strategy for reducing rural poverty by increasing the quality of lands the poor already own. More generally, many of the world's poor suffer from "ecological poverty," in which their livelihoods are constrained by the impoverishment of the natural resources on which they rely. In such settings, ecological restoration can go hand in hand with poverty reduction (Agarwal and Narain 2000).

Politically, investment is likely to be the least controversial route to natural-asset building because it adds to the stock of natural capital without impinging directly on the rights of others. The poor obtain assets as the total asset pie grows, but no one else loses assets they already have. In this respect, such a progressive investment strategy is akin to the "redistribution with growth" strategy advocated by reform-minded economists at the World Bank in the

1970s. The strategy assumed that redistribution of the existing national income
pie was politically infeasible and instead sought to channel increments from an
expanding pie into the hands of the poor (Chenery et al. 1974). The investment route to natural-asset building applies this logic to stocks of assets rather
than to flows of income.

Redistribution

Redistribution is a second route to increasing the stock of assets held by
the poor. In the case of natural capital, this route is particularly relevant to non-
renewable resources such as land and minerals, the supply of which cannot
be increased by investment. We can expect asset redistribution to be more
controversial than progressive strategies for investment. But when inequalities
in asset ownership are great, redistribution can offer the single most effective
way to build the asset base of the poor. As Oliver and Shapiro (1995, 9) remark:

> Our analysis clearly suggests the need for massive redistributional
> policies in order to reforge the links between achievement, reward,
> social equality, and democracy. These policies must take aim at the
> gross inequality generated by those at the very top of the wealth
> distribution. Policies of this type are the most difficult ones on
> which to gain consensus but the most important in creating a
> more just society.

Land reform—the transfer of rights from large landowners to tenant farmers
and landless laborers—is the best-known example of redistribution-led natural-
asset building. Land reform was a key element in the successful post–World War
II economic development strategies of such countries as China, Taiwan, and
Korea. The potential for redistribution, however, is not limited to the agricultural sectors of developing countries. In inner-city Boston, the Dudley Street
Neighborhood Initiative won the power of eminent domain in the course of a
struggle for community-based redevelopment of vacant lots. This example of
urban land reform is recounted by Greg Watson in Chapter 14.

In the bundle of sticks that constitutes the rights to a property, redistribution can involve specific sticks rather than the whole bundle. Land reforms,
for example, can give tenants "occupancy rights"—the right to till the land,
without threat of eviction, in return for a legally specified share of the
crop—rather than full title to the land. In Chapter 3, K. A. Dixon discusses
brownfields redevelopment cases in which local communities have won
certain rights—such as the right to participate in land-use decisions or to
share in employment opportunities—without taking outright ownership of
redeveloped land. In Chapter 13, Cecilia Danks considers the potential for
redistributing employment to reduce poverty in communities that are

dependent on publicly owned forests. In effect, the right to employment can serve as a vehicle for access to income from natural assets.

Internalization *of positive externals.*

When the poor own natural assets that generate benefits to others, for which they currently receive no reward, internalization offers another route to asset-building. For example, small farmers around the world who sustain crop genetic diversity play a key role in long-term world food security by providing the raw material for adaptations to new pests, plant diseases, and climate changes. Yet the farmers who perform this vital service today receive no compensation for doing so. In the language of economics, they generate "positive externalities" for others. As Stephen Brush suggests in Chapter 10, policies to reward farmers for this service—that is, to internalize some of the benefits that flow from their management of natural assets—could help both to reduce poverty and to safeguard invaluable biological resources.

Similarly, farmers and forest owners in watersheds that serve metropolitan areas provide an ecological service by regulating the quantity and quality of water that flows from their land. In effect, they are engaged in two forms of production: the production of crops, livestock, and timber, for which they are compensated by the market; and the production of water, for which they are not compensated. In some cases, the value of the latter exceeds that of the former. Devon Peña reports, for example, that the value of the ecological services provided by the "anthropogenic wetlands" of acequia farmers in the Upper Rio Grande bioregion is comparable to the value of their agricultural produce. In Chapter 11, Constance Best reports that the value of carbon sequestration services provided by forests can exceed their value as timber. Again, mechanisms to reward cash-poor farmers and forest owners for providing these ecological services could help to reduce poverty and create incentives to keep providing them.

In pursuing internalization strategies, several key issues arise: Who will finance payments for ecological services? How will compensation be delivered, with what mix of individual and community rewards? To what extent should compensation mechanisms preferentially benefit the poor, rather than simply rewarding all providers of ecological services regardless of their wealth or income? Finally, insofar as the internalization of benefits increases the market value of the natural assets, how can the poor defend these assets from others who might seek to wrest control of them? If these issues are properly resolved, internalization can be a promising route for natural-asset building, because the assets in question are already in the hands of the poor and a compelling case based on efficiency can be made for internalizing environmental externalities.

Appropriation

Appropriation, the final route to natural-asset building, pertains specifically to open-access resources. These resources are nobody's property, and so they are vulnerable to overuse in what Garrett Hardin (1968) termed the "tragedy of the commons." The classic case is an open-entry grazing commons, where each livestock owner gets the full benefit of grazing his animals, while bearing only a small fraction of the cost of thereby reducing the forage available to all. In the absence of either government regulation or privatization, overgrazing is the predictable result. Research by such scholars as Elinor Ostrom (1990) has drawn attention to a third possible solution, based on the difference between an open-access commons and property owned in common. Throughout the world, we find common-property regimes with informal but effective rules that have supported the sustained joint use of such natural resources as grazing lands, forests, and fisheries. Instead of the "tragedy of the commons," therefore, it is more precise to speak of the "tragedy of open access."

In practice, open access often leads to another tragedy as well: the appropriation of natural resources by the powerful at the expense of the powerless. In theory, open-access resources are freely available to all, yet in practice open access can be quite inequitable. In the scramble for "free" natural resources, some people are more equal than others. In open-access fisheries, for example, the advantage goes to those who can field the most efficient—or ruthless— extractive fishing technologies. In the case of environmental sinks, everyone may have the same right to pollute the airsheds, lands, and bodies of water into which we discard wastes, but not all have equal means to do so. The law that prescribes the same penalty for anyone who steals a loaf of bread—whether the thief is a starving mother or a millionaire—is a hollow form of equality. So too is the fact that a poor family living near a chemical factory has the same right to pollute the air as the factory's owners.

The democratic appropriation of rights to open-access natural resources could address both tragedies. In Chapter 7, for example, Peter Barnes and Marc Breslow propose to establish a "sky trust" funded by fees on carbon emissions, with the revenues disbursed equally to every person in the United States. The environmental goal is to reduce the burning of fossil fuels and the threat of global warming by charging rent for airborne carbon storage, at present an open-access resource. Lower-income households, which generally consume less of everything, including fossil fuels, would pay less into the fund than upper-income households; but all would receive the same payout per person. With the fees calibrated to cut carbon emissions enough to meet the targets in the Kyoto global climate accord, the effect of the sky trust would be to increase the net incomes of the poorest 10 percent of families by about 5 percent, while reducing those of the richest 10 percent by slightly less than 1 percent. The majority of U.S. households would receive more in dividends than they would pay in higher fuel prices.

Community struggles against toxic pollution offer another example of natural-asset building via the appropriation route. Communities are claiming the right to protect airsheds and bodies of water that have been treated in the past as open-access environmental sinks. Indeed, the right to live in a clean and healthy environment—a right increasingly affirmed in state constitutions and judicial decisions throughout the world (Popovic 1996, Boyce 2000)—implies a radically egalitarian distribution of rights to this subset of natural assets. Insofar as communities are able to secure these rights, they strengthen their bargaining positions with would-be polluters. The benefits from this type of community-based natural-asset building include better health, improved environmental quality, and higher property values.

In theory, communities could also gain income as compensation for any pollution they are willing to accept within the bounds set by environmental regulations. Such compensation—an application of the "polluter pays" principle—would not imply that regulatory agencies should relax pollution standards. Rather it is based on the principle that as owners of their environment, communities have a right to compensation for pollution within the legal limits.

The four routes to natural-asset building often overlap in practice. Forest stewardship, for example, can combine the internalization of benefits generated by forest ecosystems with new investment in watershed management. Brownfields redevelopment can combine the appropriation of the right to a clean environment, the redistribution of property rights from absentee landowners to community-based organizations, and investments in cleanup and new development. Alone or in combination, these routes can expand the natural-asset base of the poor, increasing their access to the income and nonincome benefits that flow from natural resources.

Democratizing Environmental Ownership

Natural-asset-building strategies must be consonant with a society's political economy and its ideas of normative justice. In the United States, a long tradition in political thought holds that property rights and democracy go hand in hand. Democracy prevents a political elite from usurping citizens' property rights; widely dispersed property ownership protects democracy against subordination to an economic elite. This relationship rests on an egalitarian foundation: all citizens have the right to vote, and all have the right to own property. For democracy to flourish, citizens not only must hold these rights in theory but also must exercise them in practice. When wealth is concentrated in the hands of a few, the mutually supportive relationship between property rights and democracy is supplanted by a relationship of tension, as the rich seek to translate their economic power into political control, and the poor seek to use their political majority for economic gain.

The link between land and liberty was evident to the American revolutionaries of the late eighteenth century. With the subsequent growth of the U.S. economy and the ascendance of the manufacturing and service sectors, the Jeffersonian vision of independent, landowning farmers as the cornerstone of American democracy faded. Yet the close relationship between wealth and power—and hence between the distribution of assets and the viability of democracy—remains as relevant today as it was during the founding of the Republic. And today, no less than in our agrarian past, natural resources and environmental sinks continue to undergird the economies of the United States and other industrialized countries. Though it is hard to assign values to benefits that bypass the market, Robert Costanza and colleagues (1997) have estimated the annual value of ecosystem services worldwide to be $33 trillion—nearly double the value of the gross world product.[7]

Thomas Paine's egalitarian claim that land is a gift in common to the human race applies equally to other natural resources. Building the natural assets held by the poor fosters a more equitable distribution of this inheritance and can strengthen the foundations of a democratic society.

States and Markets

The degree to which a society can be called democratic or oligarchic is not a matter of whether it accords a larger role in economic affairs to the market or to the state. States and markets function democratically when power and wealth are widely diffused and oligarchically when they are highly concentrated.

Societies lie on continuums defined both by their degree of democracy and by their institutional mix of the state and the market (see Figure 1.2). For the past two centuries, the contending ideologies of right and left have often sought to collapse these two dimensions into a single axis. The right has identified democracy with the market and oligarchy with the state, while the left has adopted the converse view.[8] Whichever way the axes are rotated, however, neither the market nor the state has proved to be a reliable shortcut to democracy.

For example, many economists advocate tradable emission permits—pollution allowances that can be bought and sold—as a market-based alternative to "command-and-control" pollution regulations. Such permits represent a movement along the state-market continuum in the direction of the market. In the 1990 Clean Air Act amendments, Congress introduced tradable permits

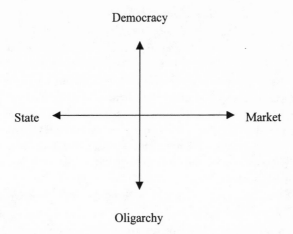

Figure 1.2. Two Continuums: Democracy-Oligarchy and Market-State.

for emissions of sulfur dioxide (SO_2), a health hazard and a major source of acid rain. Aiming to cut total SO_2 emissions to less than half their 1980 level by the year 2000, the government issued a limited number of permits for emissions by electric power plants and allowed them to be traded among the utilities. Firms that could cut emissions cheaply (relative to the price of permits) did so, while other firms bought permits. This flexibility, compared to the conventional one-rule-fits-all approach to pollution regulation, theoretically achieves the overall pollution reduction goal at the least total cost. Yet permit trading schemes have certain drawbacks compared to conventional regulations. For instance, the administrative costs of compliance monitoring may be higher when firms are free to choose different technologies for pollution control than when specific technologies are mandated by the government. In addition, the clustering of permits in particular geographical areas might create pollution "hot spots" even as national or regional emission targets are met. The balance between the pros and cons of each policy will vary from case to case.

Are tradable emission permits intrinsically more democratic than conventional pollution regulations? Some advocates of "free-market environmentalism," who axiomatically identify markets with democracy, advance this claim. Yet the degree to which a permit trading scheme can be called democratic depends crucially on how it is implemented: how the pollution reduction goals are determined and how permits are distributed. If the public is well-informed about the extent and effects of pollution and participates in defining pollution reduction targets, and if safeguards are put in place to prevent the emergence of hot spots where the residents are exposed to excessive pollution, then a permit trading scheme is more democratic than if the public is ill-informed and there are no safeguards to prevent hot spots. If the permits are auctioned off every year and the resulting revenue is shared equally among the citizenry, as in the "sky trust" proposed by Barnes and Breslow in Chapter 7, then the scheme is more democratic than if the permits are handed out for free to polluters—in effect, ratifying their prior appropriation of environmental sinks—as happened in the case of SO_2 permits. Similarly, the degree to which conventional pollution regulations can be considered democratic depends on the extent of public engagement in decision-making and on how the resulting costs and benefits are shared.

Just as tradable emission permits or "green taxes" can give firms an incentive to limit pollution, so compensation payments or "green subsidies" can give owners of natural resources incentives to manage them well and provide ecosystem services such as watershed management, biodiversity conservation, and carbon sequestration. In the parlance of economists, the former instruments serve to internalize "external costs" (or "negative externalities"), the latter to internalize "external benefits" (or "positive externalities"). In both cases, government action must create these instruments to redress the failure of the market to provide adequate incentives for environmental protection.

Yet government failure can be just as serious as market failure. There is no guarantee that the state will accurately calibrate its interventions to redress market failures and advance the public good. The market responds to the price signals that emerge from a given distribution of wealth and income, whereas the state responds to the political signals that emerge from a given distribution of power. It is no accident, for example, that public monies ostensibly meant to serve the national interest in timber production and forest management have disproportionately flowed to wealthy forest owners, as Deborah Brighton observes in Chapter 12.

Democratic accountability, founded on an equitable distribution of wealth and power, is the best way to make sure that the benefits of government interventions go to the public instead of being captured by a powerful few. It is also the best way to ensure that those interventions correct market failures rather than exacerbating them. The results will be as imperfect as democracy itself, but they are likely to be better than the practical alternatives. In Winston Churchill's famous words, "Democracy is the worst form of government—except all those other forms that have been tried." The key challenge in framing environmental policies is not to strike the right balance between states and markets—important as that may be—but to ensure that the policy mix is chosen democratically, with equal voice given to all whose lives and well-being are affected.

Sanctified and Instrumental Property Rights

Throughout U.S. history, property rights to natural resources have undergone reallocation and redefinition. In Chapter 2, Gerald Friedman traces the long-standing conflict in American jurisprudence between "sanctified" and "instrumental" conceptions of property. In the sanctified view, property rights can and should be clearly defined and perfectly secure; indeed, this is perceived as an overarching social end in itself. In the instrumental view, by contrast, property rights are a means toward more fundamental ends, such as efficiency, growth, and justice (or injustice, as in the case of property restrictions designed to enforce racial discrimination). Both schools of thought recognize that property rights are socially constructed—creations of human law, not divine ordination—but proponents of the sanctified view tend to regard this construction as a fait accompli, whereas proponents of the instrumental view see it as a more open-ended process, permitting reconstruction in response to ongoing changes in values, technology, and institutions.

The mainstream view of property rights in the United States has been firmly instrumental, as Friedman documents. Early in the nineteenth century, for example, the courts redefined property rights to remove impediments to both private entrepreneurship and public infrastructure. In 1877, the Supreme Court declared that "a government may regulate the conduct of its citizens toward each other, and, when necessary for the public good, the manner in which each shall use his own property."[9] In the latter half of the twentieth century, Congress and the states further redefined property rights to protect the environment and occupational health and safety.

In recent decades, under the banner of "free-market environmentalism," some authors have argued not only for greater reliance on market-based instruments to protect the environment but also for a radical shift toward the sanctified view of property rights. They portray any government regulations that constrain what firms or individuals can do with property as "takings" for which the government ought to compensate property owners. In this view, landowners are deemed to hold all property rights not explicitly withheld by prior law or explicitly held by others. There are no ambiguities about the prerogatives of ownership: unless already specified otherwise, all sticks in the property-rights bundle belong to those who hold the biggest stick, the title. For instance, even though the right to drain a wetland and build on it is not explicitly granted by prior law, any government action that blocks such development is construed as taking that right from the landowner—a default position that dismisses the rights of everyone else. This line of reasoning conveniently ignores the extent to which the private property now to be sanctified was itself created by the usurpation of other property rights, notably those of Native Americans—a point Winona LaDuke makes eloquently in Chapter 8.

It also ignores the extent to which current private property values are augmented by "givings" resulting from government actions, such as proximity to
publicly funded roads and other infrastructure.

Economist Daniel Bromley (1993, 672) describes the pursuit of compensation for takings as a "demand to be paid for no longer being allowed to undertake activities now declared to be illegal," and compares it to extortion. Laws
generally do infringe on people's right to do whatever they wish—otherwise
the laws would be unnecessary—and in some cases, this reduces the value of
a property below what it would otherwise be. The claim that any such impacts
represent "takings" presumes not only that property rights already have been
perfectly specified but also that the law already has been perfectly specified, at
least insofar as it affects property values. Hence there is no scope for new laws
or regulations, unless these are accompanied by side payments to those whose
property values would be adversely affected. Such a stance, in effect, would
turn legislation into a market exchange.

In practice, property rights are neither fully specified nor immutable. As
societies change over time, so do the ways in which they define and allocate
property. Bromley (1993, 653) remarks:

> To have a right is to have the ability to require some authority sys-
> tem to act in your behalf—that is, to act so as to protect your partic-
> ular interest against the interests of others. . . . In the starkest possible
> terms, what I own is a function of what the other members of the
> polity say I own—*not what I say I own*. [Emphasis in the original.]

What others say that a person owns can, and does, change over time. Until the
U.S. Civil War, for example, many states explicitly recognized property rights
in human slaves. As Gerald Friedman observes, the abolition of slavery represented a huge (and uncompensated) redefinition of property rights, brought
about by changes in ethical values and in balances of power.

The plasticity of property rights, and their role as an instrument in pursuit of
a society's broader goals, has far-reaching implications for natural-asset-building
strategies. First and foremost, this plasticity suggests that there is considerable
scope for building natural assets via the routes of redistribution, internalization,
and appropriation—all of which involve the reconfiguration of property
rights—as well as via the route of investment.

Second, once we reject the sanctified view of property rights and the pre-
sumptive allocation of all unspecified rights to landowners, there is no compelling
reason for proponents of market-based approaches to environmental protection
to object to allocations of property rights that favor the poor. If, as free-market
environmentalists often assert, well-defined property rights foster efficient outcomes regardless of how the rights are distributed, why not allocate emerging
rights in natural assets—including rights to environmental sinks—equally among

all citizens? Indeed, if a society's objectives include poverty reduction and the equitable distribution of wealth and power, there are strong grounds to prefer an egalitarian allocation over the assignment of these rights to those already best endowed with assets. In addition, as discussed above, there are good environmental reasons to favor an equitable distribution of rights to natural assets.

A final implication of the plasticity of property rights is that successful efforts to build natural assets held by the poor inevitably bring the risk that more powerful parties will then attempt to wrest control of those assets by legal, illegal, or quasi-legal means. There is a danger, in other words, that the poor will no longer be too poor to rob but will remain too weak politically to defend themselves from their would-be robbers. It would be a cruel irony if investments in ecological restoration by small farmers or woodlot owners, or the internalization of benefits from the ecological services they provide, were to prompt the powerful to deprive them of their land. This risk does not diminish the case for natural-asset-building strategies, but it means that one important element of such strategies must be an effort to strengthen the capacity of the poor to defend their assets. Struggles to democratize environmental ownership therefore require parallel struggles to democratize the political framework, including efforts to organize communities, protect human rights, and improve access to legal assistance. Natural-asset-building strategies neglect these elements of social and political capital at their peril— or, more precisely, at the peril of those they aim to assist.

The essays in this volume demonstrate that building natural assets can do much to advance the goals of poverty reduction, environmental protection, and environmental justice. Yet the very features of natural assets that make successes possible—the ongoing historical reconfiguration of property rights to natural resources and the human capacity to increase or deplete the stock of natural assets—carry the possibility of failure, too. In the twenty-first century, we can expect that many critical issues of environmental ownership will be resolved for better or worse. The challenge we face is to resolve them for the better.

Acknowledgments

I am grateful to Michael Conroy, Barry Shelley, Rachel Bouvier, T. Robert Fetter, and Karen Graubart for their comments and to all the participants in the Natural Assets Project for their insights into the issues discussed here.

Notes

1. See Shapiro and Wolff (2001), Danziger and Waldfogel (2000), and Saegert et al. (2001).
2. For a discussion of the bundle-of-sticks metaphor in property law, see Ross (1989).

3. As Anderson et al. (2000, 159) remarked, "The assignment of property rights affects peoples' perceptions of the allocation of moral responsibility." For a survey of literature on the disparity between willingness-to-pay and willingness-to-accept, see Brown and Gregory (1999).

4. Egalitarian asset-building strategies can also help to build "moral capital" in the form of a stronger sense of responsibility toward other people. Recent studies have shown that when wealth is more equally distributed, individuals are more inclined to cooperate for mutual benefit (Bowles and Gintis 1998; Ben-Ner and Putterman 2000). By extension, they are also less willing (as well as less able) to impose negative externalities on others.

5. See the chapters in this volume by K. A. Dixon, Raquel Pinderhughes, Cecilia Danks, and Stephen Brush, respectively.

6. For discussions of the relationship between farm size and productivity, see Berry and Cline (1979), Strange (1988), and Netting (1993).

7. Recognizing the inadequacy of gross national product (GNP) as a measure of income, a U.S. National Academy of Sciences panel recently concluded that "the development of environmental and natural-resource accounts is an essential investment for the nation" (Nordhaus and Kokkelenberg 1999, 10).

8. Both identifications typically invoke idealized pictures of the market and the state. "Proponents of central planning tend to compare the market as it actually works with the government as it would work under ideal circumstances," observes an ardent partisan of the market (De Alessi 1998, 3). Yet, in the same fashion, proponents of the market tend to compare the state (or "central planning," to use their preferred epithet) as it actually works with the market as it would work under ideal circumstances. For example, the same author baldly claims that "the existence of a market in which private rights can be exchanged implies that future consequences are instantaneously capitalized into current transfer prices and reflected in owners' wealth" (De Alessi 1998, 10).

9. *Munn v. Illinois*. For discussion, see Gerald Friedman in Chapter 2.

References

Agarwal, Anil, and Sunita Narain. 2000. "Redressing Ecological Poverty Through Participatory Democracy: Case Studies from India." Working Paper No. DPE-00-01. Amherst, Mass.: Political Economy Research Institute.

Anderson, Johan, Dan Vadnjal, and Hans-Erik Uhlin. 2000. "Moral Dimensions of the WTA-WTP Disparity: An Experimental Examination." *Ecological Economics* 32:153–62.

Ben-Ner, Avner, and Louis Putterman. 2000. "Values Matter." *World Economics* 1(1): 39–60.

Berry, R. Albert, and William R. Cline. 1979. *Agrarian Structure and Productivity in Developing Countries*. Baltimore: Johns Hopkins University Press.

Bowles, Samuel, and Herbert Gintis. 1998. "Is Equality Passé? *Homo Reciprocans* and the Future of Egalitarian Politics." *Boston Review* 23(6): 4–10.

Boyce, James K. 1994. "Inequality as a Cause of Environmental Degradation." *Ecological Economics* 11:169–78.

————. 2000. "Let Them Eat Risk? Wealth, Rights, and Disaster Vulnerability." *Disasters* 24(3): 254–61.

Boyce, James K., Andrew R. Klemer, Paul H. Templet, and Cleve E. Willis. 1999. "Power Distribution, the Environment, and Public Health: A State-Level Analysis." *Ecological Economics* 29:127–40.

Bromley, Daniel. 1993. "Regulatory Takings: Coherent Concept or Logical Contradiction." *Vermont Law Review* 17(3): 647–82.

Brooks, N., and R. Sethi. 1997. "The Distribution of Pollution: Community Characteristics and Exposure to Air Toxics." *Journal of Environmental Economics and Management* 32:233–50.

Brown, Thomas C., and Robin Gregory. 1999. "Why the WTA-WTP Disparity Matters." *Ecological Economics* 28:323–35.

Bullard, Robert D. 1990. *Dumping in Dixie: Race, Class, and Environmental Quality.* Boulder: Westview Press.

Bullard, Robert D., ed. 1994. *Environmental Justice and Communities of Color.* San Francisco: Sierra Club Books.

Chenery, Hollis, Montek S. Ahluwalia, C. L. G. Bell, John H. Duloy, and Richard Jolly. 1974. *Redistribution with Growth.* New York: Oxford University Press.

Costanza, Robert, Ralph d'Arge, Rudolf de Groot, Stephen Farber, Monica Grasso, Bruce Hannon, Karin Limburg, Shahid Naeem, Robert V. O'Neill, Jose Paruelo, Robert G. Raskin, Paul Sutton, and Marjan van den Belt. 1997. "The Value of the World's Ecosystem Services and Natural Capital." *Nature* 387:253–60.

Cronon, William. 1995. "Introduction: In Search of Nature." In *Uncommon Ground: Toward Reinventing Nature,* edited by William Cronon. New York: W. W. Norton.

Danziger, Sheldon, and Jane Waldfogel, eds. 2000. *Securing the Future: Investing in Children from Birth to College.* New York: Russell Sage Foundation Press.

De Alessi, Louis. 1998. "Private Property Rights as the Basis for Free Market Environmentalism." In *Who Owns the Environment?* edited by Peter J. Hill and Roger E. Meiners. Lanham, Md.: Rowman & Littlefield.

Friedman, Milton, and Rose Friedman. 1980. *Free to Choose: A Personal Statement.* New York: Harcourt Brace Jovanovich.

Hardin, Garrett. 1968. "The Tragedy of the Commons." *Science* 168 (December 13).

Jansson, AnnMari, Monica Hammer, Carl Folke, and Robert Costanza, eds. 1994. *Investing in Natural Capital: The Ecological Economics Approach to Sustainability.* Washington, D.C.: Island Press.

Mittal, Aunradha, with Joan Powell. 2000. "The Last Plantation." *Institute for Food and Development Policy Backgrounder* 6(1).

Nash, Roderick F. 1990. *The Rights of Nature: A History of Environmental Ethics.* Madison: University of Wisconsin Press.

Netting, Robert M. 1993. *Smallholders, Householders: Farm Families and the Ecology of Intensive, Sustainable Agriculture.* Stanford, Calif.: Stanford University Press.

Nordhaus, William D., and Edward C., Kokkelenberg, eds. 1999. *Nature's Numbers: Expanding the National Economic Accounts to Include the Environment.* Washington, D.C.: National Academy Press.

Oliver, Melvin L. and Thomas M. Shapiro. 1995. *Black Wealth/White Wealth: A New Perspective on Racial Inequality.* New York: Routledge.

Ostrom, Elinor. 1990. *Governing the Commons: The Evolution of Institutions for Collective Action*. Cambridge: Cambridge University Press.

Paine, Thomas. [1796] 1920. *Agrarian Justice*. Reprinted in M. Beer, ed. *The Pioneers of Land Reform*. New York: Alfred A. Knopf.

Popovic, Neil A. F. 1996. "Pursuing Environmental Justice with International Human Rights and State Constitutions." *Stanford Environmental Law Journal* (June).

Ross, Thomas. 1989. "Metaphor and Paradox." *Georgia Law Review* 23:1053–84.

Saegert, Susan, J. Phillip Thompson, and Mark R. Warren, eds. 2001. *Social Capital and Poor Communities*. New York: Russell Sage Foundation Press.

Sen, Amartya K. 2000. *Employment, Technology, and Development*. Oxford: Oxford University Press.

Shapiro, Thomas M., and Edward N. Wolff, eds. 2001. *Assets for the Poor: The Benefits of Spreading Asset Ownership*. New York: Russell Sage Foundation Press.

Sherraden, Michael. 1991. *Assets and the Poor: A New American Welfare Policy*. New York: M. E. Sharpe.

Strange, Marty. 1988. *Family Farming: A New Economic Vision*. Lincoln: University of Nebraska Press.

Torras, Mariano, and James K. Boyce. 1998. "Income, Inequality, and Pollution: A Reassessment of the Environmental Kuznets Curve." *Ecological Economics* 25:147–60.

CHAPTER 2

"A Question of Degree": The Sanctity of Property in American Economic History

Gerald Friedman

The life of the law has not been logic: it has been experience. The felt necessities of the time, the prevalent moral and political theories, intuitions of public policy, avowed or unconscious, even the prejudices which judges share with their fellow-men, have had a good deal more to do than the syllogism in determining the rules by which men should be governed.

—Oliver Wendell Holmes, *The Common Law*

Society makes property. And by defining property, a society fundamentally shapes its economy, its production mix, and its distribution of income. Societies differ in the *extension* of ownership, the range of assets that individuals may own. These may include natural assets (for example, land, animals, genomes, water), human-made assets (for example, buildings, goods, patent protection for ideas and inventions), and even living humans. Societies also differ in the *intensive* rights they accord to owners of assets. Intensive rights include the right to sell or rent the property, the regulation of prices owners can charge, and the assignment of responsibility for spillover costs when one property owner's actions affect others, as in cases involving pollution, land erosion, traffic congestion, and business competition. In short, extensive property rights govern what people can own as property; intensive rights govern what they can do with it.

A society can allow individuals to exploit their property in ways that damage neighboring property, or it may protect neighbors by restricting actions that affect others. The intensive rights established by property law therefore have distributional effects. Where property owners have the right to pollute, for example, their neighbors' well-being or income declines due to the loss of clean air and water or the cost of paying the polluter to refrain from polluting. Alternatively, without this privilege, polluters are poorer because they must mitigate their pollution or buy from neighbors the right to pollute.

Few dispute that property law has important distributional effects, but some analysts choose to focus on efficiency rather than distributional issues. In a pioneering article, Ronald Coase (1960) argued that regardless of the allocation of property rights, any clear demarcation can lead to the same efficient social outcome and the same level of production of goods and services. Whether polluters must buy the right to pollute from their neighbors or neighbors must pay polluters to stop polluting, free market exchange will ensure that pollution continues wherever mitigation costs more than the value that individuals assign to clean air, and it will be curtailed wherever mitigation is cheaper.

Coase's article had an enormous impact on economic theory and led many economists to neglect distribution while focusing on the efficiency implications of different legal regimes.[1] But the neat separation of outcomes from distribution holds only in the special cases where all consumers are identical or production is at constant returns to scale (so that costs do not change with the volume of output).[2] Moreover, Coase himself intended his article to demonstrate the importance of transaction costs—the expenses involved in negotiating and enforcing contracts—and their role in preventing efficient outcomes through private exchange or bargaining.

A long tradition in social theory warns of a conflict between individual liberty to manage private property and the rights of the majority to govern in a democratic polity. But all property rights give individuals state-sanctioned monopolies and restrict the liberties of others. This chapter discusses how property law in the United States has been modified over time in response to changes in technology and in society's values. It explores the long-standing tension in American jurisprudence between two views of property: a *sanctified* view, which holds that property should be free of public interference, and an *instrumental* view, which understands property as a means to advance social goals. This chapter argues that, historically, property rights have been defined instrumentally in the United States. Rather than being disputes over principles of natural liberty and justice, debates about property regulation involve fundamental societal choices about which property is to be protected and which rights are to prevail.

Locke, Labor, and Right: Property's Origin and Justification

The concept of private property continues to bedevil economic theory. Of course, many economists happily ignore the issue, characterizing commodities in one dimension: owned or not owned. Others recognize multiple dimensions of property but still treat property rights as a relationship between people and objects (Barzel 1997; Libecap 1989). Defined as a relationship between people and things, property rights are independent of society; Robinson Crusoe, too, has property rights.[3]

As a relationship between people and the things they create, property rights acquire moral legitimacy and economic significance as a reward for labor that shapes the nonhuman material world. Labor, John Locke states, "in the beginning, gave a right of property" (Locke 1952 [1690], 17, 27). There is an "unquestionable" right to property in an individual's own labor because

> though the earth and all inferior creatures be common to all men, yet
> . . . [t]he labor of his body and the work of his hands, we may say, are
> properly his. Whatsoever then he removes out of the state that nature
> has provided and left it in, he has mixed his labor with, and joined to
> it something that is his own, and thereby makes it his property. . . .
> For this labor being the unquestionable property of the laborer, no
> man but he can have a right to what that is once joined to, at least
> where there is enough and as good left in common for others.

Thus Locke sanctifies property as an essential natural right. Because property is a physical manifestation of past labor, to take it is to take labor, to make one a slave. Property then owes nothing to society; on the contrary, property owners form society and government to protect property (Smith 1999). Property, the source and purpose of social organization, becomes an end in itself. Popular in the early American republic, Lockean arguments continued to be cited by late-nineteenth-century Supreme Court justices arguing against public regulation of intensive property rights (Ely 1998).[4]

Some others use instrumental arguments, defending intensive private property rights as valuable incentives to entrepreneurs (North 1981). But such instrumental arguments cannot sanctify property; they cannot make it an end in itself, an unquestioned right transcending all other considerations. Instead, by making property a mere means to higher ends, instrumental reasoning undermines the defense of intensive property rights. As an instrument, a particular form of property may be convenient, but it can never be necessary.[5]

Locke's own defense of property was considerably less absolute than one might conclude from a quick reading of the famous passage cited above (Horne 1990; Katznelson 1998, 77). Even there, Locke recognized a social dimension in which property rights are limited by other natural rights, including a universal right to share nature's bounty, leaving "enough and as good" for others. Citing biblical authority, Locke (1952 [1690], 19) argues that

> the same law of nature that does by this means give us property
> does also bound that property too. "God has given us all things
> richly" (1 Tim. vi. 17), is the voice of reason confirmed by

inspiration. But how far has he given it to us? To enjoy. As much
as any one can make use of to any advantage of life before it
spoils, so much he may by his labor fix a property in; whatever is
beyond this is more than his share and belongs to others.
Nothing was made by God for man to spoil or destroy.

It was the invention of money as a store of wealth that, to Locke's regret,
allowed some to monopolize a "disproportionate and unequal possession of
the earth." This side of Lockean property theory leads to a natural-rights argument for curbs on individual accumulation, a perspective later developed by,
among others, the great transatlantic radical Thomas Paine.

Modern advocates of sanctified property rights have regretted Locke's
extended discussion. Charging that Locke was confused in his biblical exegesis,
Richard Epstein acknowledges that Locke created "no little difficulty" for the
defense of intensive property rights (Epstein 1985, 10). As a relationship
between people and things, property rights can be defended as socially
neutral: accumulating property in the fruits of one's labor does not detract
from what is available for others. But recognizing the social dimensions
acknowledges a distributive aspect to property by which one's property rights
can harm others by monopolizing resources previously available to all (see
Fried 1998, 19, 24, and Horwitz 1992, 128).

American Exceptionalism, the Sanctity of Property, and the Police Powers

A convention, even an organizing myth, in the study of American history
holds that the United States is uniquely devoted to individualism and to property rights. Owing much to Louis Hartz and his classic work, *The Liberal
Tradition in America* (1955), the United States is held to be quintessentially
liberal and classically Lockean. This national ethos sanctifies private property
and individual initiative (Lipset 1996; Friedman 1999).

This vision has always been narrow. Some Americans accumulated property
in the Lockean way, by mixing their labor with land and materials. But more
became wealthy through military conquest and theft, following the example
of the original Norman lords who followed William to England. White
Americans became rich by enslaving millions of Africans and using military
force to expropriate land held by Native peoples. Even the American
Revolution of 1776, fought to uphold liberal ideals, became the occasion for
massive theft. Rebels, seizing the property of those loyal to the king, confiscated
two-thirds of the property in New York City and its suburbs (Flick 1901, 153).
British property received as little consideration: debts owed to British creditors

were summarily annulled; some states, including Virginia, closed their courts to suits by British subjects (Ely 1998, 35).

Fearing a wholesale assault on property, prominent rebels worked to secure property as "the guardian of every other right" (Ely 1998, 26; Tomlins 1993, 60; Foner 1976, 133). Conservative fears led the Constitutional Convention of 1787 to restrict the authority of state governments to interfere with contracts and led to the enactment of the Fifth Amendment protecting property from seizure without compensation and due process (Rakove 1996, 314–15; Ely 1998, 43–54; Jacobs 1954, 4–5). Notwithstanding the constitutional protection of property, American states continued to reallocate wealth. The Thirteenth Amendment to the U.S. Constitution enshrines the principle of property confiscation: the uncompensated expropriation of slave property under that amendment redistributed nearly $3 billion, half the South's total wealth, making slave emancipation in the United States one of history's largest expropriations of property.[6]

Throughout the colonial and antebellum period, state and local governments interfered regularly with private property to promote a healthy economy and sustain troubled citizens. Most localities, for example, set bread and transportation prices; regulated wages and entry to occupations; and restricted trade in foodstuffs and the activities of liquor dealers, prostitutes, and taverns (Handlin and Handlin 1947; Bourgin 1989; Novak 1996). Local governments regularly invoked the principle of eminent domain to advance social ends at the expense of private property holders.

The term *eminent domain* entered English law through Locke, who grounded it in the consent of the population as delegated to the legislature (Eagle 1996, 8). But American lawyers, grounding it on purely instrumental considerations, expanded the concept far beyond Locke's vision. Implicitly denying the sanctity of private property rights, the Vermont Constitution of 1791 proclaimed: "Private property ought to be subservient to public uses, when *necessity* [emphasis added] requires it" (Ely 1998, 33). The United States Supreme Court similarly grounded eminent domain on convenience and instrumental considerations. In *Kohl v. United States* (1875), it declared eminent domain "the offspring of political necessity . . . inseparable from sovereignty."

Eminent domain was one example of government promoting the "public good" at the expense of individuals' intensive property rights. Such regulation reflects common law maxims dating back to medieval England: *salus populi suprema lex est* ("the welfare of the people is the supreme law") and *sic utere tuo ut alienum non laedas* ("use your own so as not to injure another"). These doctrines provided the "legal basis for extensive public regulation of property to reflect the reciprocal interests and rights of all citizens" (Novak 1996, 42).

Using this logic, antebellum local and state governments assumed extensive powers to regulate property. In 1837, for example, the Illinois legislature needed three typed pages to catalogue all the powers over property to be held by the new city of Chicago. In addition to regulating and licensing ferries and preventing "the rolling of hoops, playing at ball, or flying of kites . . . having a tendency to annoy persons," the new city could "compel the owner or occupant of any grocery, cellar, tallow-chandler's shop, soap factory, tannery, stable, barn, privy, sewer, or other unwholesome, nauseous house or place, to cleanse, remove, or abate the same" (Novak 1996, 3–6). Other cities assumed similarly extensive powers over property. New York City needed several pages to set rates on the East River ferry, enumerating the price of transporting items ranging from fat ox, steer, or bulls (25 cents) to cords of nutwood (50 cents), empty milk kettles (1 cent), children's corpses (25 cents), and corpses of adults (50 cents) (Novak 1996, 118–20). Local governments regularly seized houses used for immoral purposes, filled privately owned mill-creeks accused of "endangering the public health," banned dangerous chemicals, and blocked fires by destroying private dwellings and warehouses without paying compensation. Officials regulated access to dozens of trades, including those associated with public health—such as medicine and butchering—but also including others of economic but not health consequence—such as the right to trade and to buy and sell produce (Novak 1996, 84–94). Where regulation failed to achieve the public purpose, officials took direct action. In 1872, for example, Jersey City's street commissioner led 25 armed police officers into a plant owned by the Manhattan Fertilizing Company and proceeded to "abate" the nuisance the plant's operation caused by destroying machinery and carrying away essential parts (Novak 1996, 226).

Such acts were justified under what is called the state's "police powers" or "limits set to property by other public interests." This justification involves a fundamentally instrumental view of property law, as New York's Justice Woodworth enunciated in the 1827 case of *Vanderbilt v. Adams:* "The sovereign power in a community . . . ought to prescribe the manner of exercising individual rights over property. . . . The powers rest on the implied right and duty of the supreme power to protect all by statutory regulations, so that, on the whole, the benefit of all is promoted." The classic statement on the police power was made by Massachusetts Chief Justice Lemuel Shaw in *Commonwealth v. Alger* (1851), in which he upheld legislation regulating property in Boston harbor and restricting building beyond the wharf line:

> We think it is a settled principle, growing out of the nature of well ordered civil society, that every holder of property, however absolute and unqualified may be his title, holds it under the implied liability that his use of it may be so regulated that it shall not be injurious to the equal enjoyment of others having an equal right to the enjoyment of their property, nor injurious to the rights of the community. All property in this commonwealth . . . is derived directly or indirectly from the government, and held

subject to those general regulations, which are necessary to the common good and general welfare. Rights of property, like all other social and conventional rights, are subject to such reasonable limitations in their enjoyment as shall prevent them from being injurious, and to such reasonable restraints and regulations established by law, as the legislature . . . may think necessary and expedient.

Chief Justice Shaw noted that "it is much easier to perceive and realize the existence and sources of this power than to mark its boundaries, or prescribe limits to its exercise." Indeed, by using elastic terms such as "public interest" and "the common good and general welfare," Shaw defined the police powers to accommodate many uses. Jersey City used the police powers to restrain noxious factory emissions. Southern state governments used them to restrict property sales to African-Americans and their employment in certain occupations in order to uphold racial segregation. In both cases, property rights were socially defined to achieve social goals; only the goals differed.[7]

Redistributing Property Rights to Promote Economic Growth

Property rights have been reallocated throughout American history to advance both private interests and public interests. Whether effected by legislative processes or by judicial reinterpretation of established law, these changes in property rights have been based in pragmatic considerations and instrumental reasoning. Property law has been made, interpreted, and refashioned to serve the society's broader goals, not to accord with immutable principles.

Subsidizing Public Infrastructure by Reallocating Property Rights

In 1837, Supreme Court Chief Justice Roger Taney used instrumental arguments in abrogating the contractual rights of the Charles River Bridge Company to operate the sole bridge over the Charles River between Boston and Cambridge (*Charles River Bridge v. Warren Bridge*). Protecting the company's property rights, Taney found, was inconvenient. It would threaten the "millions . . . which have been invested in railroads and canals, upon lines of travel which had been occupied by turnpike corporations. . . . We shall be thrown back to the improvements of the last century, and obliged to stand still." Here again, as throughout American law, property rights established to advance social goals were overturned when they impeded those objectives.

Eager to promote industry and commerce, early-nineteenth-century governments encouraged road, canal, and railroad building. But infrastructure construction risked damaging other property, including causing a loss in value to property bypassed by improvements. Under the traditional interpretation of the doctrine of *sic utere tuo ut alienum non laedas* ("use your own so as not to injure another"), investors would be responsible for these costs and could be forced to compensate neighbors for damages and losses. Because this would raise the cost of infrastructure investments, the traditional interpretation of the *sic utere* doctrine would hinder the government's purposes. Courts and state officials therefore sought to free investors by reinterpreting *sic utere* and by reinterpreting property rights to include the right to burden neighbors with the spillover costs of their actions on neighboring property.

The transformation of *sic utere* began in 1823 in the precedent-setting Massachusetts case of *Callender v. Marsh*. Callender sued for damages when street reconstruction work exposed his Boston home's foundation. His attorney cited the standard sources including the *sic utere* doctrine (carried over from English common law) to argue for compensation. The defense countered with a novel instrumental argument: American circumstances require road construction, and if "such an action" as Callender's "can be sustained, it will put a check to all improvements in our highways."

This argument resonated with Massachusetts judges, who denied Callender compensation. Similar conclusions were reached in New York in *Lansing v. Smith* (1828). Walter Quackenbush sued New York State for damages when his docks lost value after the state constructed a new boat basin at Albany. As Massachusetts did in *Callender v. Marsh,* the New York court rejected Quackenbush's claims on purely instrumental grounds. "Every great public improvement," it held, "must of necessity, more or less affect individual convenience and property; and where the injury sustained is remote and consequential, it is *damnum absque injuria* [injury for which no compensation is due] and is to be borne as a part of the price to be paid for the advantages of the social condition." This, the court concluded, "is founded upon the principle that the general good is to prevail over partial individual convenience."

Subsidizing Private Entrepreneurship

By freeing government to erect public improvements at the expense of neighboring property holders, case law like *Lansing* and *Callender* shifted to some individuals the cost of achieving social goals (Horwitz 1977, 70). Other precedents extended these instrumental principles to private actions. Writing in *Thorpe v. Rutland and Burlington Railroad Company* (1855), for example, Vermont's chief justice, Isaac Redfield, upheld a law requiring railroads to fence their lines because the "police power of the state extends to the protection of the lives, limbs, health, comfort, and quiet of all persons, and the protection of all property within the state according to the maxim, *sic utere tuo ut alienum non laedas*. The use here of the *sic utere* maxim provides a window into the social construction of property. Justice Redfield invoked it to sustain restrictions on intensive property rights because he recognized that actions taken by one property owner affect others even when performed on their own property. But *sic utere* is a principle, not a rule; it provides no guidance in cases between individuals with competing property interests (Holmes 1894, 11).[8] Nineteenth-century judges such as Redfield redefined property and *sic utere* to facilitate entrepreneurial activity even at the cost of harming the property of others. The words *sic utere* survived but were now used to protect entrepreneurs' right to act over the claims of passive neighbors to enjoy their property undisturbed. Injury became passive, reinterpreted to mean preventing property owners from using property.

Here the seminal case was New York's *Palmer v. Mulligan* (1805), in which a downstream user sued for damages when a dam obstructed the flow of water to his property. The court ruling in favor of the dam owner turned on the equal right of a new arrival to do what older occupants had done. Speaking for the court, Judge Livingston concluded:

> Defendants had the same right opposite their ground. . . . [*Sic utere*] must be restrained within reasonable bounds so as not to deprive a man of the enjoyment of his property, merely because of some trifling inconvenience or damage to others. . . . Were the law to regard little inconveniences of this nature, he who could first build a dam or mill on any public or navigable river, would acquire an exclusive right, at least for some distance, whether he owned the contiguous banks or not. . . . The public, whose advantage is always to be regarded, would be deprived of the benefit which always attends competition and rivalry.[9]

This transformation of the *sic utere* rule owed nothing to Lockean concepts of sanctified private property. It was neither a general attack on, nor a general reaffirmation of, property rights: by reallocating rights, it affirmed some property against other property. By minimizing the legal risk to entrepreneurs, the new doctrine promoted entrepreneurship. This is an example of what legal historian Willard Hurst (1956, 6) saw as one of the working principles of the U.S. legal order: "the release of creative human energy." Had entrepreneurs been required to compensate neighbors for consequential damages, efficient projects may still have been undertaken. In theory, projects worth more than the damages inflicted would still have gone forward. But shifting the burden to the injured parties favored entrepreneurs by putting all the risk and transaction costs on the neighbors.[10]

Reining in an Excess of Democracy?

The Civil War inaugurated a new era in American politics, demonstrating through war and emancipation the power of the national state to expand freedom. Reformers looked for more. Labor activists sought to "engraft republican principles into our industrial system." "The Declaration of Independence," railroad trainman C. F. Bracey argued, "was not made for such purposes as the trusts of today are enforcing upon us. The strike of '61 was to free the colored slave, but the working people today are nothing more or less than slaves of the combined trusts" (Foner 1998, 99, 124–25).

But the war also fostered forces opposed to these demands for reform by promoting large-scale financial and industrial capital and a newly centralized banking system based in New York (Bensel 1984, 1990). Angry workers and farmers pushed for new laws to expand public regulation of property and achieved some dramatic successes, including the enactment of laws regulating the length of the workday and setting railroad rates. Despite objections from business leaders, such legislation even passed muster with the Supreme Court. Well into the 1880s, the Supreme Court continued to accept broad regulation of intensive property rights.

Most alarming to business interests concerned with the rising tide of popular radicalism was the 1877 Supreme Court decision in *Munn v. Illinois*. A Chicago grain elevator challenged an Illinois law regulating the prices charged by railroads, warehouses, and grain elevators. Plaintiffs charged that the law violated the Constitution's contract clause and the Fourteenth Amendment's protection against state interference with the rights of citizens. Recently enacted to protect the civil liberties of freed slaves in the South, the Fourteenth Amendment was now invoked as a constitutional guarantee of property, privileging the intensive private property rights of some from state interference.

The Supreme Court rejected this view, upholding "powers inherent in every sovereignty. . . . A government may regulate the conduct of its citizens toward each other, and, when necessary for the public good, the manner in which each shall use his own property." Chief Justice Waite quoted England's Lord Chief Justice Hale in saying that when property was "affected with a public interest, it ceases to be *juris privati* [subject to private regulation] only." Citing the doctrine of *salus populi suprema lex est* ("the welfare of the people is the supreme law"), Waite added:

> When the owner of property devotes it to a use in which the public has an interest, he in effect grants to the public an interest in such use, and must to the extent of that interest, submit to be controlled by the public, for the common good, as long as he maintains the use. He may withdraw his grant by discontinuing the use.

In a sweeping assertion of the scope of public power in a democracy, Waite acknowledged few restraints on state regulation. Regulated property "is entitled to a reasonable compensation for its use," but final judgment on compensation remains with the legislature. Acknowledging that this legislative power might be abused, he urged citizens to go for redress "to the polls, not to the courts."

Advocates of property rights were appalled at this expansive reading of the police powers. Dissenting Justice Stephen Field warned that "the principle upon which the opinion of the majority proceeds is . . . subversive of the rights of private property." "If this be sound law," he warned, then "all property and all business in the State are held at the mercy of a majority of its legislature." *Munn* made property but one among many interests, just another instrument to achieve social ends with no more constitutional protection than is accorded other interests.

Responding to popular unrest and the *Munn* decision, American lawyers and judges set out to sanctify private property. They sought to curb the scope of state regulation dramatically, limiting states' police powers to restraints founded on the entrepreneur-friendly form of the *sic utere* doctrine.

Initially, state courts had taken the lead in erecting new foundations for a sanctified, rather than instrumental, notion of private property. Even before the Civil War, in *Wynehamer v. People* (1856), the New York Court of Appeals overturned legislation outlawing liquor sales, ruling that when it was applied to liquor owned when the law took effect, the legislation was a deprivation of property without due process. This was the first time that due process was found to protect property rather than persons.

Wynehamer found few echoes for nearly 30 years, but after *Munn* it was taken up with a vengeance. In *In re. Jacobs* (1885), the New York Court of Appeals overturned legislation prohibiting the manufacture of cigars in tenements because it "interferes with the profitable and free use of his property by the owner," and thereby "deprives him of his property and some portion of his personal liberty." Dramatically applying individual liberty to the defense of property, Judge Earl warned that

> liberty, in its broad sense as understood in this country, means the right, not only of freedom from actual servitude . . . but the right of one to use his faculties in all lawful ways to live and work. . . . All laws, therefore, which impair or trammel these rights . . . are infringements upon his fundamental rights of liberty.

The legislature had based the act on the state's police powers, claiming it was needed "to improve the public health." Ominously for advocates of state regulation, the court felt entitled to review this claim. Ruling that the law really "had no relation whatever to the public health," Judge Earl warned that "under the mere guise of police regulations, personal rights and private property cannot be arbitrarily invaded."

In re. Jacobs inaugurated a period of unprecedented judicial activism by state courts in defense of property rights. In *Godcharles v. Wigeman* (1886), the Pennsylvania Supreme Court overturned a law requiring payment in lawful money (rather than company scrip) because it was "an insulting attempt to put the laborer under legislative tutelage" by preventing workers from selling their labor on any terms they were willing to accept. But the laissez-faire prejudices of the era's judges were perhaps best exemplified by the West Virginia Court of Appeals. In *State v. Goodwill* (1889), the court held that laws requiring payment in money were unconstitutional because government should not "do for its people what they can best do for themselves. The natural law of supply and demand is the best law of trade."

Justice Stephen J. Field and the Construction of Sanctified Private Property

The U.S. Supreme Court was slow to join the attack on state regulation, but Justice Stephen J. Field challenged the concept of the police power in 1872 in his dissenting opinion in the *Slaughter-House* case (*Butchers' Benevolent Association of New Orleans v. The Crescent City Live-Stock Landing and Slaughter-House Company*). The case arose from a challenge to a Louisiana law restricting the slaughtering of animals in New Orleans to a newly constructed, centralized and regulated facility. Citing Chief Justice Shaw in *Commonwealth v. Alger* (1851), the Louisiana Supreme Court approved the law, finding that "the sacrifice of the individual right in this case is of no consequence in view of the general benefit and commerce of a great commercial community."

Appealing to the Supreme Court, the New Orleans butchers were represented by Field's predecessor on the Court, John A. Campbell, a Democrat and the Confederacy's assistant secretary of war (Foner 1988, 530). Serving before the Civil War, Campbell had ruled, in the *Dred Scott* case, that African-Americans could not be citizens of the United States. Fifteen years later, he invoked free-labor principles to urge the Court to protect a citizen's right to intensive property rights. Citing the struggle against feudalism, Campbell argued that the New Orleans regulations marked a step back to a time "when the prying eye of the government followed the butcher to the shambles and the baker to the oven."

The New Orleans butchers lost their case on a vote of 5–4, but Campbell's arguments resonated with judges and lawyers who feared rising pressures to extend regulation and to redistribute income, property, and power. Today, Justice Field's dissent is remembered better than Justice Miller's majority opinion, with its conventional citations in support of the police powers. Like

Campbell, Field argued that Louisiana violated fundamental rights of free labor. Quoting extensively from Adam Smith, he grounded his defense of intensive property rights on Lockean precepts that because free labor is the ultimate source of property, property is an "essential part of liberty . . . in the American sense of the term." [11]

It would take two decades before Field's views were accepted by the Supreme Court. In 1897, in *Allgeyer v. Louisiana,* the Court struck down a state law prohibiting the sale of insurance without a Louisiana state license as an intrusion on rights guaranteed by the Fourteenth Amendment. Echoing New York's *In re. Jacobs,* Justice Rufus W. Peckham argued that an individual's liberty embraced a right to "work where he will; to earn his livelihood by any lawful calling; to pursue any livelihood or avocation, and for that purpose to enter into all contracts."Writing for the Court in *Lochner v. New York* (1905), Peckham similarly found that a New York law restricting working hours for bakers was unconstitutional because it "necessarily interferes with the right of contract between the employer and employes [sic]," violating the "general right to make a contract in relation to his business . . . protected by the Fourteenth Amendment of the Federal Constitution."The reasoning in *Allgeyer* and *Lochner* was sustained in later decisions, such as *Adkins v. Children's Hospital* (1923), where the Court overturned a minimum wage law for the District of Columbia, ruling that it unconstitutionally seized the property of workers and businesses by intruding on their "freedom of contract."

Property, Instrumentalism, and the New Deal

By the 1920s, freedom of contract and the sanctity of property seemed to be firmly embedded in American law. But the foundations of this legal triumph were weaker than they appeared. Notwithstanding appeals to John Locke, the case for sanctified property rested more on Adam Smith, and on the economic theory that this view of property would advance public interests. Justice Oliver Wendell Holmes exposed this weakness in the legal defense of property rights by showing that it, too, was rooted in instrumentalism. Stripped of its universal claims, property law was vulnerable to a revolution in the 1930s when the political consensus in favor of *laissez faire* economics collapsed.

Oliver Wendell Holmes and Pennsylvania Coal

Shortly before *Adkins,* another Supreme Court ruling seemed to commit the Court to a sanctified view of intensive property rights. In *Pennsylvania Coal Co. v. Mahon* (1922), the Court overturned a Pennsylvania law restricting coal mining to maintain underground support for the surface. The Court found that

> the general rule at least is, that while property may be regulated to a certain extent, if regulation goes too far it will be recognized as a taking. . . . In general it is not plain that a man's misfortunes or necessities [i.e., the damage suffered by the owner of the surface undermined by mining] will justify his shifting the damages to his neighbor's shoulders [i.e., onto the owner of the mine]. . . . Strong public desire to improve the public condition is not enough to warrant achieving the desire by a shorter cut than the constitutional way of paying for the charge. . . . This is a question of degree.

Cited more than 100,000 times in the next 75 years, *Pennsylvania Coal* remains "good law" today. By extending the protection of property from security against absolute seizure to protection against loss of value, Holmes established a new legal doctrine and a new field of law, now entitled "takings." The case appeared to mark the final reversal of *Munn* because it invoked a vision of property as inviolable against state intrusion without compensation. But note the last phrase: "This is a question of degree." Using *Pennsylvania Coal* as a Trojan horse, Holmes here explicitly reinserted instrumental and pragmatic reasoning into property law, overturning 50 years of judicial activism based on a Lockean vision of property rights that began with Justice Field's dissenting opinion in the *Slaughter-House* case.

Holmes had already dissented in *Lochner*. Against the majority's absolutist defense of intensive property rights, Holmes insisted on a balancing of competing interests. Defeated, he chose his dissenting words carefully to build a case for an alternative law. Dismissing the Court's professed belief in natural rights, he accused it of following "Mr. Herbert Spencer's *Social Statics.*" Denying his opponents any moral high ground, Holmes characterized their position as instrumental, accusing them of using property as a means to the goals of efficiency and prosperity. He thus reduced the grounds for disagreement to a dispute over economic models.

This was not Holmes's first challenge to prevailing forms of legal reasoning defending intensive property rights. In *The Common Law* (1881), he rejected simple arguments for absolute property rights with the original and fertile observation that they conflicted with the premises of a competitive market economy. "The law," Holmes observed, "does not even seek to indemnify a man from all harms." For example, Holmes notes that one may establish a business even when this reduces "the custom of another shop-keeper, perhaps to the ruin of him." But the law permits new entrants to hurt established businesses on grounds of "policy without reference to any kind of morality" (Holmes 1881, 115, 128).[12]

In "Privilege, Malice and Intent" (1894), Holmes used competitive injury to argue for an instrumental approach that balances competing property interests rather than applying syllogistic reasoning (Horwitz 1992, 130–35). On the Supreme Court, he applied this approach in *Diamond Glue Co. v. United States Glue Co.* (1903). "In modern societies," he wrote,

> every part is related so organically to every other that what affects any portion must be felt more or less by all the rest. Therefore, unless everything is to be forbidden and legislation is to come to a stop, it is not enough to show that in the working of a statute there is some tendency logically discernible to interfere with commerce or existing contracts. Practical lines must be drawn and distinctions of degree must be made.

Seen in this context, Holmes's ruling in *Pennsylvania Coal* did not sanctify property. Instead, he founded the "takings doctrine" on a balance of competing interests. Compensation is not necessarily due property owners; instead, restitution depends on circumstances. Property should not be left without "reasonable" use; but "reasonable" is deliberately unspecific. Interference that goes "too far" is a "taking" requiring recompense, but how much is "too far" is to be evaluated by judges considering the particular circumstances. Neither the individual owners of private property nor the public has absolute rights; instead, competing interests must be weighed and balanced. Judges must weigh competing interests on a case-by-case basis because, although property owners should not be arbitrarily indisposed, "government hardly could go on if to some extent values incident to property could not be diminished." Those who today use "takings" law to defend an absolute right of property go against Holmes's clear intent, reverting to the doctrines of Field and Peckham that Holmes overturned in his decisions.

The gradual acceptance of Holmes's instrumentalist view made the 1920s the last gasp for the sanctity of property rights. The decade that began with *Adkins* ended with the spread of the "Legal Realism," which by 1930 dominated some major law school faculties (Horwitz 1992; Fisher et al. 1993). Following Holmes, the realists insisted that the law was to be studied instrumentally using the tools of empirical social science.

New Priorities in the New Deal

Retreat became rout when the political support for sanctified property rights collapsed during the Great Depression of the 1930s. Rallying around President Franklin Delano Roosevelt and the New Deal, a new breed of liberals promoted government regulation to relieve distress and reform capitalism. Even the Supreme Court retreated from the absolute defense of intensive property rights. Scholars have highlighted a "constitutional revolution of 1937" after two conservative judges resigned. But landmark decisions like *West Coast Hotel Co. v. Parrish* (1937), *National Labor Relations Board v. Jones and Laughlin Steel Corp.* (1937), *United States v. Carolene Products Co.* (1938), and *United States v. Darby* (1941) were prefigured by earlier decisions reflecting a new instrumental approach to property rights.

Most remarkable was *Home Building and Loan Association v. Blaisdell* (1934), in which the Supreme Court accepted a Minnesota moratorium on mortgage foreclosures during a legislatively declared economic emergency. Speaking for the Court, Chief Justice Charles Evans Hughes denied property any sanctity, declaring instead that constitutional protection was not "to be applied with literal exactness like a mathematical formula, but . . . requires construction to fill out details . . . in harmony with the reserved power of the State to safeguard the vital interests of her people." The test for legislation should be "whether the end is legitimate and the means reasonable and appropriate." Here is the social and the instrumental interpretation of property erected into constitutional doctrine. Hughes concluded by denying any privilege to property:

> Economic conditions may arise in which a temporary restraint of enforcement of contracts will be consistent with the spirit and purpose of the contract clause, and thus be within the range of the reserved power of the State to protect the vital interests of the community. . . . Since the contract clause is not an absolute and utterly unqualified restriction of the States' protective power, the legislation is clearly so reasonable as to be within the legislative competency. . . . Whether the legislation is wise or unwise as a matter of policy does not concern the Court.

The Court became even more amenable to Roosevelt's reform program after his reelection in 1936 and his attempt to "pack" the Court in 1937. No decision marked the Court's new approach so clearly as *United States v. Carolene Products Co.* (1938). Rejecting property rights arguments, the Court found that a law forbidding milk adulteration was a reasonable use of state regulatory authority. But more important than the decision itself was Footnote Four of Justice Stone's opinion, in which the Court majority explicitly separated property from the bundle of sanctified civil liberties guaranteed by the Bill of Rights. Following the lead of Justice Hughes in *Blaisdell,* Stone announced that the Court would defer to elected legislators in assessing regulations on property, because the Court believed legislatures are better able to perform the necessary balancing of contending economic interests. In contrast, Stone warned that intrusions on personal liberties, such as free speech or religious practices, would be examined carefully.

Environmental Protection and the "Takings" Counteroffensive

Since *Carolene,* the Supreme Court has allowed democratically elected legislators wide discretion in choosing the objects of social policy, even when
they have dramatically restricted the actions of property holders. The
Wisconsin Supreme Court case of *Just v. Marinette County* (1972) illustrates
well the judiciary's post-*Carolene* posture. In *Just,* the Wisconsin court rejected
Ronald and Kathryn Just's challenge to state regulations preventing them
from filling wetlands. Moving beyond the traditional police powers, the
Wisconsin court denied property owners any "absolute and unlimited right
to change the essential natural character of [their] land." Zoning regulations,
the court acknowledged, "must be reasonable" but may be established "to
prevent harm to public rights by limiting the use of private property to its
natural uses." There was no "taking" of property, as defined under
Pennsylvania Coal, because the "uses consistent with the nature of the land
are allowed."

Just v. Marinette has not been tested in the Supreme Court and has been
accepted in only two other states, New Jersey and Minnesota. But the Court
has continued to apply a "balancing test" in assessing property regulations. In
Penn Central Transportation v. New York (1978), for example, the Penn Central
Transportation Company sued the New York Landmarks Preservation
Commission for damages when the commission vetoed construction above
Grand Central Station. Rejecting the suit, Justice William Brennan gave three
criteria to determine due compensation—criteria that were sufficiently
vague and elastic to provide little protection for the rights claimed by some
property holders.

Property rights advocates did better in "takings" litigation after the election
of President Ronald Reagan in 1980, but they have not yet succeeded in
moving the law away from the instrumental and "balanced" approach cham-
pioned by Holmes. Led by a Reagan appointee, Antonin Scalia, the Court
made a series of decisions beginning in 1987 that seemed to turn away from
the Court's post-*Carolene* stance of deferring to elected legislatures and
balancing competing interests in assessing property regulations. In *First English
Evangelical Lutheran Church v. County of Los Angeles* (1987), for example, the
Court required Los Angeles County to pay compensation after the flood
control district prohibited rebuilding a flood-damaged campground because
the "regulation depriv[ed the] owner of *all* [emphasis added] use of property."

Environmentalists and others opposed to a return to the legal sanctification
of property feared *First English.* But liberal judges Brennan and Marshall
supported the decision because it broke no new constitutional ground but
merely reaffirmed established principles from *Pennsylvania Coal. However,
Nollan v. California Coastal Commission* (1987), decided in the same year, was
different because it imposed a new standard on regulations. The Nollans, owners

of an oceanfront lot nestled between public parks to the north and south, sought to replace their dilapidated bungalow with a three-bedroom house similar to other structures in the area. The California Coastal Commission gave the required permit only after the Nollans granted a public easement between the mean high-tide line and the seawall behind their house to allow public passage along dry sand between the parks to the north and south. The commission justified the requirement by saying that the larger house would contribute to a "wall of residential structures" that "would prevent the public psychologically . . . from realizing a stretch of coastline exists nearby that they have every right to visit" (Eagle 1996, 255).

In *Nollan,* the Supreme Court overturned the California Coastal Commission and established new criteria for judicial review of property regulations. Writing for the Court, Justice Antonin Scalia admitted that placing "a condition on the granting of land-use permit" is not, as in First English, "a 'taking' within the meaning of the Fifth Amendment." But "the evident constitutional propriety disappears . . . if the condition substituted for the prohibition utterly fails to further the end advanced as the justification for the prohibition." In other words, Scalia argued that requiring an easement does not serve the stated purpose of protecting the access to the beach. As an arbitrary "taking" that reduces the value of property for no good reason, it therefore requires compensation. Scalia concluded by pronouncing a new standard:

> The lack of nexus between the condition and the original purpose of the building restriction converts that purpose to something other than it was. The purpose then becomes, quite simply, the obtaining of an easement to serve some valid governmental purpose, but without payment of compensation. . . . Unless the permit condition serves the same governmental purpose as the development ban, the building restriction is not a valid regulation of land use but "an out-and-out plan of extortion."

This time Brennan and Marshall dissented. Rejecting Scalia's second-guessing of state officials, they upheld the post-*Carolene* standard that "the proper standard for review . . . is whether the state could rationally have decided that the measure adopted might achieve the state's objective." But after these liberal icons retired in 1990 and 1991, the Court moved to impose additional restrictions on state regulation. In *Lucas v. South Carolina Coastal Council* (1992), for example, the Court ordered compensation to a South Carolina landowner for loss of value after the new state Beachfront Management Act forbade construction on his land. Writing for the Court, Justice Scalia sought to reestablish an absolute standard, a renewed sanctification of intensive property rights. "Our decision in [*Pennsylvania Coal Co. v.*] *Mahon,*" he warned,

> offered little insight into when, and under what circumstances, a given regulation would be seen as going "too far" for purposes of the Fifth Amendment. In 70-odd years of succeeding "regulatory takings" jurisprudence, we have generally eschewed any "set formula" for determining how far is too far, preferring to "engag[e] in . . . essentially ad hoc, factual inquiries."

Now Scalia urged the Court to abandon "ad hoc" rules and "balancing tests" to establish firm categorical rules requiring compensation not only for land seizures but also for regulations that "deny the property owner all 'economically viable use of his land'." Openly voicing his distrust of elected legislators, Scalia warned, as he had in *Nollan,* that judges need to evaluate regulations carefully to ensure against the "risk that private property is being pressed into some form of public service under the *guise* [emphasis added] of mitigating serious public harm."

The Court refined its new standards in *Dolan v. City of Tigard* (1994), in which it instructed courts to shift some of the burden of proof in regulation cases from property owners to the government. The case arose when the city of Tigard, Oregon, allowed Florence Dolan to expand her plumbing supply store only on the condition that she dedicate land for a public greenway along a neighboring creek and provide a pedestrian and bicycle pathway to relieve traffic congestion. Again second-guessing local officials, Chief Justice William Rehnquist concluded that the city had "not met its burden of demonstrating that the additional number of vehicle and bicycle trips generated by Dolan's development reasonably relates to the city's requirement for a dedication of the pathway easement."

The *Nollan, Lucas,* and *Dolan* decisions signal a new era of heightened scrutiny of property regulation that could signal a return to the pre–New Deal era of sanctified property rights. But much judicial practice and precedent still stands against this. In 1987, the same Court that ruled in *Nollan* accepted, in *Keystone Bituminous Coal Association v. DeBenedictis,* a Pennsylvania law remarkably similar to the one overturned by Holmes's Court in *Pennsylvania Coal.* Using pragmatic and instrumental reasoning based in Holmes's case law, the Court in *Keystone* concluded that restricting the property rights of the owners of subsurface rights was reasonable to protect surface property and therefore was not a "taking" requiring compensation. The ability of the Court to reverse precedent so easily demonstrated how Holmes grounded takings law in pragmatic and instrumental considerations rather than in a sanctified vision of property.

If Rehnquist's Court did not categorically accept Scalia's view of *Nollan, Lucas,* and *Dolan,* then it should not be surprising that many lower-court judges also hesitated to resanctify property. This caution has clearly frustrated property rights advocates. In *Claude Lambert et ux. v. City and County of San Francisco et al.* (2000), for example, Justice Scalia berated his fellow judges. Reminding them that "the object of the Court's holding in *Nollan* and *Dolan* was to protect against the State's cloaking within the permit process 'an out-and-out plan of extortion'," he complained that this was current zoning practice in San Francisco and other localities, where municipal officials regularly require payments to approve zoning changes. The acceptance by lower courts of such practices, Scalia warned, calls "into question [their] willingness to hold state administrators to the Fifth Amendment standards set forth by this tribunal." Scalia's disappointment must have been enhanced when only two of his fellow justices joined his dissent.

Conclusion: Means and Ends in Property Law

Notwithstanding Justice Scalia, Footnote Four of *Carolene* remains good law. Placed behind other constitutionally guaranteed rights, property is protected only as a means, an instrument to achieve other social ends, rather than as a sanctified natural right. Since *Carolene* was propounded, the Supreme Court has approved almost all legislation regulating property, recognizing the power of elected legislatures to be "as broad as the economic needs of the nation."[13] At the same time, the Supreme Court has established itself as the watchdog of the civil liberties guaranteed by the Bill of Rights and the Fourteenth Amendment, elevating these above any property owner's claim to a right to pollute or to discriminate on the basis of gender, race, or religion.

Treating property as a social construction, the post-*Carolene* Court has based property law on two pillars: the reciprocal nature of damage and a conception of property as an instrument rather than a sanctified right. Courts have treated property rights as only one of several competing rights that all must be balanced. Each asserted property "right" must be assessed in terms of the costs to other citizens and property holders and with possible alternative means to achieve the desired social ends. Property holders may be given broad discretion, but viewed as instruments, property rights can never be absolute, never sanctified as ends in themselves.

It is this social and instrumental conception of property that most disturbs those who would return to a simple law, defending property as a natural right, a physical representation of individual labor. Appalled at the inconsistencies, the confusion, and the lack of rigor inherent in a pragmatic approach that reviews each situation on a case-by-case basis, they yearn for the simplicity of absolute and sanctified property rights. But Holmes and his case law are not alone responsible for the persistence of his pragmatism and his "balancing tests." Property law, as Holmes recognized, is always "a question of degree" because there are always rival property rights requiring balance. In practice, those who would sanctify property as a "natural right" would not accord equal stature to all property and all rights; instead, they would protect some aspects of the property rights in land at the expense of the rights of other property and of other civil rights. Property law can simply sanctify some property, but only by disregarding other property and other rights. It is these competing interests that force judges to make pragmatic judgments. They are driven to view property as an instrument because that is the only way to deal with competing interests and rights. Holmes understood this, and that is why his decisions are still law today.

Notes

1. Extending Coase's analysis, some argue that legal systems will move toward efficient property rights regimes that minimize legal costs (Posner 1992).
2. Distribution will not affect demand patterns where economic agents have identical preferences regardless of income. Changes in demand will not affect prices if there are constant returns to scale because increases or reductions in output will leave costs constant.
3. This is the view of some scholars of the American land claim movement in the West, who have shown how groups of individuals established property rights prior to the formal organization of local governments (Hurst 1956, 3–5; Umbeck 1977, 1981).
4. Note Justice Field's dissent in the *Slaughter-House* case cited below.
5. This point is made repeatedly by Richard Ely (1971). Presumably, it contributes to Richard Epstein's rejection of instrumental reasoning (as used, for example, by Posner) (Epstein 1985; Mercuro and Medema 1997, 73).
6. This expropriation would be worth over $300 billion in current dollars. In other cases, such as the British Empire, compensation covered some of the slave owners' lost property. Following this precedent, President Lincoln was prepared to offer $400 million in compensation if the Confederate states would lay down their arms (Connor 1920, 166–68).
7. One of the few victories won by liberals before the Supreme Court in the early twentieth century came in *Buchanan v. Warley* (1917), in which the Court overturned a Louisville, Kentucky, ordinance prohibiting blacks from living in neighborhoods in which the majority of homes were occupied by whites. The law was overturned as a violation of the rights of property owners to sell their property.
8. This insight led to Holmes's instrumental reasoning and his explicit weighing of costs and use of "balancing rules" for the adjustment of differences in cases involving externalities, most famously in *Pennsylvania Coal Co. v. Mahon*. His line of reasoning is still good law, as shown in *Penn Central Transportation v. New York* 438 U.S. 104 (1978).

9. *Palmer v. Mulligan* was to be used as precedent many times, including in New York, *Platt v. Johnson and Root* 15 Johns New York (1818), and Massachusetts, *Tyler v. Wilkinson* (1827).
10. The significance of this subsidy to entrepreneurial activity is discussed in Horwitz (1977). The magnitude is questioned in Epstein (1982) and Schwartz (1981).
11. By citing Smith rather than Locke, Field avoided Locke's lapse into biblical exegesis.
12. This is discussed further in Horwitz (1992, 127ff.).
13. Majority decision in *American Power and Light Co. v. Securities and Exchange Commission* 329 U.S. 90 (1946).

References

Barzel, Yoram. 1997. *The Economic Analysis of Property Rights*. Cambridge: Cambridge University Press.

Bensel, Richard Franklin. 1984. *Sectionalism and American Political Development 1880–1980*. Madison: University of Wisconsin Press.

———. 1990. *Yankee Leviathan: The Origins of Central State Authority in America, 1859–1877*. Cambridge: Cambridge University Press,

Bourgin, Frank P. 1989. *The Great Challenge: The Myth of Laissez Faire in the Early Republic*. New York: Scribner's.

Coase, Ronald. 1960. "The Problem of Social Cost." *Journal of Law and Economics* 3:2–44.

Connor, Henry G. 1920. *John Archibald Campbell: Associate Justice of the United States Supreme Court*. Boston: Little, Brown.

Eagle, Steven. 1996. *Regulatory Takings*. Charlottesville, Va.: Michie Law Publishers.

Ely, James W., Jr. 1998. *The Guardian of Every Other Right: A Constitutional History of Property Rights*. New York: Oxford University Press.

Ely, Richard. 1971 [reprint of 1914 edition]. *Property and Contract in their Relation to the Distribution of Wealth*. 2 volumes. Port Washington, N.Y.: Kennikat Press.

Epstein, Richard. 1985. *Takings: Private Property and the Power of Eminent Domain*. Cambridge: Harvard University Press.

Fisher, William W. III, Morton J. Horwitz, and Thomas A. Reed, eds. 1993. *American Legal Realism*. New York: Oxford University Press.

Flick, Alexander C. 1901. *Loyalism in New York during the American Revolution*. New York: Columbia University Press.

Foner, Eric. 1976. *Tom Paine and Revolutionary America*. London: Oxford University Press.

———. 1988. *Reconstruction: America's Unfinished Revolution, 1863–1877*. New York: W. W. Norton.

———. 1998. *The Story of American Freedom*. New York: W. W. Norton.

Fried, Barbara H. 1998. *The Progressive Assault on Laissez Faire: Robert Hale and the First Law and Economics Movement*. Cambridge: Harvard University Press.

Friedman, Gerald. 1999. *State-Making and Labor Movements*. Ithaca, N.Y.: Cornell University Press.

Handlin, Oscar and Mary Flug Handlin. 1947. *Commonwealth: A Study of the Role of Government in the American Economy: Massachusetts, 1774–1861.* Cambridge: Harvard University Press.

Hartz, Louis. 1955. *The Liberal Tradition in America: An Interpretation of American Political Thought since the Revolution.* New York: Harcourt Brace Jovanovich.

Holmes, Oliver Wendell. 1881. *The Common Law.* Boston: Little, Brown.

———. 1894. "Privilege, Malice, and Intent." *Harvard Law Review* 8 (April): 1–14.

Horne, Thomas. 1990. *Property Rights and Poverty: Political Argument in Britain, 1605–1834.* Chapel Hill: University of North Carolina Press.

Horwitz, Morton J. 1977. *The Transformation of American Law, 1780–1860.* Cambridge: Harvard University Press.

———. 1992. *The Transformation of American Law, 1870–1960.* New York: Oxford University Press.

Hurst, James Willard. 1956. *Law and the Conditions of Freedom in the Nineteenth-Century United States.* Madison: University of Wisconsin Press.

Jacobs, Clyde E. 1954. *Law Writers and the Courts: The Influence of Thomas M. Cooley, Christopher G. Tiedeman, and John F. Dillon upon American Constitutional Law.* Berkeley: University of California Press.

Katznelson, Ira. 1998. *Liberalism's Crooked Circle: Letters to Adam Michnik.* Princeton: Princeton University Press.

Libecap, Gary. 1989. *Contracting for Property Rights.* Cambridge: Cambridge University Press.

Lipset, Seymour Martin. 1996. *American Exceptionalism? A Double-Edged Sword.* New York: W. W. Norton.

Locke, John. [1690] 1952. *The Second Treatise of Government.* Indianapolis: Bobbs-Merrill.

Mercuro, Nicholas, and Steven G. Medema. 1997. *Economics and the Law: From Posner to Post-Modernism.* Princeton: Princeton University Press.

North, Douglas C. 1981. *Structure and Change in Economic History.* New York: W. W. Norton.

Novak, William J. 1996. *The People's Welfare: Law and Regulation in Nineteenth-Century America.* Chapel Hill: University of North Carolina Press.

Posner, Richard. 1992. *Economic Analysis of Law.* Boston: Little, Brown.

Rakove, Jack N. 1996. *Original Meanings: Politics and Ideas in the Making of the Constitution.* New York: Knopf.

Schwartz, Gary T. 1981. "Tort Law and the Economy in Nineteenth Century America: A Reinterpretation." *Yale Law Journal* 90:1717–75.

Smith, Vernon L. 1999. "Property Rights as a Natural Order: Reciprocity, Evolutionary and Experimental Considerations." In *Who Owns the Environment?* edited by Peter J. Hill and Roger Meiners. Lanham, Md.: Rowman & Littlefield.

Tomlins, Christopher. 1993. *Law, Labor, and Ideology in the Early American Republic.* Cambridge: Cambridge University Press.

Umbeck, John. 1977. "The California Gold Rush: A Study of Emerging Property Rights." *Explorations in Economic History* 14:197–206.

———. 1981. "Might Makes Right: A Theory of the Formation and Initial Distribution of Property Rights." *Economic Inquiry* 19:38–59.

Cases Cited

Adkins v. Children's Hospital, Supreme Court of the United States 261 U.S. 525 (1923).

Allgeyer v. Louisiana, Supreme Court of the United States 165 U.S. 578 (1897).

American Power and Light Co. v. Securities and Exchange Commission, Supreme Court of the United States 329 U.S. 90 (1946).

Buchanan v. Warley, Supreme Court of the United States 245 U.S. 60 (1917).

Butchers' Benevolent Association of New Orleans v. The Crescent City Live-Stock Landing and Slaughter-House Company, Supreme Court of the United States 83 U.S. 36 (1872).

Callender v. Marsh, Supreme Court of Massachusetts, Suffolk 18 Mass. 418 (1823).

Charles River Bridge v. Warren Bridge, Supreme Court of the United States 36 U.S. 420 (1837).

Claude Lambert et ux. v. City and County of San Francisco, et al., Supreme Court of the United States 120 U.S. 1549 (2000).

Commonwealth v. Alger, Supreme Court of Massachusetts, Suffolk and Nantucket 61 Mass. 53 (1851).

Diamond Glue Co. v. United States Glue Co., Supreme Court of the United States 187 U.S. 611 (1903).

Dolan v. City of Tigard, Supreme Court of the United States 114 U.S. 2309 (1994).

First English Evangelical Lutheran Church of Glendale v. County of Los Angeles, Supreme Court of the United States 482 U.S. 304 (1987).

Godcharles v. Wigeman, Supreme Court of Pennsylvania 113 Pa. 431 (1886).

Home Building and Loan Association v. Blaisdell, Supreme Court of the United States 290 U.S. 398 (1934).

Hudson County Water Co. v. McCarter, Supreme Court of the United States 209 U.S. 349 (1908).

In re. Jacobs, Appeals Court of New York 98 N.Y. 98 (1885).

Just v. Marinette County, Supreme Court of Wisconsin 56 Wis. 2d 7 (1972).

Keystone Bituminous Coal Association v. DeBenedictis, Supreme Court of the United States 480 U.S. 470 (1987).

Kohl v. United States, Supreme Court of the United States 91 U.S. 367 (1875).

Lansing v. Smith, Supreme Court of Judicature of New York 8 (Cow.) N.Y. 146 (1828).

Lochner v. New York, Supreme Court of the United States 292 U.S. 198 (1905).

Lucas v. South Carolina Coastal Council, Supreme Court of the United States 2886 U.S. (1992).

Munn v. Illinois, Supreme Court of the United States 94 U.S. 113 (1877).

National Labor Relations Board v. Jones & Laughlin Steel Corp., Supreme Court of the United States 301 U.S. 1 (1937).

Nollan v. California Coastal Commission, Supreme Court of the United States 483 U.S. 825 (1987).

Palmer v. Mulligan, Supreme Court of Judicature of New York 3 Cai.. R. N.Y. 307 (1805).

Penn Central Transportation v. New York, Supreme Court of the United States 438 U.S. 104 (1978).

Pennsylvania Coal Co. v. Mahon, Supreme Court of the United States 260 U.S. 393 (1922).

Platt v. Johnson and Root, Supreme Court of Judicature of New York 15 Johns N.Y. 213 (1818).

State v. Goodwill, Supreme Court of Appeals of West Virginia 33 W.Va. 179 (1889).

Thorpe v. Rutland and Burlington Railroad Company, Supreme Court of Vermont, Chittenden County 27 Vt. 140 (1854).

Tyler v. Wilkinson, Circuit Court, D. Rhode Island, 24 F. Cas. R. I. 472 . (1827).

United States v. Darby, Supreme Court of the United States 312 U.S. 100 (1941).

United States v. Carolene Products Co., Supreme Court of the United States 304 U.S. 144 (1938).

Vanderbilt v. Adams, Supreme Court of Judicature of New York 7 Cow. 349 N.Y. (1827).

West Coast Hotel Co. v. Parrish, Supreme Court of the United States 300 U.S. 379 (1937).

Wynehamer v. People, Court of Appeals of New York 13 N.Y. 378 (1856).

PART II

RECLAIMING ENVIRONMENTAL SINKS

The rights to life, liberty and the pursuit of happiness proclaimed in the U.S. Declaration of Independence can be understood to encompass the right to live in a clean and safe environment. Indeed, a number of state constitutions explicitly guarantee this right. "All persons are born free and have certain inalienable rights," declares the constitution of the state of Montana. "They include the right to a clean and healthful environment." In the same vein, Pennsylvania's constitution asserts, "The people have a right to clean air, pure water, and the preservation of the natural, scenic, historic and esthetic values of the environment."

There is an inherent tension between this constitutional right and the treatment of air, water, and lands as open-access sinks into which polluters can discharge wastes free of charge or social control. With the advent of government regulations on pollution, and the creation of the Environmental Protection Agency (EPA) in 1970, Americans have moved to resolve this tension by setting constraints on the use of environmental sinks. Access to sinks is no longer completely open. Intense debate persists, however, over the desirable degree of pollution control.

In the past two decades, the environmental justice movement has introduced an important new dimension to this debate, focusing attention not only on the total amount of pollution society should allow but also on its distribution and in particular on the disproportionate environmental burdens often imposed on people of color and low-income communities. Among the landmark achievements of the environmental justice movement is the 1994 executive order issued by President Clinton that directs each federal agency to take steps to identify and rectify "disproportionately high and adverse human health or environmental effects of its programs, policies, and activities on minority populations and low-income populations."

In seeking to assert democratic control over environmental sinks, efforts to control pollution and to promote environmental justice exemplify the *appropriation* route to building natural assets. The chapters in Part 2 examine a variety of strategies to appropriate environmental sinks. K. A. Dixon discusses brownfields, underused lands whose redevelopment is impeded by unresolved issues of liability for past contamination. Manuel Pastor reviews evidence of environmental injustice and suggests that building "social capital" can help communities to combat it. Paul Templet documents the connection between subsidies to polluters and the inequitable distribution of political power, and concludes that campaign finance reform ought to be seen as an environmental issue. Nicolaas Bouwes, Steven Hassur, and Marc Shapiro describe a pioneering EPA initiative that can help to empower communities by increasing their access to information about toxic hazards. Peter Barnes and Marc Breslow propose to charge polluters for emitting carbon dioxide into the atmosphere and to distribute the revenues equally to all citizens. These chapters demonstrate that policies to reclaim environmental sinks, by transforming them from open-access resources into democratically appropriated natural assets, not only can protect the environment but also can improve the health and economic well-being of low-income people.

CHAPTER 3

Reclaiming Brownfields: From Corporate Liability to Community Asset

K. A. Dixon

Across the United States, many impoverished communities live near polluting industries and the potentially contaminated properties that such industries have left behind as idle or underused land. These properties, known as brownfields, can adversely affect human health and safety, the environment, property values, and the aesthetic quality of nearby neighborhoods. The poverty of local residents is exacerbated by their close proximity to lands that have been used and abused as environmental sinks.

For many low-income and predominantly minority communities, such incompatible neighbors are a fact of life. But they do not have to be. Throughout the country, citizens are reenvisioning brownfields—previously viewed only as liabilities—as potential community assets. Through creative redevelopment efforts, they are transforming these properties into resources that contribute substantial benefits to the surrounding community: a cleaner and safer environment, new jobs, new housing, new commercial or retail space, restored open space, and other public amenities. Brownfield redevelopment can give nearby residents an opportunity to participate democratically in neighborhood revitalization plans to ensure that the results more closely reflect their visions and goals. In such cases, brownfield redevelopment becomes more than a strategy to clean up and reclaim a contaminated parcel of land. It becomes a process of community asset-building that helps to restore the physical and social fabric of neighborhoods and to recreate vibrant, livable communities.

What Are Brownfields?

The U.S. Environmental Protection Agency (EPA) defines brownfields as "abandoned, idled, or under-used industrial and commercial facilities where expansion or redevelopment is complicated by real or perceived environmental contamination."[1] The General Accounting Office (1987, 4) estimates that there are more than 425,000 brownfields across the nation, posing a threat to public health and the environment, contributing to neighborhood blight, and diminishing local tax revenues.

The ownership of brownfield properties is mixed. Some sites are in private hands; others are owned by the federal government or by local or state governments. Still others are "orphan sites" for which there are no recognized "potentially responsible parties" to pay for contamination cleanups because such parties no longer exist, are insolvent, or are unknown. Each site has its own industrial history and quality of infrastructure. Site size can vary from a half-acre former dry-cleaning establishment to a 900-acre defunct manufacturing facility. Contamination levels also differ, from none at all to severe contamination. But what all sites have in common is the perception that they are contaminated, and that perception makes redevelopment more difficult.

Brownfields often are divided into three broad categories. The first includes well-located sites that are lightly contaminated and can be redeveloped through private market transactions, without public subsidies or other forms of external intervention. Second, some sites are well-located but have moderate to high levels of contamination or other problems such as aging infrastructure or liability issues. These sites require public subsidies or other types of external intervention to attract private-sector investment. The third category comprises sites so severely contaminated and/or poorly located that a great deal of public support and expenditure is required to clean and redevelop the property.[2]

Brownfields also can be categorized according to the degree of community ownership of the sites. Ownership includes not only actual title to the property but also the degree to which the local community determines what happens on the site. The continuum of community ownership ranges from cases in which the property and the redevelopment process are fully in private external hands (zero percent community ownership) to cases in which sites are owned and managed by democratic, community-based organizations (100 percent community ownership). Public-sector ownership lies between these two poles, its position on the continuum depending on the extent of community participation in the redevelopment process. Even under private corporate ownership, however, the community typically still has some rights with regard to the property:

> Privately-owned land is a community resource, as well as a private
> one, and local land use laws and zoning ordinances allow for public

participation in deciding what is the appropriate use of a piece of
land. Local, state, and federal tax breaks and redevelopment assistance only strengthen the argument that the community has a
legitimate role to play in land use and development decisions that
will affect their environment. (Dalton 1998, 4.)

Agreements can be crafted that guarantee jobs to local residents, implement
various forms of joint land use, and set limits on environmental externalities.
Such agreements represent intermediate points on the community ownership continuum.

In all these categories, one class of brownfields poses a particular challenge:
sites mothballed by corporate owners who prefer to leave them idle rather
than redevelop them. These owners do not try to sell, remediate, or redevelop
the land. Instead, they hold the land simply to avoid paying cleanup costs: it is
less expensive, and less of a headache, to keep the property dormant or barely
operating. To sell or redevelop the mothballed site would expose the owner
to a greater risk that others—the public, state regulatory agencies, or the
EPA—might discover the site's flaws and possible liabilities. Although it may
be financially advantageous for corporate owners to mothball these sites, the
local community pays the external costs of such inaction, including unabated
environmental degradation, related health effects, and the opportunity costs
of forgone jobs and lost tax revenues.

Who Benefits from Brownfield Redevelopment?

A number of stakeholders stand to gain when contaminated urban properties
are redeveloped. Local residents benefit from the positive environmental and
health effects of cleaner air, water, and soil. Residents of the city periphery
benefit because land recycling diminishes the need to develop open space, thus
combating suburban sprawl. Reclaimed sites provide business and industry
with opportunities to locate near customers, potential employees, and transportation routes. Everyone gains from the resulting improvements in urban
infrastructure and amenities. Local governments benefit when brownfield
parcels return to the tax ledger.

By attracting additional economic activity to the community, brownfield
redevelopment can create new job opportunities for area residents. In her
report *Working on Brownfields,* Paula Doogan (1998, 3) observes that "the con-
fluence of brownfields, on the one hand, and employment problems, on the
other, is striking." The same process that creates brownfields dislocates workers
as industries close down or operate minimally. Conversely, the reclamation of
these sites increases employment opportunities. Jobs are created at three stages

in the redevelopment process: the assessment and remediation stage, the new construction stage, and the reuse stage. "No brownfields cleanup project exists in a vacuum," Doogan writes. "All are part of economic development and environmental cleanup undertakings that aim to bring renewed economic activity, improved living conditions, and healthier fiscal situations, in short—JOBS—to their communities." Because many brownfields are located in low-income communities, areas particularly likely to suffer from unemployment and lack of economic opportunities, brownfield redevelopment can create jobs where they are most needed. Depending on the stage of redevelopment and the end use of the site, new employment can include a mix of permanent and temporary jobs requiring diverse skill levels.

Not all brownfield projects create permanent jobs, however, and those that do create jobs do not automatically employ the people who live closest to the site. Unless stakeholders in the redevelopment process are committed to the principle of hiring local residents, employment benefits may go to others. Typically, projects that are committed to local employment are those with some degree of community participation and public-sector involvement.

Barriers to Brownfield Redevelopment

Unfortunately, the multiple benefits of brownfield redevelopment are often blocked by multiple barriers. The costs of cleaning up and redeveloping brownfields are often greater than the costs of developing undeveloped open space. An array of factors drives up these costs, creating significant barriers to brownfield redevelopment.

First, the fact that brownfields are perceived to be contaminated means that property owners, developers, and lenders fear the liability risks associated with such sites. Under current federal law, liability at contaminated sites—from Superfund sites to the most lightly tainted brownfields—is joint, several, and retroactive. That is, everyone in the chain of title can be held liable for contamination that has already occurred, for future contamination, and for any contamination of neighboring properties. All these parties could be held responsible for the cleanup costs. The magnitude of liability and its associated costs (including assessment, remediation, third-party damages, and litigation fees) vary from site to site and depend not only on the level of contamination but also on the willingness of the potentially responsible parties to engage in redevelopment activities and on their ability to manage risk.

Steps have been taken at the state and federal levels to allay these fears and to reduce the risk of liability. In 1996, the federal government enacted legislation to reduce the liability of institutions that make loans to brownfield redevelopment projects.[3] Many state governments have established grant and loan funds to assist in the redevelopment of contaminated sites. Despite these efforts, however, the risk of liability claims remains a significant barrier to brownfield redevelopment.

Other site characteristics can pose additional barriers to redevelopment. Many brownfields support aging and obsolete infrastructure unsuitable to modern manufacturing techniques. Often, brownfield parcels are too small to support cost-effective redevelopment, and the difficulties associated with land assembly prevent interested parties from forming larger, more viable properties. Such factors as limited access to transportation routes, a high incidence of crime, neighborhood physical decay, and the insufficient availability of a qualified workforce may also serve to deter redevelopment. Brownfield projects can take a long time to complete, often much longer than conventional development projects. Assessing and remediating a contaminated site, securing the necessary environmental regulatory permits and approvals, and arranging financing can extend the timeline considerably, and time can make or break a redevelopment deal.

Finally, one of the most significant barriers to transforming brownfield liabilities into community assets is the way most stakeholders define redevelopment. In the context of brownfields, redevelopment generally refers to market-driven commercial or industrial end uses that are expected to generate profits (Mallach 1998, 7). Such use, of course, should be a serious option among the redevelopment possibilities; often, the results can significantly benefit low-income communities. But such redevelopment may not always be what communities most need or want. Preferred end uses may include low-income housing, public parks, community gardens, or greenhouses, the benefits of which cannot be judged simply in terms of the number of jobs or the level of market activity generated. Securing support and financing for non-revenue-producing end uses such as parks and open space, however, is often very difficult. Conditions on available funding can restrict the ability of communities to implement their own visions of what is best for their neighborhood.

Who Can Make It Happen? Partnerships for Brownfield Redevelopment

Despite these formidable barriers, brownfield redevelopment activity has increased substantially in recent years and has gained prominence on the national political agenda. Projects have garnered support from a broad range of stakeholders: federal agencies, state and local governments, community-based organizations, business enterprises, and a scattering of private financial institutions. These actors play distinctive roles, but their ability to work together in creative partnerships enhances the possibility that redevelopment efforts will serve the needs of poor communities.

The EPA has provided national leadership in encouraging brownfield redevelopment, launching a campaign to "prevent, assess, safely clean up, and sustainably reuse" brownfields.[4] The EPA addresses redevelopment issues on several fronts, including financing, liability concerns, and education. The agency offers grants and loans to cities, states, and tribes that are redeveloping a publicly owned site or working to set up a brownfields program. As part of this program, the EPA requires that applicants notify and actively involve the local community in planning and development decisions. The agency also provides clarification and guidance on liability and cleanup issues and has instituted a new program to link brownfield projects to job training and workforce development. Finally, the EPA has worked in partnership with state governments to develop Voluntary Cleanup Programs to facilitate brownfield redevelopment and to encourage private sector involvement.

Federal support for brownfield redevelopment is not limited to the EPA. The Department of Housing and Urban Development (HUD), the Economic Development Agency, the Department of Transportation, the Department of Energy, and other federal agencies participate in an interagency brownfield redevelopment working group coordinated by the EPA. The programs of these agencies augment those of the EPA by providing loans and grants, technical assistance and training, clarification of liability issues, and support for efforts to develop state brownfield programs.

States and municipalities also play important roles in brownfield redevelopment, as the examples we will discuss shortly illustrate. State and local programs are particularly important in cases where the sites are small, moderately to highly contaminated, poorly located, or some combination thereof, thus making redevelopment less attractive to private investors. Municipal governments, in particular, can be a source of important technical assistance, financing, and other support that local communities need to engage in complex redevelopment activities.

In addition to federal, state, and municipal initiatives, local residents and community-based organizations have taken leading roles in the redevelopment of brownfields in a number of cities, including Pittsburgh, San Diego, Minneapolis, and Birmingham. Private, nonprofit community development corporations (CDCs) have been particularly important contributors of planning and organizing expertise to the redevelopment process. The CDCs often wear many hats, serving simultaneously as project managers, financial intermediaries, developers, and community organizers. They often take on projects the business sector avoids and fill gaps left by local government and federal initiatives. Community support and participation are often hallmarks of brownfield projects with a significant degree of CDC leadership and frequently play a crucial role in the successful completion of the projects.

Finally, private businesses and financial institutions are often key players in successful brownfield redevelopment, providing a major portion of the investment funds. Not all brownfield projects lend themselves to a high degree of community decision-making, and not all communities have the wherewithal to pursue such strategies. However, strictly private development projects—in which one private owner sells the property to another private owner without public-sector involvement—are less likely to present opportunities for community involvement.

The partnerships forged among public agencies, community-based organizations, and private firms during the development process are of fundamental importance in increasing the chances of successful brownfield redevelopment (Pepper 1996; Van Horn et al. 1999). Establishing effective working relationships among all participants reduces the risk that the transfer and subsequent redevelopment of the asset will be derailed by one disgruntled stakeholder or slowed by the inability to reach consensus. Such partnerships are not easy to form or maintain, however, because the primary interests of the different stakeholders are often contradictory. "The durability of partnerships for initiating and coordinating urban social change," Jezierski (1995, 300) observes, "requires constant efforts to institutionalize conflicting interests and construct legitimacy for development policy and for the partnership itself." Despite the difficulties of reconciling stakeholder interests, the benefits of building and maintaining effective partnerships make it a wise investment.

Building Community Brownfield Assets

In financial markets, one party's liability is another party's asset. For example, in a home mortgage, the liability on the homeowner's balance sheet corresponds to an asset on the bank's. Similarly, if a brownfield site is a potential or actual liability to its current owner, then it represents an asset to other parties, including local residents who could sue for damages and/or force the owner to clean up the site. This is not to suggest that proximity to contaminated sites is desirable for a community. But once the environmental damage has been done, the community has a claim for just compensation and redress of the injury it has suffered. In this admittedly unconventional sense, brownfields are latent community assets. The question is how to transform them into performing assets that provide flows of benefits to the surrounding community.

The extent to which low-income communities are able to convert these assets and obtain their benefits depends, in large part, on how far they are able to move along the ownership rights continuum toward increased participation in and control of the redevelopment process. The spectrum of community participation ranges from simple public notification, to varying degrees of direct input into decisions about such issues as hiring and workforce development planning, to management of the redevelopment process, to ownership of the reclaimed site itself.

Community Notification

Many municipalities have community notification requirements for developers who undertake brownfield projects. These may include public hearings that community residents can attend to learn about the project and the job opportunities redevelopment will generate and to voice concerns. Although valuable, community notification alone does not result in truly shared decision-making power, and it often occurs too late in the redevelopment process to allow local residents to participate meaningfully.

Community Participation in Developing Hiring Goals

From the outset, project stakeholders and local residents can work with future tenants of the redeveloped site to anticipate the number of workers who will be hired and what job skills they will need. Federal, state, and local employment and training programs can then be coordinated to provide training and employment-related assistance. When site redevelopment is completed, local residents will be better equipped with the skills necessary to compete successfully for jobs. Such training efforts can be complemented by municipal tax incentives or other policies to encourage the hiring of local residents.

Such a strategy is being employed at the North Birmingham Industrial Redevelopment Project in Birmingham, Alabama.[5] The city and a number of community organizations are coordinating the redevelopment of this 900-acre site, which includes active industrial facilities, derelict and abandoned buildings, dilapidated housing, and vacant space. The site is well-located, being close to the center of town, the Birmingham International Airport, and several interstate highways and rail lines. A mixed-use redevelopment is planned, consisting of light industrial and commercial uses, community amenities, residential areas, and public open space. The North Birmingham project was among the first to be designated an EPA brownfield pilot project. The $200,000 pilot grant was used to set up the Birmingham Environmental Clearinghouse, a nonprofit organization designed to conduct community outreach and education on environmental issues. The clearinghouse in turn helped to form the North Birmingham Economic Revitalization Corporation to coordinate the economic redevelopment on the site.

A primary focus of the project is job creation, and the redevelopment is expected to create more than 2,000 new jobs at the site. Project coordinators are working to ensure that primarily local residents are hired for these jobs. The site is within a state enterprise zone where tax benefits encourage local hiring. In addition, community organizers and local residents intend to work with each potential tenant to ascertain how many employees and what types of skills the company will require, so that local people can be trained before-

hand. These efforts have already scored some success. The first three companies to locate on the site have created approximately 200 jobs, more than half
of them filled by local residents. If assets are broadly understood as claims on
future income streams, such employment gains can be considered a form of
asset-building. In this case, however, there is no formal agreement between
the employers and the local community that guarantees local residents access
to the new jobs, so their claim on the employment "asset" remains tenuous.

Taking community input a step further, some brownfield projects have
included formal agreements that commit end users to a certain percentage of
local hiring. Although they still need proper training and skills, local residents
find themselves with a leg up in the hiring process. A good example is the
Quarry Retail Project in Minneapolis, which not only removed a significant
environmental hazard from a low-income neighborhood and brought much-
needed retail services but also increased the number of jobs on the site from
less than 250 to around 2,000. The developer of the site, recognizing the complexity of the project and responding to government offers of financial and
technical assistance and tax incentives, agreed to cooperate with both the city
of Minneapolis and a neighborhood task force representing local residents.[6]
Working within this cooperative arrangement, the city set project employment goals to ensure that a fair portion of the new jobs went to local and
minority residents. Both the developer and two of the project's largest tenants
pledged to hire locally, and the project surpassed its 20 percent minority
hiring goal, achieving a level of 25 percent (Pepper 1996, 76). Although the
city provides some funds for training programs, many of the retailers in the
new development provide job training to potential employees. In addition,
retailers have attended community meetings to announce job openings and
take applications for employment.

This experience has been replicated and strengthened elsewhere. Many private firms receive public subsidies to redevelop brownfields. Such subsidy
arrangements can include a condition that the firm or developer agree to hire
local residents, in some cases with priority given to residents who have been
unemployed for long periods. Several cities—including San Francisco,
Berkeley, and Boston—have used this strategy. In the event that a firm or
developer fails to live up to its performance commitments, it is required to
reimburse the city for the benefits it received (Krumholz 1995, 181).

Owning the Redevelopment Process: The Southside Works Project

Successful brownfield projects typically result from an effective collaborative
planning process that involves "a search for voluntary, consensual solutions to
environmental problems through joint participation by federal, state, and local
agencies; business and industry; environmental groups; other interested

nongovernmental organizations; and citizens" (Vig and Kraft 1999, 382). If we take a broad view of asset-building, community participation in the redevelopment process, if sufficiently meaningful and intensive, can approach asset ownership. Even though the community does not own the property in the traditional sense, it "owns" the process by which decisions about redevelopment are made. Beyond securing employment opportunities, low-income residents can secure the right to determine the destiny of the place in which they live.

The LTV Southside Works project in Pittsburgh illustrates a collaborative approach in which there has been a high degree of community ownership of the decision-making process. The LTV site is a 130-acre parcel of land with approximately a mile of frontage on the south side of the Monongahela River. The site is located centrally within the city of Pittsburgh and is close to most of the city's major areas of employment. The surrounding residential community, known as the Southside, is a racially diverse, predominantly blue-collar neighborhood. Southside has a decades-long history of activism and community advocacy, and the neighborhood supports several community-based organizations, including the Southside Local Development Corporation (SSLDC), a CDC. Out of a community meeting organized by the SSLDC in 1985, the Southside Steering Committee was formed to develop long-range strategies for neighborhood redevelopment. Based on the work of this committee, the community created the Southside Planning Forum, an umbrella organization for all neighborhood groups including the Southside Community Council, the Southside Business Alliance, SSLDC, and Friends of the Southside Branch Library. The planning forum meets monthly and operates by consensus.

When the LTV Southside steel plant closed its doors in 1986, the community had the organizational capacity to take a proactive approach to redeveloping the site. LTV Steel itself went to the SSLDC to seek advice about what to do with its land. Contamination was not all that extensive, but the property nevertheless would have been very difficult to sell on the private market. More than a hundred residents took part in a series of community meetings in 1991 to solicit opinions and input. With the help of the SSLDC, and with funding from LTV Steel, the community developed a set of 10 recommendations for redevelopment and end uses of the site (see the accompanying box). These were adopted by the planning forum and have served to guide the ongoing redevelopment process. Similar recommendations have been adopted by other Pittsburgh communities engaged in redevelopment efforts.

Even more important, the Southside Planning Forum entered into a legally binding agreement with the Urban Redevelopment Authority (URA), the redevelopment agency of the city and eventual site owner, covering reuse of the site. To ensure community participation in the process, the agreement specified (1) a planning process to include conceptual plans, socioeconomic assessment, traffic analysis, market analysis, selection of qualified developers, and

Box 3.1. Recommendations from *A Community-Based-Planning Evaluation: LTV Steel's Southside Mill Site*

1. Planning for the site should be consistent with the Southside Neighborhood Plan.
2. The property should be zoned as a Special Planned District to promote flexible development while also assuming maximum public review.
3. Development should not overburden local streets or available public services.
4. There should be a high level of public participation in the redevelopment process.
5. Planning for and development of the site should respond more to long-term objectives than to short-term opportunities.
6. Mixed-use development is encouraged to provide flexibility, respond to market opportunities, assure expeditious development, and ensure variety in keeping with the existing community.
7. Development of the property should be directed to markets that complement rather than duplicate those already existing in the community.
8. Development of the site should be master-planned, paying attention to the outlying parcels to the south of East Carson St. so that development is to scale and in character with surroundings.
9. The riverfront should be treated as an amenity for public access.
10. Interim uses are strongly discouraged.[†]

[†]When engaging in long-term planning, some parcels will be developed later than others. It may be tempting for some stakeholders (such as the public sector) to want to use these parcels "temporarily" for uses other than those for which they were intended. Storage is an example of such an interim use. Such uses are discouraged in order to avoid the permanent establishment of activities that are not compatible with the community's vision.

Source: Sasaki Associates (1996).

a final land development plan; (2) a planning team to include representatives from the community, the URA, the city planning office, and other appropriate individuals; and (3) additional measures to promote public participation, including the dissemination of information to community meetings, community consensus on the master plan, and financial and technical assistance to enhance the forum's ability to participate in the planning process.

This agreement codified the residents' right to take an active leadership role in the redevelopment of the site. It did not guarantee a problem-free project, of course. There have been, and no doubt will continue to be, bumps along the road as redevelopment of the site continues.[7] It will be several years before the project's economic impact on the community can be accurately assessed, but what has been accomplished so far is impressive. The plan for the site envisions a mixed-use, pedestrian-friendly development to evolve over a number of years. It features more than 300 new housing units; 250,000 square feet for retail space; 180,000 square feet for flexible use, product distribution, and entertainment enterprises; and 1.6 million square feet for offices and research and development (Urban Redevelopment Authority 1999, 1). It is expected that more than 6,000 new jobs will be created, and the SSLDC is negotiating with the URA to ensure that a significant portion of these jobs go to local residents. Though the community does not hold title to the property, it thus has gained significant control over the asset by winning the right to help determine the direction of the redevelopment process.

Several factors contributed to the Southside community's ability to take a significant degree of ownership of the process. First, it already had a well-established cadre of community-based groups that were capable of coordinating community input and decision-making. Second, the project benefited from public-sector intervention where the private market had failed. LTV Steel had no use for the site and wanted to sell it, but the company could not find a buyer willing to take on a contaminated piece of property. The URA allowed redevelopment to move forward when it stepped in to negotiate a partial liability release with LTV Steel. Subsequently, the URA bought, assessed and remediated the site.[8] Finally, the URA was open to the high level of community involvement in the Southside. In the words of the URA's Marc Knezevich (1999), "The community was an asset to this project."

Community ownership of the process need not end with the successful completion of the brownfield cleanup and physical rebuilding. The community must ensure that the end uses are appropriately managed and remain compatible with the community's redevelopment vision. To this end, Dalton (1998) suggests "Good Neighbor Agreements" between communities and the new businesses that occupy the site. Such agreements would require disclosure of how the business will operate and would stipulate the local community's right to inspect the facility. The agreements also could specify measures to guarantee that any contamination left on the site would remain contained, and they could set job creation and hiring goals.

Owning the Land: The Dudley Street Neighborhood Initiative and the Power of Eminent Domain

Boston's Dudley Street neighborhood has used a potent brownfield redevelopment tool—the power of eminent domain (see Chapter 14)—to achieve an unprecedented level of community ownership. In the early 1980s, the neighborhood was in serious decline, characterized by high levels of poverty, unemployment, crime, and pollution and by inadequate public services. Following a rash of arson, more than 20 percent of the lots in the 1.5-square-mile community were vacant (Wallsjasper 1997). Yet the neighborhood was home to a diverse group of African-American, Latino, Cape Verdean, and white citizens who shared a vision of their community beyond the empty lots, dilapidated buildings, and unsafe streets and who were determined to work together to make this vision a reality.

The revitalization of the Dudley Street area began in 1984, when local residents came together to form the Dudley Street Neighborhood Initiative (DSNI). DSNI is a nonprofit group whose mission is to "empower Dudley residents to organize, plan for, create, and control a vibrant, diverse and high-quality neighborhood in collaboration with community partners" (Dudley Street Neighborhood Initiative 2000).[9] Working with other civic and church groups, DSNI facilitated a community visioning process to help local residents determine the economic, environmental, and cultural future of the neighborhood. A central issue that emerged was how to deal with the vacant lots that riddled the neighborhood. Residents recognized that the best way to achieve their goals would be to gain control over these assets. The city of Boston had acquired about half the empty lots through tax delinquency. Private individuals, many of whom were hoping to capitalize on any potential redevelopment of the area, held the remainder. Eventually, after several years of public mobilization and court challenges, the city's redevelopment authority granted DSNI the right to eminent domain—a right usually reserved for public-sector agencies and not traditionally used in favor of low-income neighborhoods—throughout a 60-acre portion of the neighborhood. Armed with this powerful tool, the community was able to obtain title to unused land in the neighborhood and has redeveloped more than 300 vacant parcels.

Lessons for Community Organizing

In the end, it is the local community that will feel the most profound effects, positive or negative, of brownfield redevelopment. As the cases discussed illustrate, the degree to which communities are able to establish ownership of brownfield assets and gain access to the benefits that flow from them depends upon a number of factors. Perhaps most important is the ability to organize and exercise power vis-à-vis other private and public-sector actors. Communities with a history of activism and organizing usually are best prepared to meet this challenge. The presence or formation of an effective community-based organization—such as a CDC, a citizen task force, or a neighborhood association—is essential to the success of community asset-building efforts. From previous brownfield redevelopment experiences, we can glean some insights into the key elements of successful community organizing efforts.

The community first must establish a system of decision-making that facilitates the democratic formulation of both the community's long-term vision of its future and concrete decisions about the redevelopment of specific brownfield sites. A representative steering committee, task force, or planning forum should coordinate community information-sharing, participation, and decision-making. In the case of Dudley Street, for example, the residents have established a 29-seat board of directors, made up of residents from each of the area's four main ethnic groups (African-American, Latino, Cape Verdean, and white) and of representatives from seven nonprofit agencies, two churches, two businesses, and two CDCs.

Members of the decision-making body must create mechanisms through which all residents have access to the project proceedings and decisions. Ownership of the process must be shared from the beginning. A regular schedule of meetings and discussion forums can provide members of the community with opportunities to hear about options and to voice opinions. In North Birmingham, the Greater Birmingham Ministries conducted a door-to-door survey to assess housing needs and gauge resident opinion about the neighborhood's strengths and weaknesses. Telephone and mail surveys and focus groups can also be useful. Communication between local residents and their representatives must be consistent, frequent, and two-way.

Through this open process, the decision makers should develop a neighborhood master plan to articulate the community's overall vision and its particular goals for the site. The Neighborhood Plan devised by the Southside community in Pittsburgh is a good example of placing site redevelopment within the larger vision of desirable outcomes. "Without a clear view of those outcomes," Mallach (1998, 4) observes, "the most carefully conceived and broadly participatory process will sooner or later disintegrate." A neighborhood plan that codifies the community's intentions will remind all stakeholders—the community, the municipality, the developer, the end users—of the project's ultimate goals.

Much work is required to keep community residents actively and positively involved over the long haul. Obviously, not every member of the community will participate in this process, and not everyone who does participate will get everything he or she wants. There will be disagreements; compromises will be required. Relationships among stakeholders must be continually refreshed, strengthened, and possibly renegotiated as the redevelopment effort progresses. "People get impatient," remarked one community leader actively involved in the North Birmingham Industrial Redevelopment Project. "The size of the site is sometimes overwhelming, and we need to let people know that improvements to one area benefit everyone" (Davis 1999).

Resolving the Liability Issue

One of the primary reasons some sites are mothballed, instead of being sold or redeveloped, is that their corporate owners fear being held liable for cleanup costs and known or potential damages from contamination. At the same time, many of these owners probably would be glad to rid themselves of properties for which they have no profitable use. If the threat of liability were removed or substantially reduced, the owners of mothballed sites would be more likely to accept opportunities to transfer the property to new owners.

From the standpoint of the community, as noted earlier, these liabilities represent a latent asset, one for which the community has, in a very real sense, already paid by bearing the external costs of living near contaminated and abandoned sites. The possibility therefore exists to reduce corporate liability in exchange for some transfer of asset rights to the community. A reduction of corporate liability need not mean its complete elimination. Rather, the options lie along a continuum of burden sharing among three parties: the corporate owner, the community, and the public sector.

One possibility is for the community or its representative entity (a CDC or some other intermediary) to indemnify the property against legal action, effectively assuming the risk of liability itself.[10] In exchange, corporate owners donate the land to the community. In this scenario, the community and the owner in effect agree that the "price" of the land equals the value of the liability. There is no intrinsic reason, however, that the two amounts should always coincide. Agreements could also be brokered whereby the corporate owner, in exchange for release from liability, would both donate the title of the land *and* pay part or all of the cost of remediating the property. This would be possible if the corporate owner's potential liability were significant enough or if public-sector incentives made the option attractive enough. One incentive for the owner to relinquish title to the property could be an agreement to settle fines the owner might owe for environmental violations. Another could be public-sector assistance in securing permits for building elsewhere.

Depending on the state in which the site is located, the transfer of liability and the costs of remediation of the site can be negotiated through Voluntary Cleanup Programs (VCPs).[11] Under the guidance of the state VCP, the site can be assessed and remediated to meet appropriate cleanup and health standards. Many states allow for "risk-based cleanup actions" whereby the required level of remediation of a parcel depends upon its intended end use. For a site where the intended reuse is housing, for example, cleanup must meet more stringent standards than it would if manufacturing were the intended use. Upon completion of the cleanup, the original site owner receives written confirmation that it has satisfied state laws and will not be held liable by the state for any future cleanup costs or contamination. The new site owner enters into an agreement with the state that it is now the responsible party.

For the corporate owners, this is not a completely risk-free process. Protection from state liability does not protect former and current owners from third-party legal actions. Furthermore, a waiver from state liability does not translate automatically to a waiver from federal liability. In the event that more contamination is discovered in the future, the EPA can hold all former and current owners or operators of the site liable, but so far the agency has been reluctant to infringe upon state-negotiated cleanup and liability agreements. Hence, the benefits of such a negotiated transfer of property may outweigh the risks. The corporate owner disposes of a burdensome property, perhaps garnering some positive public relations, tax deductions, or other benefits in addition to a reduction in liability risks. The community obtains the property or claims to the benefits that flow from it, helping to build its natural-asset base.

Another way to resolve the liability deadlock is through environmental insurance, used alone or in conjunction with the previous options. Comprehensive insurance policies are available that shield participants from the risks that accompany brownfield redevelopment. For example, there are policies that provide coverage for first-party liability (direct state or federal action against a potentially responsible party), third-party pollution legal liability (third-party lawsuits for damages caused to neighboring sites), and unexpected cost increases incurred during an approved site cleanup. Insurance policies can be transferred along with the property, further facilitating sales of brownfield properties.

The cost of insurance can be prohibitive, however. Here again, the participation of the public sector can play a crucial role in expediting asset transfers. For example, the Massachusetts Brownfields Redevelopment Access to Capital Program provides environmental insurance for the developer and secured creditor coverage for the lender. The state-sponsored and subsidized environmental insurance is designed to protect the developer from cleanup cost overruns and from liability arising from newly discovered preexisting environmental contamination. In addition, lenders can be protected from losses due to a default related to environmental issues.[12]

Innovative Financing Arrangements

Innovative institutional arrangements may be needed to finance brownfield redevelopment projects. Local government tax policies, such as Tax Increment

Financing (TIF), may apply to the area in which the property is located; if not, the community can work with the local municipality to establish a TIF zone that includes its parcel.[13] Increasingly, Community Development Block Grants and Section 108 funds from HUD have been applied to brownfield redevelopment projects. HUD also targets monies through its Brownfields Economic Development Initiative grants. State financial support may also be available. New Jersey, for instance, offers Smart Growth Planning Grants to municipalities to encourage redevelopment and sustainable use of land resources and to discourage sprawl in suburban and rural areas. Other potential sources of support include Empowerment Zone funds, EPA pilot project grants, Local Initiative Support Council loans, and the federal Economic Development Agency.

Funding for redevelopment of brownfields is a complex business, and projects typically must cobble together a number of funding resources from federal, state, and local agencies as well as from private investment by developers and end users. This task may be beyond the experience and capacity of the local municipality or CDC, in addition to being very time-consuming. The expertise of intermediaries can be particularly helpful at this juncture. A number of nonprofit and for-profit organizations have emerged in recent years to provide financing, mediation, remediation, and technical services to brownfield stakeholders.[14]

Conclusion

The redevelopment of contaminated properties is a complex and often frustrating process. There is no avoiding the fact that it is simply easier and, at least in the short run, cheaper to develop uncontaminated properties. Yet the examples discussed here illustrate some of the innovative strategies and effective partnerships that hold promise for successful brownfield redevelopment. When the owners of brownfields are persuaded or compelled to take responsibility for their deleterious effect on the surrounding community; when the public sector provides the incentives and support that the market cannot; when the stakeholders work in a committed and cooperative fashion; and when communities organize effectively to claim their right to participate in the redevelopment process and to share in its outcomes—then and only then can brownfields be transformed from corporate liabilities into community assets. Such reclamation of environmental sinks can improve both the health and the economic well-being of those who live in their host neighborhoods.

Notes

1. Superfund sites—those listed on the EPA's National Priorities List—are excluded from the EPA definition of brownfields.

2. For a critique of this classification, emphasizing the potential values created by interdependence among sites in brownfield redevelopment, see Ackerman and Soler (2000).

3. The Asset Conservation, Lender Liability, and Deposit Insurance Protection Act of 1996 was signed into law by President Clinton as part of the 1997 appropriations bill.

4. According to the EPA's Brownfields Mission Statement, the "EPA's Brownfields Initiative will empower States, communities, and other stakeholders in economic development to work together in a timely manner to prevent, assess, safely clean up, and sustainably reuse brownfields." For more information on EPA's brownfields programs, see its web site at http://www.epa.gov/swerosps/bf/.

5. For an in-depth analysis of this and other case studies of brownfields, see the Heldrich Center for Workforce Development, "Turning Brownfields Into Jobfields: Selected Brownfields Case Studies, 12/99" at http://www.heldrich.rutgers.edu.

6. One example of this cooperative relationship is an agreement by which the developer is required to meet with local citizens twice annually for 20 years to address residents' concerns and grievances.

7. The local community knew that there would be some daunting obstacles to overcome before its vision for the neighborhood could be realized. First and foremost, who would pay for the cleanup and redevelopment of the site? LTV, although still subject to federal and third-party liability, would not be a source of funding. At the same time, the city of Pittsburgh has an extensive redevelopment agenda, and nobody knew how much money and how many resources the city would commit to the LTV site. Eventually the city decided to buy the site, with the understanding that it would work with a developer to have the site assessed and remediated. Second, there were infrastructure and real estate problems. Part of the site is located in a 100-year flood plain, and any redevelopment in this area would require careful planning. Also, the foundation of the former steel mill remained buried on site and would have to be removed or built over. Third, local residents were concerned about increased traffic and congestion that would result from redevelopment. Railroad tracks crisscross the site, creating railway easement issues. In addition, structural problems existed with the local bridges that span the Monongahela, compromising access to the area and contributing to traffic congestion. Finally, when the city began to develop its own plans for the site, those plans clashed harshly with the community's redevelopment vision: in 1992, the URA entered into an agreement to bring riverboat casino gambling to the area, contingent upon state legislative action legalizing gambling. This plan was eventually abandoned in the face of vociferous public opposition.

8. Although LTV Steel was released from state liability at the site, the firm still could be held liable in a federal or third-party action.

9. For a history of the DSNI and more information about its activities, see its web site at http://www.dsni.org/contents.htm. See also Medoff and Sklar (1994) and Chapter 16 in this volume.

10. At least one brownfields intermediary, the Chicago Land Redevelopment Institute, is exploring the option of serving as an indemnifier in the case of mothballed properties in order to encourage their transfer.

11. State VCPs offer site owners release from state liability, usually in the form of a No Further Action letter or Covenant Not to Sue, provided the cleanup is done in accordance with state laws. In addition, many state VCPs include technical assistance and financial resources.

12. According to the Massachusetts Governor's Office for Brownfields Revitalization, the state provides a subsidy of 50 percent of the insurance premium for most business projects. For more information on the Brownfields Redevelopment Access to Capital Program, see the web site of the Massachusetts Governor's Office for Brownfields Revitalization at http://www.state.ma.us/massbrownfields/.

13. Tax Increment Financing is a redevelopment strategy that uses tax revenue growth produced by an increase in the tax base of a specified area to repay the costs of investment in the area. Special assessments are made on properties that are expected to accrue particular benefits from general improvement or from an environmental activity such as brownfield cleanup. The incremental difference in tax revenues between the original assessment rate and the new, higher rate is then used by the local government to help the private sector pay for the improvement activity. Many cities and redevelopment authorities use TIF to encourage the private sector to redevelop contaminated or blighted areas.

14. Examples of nonprofit organizations include the Phoenix Land Recycling Company, the Development Fund, and the California Center for Land Recycling. More information about these and other nonprofits can be found at http://www.brownfieldsnet.org/bao.htm.

References

Ackerman, Jerry, and Stephen M. Soler. 2000. "Upsizing Brownfield Sites: Creating Value Beyond the Surface." Paper presented at the EPA Brownfields 2000 Conference. Available at http://www.brownfields2001.org/proceedings-old/.

Dalton, Kathy L. 1998. *Reclaiming Lost Ground: A Resource Guide for Community Based Brownfields Development in Massachusetts.* Boston, Mass.: Environment and Community Development Program, Lincoln Filene Center, Tufts University. Available at http://www.dsni.org/Archives/Reclaiming_lost_ground/reclaiming_lost_ground.htm.

Davis, Annie. 1999. Personal interview. 17 February. Birmingham, Alabama.

Doogan, Paula. 1998. *Working on Brownfields: The Employment and Training Connection.* Washington, D.C.: Northeast-Midwest Institute.

Dudley Street Neighborhood Initiative. 2000. "Mission Statement." Available at http://www.dsni.org/default.htm.

Jezierski, Louise. 1995. "Neighborhood and Public-Private Partnerships in Pittsburgh." In *Exploring Urban America*, edited by Roger W. Caves. Thousand Oaks, Calif.: Sage Publications.

Knezevich, Marc. 1999. Telephone interview. 2 January.

Krumholz, Norman. 1995. "Equity and Local Economic Development." In *Exploring Urban America,* edited by Roger W. Caves. Thousand Oaks, Calif.: Sage Publications.

Mallach, Allan. 1998. "Rebuilding Urban Neighborhoods: Thinking About Brownfields Sites in the Context of Neighborhood Revitalization and

Redevelopment." Paper presented to the Environmental and Occupational Health Institute, Workshop on Redefining Public Health for Brownfields Neighborhoods. 11 December. New Brunswick, N.J.

Medoff, Peter, and Holly Sklar. 1994. *Streets of Hope: The Fall and Rise of an Urban Neighborhood*. Boston: South End Press.

Pepper, Edith. 1996. *Lessons from the Field: Unlocking Economic Potential with an Economic Key*. Washington, D.C.: Northeast-Midwest Institute.

Sasaki Associates, Inc. 1996. "South Side Works Master Plan." January. Watertown, Mass.

Urban Redevelopment Authority of Pittsburgh. 1999. "LTV Southside Works Fact Sheet."

U.S. General Accounting Office. 1987. *Superfund: Extent of Nation's Potential Hazardous Waste Problem Still Unknown*. Washington, D.C.: U.S. Government Printing Office.

Van Horn, Carl, K. A. Dixon, Gregory Lawler, and Daniel Segal. 1999. *Turning Brownfields into Jobfields: A Handbook for Practitioners and Citizens on Making Brownfields Development Work*. New Brunswick, N.J.: The John J. Heldrich Center for Workforce Development, Rutgers, the State University of New Jersey.

Vig, Norman J., and Michael E. Kraft. 1999. "Toward Sustainable Development." In *Environmental Policy*, 4th ed., edited by Norman J. Vig and Michael E. Kraft. Washington, D.C.: CQ Press: A Division of Congressional Quarterly.

Wallsjasper, Jay. 1997. "When Activists Win: The Renaissance of Dudley St." *The Nation* (March 3).

Chapter 4

Building Social Capital to Protect Natural Capital: The Quest for Environmental Justice

Manuel Pastor

Throughout the United States, the idea of environmental justice has been gaining ground. Initially defined in the negative—as a reduction in the disproportionate exposure of minority residents and the poor to various hazards—environmental justice (EJ) advocates often considered it their first task to raise awareness of environmental disparities, both nationally and locally. In this effort, activists have successfully changed policies as well as projects. In 1994, President Clinton issued an executive order directing all federal agencies to take into account the potentially disproportionate burdens of pollution or hazard siting on minority and low-income communities. In 1998, the Southern California Air Quality Management District created a local Task Force on Environmental Justice, partly in response to a lawsuit filed by community advocates who contended that the district's permit trading system was leading to "hot spots" in minority neighborhoods.[1]

Although many of these victories have primarily involved reducing harm or ameliorating inequities, environmental justice can also offer hope for a more positive and harmonious vision of the social good. Claiming the right to clean air and water can be the foundation of a community movement to deploy natural assets in the service of creating community-based wealth (as, for example, in the community food strategies profiled by Raquel Pinderhughes in Chapter 16). The assertion that communities deserve equitable access to a healthy environment can strengthen the base for similar assertions about the distribution of other social resources, such as schools, housing, open space, and employment. In turn, a more equitable distribution of social goods and services can help the environment. Recent research demonstrates that lower levels of inequality are associated with higher levels of environmental protection, presumably because the fairer distribution of power makes it difficult to place hazards in someone else's backyard and thus enhances incentives to engage in source reduction and cleanup at the regional and state levels (Boyce et al. 1999; Morello-Frosch 1997).

This chapter highlights the central role of social capital—both informal networks and formal organizations that enable communities to work together for common goals—in achieving environmental justice. In particular, I draw on recent experience in the Los Angeles area. One reason for the disproportionate exposure of some groups to environmental hazards is a relative lack of social capital and social power. Some communities are isolated from others, and some lack the ability to garner the political clout necessary to resist hazard siting. Thus, a key way to achieve environmental justice is to build both "bonding" social capital that can unify or bring communities together and "bridging" social capital that can link these communities with one another and with potential allies. Building social capital, in turn, can have positive effects on both the environment and community development.

Research on Environmental Inequities

Although a 1983 report by the U.S. Government Accounting Office (GAO) was one of the first significant studies of the distribution of environmental negatives, many activists consider a 1987 United Church of Christ (UCC) report to be the landmark study. The report seemed to offer clear evidence that toxic facilities were disproportionately located in minority communities. This result lent credence to social movements that had emerged after the historic 1982 protests in Warren County, North Carolina, where a largely African-American and rural community had been chosen as the site for burial of polychlorinated biphenyls (PCBs) in a landfill (Bullard 1994).[2]

However, just as the EJ movement was gaining momentum—with the first People of Color Environmental Leadership Conference held in October 1991 in Washington, D.C.; the presidential executive order in 1994; the formation of a National Environmental Justice Advisory Committee within the U.S. Environmental Protection Agency (EPA); and the adoption of environmental justice as an issue by some mainstream environmental organizations (such as the Environmental Defense Fund; see Sandweiss 1998)—the statistical evidence for environmental inequity was being challenged. Indeed, the apparent disconnection between the strength of the social movement and the ambiguity of the available evidence has led some people to attack the EJ movement as lacking a scientific foundation (Foreman 1998).

The most important studies challenging the documentation of environmental inequity came from sociologists based at the University of Massachusetts, Amherst (UMass). They criticized the earlier UCC study on two grounds: (1) the UCC study took zip codes as its unit of analysis, large areas that do not necessarily reflect community-defined boundaries; and (2) the associations made between hazards and race were based on simple bivariate correlations (that is, relationships between two variables, without considering the potential impacts of other variables). The latter criticism was especially significant, because it suggested that racial differences in exposure might no longer be salient once controls were introduced for income, access to industry, and other relevant explanatory factors.

Using a more compact geographic unit, the census tract, and a multivariate approach, the UMass researchers offered a series of national-level studies demonstrating that the key factors associated with the placement of one form of hazard, toxic storage and disposal facilities, were income, population density, the proximity of manufacturing employees, and other variables. When these were taken into account, race generally did not have an independent impact (Anderton, Anderson, Oakes, and Fraser 1994; Anderton et al. 1994). These findings have been criticized for both methodological reasons and data inadequacies (Been 1995; Bullard 1996). Still, the work included some substantial methodological advances over previous research, and the results called into question the basis of EJ concerns, particularly those involving race.

The central Anderton et al. finding—that income matters but race does not—is important. From an ethical viewpoint, disparate impacts on the poor would be sufficient grounds for concern. If certain income groups are seeing their natural assets diminished by the use of their communities as environmental sinks, then this inequity should be addressed. Under U.S. federal law, however, racial minorities are a protected category and the poor are not.[3] Thus, for many poor communities, finding a disproportionate exposure by race is the best way to seek a public policy remedy, notwithstanding the inclusion of income as a criterion in President Clinton's executive order. The distribution of environmental inequity primarily across lines of class rather than race may be accepted by a society that views the poor simply as the inevitable losers in a market system.

Indeed, some analysts have suggested that it is precisely market dynamics that determine the location of wastes. Polluters are attracted to areas with low land values, and communities with low levels of economic activity are more likely to seek or accept such facilities as they try to encourage economic development (Been 1994). Thus, the Anderton et al. results may be seen as "rational": if income matters but race is insignificant, then perhaps the market is simply working its usual magic.

The Anderton et al. findings have been challenged by other researchers who have used better facility location data and more sophisticated Geographic Information System (GIS) and statistical techniques.[4] Although the results of these subsequent studies are somewhat mixed, the bulk of the evidence points to inequity by class *and* by race (see Been 1995 and Szasz and Meuser 1997). Still, the dynamics of the market rather than politics might be at work. Could it be that minorities and the poor are "attracted" to hazards by virtue of low housing costs that incorporate, or internalize, the environmental disadvantages? Does the apparent pattern of inequity reflect consumer choice rather than racial discrimination in siting?

Determining whether hazards were placed in minority communities or minority residents simply moved to these areas has important implications for an asset-based view of community development. Imagine that a neighborhood receives a new environmental negative. As a result, wealthier residents depart, and newer, poorer residents with a different set of risk-income tradeoff preferences arrive to take their place. A statistical snapshot across the relevant region, no matter how multivariate, will show environmental inequity even though the whole process simply reflects a desire to maximize one sort of asset—housing—by substituting it for another—access to clean air and lower-risk environments.[5]

Determining causality is also important for policy. If there really is a significant demographic transition after the siting of a hazard, then an EJ policy governing siting decisions would prove futile. Moreover, suppose that social protest leads local regulators or operators to improve their environmental record. If housing values then rise, this improvement could lead to an exodus of poorer residents: In this case, measured socioeconomic variables for the local geography will improve, but only because of gentrification and displacement. This scenario would represent little advance for the poor who previously suffered the negative externality—and it would hardly fit into an asset-based community development strategy whose goal is to uplift, not uproot, the poor.

What does the national research tell us about placement versus move-in? The UMass researchers (Oakes et al. 1996) found no evidence that hazards were placed in minority neighborhoods, but they also found no significant demographic postsiting transition. Been and Gupta (1997) found no evidence of significant postsiting changes in racial or ethnic composition, but they did find that Latino communities may be at special risk for siting. They also found that it is not the very poorest areas that receive hazards and that the areas that do receive hazards later become poorer. This finding suggests the possibility that some of the poorer population indeed moves in, a pattern consistent with the market-oriented theory.[6]

In general, however, the evidence has failed to settle the debate between a market framework that stresses choice and demographic change and a political approach that stresses unequal power and access to the decision-making process (see Hamilton 1995). The next section presents some specific evidence from one urban area, Los Angeles. The results there tend to support a more political view and also seem to reflect the role of social capital in constructing resistance to environmental negatives.

Environmental Inequities in the Los Angeles Area

In a series of papers, several colleagues and I have argued that much of the national-level work reviewed above is flawed for methodological reasons (Boer et al. 1997; Sadd et al. 1999; Pastor et al. 2001). One reason, we suggest, is that studies of the distribution of waste treatment and disposal facilities are more appropriately conducted at the regional level. Because industrial clusters are regional, the distribution of waste should also be regional. For example, furniture manufacturing is unlikely to move from Los Angeles to Seattle, and Microsoft is unlikely to leave Washington State for the Southland. We must consider who bears the brunt of the solvent-using furniture industry where it actually exists and will likely remain.

In our work on Los Angeles, we found that a multivariate regression, in which the dependent variable is whether or not a particular census tract contains or is close to a toxic storage facility, suggests that race *does* matter even after we take into account income, industrial land use, and local manufacturing employment. Moreover, the income effect is actually an inverted U shape: the poorest and the richest communities are spared, and working-class communities of color are the most likely places to find such toxic facilities (Boer et al. 1997). The reason, we suggest, is a mix of economics and politics. In some very poor communities, the low level of economic activity correlates with low pollution levels, whereas affluent communities have sufficient political power to resist various locally undesirable land uses (LULUs). Regressions using data from the Toxic Release Inventory (TRI) yield a similar set of relationships: even controlling for other factors, race influences the probability that a particular census tract will have a TRI release. We also found that the *degree* of toxicity of the releases rises with percentage of minority residents and with increases in the other key variables.[7] Income again takes an inverted U shape, suggesting that the communities most suffering the effects of environmental injustice are working-class, minority areas. Interestingly, it is exactly these areas that have been the focus of EJ organizers in Los Angeles, implying that these organizers have been appropriate in their targeting.

Figure 4.1 shows how this unequal distribution of risks plays out in terms of relative "exposure rates." We measured the percentage of all Anglos, African-Americans, and Latinos in the broader southern California area who live in a

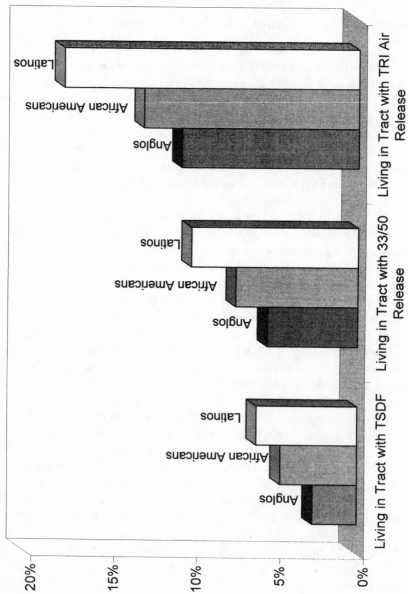

Figure 4.1. Exposure by Group to Environmental Negatives in Southern California. The figure charts the percentage of each group living in a tract with the specified release. For example, 5.4 percent of Anglos in southern California live in a tract with a 33/50 release, whereas 10 percent of Latinos in southern California live in such a tract.

census tract containing one of three potential hazards: a toxic storage and disposal facility, an air release that contains elements on the 33/50 list of high-priority (usually carcinogenic) toxics specially targeted for reduction by the EPA, or a general air release listed in the EPA's TRI. As Figure 4.1 shows, Latinos have the highest likelihood of living in a tract with these hazards and Anglos the lowest, with the probability for African-Americans being in between.

What about placement versus move-in? To explore this issue, we obtained the dates when various toxic storage and disposal facilities (TSDFs) were located in the County of Los Angeles. We geo-coded these address-date pairs (visiting a sample of them to check actual facility locations) and then drew both 1/4-mile and 1-mile circles around each site point to capture potentially affected areas. We then obtained a database that carried 1990 census tract shapes back through the 1980 and 1970 censuses; that is, the database rearranged certain demographic data from those years to fit the 1990 shapes, creating a spatially consistent time series at the census tract level.[8]

The simplest way to present the results is through a series of t-test comparisons of means. Table 4.1 compares the 1970 demographics for tracts in Los Angeles that received an in-tract or proximate TSDF over the 1970–1990 period with the demographics for those tracts that did not. The results indicate that the receiving areas indeed tended to have more minority, poor, and blue-collar residents, as well as fewer homeowners, lower initial home values and rents, and a lower percentage of college-educated residents. Population

Table 4.1. Comparison of Tracts in 1970 that Would Receive a TSDF in 1970–1990 with All Other Tracts in Los Angeles County

Demographic Characteristic	TSDF Sited within 1/4 Mile	TSDF Sited within 1 Mile	County Average
Minority share (percent)	53.2[a]	50.5[a]	31.8
African-American share (percent)	25.7[b]	20.1[a]	10.8
Latino share (percent)	22.0	25.4[a]	18.0
Household income (annual dollars)	8,197.0[a]	8,742.0[a]	10,032.0
Home value (dollars)	21,611.0[a]	22,578.0[a]	26,042.0
Median rent (monthly dollars)	116.0[a]	121.0[a]	138.0
College-educated share (percent)	7.9[a]	8.4[a]	12.6
Single family housing share (percent)	55.5[b]	63.5	64.4
Population density (persons per square mile)	6,849.0[c]	9,112.0	8,724.0
Blue-collar share (percent)	55.5[a]	53.7[a]	46.1

[a]Difference from all other tracts statistically significant at the .01 level.
[b]Difference from all other tracts statistically significant at the .05 level.
[c]Difference from all other tracts statistically significant at the .10 level.

Table 4.2. Demographic Change in Census Tracts Following a TSDF Siting versus Tracts without a TSDF Siting

| | Average Percentage Change from 1970 to 1990 | | |
Demographic Characteristic	TSDF Sited within 1/4 Mile	TSDF Sited within 1 Mile	County Average
Minority share	24.8	23.7	24.6
African-American share	−5.7	−3.6[a]	0.2
Latino share	24.8	19.1	16.7
Household income	267.0	278.0	276.0
Home value	716.0	808.0	818.0
Median rent	378.0	373.0	362.0
College-educated	5.5[b]	9.6	9.4
Single family housing share	−1.7	−3.7	−4.7
Blue-collar share	−5.1	−8.2[a]	−5.3

[a]Difference from all other tracts statistically significant at the .10 level.
[b]Difference from all other tracts statistically significant at the .05 level.

density was significantly lower in the 1/4-mile zone. This result may reflect the sensible notion that hazards should be sited in areas with fewer people, but it may simply mean they are sited in areas where a higher fraction of the land is devoted to industrial or other nonresidential use. Population density is higher (although the difference is statistically insignificant) at the 1-mile level, a worrisome finding from a public health perspective.

What happened in these tracts *after* a TSDF arrived? Table 4.2 presents the demographic changes over the 1970–1990 period in tracts that received or were near TSDFs that were sited in 1960–1970, as compared to tracts that did not receive such hazards. As the table shows, the only changes of statistical significance were a faster decline in the percentage of African-Americans and in the blue-collar presence within the 1-mile zone and a slower increase in the percentage of the college-educated in the most proximate areas. Note that there is a more rapid increase of Latinos in the affected areas (although the difference is statistically insignificant), suggesting some degree of move-in and a process of ethnic transition (from African-American to Latino), which we explore below.[9]

Of course, as we said earlier, such simple tests can mask the underlying dynamics, and multivariate strategies are therefore appropriate. For that reason, we developed a simple model of TSDF placement and subjected it to a series of regression strategies. The results indicate that both the presence of more minorities and the presence of persons with lower income levels as of 1970 were indeed statistically significant predictors (along with population density and a proxy for home ownership) of whether a census tract (particularly within 1 mile of an eventual hazard site) was to receive a hazard in the next 20 years. This pattern supports the basic tenets of a political placement hypothesis: that is, the notion that minorities and the poor may have been special targets for such facilities.[10]

Similarly, to explore the dynamics of move-in, we constructed a simple model of neighborhood demographic change and added to it variables indicating whether the neighborhood had a TSDF (within 1/4 mile or 1 mile) as of 1970 and whether it had received a TSDF during the 1960s. The effects were generally negative—that is, TSDFs led to minority move-out, not move-in—but the results were statistically insignificant. Recognizing that the processes of siting and move-in may be happening quickly, we also tried a simultaneous-equations approach that took into account both the demographic changes and siting decisions in the 1970–1990 period. The results: the political placement hypothesis again dominated and, controlling for all other factors, the placement and/or existence of a hazard continued to have a negative (albeit statistically insignificant) impact on minority move-in.

We then decided to go beyond the usual notion that minority presence *per se* leads to facility placement and look at the major minority groups separately. We found that in Los Angeles, census tracts were at peak vulnerability to a TSDF when their populations were roughly 48 percent Latino and 44 percent African-American—that is, when neighborhoods had a rough balance between similarly disenfranchised groups. Since this balance is usually present when communities are in transition, we decided to look at the degree of demographic change in the immediate past—calculated by simply adding up the absolute values of the percentage shifts in the demographics of the four largest groups—and found that this measure of "ethnic churning" was a powerful predictor of the location of hazards.

Figure 4.2 maps this ethnic churning in Los Angeles County between 1970 and 1990 against the siting of TSDFs over the same period; as can be seen visually, there is a strong correlation. A detailed statistical profile reveals that there was a significant degree of ethnic change in the decade *prior* to siting, with demographic transition slowing during and after siting. A simultaneous multivariate technique yields similar results: ethnic churning is a strong predictor of a concurrent siting of a TSDF, whereas TSDF siting has little effect on subsequent ethnic transition. Although these results do reveal some degree of postsiting move-in, our analysis suggests that the neighborhood is simply completing a process of change that first brought new minorities and, in their wake, new toxics.

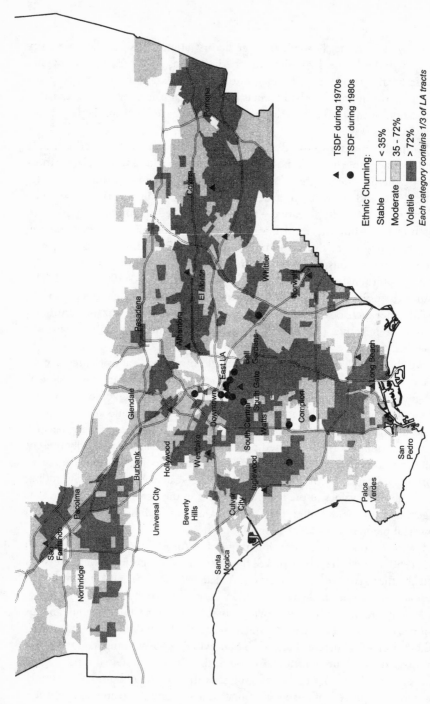

Figure 4.2. TSDFs Placed during the 1970s and 1980s and Ethnic Churning, Los Angeles County.

Social Capital, Natural Assets, and Environmental Justice

Although the patterns revealed in the Los Angeles research may seem complex, the general story is simple. First, race and income seem to matter in explaining the contemporary distribution of hazards. Second, there is strong evidence of disproportionate siting in minority neighborhoods but weak and sometimes contradictory evidence about minority move-in after siting, suggesting that the contemporary pattern is mainly a result of inequity in siting decisions. Finally, one variable that has a significant impact on the likelihood of receiving a hazard is the extent of ongoing demographic change. Taken together, these results square better with a political explanation of TSDF siting than with a market- or choice-driven analysis.

The fact that areas in the midst of demographic change are more likely to receive sites suggests the potential importance of social capital. In general, areas richer in social capital—both informal networks and formal community organizations—are better able to advocate for their needs, regardless of their level of other political and economic assets. Given the importance of race in the construction of individual and community identity, it may be unsurprising that an area that is nearly all African-American might be better able to resist a site than an area that is mixed. Intraracial bonds, and invocations of a collective history of discrimination, can be used to rally the community to its overall self-interest. By contrast, a rapidly changing social fabric can make communities less able to mount resistance to siting decisions.

The resulting challenge—one that has been central to the EJ movement— is to build solidarity and social capital across a multiracial public. This social capital can take two forms: bonding social capital among those suffering the most environmental negatives and bridging social capital that reaches out for support from other communities. Bonding involves building connections within a community via organizing, a task often facilitated by the immediacy of health issues and by the deep, visceral sense of evident injustice that environmental inequity presents. Such bonding is often complicated by the need for interethnic organizing, but it is crucial for protecting natural assets. As Cole (1992) notes, lawyers can help communities to win injunctions, but it is a mobilized community that will ensure enforcement and thus protect the local environment.

EJ activists have also sought to build bridging social capital, working to help minority communities cultivate powerful allies in other communities. This task is facilitated by the fact that the mainstream environmental movement has made progress in recognizing the importance of environmental inequity. The task is also made easier by the general public's moral sense that the environment is a public good to which communities should have free and relatively equal access. As a result, the notion of sharp disparities in the distribution of hazards—and the resulting uneven abilities to enjoy natural assets such as clean air and water—is unpopular. Instances of environmental inequity therefore present an opportunity to build alliances within and between disenfranchised communities as well as with the broader public.

The ultimate reason for building this social capital is to influence policy to ensure that communities are protected from unfair use of their wealth or assets. Although the EJ movement has not often articulated itself in these terms, we can easily see the movement as asserting community property rights over the environmental sinks of air and water (see Boyce, Chapter 2 in this volume). Indeed, the policy and political challenge for the EJ movement is to define more specifically the relevant property rights (community control over the sinks) and the relevant boundaries (at the neighborhood or regional level), and then to contest other forces (including polluters and regulatory agencies) over both issues.

Within this framework, we can argue that environmental inequity arises when the community property claim—that is, the right to determine how much pollution a neighborhood will tolerate, and for what purposes—is appropriated by others, whether by the regulatory apparatus of the state or by a private firm. If a community experiences localized environmental costs from an activity that disperses the benefits widely (for example, when toxic by-products of production that benefits an entire region are disposed of in one particular neighborhood), or if the benefits are highly concentrated in another community (as when the profits and employment opportunities generated by waste operations accrue to people outside the local area), the affected community bears environmental costs without receiving commensurate benefits. This situation represents a violation of the community's property rights.[11]

On the other hand, to the extent that a community itself chooses to trade environmental integrity for another goal, such as economic development, it is valuing the flow of benefits from one asset, such as productive capital, above that from another asset, natural capital. In such a case, some observers may not be as concerned about any apparent inequity in the distribution of environmental hazards. The affected populations are being compensated by employment and may be balancing health and jobs along their own collective "indifference curves."[12] Others will argue that this sort of "vicious choice" reflects a tradeoff with which no community should be faced.

Have the disproportionately affected communities in Los Angeles at least gained jobs and other benefits? To look at this question, I broke Los Angeles County into 58 different Public Use Microdata Areas (PUMAs), a geographic frame used in the U.S. Census Bureau's Public Use Microdata Sample. In Los Angeles, the PUMAs are geographically compact, follow recognizable community lines, and are of sufficient size to permit examination of localized labor and retail markets.[13] As of 1990, the most recent year for which data were available, the typical PUMA encompassed about 22 square miles, with an average population of about 150,000 and slightly less than 80,000 jobs.

To examine the relationship between environmental costs and employment benefits, I then used an estimate of the additional cancer risk from hazardous air pollutants in each PUMA, based on the EPA's Cumulative Exposure Index as developed by Rachel Morello-Frosch (1997). I divided the areas into three categories, ranging from least polluted to heavily polluted, then calculated the percentage of minority residents against the rate of job growth in the 1980–1994 period, based on data provided by the Southern California Association of Governments. The racial disparities, depicted in Figure 4.3, are quite clear: the cancer risk due to air pollution and the percentage of minority residents rise in tandem. The line in the figure shows the rates of job growth over the 1980–1994 period: as can be seen, the higher the level of pollution, the lower the rates of employment increase.[14] In the most polluted areas, employment actually declined.

This pattern hardly recommends a toxic-based strategy for community development. It also raises serious issues for a market-oriented theory claiming that choices are being made by communities along their self-selected indifference curves. If communities are balancing potential environmental risks against improvement in economic potential, they clearly are not getting a very

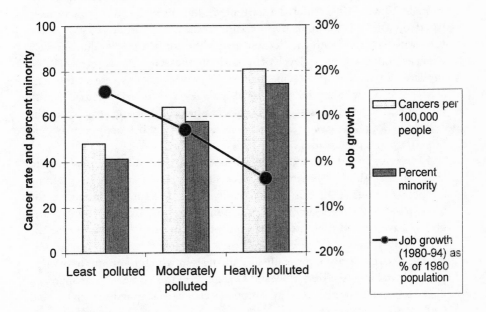

Figure 4.3. Pollution and Jobs: Is There a Tradeoff in Los Angeles County?

good deal. Instead, it looks as if environmental degradation and economic weakness go hand in hand.

The idea that there might be complementarities among various forms of capital—natural, social, human, financial, and physical—is increasingly accepted by economic researchers.[15] For example, the mutually reinforcing relationship between natural and financial capital can affect the extent of rain-forest destruction through two mechanisms. First, the financial poverty of residents can induce a short-term mentality that leads to overuse of natural assets (Kyle and Cunha 1992). Second, the lack of wealth and power in poor, forest-dependent communities weakens their resistance to timber companies, mining firms, ranchers, and other outsiders who seek to exploit natural resources (Segura and Boyce 1994). In either case, the solution is to increase a community's economic assets as a way to protect natural assets. Similarly, in the case of social and physical capital, an intriguing body of recent literature suggests that relative equality in the distribution of income tends to enhance social consensus and to improve overall economic policies and performance in both countries and regions.[16]

What is the relationship between social capital and natural capital? As we have seen, the lack of bonding social capital within a community can lead to environmental vulnerability; organizing, on the other hand, can lead to direct improvements. Yet the bridging aspect of social capital may be just as important for enhancing natural assets. In a recent dissertation, for example, Rachel Morello-Frosch (1997) offered a startling finding: using a cancer-risk variable based on the EPA's cumulative exposure index, she discovered that those California counties with the deepest inequalities of income, wealth, and race experienced the highest level of hazards in the state. Boyce et al. (1999) similarly found that greater inequalities in power—in this case at the state level—lead to weaker environmental policies and adverse public health outcomes. In short, EJ struggles to equalize hazard exposure may lower the *overall* level of pollution: forcing the commons to really be common may help in cleanup and preservation.

EJ activists have long recognized this potential, partly because they seek to avoid simply shifting hazards to other neighborhoods and thus straining alliances. As a result, EJ principles typically focus on source reduction as the ultimate goal (see, for example, Environmental Health Coalition 1998). Other groups have turned their attention from preventing new hazards toward the cleanup of lands with a legacy of toxic uses and their conversion to new productive uses, the thrust of brownfields initiatives in which EJ groups have often played a vital role (see EPA 1999 and Chapter 3 in this volume). This approach illustrates the potential synergy among social capital, physical capital, and natural assets.[17]

Conclusion: Building Social Capital to Protect Natural Capital

Environmental issues are often posed in terms of humans versus nature, a view that feeds into the notion of a jobs-environment tradeoff. Yet as Boyce (1994) argues, the issue—one found in both the realm of the environment and elsewhere in society—is that some groups of humans are positioned against others, with each group asserting its claim to some form of capital. Thus, Boyce suggests that any analysis of the environment should ask: (1) who are the net gainers from an environmentally degrading action? (2) who are the losers? and (3) what is it about the relationship between the winners and the losers that allows this pattern to be sustained?

The siting of toxic hazards, a central concern of the EJ movement, is a clear example of a situation where there are winners and losers. There remain significant methodological problems in the literature on hazard location, and debates about techniques and evidence are likely to engage social scientists and natural scientists for years to come.[18] The research reviewed in this chapter, however, presents a compelling case that there are indeed significant disparities in the allocation of hazards and suggests that these disparities are better explained by politics and power than by the impartial operation of markets.

First, the evidence indicates that environmental toxics are disproportionately located in minority neighborhoods but do not tend to be located in the poorest communities. This finding suggests that something besides simple market dynamics is influencing the placement of such hazards. Second, statistical tests in at least one urban area, Los Angeles, suggest that placement or siting is far more important than move-in, again casting doubt on the simple market theory in which minority residents are exercising choice by trading one asset (cleaner air) for another (lower housing prices). Third, there is little evidence of a positive tradeoff between pollution levels and job growth; indeed, the overall panorama suggests that more pollution leads to fewer jobs.

Finally, social capital may be important in understanding the pattern of environmental inequity and the state of natural assets. Areas experiencing the most significant demographic change—areas where the social fabric may be temporarily torn—appear to be the most vulnerable to new siting. Moreover, there is evidence that where social capital is strongest in a region or a state—as measured by the equity in the distribution of income and power—the environment is in better shape. This finding suggests that building social capital through EJ organizing can have a positive impact on a community's and a society's natural assets.

Indeed, the EJ movement can be understood as a broad effort to improve the asset base of poor people of color. It has often had more to do with the

broader social movements for racial and economic justice than with environmentalism writ small. In recent years, some dynamic new efforts have tied
environmental issues to basic economic equity. In Los Angeles, for example,
the Labor-Community Strategies Center cast transportation as an EJ issue and
organized a Bus Riders' Union that successfully sued the local transportation
authority, forcing it to reorient spending to expand the bus service used
primarily by the region's poor.[19] In San Francisco, the Urban Habitat Program
(UHP) has moved to address a wide range of challenges associated with
suburban sprawl. Arguing that environment-friendly antisprawl efforts can
steer development back to the inner city,[20] UHP proposes regional tax-sharing
as one element of a solution.

These broad challenges to urban development strategies are an appropriate
next step for the EJ movement. Environmental inequity is part of a larger
phenomenon in which older industries have abandoned central city areas and
left a weak job base, concentrated poverty, and pollution in their wake.[21]
Community development in urban America will require improving the asset
base on all sides: independent financial capital for business formation, skills and
employment for workers, stronger social capital for communities, and a cleaner
natural environment that can improve the health of residents and attract new
development. By stitching these concerns together, EJ groups are advancing a
new vision of asset-based community building.

Notes

1. Communities for a Better Environment (CBE) filed suit against an emissions-
   trading program in which oil firms could maintain dirty refineries if they
   cleaned up an equivalent amount of pollution by purchasing and then destroying
   heavily polluting older vehicles. Although such trading did yield overall benefits—especially a cleaner air basin at lower dollar costs—it imposed local burdens
   by leaving the hazards concentrated in the neighborhoods hosting the refineries.
   After CBE sued, the Air Quality Management District was forced to suspend the
   program, and the Task Force on Environmental Justice came into being. For
   details, see Kuhn (1999).
2. The GAO (1983) study grew directly out of the protest and was initiated under
   pressure from the Congressional Black Caucus.
3. Title VI of the Civil Rights Act of 1964 mandates that entities getting federal
   assistance cannot discriminate on the basis of race. Historically, Title VI has been
   attractive to civil rights litigators because it requires plaintiffs to demonstrate
   disparate outcomes rather than discriminatory intent (which is more difficult and,
   in the EJ situation, requires an extensive analysis of actual siting practices and
   histories). Although no environmentally oriented lawsuit filed solely on these
   grounds has been successful, activists have been able to file administrative com-
   plaints through the EPA alleging disparate regulatory impacts under Title VI (see
   Ramirez and Stephenson 1998; Kracov 1998).

4. As Been (1995) notes, the original Anderton, Anderson, Oakes, and Fraser (1994) and Anderton et al. (1994) studies were based on a "dirty" data set in which addresses had not been checked for inaccuracies resulting from either pure error or the fact that some firms list their business address rather than the site address in some national databases.

5. It would, however, be difficult to explain the racial (as opposed to income) pattern without resorting to the hypotheses that risk preferences are somehow different for different groups and/or that housing discrimination forces minorities to select housing from a more limited (and more polluted) pool. Although the latter hypothesis is different from a pure market-dynamics theory, the problem still lies in the movement of people and not in the placing of hazards. Of course, the policy implications are different: if it is simply choice, then individuals should be provided with full information about local hazards in order to make the best choices; if it is housing discrimination that "steers" minority movers, then this must be addressed through enforcement of existing housing laws or the enactment of more effective legislation.

6. For more extensive reviews of the EJ literature, see Szasz and Meuser (1997), Bryant and Mohai (1992), and Foreman (1998). The first two pieces generally support EJ suppositions, but Foreman (1998) is more skeptical.

7. The degree of toxicity was measured by casting the tracts into three categories: those that had no air releases as recorded in the TRI, those that had air releases that were not on the EPA's 33/50 list, and those that had 33/50 air releases. The substances on the 33/50 list are identified by the EPA as "high priority" for reduction.

8. The technical details and formal econometric results are explained in Pastor et al. (2001).

9. The relative decline in blue-collar workers may be of special interest, given the usual tradeoff theory in which such sites are said at least to bring useful employment to local residents. However, these figures are for residents, not jobs, so that issue cannot be explored directly here; we tackle the jobs-pollution issue with a different strategy below. Given these anemic results for move-in effects, we looked for evidence of more rapid changes that might have converged to the county average over time, by examining changes in the decade after that in which the areas received sites. Although the overall pattern offers some modest evidence for the move-in hypotheses—a limited increase in minorities in the 10-year periods and a decrease in housing values in one of the time periods examined—both the general pattern of statistical insignificance and certain contradictory results suggest problems with the market-dynamics or choice-driven theory. Also, as noted in the text, there is little evidence for move-in once we nest the relationships in a multivariate regression analysis.

10. There is also a bit of "smoking gun" evidence of the role of politics in placement. A report by Cerrell Associates, Inc. (1984), which provided advice to the California Waste Management Board on locating waste incinerators, stated that "all socioeconomic groupings tend to resent the nearby siting of major facilities, but the middle and upper-socioeconomic strata possess better resources to effectuate their opposition. Middle and higher-socioeconomic strata neighbor-

hoods should not fall at least within the one-mile and five-mile radii of the proposed site."

11. For example, California's 1986 Tanner Act requires that governments develop local assessment committees for siting new TSDFs that would be "broadly constituted to reflect the makeup of the community." In practice, however, the "local" community has been defined to be a large geographic unit, such as a county, and this has allowed the general and diffuse benefits to overwhelm the concentrated neighborhood costs in the process of making siting decisions (Cole 1999). For this reason, Schwartz and Wolfe (1999) recommend modifying the Tanner Act to include a provision that four of the seven committee members be from the adjacent communities; they also suggest that there be some mandate for minority representation.

12. Of course, until decision-making authority is truly democratic, there is little reason to assume that pollution outcomes reflect choice and not simply the distribution of power. For this reason, the most crucial element in the EJ agenda is general community empowerment.

13. This geographical unit—larger than the census tract but still subcounty and often subcity—is especially appropriate in a metropolitan area like Los Angeles, where the city is spread out and contains its own suburbs. Indeed, within the city itself, places like Watts may have more in common with immediately adjoining unincorporated county territories and old industrial suburbs than they do with the San Fernando Valley or the Westside. The municipal line where South Los Angeles abuts the region's inner-ring suburbs will not stand in the way of a short commute to employment or shopping—but the profound distances within the city between the San Fernando Valley and East Los Angeles often will.

14. In Figure 4.3, I define job growth as a percentage of the 1980 population. Using a base of 1980 jobs shows an even wider disparity: more polluted areas generally have more jobs per resident, but the relative strength of that job base has been steadily shrinking over time.

15. Some tradeoffs no doubt remain, but if we think in several dimensions, we can see another important point: an increase in one form of capital may improve the balancing act between two other forms. Imagine a curve describing a community's preferences between feasible mixes of environmental protection and job creation. To the extent that a community enjoys political power rooted in social capital, it can improve outcomes in each area—that is, shift the curve outward to improve the overall tradeoff.

16. On the international evidence, see, for example, Rodrik (1994) and Birdsall and Londoño (1997); on the evidence for U.S. regions, see, for example, Savitch et al. (1993), Barnes and Ledebur (1998), and Pastor et al. (2000).

17. Although some business critics have worried that the involvement of EJ groups would make brownfield development contentious, the opposite has been the case. A recent EPA study of seven of its Brownfields Pilot Study sites found that those sites with active EJ movements were less likely to result in filings under Title VI, because the communities were involved early in planning for brownfield reuse (EPA 1999).

18. New models will have to take better account of innovations in geographic research (see Bowen 1999), and analyses will need to go beyond the simple presence of pollutants to specify more exactly the relationship between proximity and exposure on the one hand and exposure and risk on the other. Attempts to quantify the hazard effect on health indicators are under way; see, for example, Morello-Frosch (1997).

19. For more on transportation issues, see Center for Community Change (1998) and Hodge (1995); for more on the Los Angeles experience, see Mann (1996).

20. As in Portland, Oregon; see Rusk 1998, 22.

21. For a full explication of this argument, see Pastor (2001).

References

Anderton, D. L., A. B. Anderson, M. Oakes, and M. R. Fraser. 1994. "Environmental Equity: The Demographics of Dumping." *Demography* 31:229–48.

Anderton, Douglas L., Andy B. Anderson, Peter H. Rossi, John Michael Oakes, Michael R. Fraser, Eleanor W. Weber, and Edward J. Calabrese. 1994. "Hazardous Waste Facilities: 'Environmental Equity' Issues in Metropolitan Areas." *Evaluation Review* 18 (April): 123–40.

Anderton, Douglas L., John Michael Oakes, and Karla L. Egan. 1997. "Demographics of the Discovery and Prioritization of Abandoned Toxic Sites." *Evaluation Review* 21(1): 3–26.

Barnes, William, and Larry Ledebur. 1998. *The New Regional Economies: The U.S. Common Market and the Global Economy.* Thousand Oaks, Calif.: Sage Publications.

Been, Vicki. 1994. "Locally Undesirable Land Uses in Minority Neighborhoods: Disproportionate Siting or Market Dynamics?" *The Yale Law Journal* 103:1383–422.

————. 1995. "Analyzing Evidence of Environmental Justice." *Journal of Land Use and Environmental Law* 11 (Fall): 1–37.

Been, Vicki, and Francis Gupta. 1997. "Coming to the Nuisance or Going to the Barrios? A Longitudinal Analysis of Environmental Justice Claims." *Ecology Law Review* 24(1): 1–56.

Birdsall, Nancy, and Juan Luis Londoño. 1997. "Asset Inequality Matters: An Assessment of the Bank's Approach to Poverty Reduction." *American Economic Review, Papers and Proceedings* 87(2): 32–37.

Boer, J. Tom, Manuel Pastor, Jr., James L. Sadd, and Lori D. Snyder. 1997. "Is There Environmental Racism? The Demographics of Hazardous Waste in Los Angeles County." *Social Science Quarterly* 78(4): 793–810.

Bowen, William M. 1999. "Comments on 'Every Breath You Take . . .': The Demographics of Toxic Air Releases in Southern California." *Economic Development Quarterly* 13(2): 124–34.

Boyce, James K. 1994. "Inequality as a Cause of Environmental Degradation." *Ecological Economics* 11:169–78.

Boyce, James K., Andrew R. Klemer, Paul H. Templet, and Cleve E. Willis. 1999. "Power Distribution, the Environment, and Public Health: A State-level Analysis." *Ecological Economics* 29:127–40.

Bryant, B., and P. Mohai. 1992. "Environmental Racism: Reviewing the Evidence." In *Race and the Incidence of Environmental Hazards: A Time for Discourse,* edited by Bunyan Bryant and Paul Mohai. Boulder, Colo.: Westview Press.

Bullard, Robert D. 1994. "Environmental Justice for All." In *Unequal Protection: Environmental Justice and Communities of Color,* edited by Robert D. Bullard. San Francisco: Sierra Club Books.

Center for Community Change. 1998. *Getting to Work: An Organizer's Guide to Transportation Equity.* Washington, D.C.: Center for Community Change.

Cerrell Associates, Inc. 1984. "Political Difficulties Facing Waste-to-Energy Conversion Plant Siting." Prepared for the California Waste Management Board. California: Cerrell Associates, Inc.

Cole, Luke W. 1992. "Empowerment as the Key to Environmental Protection: The Need for Environmental Poverty Law." *Ecology Law Quarterly* 19(4): 619–83.

———. 1999. "The Theory and Reality of Community-based Environmental Decisionmaking: The Failure of California's Tanner Act and Its Implications for Environmental Justice." *Ecology Law Quarterly* 25(4).

Environmental Health Coalition. 1998. *Toxic Turnaround: A Step-by-Step Guide to Reducing Pollution for Local Governments.* San Diego, Calif.: Environmental Health Coalition.

Foreman, Christopher H., Jr. 1998. *The Promise and Peril of Environmental Justice.* Washington, D.C.: Brookings Institution.

Hamilton, James T. 1995. "Testing for Environmental Racism: Prejudice, Profits, Political Power?" *Journal of Policy Analysis and Management* 14(1).

Hodge, David C. 1995. "My Fair Share: Equity Issues in Urban Transportation." In *The Geography of Urban Transportation,* edited by Susan Hanson. New York: Guilford Press.

Kracov, Gideon. 1998. "Has the Environmental Justice Movement Come of Age?" *The Planning Report* (August).

Kuhn, Scott. 1999. "Expanding Public Participation is Essential to Environmental Justice and the Democratic Decisionmaking Process." *Ecology Law Quarterly* 25(5): 647–58.

Kyle, Steve C., and Aercio S. Cunha. 1992. "National Factor Markets and the Macroeconomic Context for Environmental Destruction in the Brazilian Amazon." *Development and Change* 23:7–33.

Mann, Eric. 1996. *A New Vision for Urban Transportation: The Bus Riders Union Makes History at the Intersection of Mass Transit, Civil Rights, and the Environment.* Los Angeles: Labor/Community Strategies Center.

Morello-Frosch, Rachel. 1997. "Environmental Justice and California's 'Riskscape': The Distribution of Air Toxics and Associated Cancer and Non-Cancer Risks Among Diverse Communities." Ph.D. diss., University of California at Berkeley.

Oakes, John Michael, Douglas L. Anderton, and Andy B. Anderson. 1996. "A Longitudinal Analysis of Environmental Equity in Communities with Hazardous Waste Facilities." *Social Science Quarterly* 25:125–48.

Pastor, Manuel, Jr. 2001. "Geography and Opportunity." In *America Becoming: Racial Trends and Their Consequences,* Vol. 1, edited by Neil Smelser, William Julius Wilson, and Faith Mitchell. National Research Council, Commission on Behavioral and Social Sciences and Education. Washington, D.C.: National Academy Press.

Pastor, Manuel, Jr., Peter Dreier, Eugene Grigsby, and Marta López Garza. 2000. *Regions That Work: How Cities and Suburbs Can Grow Together.* Minneapolis: University of Minnesota Press.

Pastor, Manuel, Jr., Jim Sadd, and John Hipp. 2001. "Which Came First? Toxic Facilities, Minority Move-in, and Environmental Justice." *Journal of Urban Affairs* 23:1–21.

Ramierez, Kenneth, and Shanda M. Stephenson. 1998. "The Current Status of Environmental Equity: Why the Future is Uncertain." *St. B. Texas Environmental Law Journal* 28.

Rodrik, Dani. 1994. "King Kong Meets Godzilla: The World Bank and the East Asian Miracle." In *Miracle or Design: Lessons from the East Asian Experience,* edited by A. Fishlow. Washington, D.C.: Overseas Development Council.

Rusk, David. 1998. "St. Louis Congregations Challenge Urban Sprawl." *Shelterforce* 97 (January/February).

Sadd, James L., Manuel Pastor, Jr., J. Tom Boer, and Lori D. Snyder. 1999. "'Every Breath You Take . . .': The Demographics of Toxic Air Releases in Southern California." *Economic Development Quarterly* 13(2).

Sandweiss, Stephen. 1998. "The Social Construction of Environmental Justice." In *Environmental Injustices, Political Struggles: Race, Class, and the Environment,* edited by David E. Camacho. Durham, N.C.: Duke University Press.

Savitch, H. V., David Collins, Daniel Sanders, and John Markham. 1993. "Ties That Bind: Central Cities, Suburbs, and the New Metropolitan Region." *Economic Development Quarterly* 7(4).

Schwartz, Michelle Leighton, and Mark R. Wolfe. 1999. "Reevaluating the California Tanner Act: Public Empowerment v. Efficient Waste Disposal." *California Real Property Journal* 13(2).

Segura, Olman, and James K. Boyce. 1994. "Investing in Natural and Human Capital in Developing Countries." In *Investing in Natural Capital: The Ecological Economics Approach to Sustainability,* edited by AnnMari Jansson et al., Washington, D.C.: Island Press.

Szasz, Andrew, and Michael Meuser. 1997. "Environmental Inequalities: Literature Review and Proposals for New Directions in Research and Theory." *Current Sociology* 45(3): 99–120.

United Church of Christ, Commission for Racial Justice. 1987. *Toxic Wastes and Race in the United States: A National Report on the Racial and Socio-Economic Characteristics of Communities with Hazardous Waste Sites.* New York: Public Data Access, Inc.

U.S. Environmental Protection Agency. 1999. *Brownfields Title VI Case Studies: Summary Report.* Washington, D.C.: U.S. Environmental Protection Agency. See http://www.epa.gov/brownfields.

U.S. General Accounting Office. 1983. *Siting of Hazardous Waste Landfills and Their Correlation with Racial and Economic Status of Surrounding Communities.* Washington, D.C.: U.S. General Accounting Office.

CHAPTER 5

Defending the Public Domain: Pollution, Subsidies, and Poverty

Paul Templet

> Freedom has appeared in the world at different times and under various forms; it has not been exclusively bound to any social condition, and it is not confined to democracies. Freedom cannot, therefore, form the distinguishing characteristic of democratic ages. The peculiar and preponderating fact which marks those ages as its own is the equality of conditions; the ruling passion of men in those periods is the love of this equality.
>
> —Alexis de Tocqueville, *Democracy in America*

In recent decades, industry has come under criticism for failing to cover the environmental costs of doing business. When companies are allowed to pollute or to use natural resources without paying their full price, in effect they are appropriating natural capital—land, air, and water—without compensation to society at large.

Economists have paid a good deal of attention to the inefficiencies that result when companies "externalize" production costs in the form of environmental damage. But few have looked at the broader effects of externalities on public welfare, particularly on the distribution of wealth. The research summarized in this chapter suggests that externalities are important contributors to economic inequality and poverty in the United States. Some degree of inequality is to be expected in any society. But massive disparities are unacceptable in a culture that upholds the principle that all people are created equal—and these disparities are all the more intolerable when fueled by the seizure of common assets.

The impetus for the research presented here comes from the four years I spent as Secretary of the Department of Environmental Quality (DEQ) for the state of Louisiana. I was a scientist at Louisiana State University (LSU) in 1987

when Buddy Roemer, a reform-minded candidate, was elected governor. After
his election, Roemer advertised in the *Wall Street Journal* for positions in his
cabinet, an unconventional approach in a state known for political patronage.
I had hosted the first Earth Day at LSU in 1970 and had led the development
of the state's coastal management program. I had never met the governor, but
I liked what I had heard him say about pollution. Having complained for years
about environmental destruction in Louisiana, I thought it was time to "put
up or shut up." So I applied, along with a couple hundred others, to be
environmental secretary. I got the job.

During my tenure, the DEQ expanded its capacity, helped draft new
laws, drew up new regulations, and stepped up enforcement. With nearly
every move to tighten pollution control, we heard from industry and from
economists on corporate payrolls that we would run jobs out of the state.

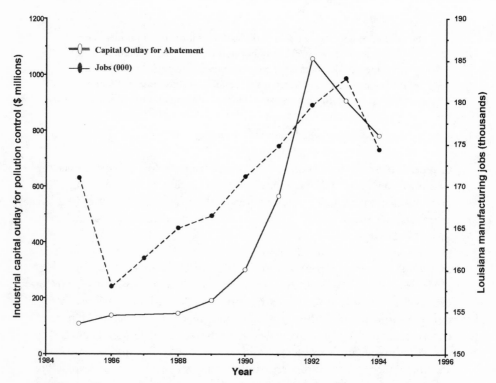

Figure 5.1. Louisiana Pollution Abatement Capital Outlay and Manufacturing Jobs.
Sources: U.S. Bureau of the Census, *State and Metropolitan Area Data Book;* U.S. Department of
Commerce, *Current Industrial Reports, Pollution Abatement Costs and Expenditures;* U.S.
Department of Commerce, Economics and Statistics Administration, *Annual Survey of
Manufactures, Statistics for Industry Groups and Industries 1989.*

That assertion didn't make a lot of sense to me, because at the time Louisiana had neither adequate jobs nor a clean environment. The state's unemployment rate was 12 percent in 1987, the highest in the country. The state also led the nation in toxic discharges, according to the Toxics Release Inventory issued by the U.S. Environmental Protection Agency (EPA) in 1989. It seemed to me that environmental protection would foster jobs rather than diminish them and that a clean environment would be good for people and for the economy. But I needed hard data and analysis to back up this hypothesis.

By the end of my four-year term, amid much controversy, we had cut the state's toxic discharges in half. We implemented new regulations and passed new laws, including an air toxics law enacted a year before the 1990 federal Clean Air Act amendments. At the same time, enforcement went up by a factor of five. We began to condition industrial property tax exemptions on environmental criteria (Templet and Farber 1994; Farber et al. 1995). Contrary to the warnings from industry, investment and jobs in Louisiana rose as firms increased their spending on pollution abatement (Figure 5.1). Many jobs were generated by the sixfold rise in spending on industrial pollution control. Other socioeconomic indicators also began to improve (Templet 1995c). When I returned to the university in 1992, I decided to pursue systematic research on these issues.[1]

Externalities as Subsidies

All economies depend fundamentally on nature. The environment provides the economy with the natural resources needed to produce goods and services and provides a place to dispose of wastes from production and consumption (Figure 5.2). A diminished environmental base threatens economic welfare. If, for example, industry discharges more waste than the environment can assimilate, then toxins accumulate in fish and wildlife and threaten commercial and sport fishing. Acid rain and air pollution damage crops and trees, harming agriculture and forestry. On the other hand, cities and regions that maintain clean air and aesthetic appeal are more likely to attract business and tourism. If ground and surface water are kept relatively clean, minimal treatment is needed for human consumption, so the public spends less. And conservation leaves more resources available for future generations.

We can view the environment as infrastructure, contributing to the economy in much the same way as do man-made systems for water delivery and waste disposal. Just as the public welfare suffers when our built infrastructure is poorly maintained, so we suffer when the environment is abused. Those who pollute without paying the costs are depreciating capital that belongs to society at large. But although society ordinarily penalizes those who steal or embezzle

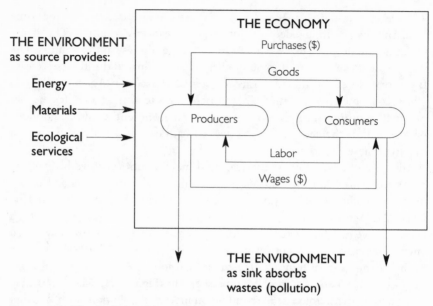

Figure 5.2. The Relationship of the Economy to the Environment.

public *financial* capital, we persist in allowing the unauthorized appropriation of public *natural* capital, despite the fact that natural capital is arguably more valuable to humankind than the entire stock of man-made capital (Costanza et al. 1997).

When producers externalize costs, they reap a subsidy. A firm releasing toxins to the environment, for example, is spared the expense of controlling that pollution, instead appropriating natural capital by using the environment as a sink. The result of this implicit subsidy is greater corporate profit, but people who are affected by the pollution are burdened with health problems and diminished quality of life. Natural wealth is redistributed in a way that exacerbates socioeconomic inequalities.

Producers also receive subsidies in the form of preferential energy prices and favorable tax rates. In these instances, the public pays the cost directly. One way in which vested interests manage to create subsidies for themselves is through political power. The more campaign contributions members of Congress receive from industry, for example, the more they tend to vote in favor of industry and against environmental protection (Templet 1995b).

Subsidies foster inequality in three ways. First, they diminish the productivity, disposable incomes, health, and quality of life of those who bear their cost. Second, subsidies help the recipients to bolster their power, which they can use to manipulate both markets and government policies to their advantage. Third, subsidies deprive the government of revenues that it might otherwise use for education, health care, and other programs that reduce inequality. In the research presented here, I examine the first two effects, leaving aside fiscal impacts, by exploring the correlations between subsidies and environmental and socioeconomic indicators in the 50 states. The aim is to document how externalities contribute to inequality and poverty and to consider how the public can reappropriate natural capital.

Measuring Subsidies

Absolute subsidies are difficult to measure because they can be calculated only by comparison to a hypothetical, subsidy-free world. Instead of attempting to measure absolute subsidies, I calculate each of the three subsidies discussed below relative to the U.S. average. Although those states paying below-average subsidies are still paying subsidies, their value is negative relative to the mean. If states with lower subsidies can be shown to have higher public welfare, then one can infer that a reduction in subsidies would benefit public welfare in all states and that those states with the biggest subsidies have the most to gain.

The Pollution Subsidy

State laws and regulations generally require that industry internalize pollution costs to some degree (Templet 1993). Although there are also federal laws to regulate emissions, states have considerable latitude in administering them. Thus, spending on pollution control varies considerably from one state to another.[2] For the purposes of this study, I define the pollution subsidy as the degree to which a state falls short of the nationwide average in spending to control pollution. Of course, states with more industries using toxic chemicals should spend more on pollution control. The pollution subsidy is therefore specified as the costs that manufacturers avoid by spending less than the national average per pound of toxic pollution, times the total pounds released in the state.

I use data on spending for pollution control from the Current Industrial Reports of the U.S. Bureau of the Census (1992). Regrettably, the Census Bureau no longer collects this information, because after the Republican Party gained a majority in Congress in 1994, lawmakers cut the bureau's budget and eliminated this function. The data on pounds of toxic releases are drawn from the EPA's (1991) Toxics Release Inventory. For interstate comparisons, I then calculate the pollution subsidy, based on these data, in dollars per capita. The results are presented in the first column of Table 5.1.

Table 5.1. Relative Subsidies in the 50 States ($ per capita)

State	Pollution Subsidy	Energy Subsidy	Tax Subsidy	Total Subsidy
Alabama	59	103	196	357
Alaska	192	218	−396	13
Arizona	98	57	155	310
Arkansas	48	43	129	220
California	−48	−100	−51	−200
Colorado	−51	−104	2	−153
Connecticut	−38	−315	39	−313
Delaware	−243	6	−242	−479
Florida	17	175	232	424
Georgia	−26	−11	38	1
Hawaii	−22	10	257	244
Idaho	2	−27	21	−5
Illinois	−22	−180	35	−167
Indiana	32	40	29	101
Iowa	30	−43	−105	−117
Kansas	172	−90	−14	68
Kentucky	−42	−171	45	−169
Louisiana	410	183	286	879
Maine	−103	−119	−26	−248
Maryland	−47	−41	−142	−230
Massachusetts	−12	−427	−301	−740
Michigan	−11	−335	−207	−553
Minnesota	10	−231	−114	−336
Mississippi	170	85	156	410
Missouri	11	−85	113	39
Montana	283	−121	−260	−98
Nebraska	46	−95	−63	−112
Nevada	7	−111	450	346
New Hampshire	−7	−515	−240	−762
New Jersey	−77	−222	−126	−426
New Mexico	65	−75	283	274
New York	−27	−121	−253	−401
North Carolina	28	12	−3	36
North Dakota	7	53	58	118
Ohio	−17	−102	−31	−149
Oklahoma	29	107	126	262
Oregon	−16	−57	−404	−477
Pennsylvania	−38	−44	−40	−122
Rhode Island	−43	−201	−98	−342
South Carolina	−5	83	63	140
South Dakota	13	−66	127	73
Tennessee	174	−59	309	424
Texas	14	159	142	315
Utah	411	−11	42	441
Vermont	−16	−326	−123	−465
Virginia	30	80	−41	69
Washington	−39	−49	442	354
West Virginia	3	67	172	243
Wisconsin	−44	−155	−140	−339
Wyoming	102	−107	−115	−120

[a]Figures for subsidies represent spending relative to the nationwide average (see text).

The Energy Subsidy

To varying degrees in different states, residents pay more for energy than industry does. In effect, consumers thereby subsidize industry. If the price differential is great, residents may not be able to afford enough fuel for themselves, or they may have to forgo other wants. To measure the energy subsidy to industry, I collected data on energy expenditures by the industrial sector in each state from the U.S. Energy Information Agency. I also collected data on the ratio of residential to industrial prices. Nationally, residents pay approximately twice what industry pays per unit of energy. Some of this disparity can be justified on the basis that firms consume energy in large volumes and that the cost of delivering energy to a firm is therefore cheaper than the cost of delivering the same amount to multiple households. But price differentials vary widely, with the ratio of residential to industrial prices ranging from 1.01 in New Hampshire and Massachusetts to 4.0 in Alaska and 3.9 in Louisiana.[3] The energy subsidy is defined here as how much more the industrial sector in each state would spend if the residential-to-industrial price ratio were equal to the U.S. average. Again, the subsidy is normalized by the state's population.[4] The results are presented in the second column of Table 5.1. (For a more detailed analysis of energy price disparity, see Templet 2001).

The Tax Subsidy

Most states rely on a mix of sales, income, and property taxes to generate public revenues. Some of these taxes are more progressive than others in their distributional impacts. In general, income and property taxes tend to be progressive; that is, they take a larger share of income from the rich than from the poor. Sales taxes, by contrast, take a fixed share of the amount consumed. Because those with modest incomes generally spend a higher proportion of their incomes on consumption than do the rich, sales taxes tend to be regressive.

To obtain a measure of the tax subsidy to business, I calculated for each state the ratio of regressive taxes collected to progressive taxes collected—considering property and income taxes to be progressive and sales taxes to be regressive—and compared that ratio to the U.S. average. A state that relies more heavily than average on regressive taxes is considered to provide a subsidy to those with high incomes and large property holdings, a subsidy paid for by those with low incomes and little property. I then divide the total dollar value of this subsidy by state population.[5] The results are reported in the third column of Table 5.1.

The Total Subsidy

The total state subsidy per capita is the sum of the pollution, energy, and tax subsidies per capita. The totals are presented in the final column of Table 5.1

Total Annual Subsidy per Capita ($)

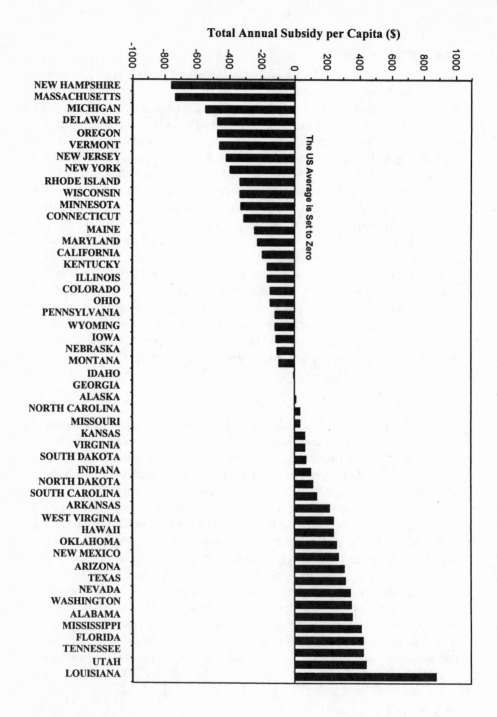

Figure 5.3. Total Subsidy by State Relative to the National Average.

and depicted in Figure 5.3. In general, the states with relatively high subsidies tend to be in the South and to a lesser extent the West. The Northeast and Midwest tend to grant fewer subsidies.[6]

The Results of Subsidies

Having calculated these subsidies, I examined their relationships to various measures of environmental and economic performance. To relate these measures to subsidies, I estimated statistical correlations across the 50 states by means of simple linear regressions. This section presents the key results.

Subsidies and Environmental Performance

To examine the relationships between subsidies and environmental performance, I used the state-level measures of environmental policy and environmental quality developed by the Institute for Southern Studies (Hall and Kerr 1991). The Green Policy index incorporates 77 indicators, including the existence of state policies on recycling, toxic waste management, and air pollution, as well as ratings of state environmental programs. The Green Conditions index is based on 179 other indicators, including measures of air and water pollution and toxic chemical releases. In both cases, the higher the score, the poorer the state's environmental status.

Not surprisingly, the correlation between the pollution subsidy and the Green Policy index was significant ($r = .52$): the higher the pollution subsidy, the lower the state ranked in the strictness of its environmental standards and enforcement. The energy subsidy is also significantly related to the Green Conditions index ($r = .47$) and Green Policy index ($r = .52$), indicating that as the energy subsidy increases, environmental protection grows weaker. The tax subsidy, too, is associated with worse environmental performance; its correlation with the Green index (a combination of the quality and policy indices) is statistically significant ($r = .44$).

Subsidies and Economic Performance

The pollution subsidy correlates with worse economic performance in terms of poverty, income disparity, unemployment, and average personal income. These findings run counter to the claim that the benefits and costs of pollution control are regressive, with costs falling disproportionately on the poor while benefits accrue elsewhere (Baumol and Oates 1988). Instead, as firms externalize more costs, poverty and income disparity increase and incomes decline. This finding suggests that spending to control pollution constitutes a progressive policy in terms of income distribution. The benefits may be more than just economic because it is the poor, and often minorities, who are most likely to live near polluting facilities.[7] The energy subsidy displays similar correlations: it is significantly and positively related to poverty ($r = .46$), unemployment ($r = .51$), and income disparity ($r = .49$), and negatively related to personal income ($r = -.45$). Because the tax subsidy is regressive, drawing from the poor and middle class and benefiting the wealthy, it is no surprise that higher tax subsidies lead to more poverty ($r = .42$) and to wider income disparity ($r = .31$).

I also examined the relationship between the pollution subsidy and job growth in the late 1980s and found the correlation to be significant and negative ($r = -.41$), indicating that as firms avoid the costs of pollution control, the state forgoes jobs. This finding is consistent with Louisiana's experience from 1988 to 1992 under the Roemer administration, when manufacturers increased spending on pollution control by 600 percent, toxic releases dropped by more than 50 percent, and manufacturing employment in the state grew by approximately 25,000 jobs.[8]

In the realm of profits, on the other hand, one would expect that subsidies would have a positive effect. Data on corporate profits are not available by state, but we can use a surrogate measure—value added in manufacturing—to test whether profits increase when the pollution subsidy rises.[9] Value added is normalized by the number of manufacturing jobs to adjust for differences in size across states. I found that value added per job is indeed significantly and positively related to the pollution subsidy, suggesting that corporate profits rise when pollution control costs are avoided. Louisiana, for example, leads the nation in value added per manufacturing job, at nearly double the national average. It also leads the nation in toxic pollution per job, at more than 10 times the natural average.[10] The energy subsidy likewise shows a significant and positive relationship with value added per job in manufacturing. These gains in corporate profits are the flip side of the losses imposed on lower-income residents.

If firms were to invest these added profits within the state, then they might contribute to public welfare over time through increased employment and income. In that case, some of their de facto appropriation of natural capital might be justified. In fact, however, most of the profits go to shareholders and managers, who often reside in other states. In general, profits tend to leak from high-subsidy, low-income states to low-subsidy, high-income states, fueling interstate inequality. I return to this issue below.

Making Connections

As pollution, energy, and tax subsidies mount, poverty and income disparity increase. Profits rise but mostly leak out of the state, reducing income. Unemployment rises, also reducing income. Natural capital is depleted; toxic

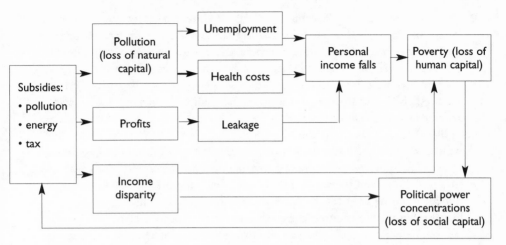

Figure 5.4. Connections among Subsidies, Poverty, and Political Power.

emissions rise. The connections extend further. Poorer environmental quality is associated with worse public health (Boyce et al. 1999), and increased morbidity, mortality, and health care costs are a further drag on the economy. At the same time, disparities of income within and between states foster the concentration of political power in fewer hands. A vicious circle ensues, whereby more concentrated power leads to more subsidies, which again lead to more poverty, inequality, and concentrated power. Figure 5.4 illustrates some of these interconnections.

Subsidies and Political Power

A troubling correlate of high subsidies is low voting rates. An active voting public is crucial to a democratic society and is one indicator of the extent of social capital. Among states with above-average total subsidies, participation in federal elections is, on average, 15 percent lower than the national average. Citizens in high-subsidy states may well feel disenfranchised, perceiving that their elected representatives cater to special interests. They may doubt that voting will change anything. Yet low voter participation itself contributes to the further concentration of power.

Those receiving subsidies can use the additional financial capital in a number of ways. One obvious way is to spend more on campaign contributions and to hire more lobbyists to protect and augment the subsidies. Industrial corporations are major contributors to political campaigns. In making contributions, special interests not only help to elect representatives who serve their interests but may also influence choices for appointed positions.

In my experience as a cabinet official in Louisiana's state government, I found that the quality of public leadership declines as special interests increase their sway. Even federally funded programs tend to languish. State agencies become less responsive to citizens, who in turn withdraw from the political process. The state becomes a less attractive place in which to live and do business. The cumulative result is institutional failure, the erosion of democracy, and the loss of social capital.

Decision makers hear the common refrain that higher environmental standards will drive away firms and jobs and lower economic welfare. Yet a growing body of research supports my findings to the contrary. For example, Meyer (1992) found that worker productivity, employment, and economic growth are lower in states with poorer environmental rankings. Cannon (1993) likewise found that economic growth rates were lower in states with poorer environmental records. The fact that environmental protection and economic performance can go hand in hand must be impressed upon public officials.

Leakage

Large companies are the biggest beneficiaries of subsidies: they use the most energy and other resources, discharge the most waste, and have the largest incomes and property holdings. If all the profits generated by subsidies were to remain in the state, the recycling of the extra income might counter at least some of the harm that subsidies inflict on public welfare. Many of the profits are exported, however, to shareholders and managers living in other states. In fact, value added per job—the surrogate measure for profits—is positively and significantly related to the share of gross state product that leaves the state. The greater the subsidies, the greater the profits and the greater the rate of leakage.

Louisiana again offers a case in point. It has the highest subsidies in the country, as well as the highest value added per manufacturing job. Yet only two-thirds of the annual gross state product accrues as income within the state (U.S. Bureau of the Census 1997). The remainder, roughly $5,000 per person annually, is exported to other states (and to other countries, since some firms are foreign-owned). If Louisiana retained this profit, the state's per-capita income would be close to the U.S. average.

Leakage is a major source of income disparities among states. It drains income from states that use the most resources and generate the most pollution—states that rely heavily on such industries as mining, manufacturing, and logging. These states tend to be poorer than average. The profits leak to richer states, which tend to pay smaller subsidies and import net income (that is, their total income can exceed their state product). As leakage declines, income rises; as income declines, leakage rises. The situation is analogous to colonialism, in which the mother country draws resources and other wealth from the colony, proffering little compensation in return. In this respect, the United States displays a kind of internal colonialism.

Policy Recommendations

Society can improve both public welfare and environmental quality by cutting subsidies and by taking back the commons to restore natural capital to citizens. Campaign finance reform is crucial if we are to elect officials who will work for change, despite opposition from entrenched interests who defend the status quo.

Cutting Subsidies

The pollution subsidy is a sink subsidy: it is based on cost-free access to the pollution-absorbing capacity of the environment. We need laws, regulations, and enforcement to minimize industrial discharges and to reappropriate this national asset. Economic incentives can be useful—in particular, to reach goals beyond minimal thresholds—but they are not sufficient by themselves. It has been found that state inspections of facilities, for example, have more impact on environmental performance than do incentives (Dasgupta et al. 2001).

One way to give firms a greater incentive to reduce pollution is to award tax exemptions based on environmental performance. In Louisiana, we devised an environmental scorecard to rate firms, and we conditioned a firm's property tax exemption on its annual score.[11] The rating was based on level of toxic discharges per job and on compliance with environmental regulations; that is, how many penalties a firm had incurred over a designated time period. Firms could also apply for bonus points; for example, by submitting a waste reduction plan or locating in areas needing development. Depending on its score, a firm could receive 50 to 100 percent of the requested exemption. Each percentage point could mean hundreds of thousand of dollars, so the incentive to perform well was substantial. Unfortunately, industry opposed the incentive vociferously, and after Buddy Roemer was defeated for a second term, the new governor's first official act was to eliminate the scorecard.

The energy subsidy is a source subsidy: it reduces the cost of obtaining a natural resource. There is no particular reason that industry should enjoy drastically cheaper energy than the public does. Some discount for volume may be justified, but economies of scale do not explain why residents pay four times more than industry in Louisiana and Alaska, while the average U.S. resident pays only twice the industrial price. The huge price differences in certain states reflect political power. Eliminating the energy subsidy would return natural assets to citizens in the form of reduced pollution and more equitable energy prices.

One way to gauge a fair price for energy is to use the nationwide average ratio of residential to industrial prices as a standard. Cutting above-average subsidies would not internalize all costs, but it would be a step in that direction. Energy prices that reflected all costs, including the associated security and environmental costs, would be much higher than current U.S. prices, and nearer to those of Europe. Higher prices for industrial energy would encourage greater efficiency in industry in the United States, which is currently among the least energy efficient of industrialized countries and thus contributes the most to global climate change. Nationally, empirical data show a significant and positive relationship ($r = .67$) between industrial energy prices and economic growth (Templet 1999). Higher industrial energy prices apparently have not stifled economic growth.

In the area of taxation, a shift from regressive sales taxes to taxes on resource use and waste releases would create stronger incentives to conserve resources and to reduce pollution.[12] Environmental taxes would require payment for the privilege of using natural capital as source or sink. Citizens who use less would benefit from lower taxes, less pollution, and conservation. Pollution-related health spending would also decline. The distribution of income, property, and sales taxes could also be adjusted to establish a reasonable ratio of regressive to progressive taxes. Again, the current U.S. average ratio might serve as an initial standard. States with above-average tax subsidies could reduce their sales taxes and correspondingly raise income and/or property taxes, in addition to raising revenues from source and sink taxes.

Campaign Finance Reform

All these reforms will be difficult to enact. Entrenched interests that benefit from current subsidies will use their political power to fight change. The correlations among the size of campaign contributions, congressional environmental voting records, and state subsidies to industry do not establish a conclusive case, but they do suggest that campaign contributions help promote subsidies for special interests. Campaign finance reform is essential to curb the purchase of influence through campaign contributions and to make room for progressive environmental policies.

Conclusion

When firms externalize environmental costs, they appropriate de facto property rights to natural capital. They capture subsidies, and the public pays the price. These firms often use political clout to advance their interests. The resulting state policies tend to make the state less attractive to other firms, reducing the diversity of businesses (Templet 1996). Communities may be left with a "company town" syndrome. They grow poorer, more polluted, more subject to boom-and-bust cycles, and more dependent on the industries that are reaping the benefits. As concentrated wealth fosters concentrated power, public policy embraces subsidies even more. The result is a spiral of public and, ultimately, private decline. Although corporations can eventually pick up and go elsewhere, the public as a whole cannot.

This negative scenario can be averted by requiring businesses to internalize their costs. We can reduce or eliminate pollution, energy, and tax subsidies in favor of a more equitable system. We can shift to progressive taxes and to taxes on the things we want to avoid—excessive resource use and pollution. A tax on resource use will promote conservation and improvements in efficiency. A tax on waste releases will encourage firms to pollute less, improving efficiency, health, and quality of life. By reallocating natural capital to the public domain, we can both protect the environment and reduce poverty. As Alexis de Tocqueville pointed out more than 150 years ago, equality is a defining characteristic of a democratic society. Environmental abuse is bad not only for our health but also for our ideals.

Notes

1. In 1991, Buddy Roemer lost his bid for a second term as governor, in the face of much soft-money spending by industry to defeat him. Although some of our reforms were rolled back by the next two governors, others remained in place.
2. The effectiveness of state policy depends not only on laws and regulations but also on enforcement. In Louisiana, the state imposed only 25 percent as many penalties in 1997 as it did per year when Governor Roemer was in office from 1988 to 1992. The size of the penalties also dropped, with the cumulative amount of fines in 1997 less than 10 percent of the 1989 level. Not surprisingly, pollution in Louisiana is increasing again: lax enforcement means greater subsidies.
3. These data are based on 1989 prices. In 1995, the ratio of residential to industrial energy prices in Louisiana had risen to 4.4.
4. For details regarding these calculations, see Templet (1995a).
5. For details, see Templet (1995a). As would be expected, the tax subsidy per capita is significantly and negatively correlated with the "tax fairness" score constructed by the Corporation for Enterprise Development (1995), a nonprofit research and policy organization that monitors economic development in the 50 states.
6. In addition to pollution, energy, and tax subsidies, many southern states liberally grant direct subsidies to attract industry. The South and West industrialized later than other regions, which may help to explain their tendency to allow industry to externalize costs more—much as developing countries often do (Templet 1996).
7. See Chavis and Lee (1987), Bullard (1990), and Chapters 4 and 6 in this volume.
8. As Table 5.1 shows, manufacturing jobs in Louisiana had been declining prior to

1988. After 1992, when pollution spending began to decline again under a new administration, manufacturing jobs fell once again. The contribution of pollution-control spending to jobs is even more impressive when compared to other state schemes to promote employment. A study by Management Information Services (American Chemical Society 1993) found that every additional million dollars spent on pollution control creates 22 jobs in the pollution-control sector alone (not counting multiplier effects on employment in other sectors). By contrast, Louisiana has had little success with tax incentives designed expressly to create jobs: Louisiana has lost about 15,000 manufacturing jobs since 1980, while paying out over $5 billion in tax subsidies.

9. Value added is the value of shipments minus the cost of raw materials. Subtracting other production costs from value added would yield profits.

10. In 1990, Louisiana's Toxics Release Inventory emissions per job in the emitting sector amounted to 2,496 pounds, compared to a U.S. average of 188 pounds (Templet 1995b).

11. For details, see Templet et al. (1991), Templet and Farber (1994), and Farber et al. (1995).

12. For reviews of tax-shifting experience in other countries, see Roodman (1999) and Ekins (1999).

References

American Chemical Society. 1993. "Currents." *Environmental Science & Technology* 27(5): 771.

Baumol, W. J., and W. E. Oates. 1988. *The Theory of Environmental Policy*. 2nd ed. Cambridge: Cambridge University Press.

Boyce, J. K., A. R. Klemer, P. H. Templet, and C. E. Willis. 1999. "Power Distribution, the Environment, and Public Health: A State Level Analysis." *Ecological Economics* 29:127–40.

Bullard, R. D. 1990. *Dumping in Dixie: Race, Class and Environmental Quality*. Boulder, Colo.: Westview Press.

Cannon, F. 1993. "Economic Growth and the Environment." In *Economic and Business Outlook*. San Francisco: Bank of America, Economics-Policy Research Department.

Chavis, B. F., and C. Lee. 1987. *Toxic Wastes and Race in the United States*. New York: Commission for Racial Justice, United Church of Christ.

Corporation for Enterprise Development. 1995. *The 1995 Development Report Card for the States*. Washington, D.C.: Corporation for Enterprise Development.

Costanza, R., R. D'Arge, R. de Groot, S. Farber, M. Grasso, B. Hannon, S. Naeem, K. Limburg, J. Paruelo, R. V. O'Neill, R. Raskin, P. Sutton, and M. van den Belt. 1997. "The Value of the World's Ecosystem Services and Natural Capital." *Nature* 387:253–60.

Dasgupta, S., B. Laplante, N. Mamingi, and H. Wang. 2001. "Inspections, Pollution Prices and Environmental Performance: Evidence from China." *Ecological Economics* 36(3): 487–98.

Ekins, P. 1999. "European Environmental Taxes and Charges: Recent Experience, Issues and Trends." *Ecological Economics* 31:39–62.

Farber, S., R. Moreau, and P. H. Templet. 1995. "A Tax Incentive Tool For Environmental Management: An Environmental Scorecard." *Ecological Economics* 12:183–89.

Hall, B., and M. L. Kerr. 1991. *1991–1992 Green Index: A State-By-State Guide to the Nation's Environmental Health.* Washington, D.C.: Island Press.

Meyer, S. M. 1992. "Environmentalism and Economic Prosperity: Testing the Environmental Impact Hypothesis." Working Paper Series No.1. Cambridge: Project on Environmental Politics and Policy, Massachusetts Institute of Technology.

Roodman, D. M. 1999. "Building a Sustainable Society." In *State of the World 1999.* Worldwatch Institute. New York: W. W. Norton.

Templet, P. H. 1993. "The Emissions-to-Jobs Ratio; A Tool for Evaluating Pollution Control Programs." *Environmental Science and Technology* 27(5): 810–12.

———. 1995a. "Equity and Sustainability; An Empirical Analysis." *Society and Natural Resources* 8:509–23.

———. 1995b. "Grazing the Commons: Externalities, Subsidies and Economic Development." *Ecological Economics* 12:141–59.

———. 1995c. "The Positive Relationship Between Jobs, Environment and the Economy: An Empirical Analysis." *Spectrum* (Spring): 37–49.

———. 1996. "The Energy Transition in International Economic Systems: An Empirical Analysis of Change During Development." *International Journal of Sustainable Development and World Ecology* 3:1–18.

———. 1999. "Diversity and Development in Economic Systems; An International Empirical Systems Analysis." *Ecological Economics* 30:223–33.

———. 2001. "Energy Price Disparity and Public Welfare." *Ecological Economics* 36:443–60.

Templet, P. H., and S. Farber. 1994. "The Complementarity Between Environmental and Economic Risk: An Empirical Analysis." *Ecological Economics* 9:153–65.

Templet, P. H., J. Glenn, and S. Farber. 1991. "Louisiana Ties Environmental Performance to Tax Rates." *Environmental Finance* (Autumn).

Tocqueville, Alexis de. 1835 [1961 translation]. *Democracy in America,* Vol. II, Book 4. Translated by Henry Reeve. New York: Schocken Books.

U.S. Bureau of the Census. 1992. *Current Industrial Reports, Pollution Abatement Costs and Expenditures.* MA200(90)-1. Washington, D.C.

———. 1997. *Statistical Abstract of the U.S.: 1997.* 117th ed. Washington, D.C.

U.S. Environmental Protection Agency. 1991. *Toxics in the Community, National and Local Perspectives, The 1989 Toxics-Release Inventory National Report.* EPA 560/4-91-014. Washington, D.C.: U.S. Government Printing Office.

CHAPTER 6

Information for Empowerment: The EPA's Risk-Screening Environmental Indicators Project

Nicolaas W. Bouwes, Steven M. Hassur, and Marc D. Shapiro

Public access to information can drive environmental change more effectively than regulations alone. Recognizing this fact, some regulatory agencies are now using public education to advance their objectives. Right-to-know legislation, such as the Emergency Planning and Community Right-to-Know Act of 1986 (EPCRA), provides the basis for many of the U.S. Environmental Protection Agency's (EPA's) information disclosure initiatives. By requiring that the public be informed about releases of toxic chemicals in their communities, EPCRA—through its Toxics Release Inventory (TRI) in particular—can help to empower community residents, heighten industry accountability to the citizenry, and support efforts to ensure environmental justice.

The availability of basic data is necessary, but not necessarily sufficient, to accomplish environmental justice objectives. The challenge is to verify the existence of *disparate impacts* (for example, disparities correlated with race and income) and to identify where they occur, who is impacted, and who is responsible. To answer such questions correctly, it is necessary to translate raw data into accessible and meaningful information. The Risk-Screening Environmental Indicators (RSEI), a unique computer tool developed by the EPA's Office of Pollution Prevention and Toxics, can translate toxic chemical release data into more meaningful risk-related information for use by activists,

The views expressed in this paper are solely those of the authors and do not necessarily reflect the views or policies of the U.S. Environmental Protection Agency or ICF Consulting, Inc.

researchers, and policy makers in analyzing disparate impacts by race and income and in properly focusing risk-reduction efforts in communities.

This chapter describes how the RSEI project builds on the TRI data to assess risks from toxic chemical releases in the United States, by taking into account the toxicity of various chemicals and the geographical patterns of their dispersal in the environment. Drawing on these data, we then conduct a national-level statistical analysis of the relationship between airborne releases of toxic chemicals and demographic characteristics of the exposed populations, focusing on characteristics of concern to environmental justice advocates: notably, race, ethnicity, and income. Our research suggests that blacks, Asian-Americans, and Hispanics face significantly greater risks than whites and non-Hispanics.

A Community's Right to Know

In the early morning of December 3, 1984, methyl isocyanate, a highly toxic chemical used in production of an insecticide, escaped from the Union Carbide facility located in Bhopal, India, a heavily populated area of 800,000 people. This accidental release killed 2,000 people immediately and injured approximately 300,000 others. It is estimated that an additional 8,000 may have died later as a result of their exposure. City health officials had not been informed of the toxicity of the chemicals used at the Union Carbide factory. There were no emergency plans or procedures in place and no local knowledge of how to deal with the poisonous cloud.

Because Union Carbide was an American-held company, Congress and the public had to confront the possibility that such an incident could occur at a similar facility in the United States. In fact, in 1985, Union Carbide accidentally released this same chemical in Institute, West Virginia, injuring 140 people. In response to these tragedies, Congress passed EPCRA the following year. Provisions of this act promote emergency planning to minimize the effects of an accident such as the one that occurred at Bhopal and mandate that the public be provided with information about releases of toxic chemicals in all U.S. communities.

The Toxics Release Inventory

Section 313 of EPCRA established the TRI. This regulation requires private firms in manufacturing and several other industrial sectors, and federal government facilities, to report releases of toxic chemicals into the air, water, or land if they meet certain thresholds in terms of number of employees and use of chemicals.[1] In 1997, 21,490 facilities reported TRI releases; more than 43,000 facilities have reported TRI data since 1987. The TRI offers the public direct access to information. The EPA compiles the toxic chemical release data submitted by facilities nationwide into a publicly accessible database. Each year, the EPA publishes a TRI Public Data Release with various presentations of the data collected for that reporting year; it also posts these data on the EPA website.

How Are TRI Data Used?

Many private and public groups use TRI data. Concerned citizens use TRI to raise and answer questions about chemicals in their local communities and about the possible risks to public health and the environment. National newspapers—including *USA Today,* the *New York Times,* and the *Wall Street Journal*—regional newspapers, and scores of trade and labor union publications have run stories on TRI findings. TRI serves as a public "report card" for the industrial community, creating public relations incentives for waste reduction and providing local residents and public interest groups with credible grounds on which to pressure company executives and public officials for changes in industrial practice and public policy. Between 1989 and 1994 alone, public interest and community groups published more than 200 reports using the TRI data (Orum 1994). There is considerable anecdotal evidence that information made available through right-to-know laws has contributed significantly to community organizing efforts to change facility emission behavior (see, for example, Lynn et al. 1992; MacLean 1993; and Settina and Orum 1990, 1991). Industry leaders have acknowledged the effect on their behavior: in a survey of roughly 200 corporate counsels, over half indicated that "pressure from community activists has affected [their] company's conduct—sometimes forcing a reduction in pollution" (Lavelle 1993).

State and local agencies rely on TRI to establish emergency planning procedures, to formulate and pass legislation, and to enable toxic waste monitoring in communities. Many states have passed right-to-know legislation that expands the data collected under TRI and, in some cases, mandates reductions in emissions. In Louisiana, the TRI data prompted the passage in 1989 of a new air toxics law requiring a 50 percent reduction of emissions by 1994. Several states have established programs at universities, such as the Toxics Use Reduction Institute at the University of Massachusetts, Lowell. Most state environmental protection departments provide technical assistance to help businesses reduce toxic releases and other forms of pollution.

Federal agencies use TRI to prepare and implement environmental legislation and to monitor national health risks. The EPA applies TRI as a baseline to measure emission reductions mandated by the Clean Air Act amendments of 1990. TRI also is used to monitor compliance with other laws; to target areas where enforcement of other regulations is needed; to gauge the need for additional regulatory efforts to clean up water, air, and solid waste problems; and to develop strategies for assessing pollution prevention programs.

Academics rely on TRI data for environmental research and education. For example, the Environmental Studies Program at Dickinson College in Pennsylvania requires its students to prepare toxic waste audits of communities or facilities, using TRI as a resource. TRI reports are often pivotal in studies of chemical use and in the development of alternative technologies for preventing toxic releases.

What Do TRI Data Show?

Since the inception of the TRI, there have been significant reductions in the pounds of TRI chemicals released to the environment. From 1988 to 1997, on-site air releases of "core" TRI chemicals (those that have had no change in their reporting requirements since TRI's establishment in 1987) decreased by 55 percent in terms of weight. Reductions in the reported air releases of TRI chemicals were greatest in the earlier reporting years. In many cases, the "low-hanging fruit" has now been picked, and the expenditures required to reduce emissions further will be higher. Yet there are still significant quantities of toxic chemicals released to the environment in the United States. In 1997, facilities reported that they released 1.3 billion pounds of TRI chemicals into the air; on-site releases to all pathways plus off-site waste transfers amounted to 5.8 billion pounds.

TRI data on the quantity of emissions alone do not reveal the extent to which public health is at risk. The evaluation of risk requires consideration not only of how much of a chemical is released but also of the toxicity of that chemical and the exposure associated with that release. The toxicity of the TRI chemicals varies greatly; the human health impacts of the various carcinogens and noncarcinogens in the inventory can differ by up to seven and eight orders of magnitude, respectively. That is, a single pound of one of the most toxic chemicals, such as acrolein or methyl isocyanate, is toxicologically equivalent to 100 million pounds of the least toxic of these substances. The human health effects of some TRI chemicals depend upon the exposure pathway. Friable asbestos, for instance, is a highly potent carcinogen when exposure occurs via inhalation, but it is not considered toxic when ingested. And from the perspectives of both public policy and risk screening, it is important to know the number of individuals exposed.

These factors can have a major impact on the ranking of risks associated with TRI releases. Table 6.1 compares the rankings of the 50 U.S. states (plus Washington, D.C.; Puerto Rico; and the Virgin Islands) for total air releases of TRI chemicals in 1997 in terms of three measures: the number of pounds released; the hazard associated with those releases, obtained by incorporating

Table 6.1. Rankings Based on Air Releases of TRI Chemicals in 1997[a]

Rank	Pounds		Hazard		Total Risk	
	State	Percentage	State	Percentage	State	Percentage
1	TX	8.10	OH	9.30	OH	10.70
2	TN	6.20	SC	9.30	IL	9.90
3	LA	5.60	MO	8.30	PA	8.00
4	OH	5.00	TX	7.70	TX	6.80
5	UT	4.90	PA	5.80	IN	5.70
6	IL	4.90	IL	5.10	MO	4.60
7	AL	4.70	IN	4.70	CA	4.50
8	IN	4.30	AL	3.40	MI	4.50
9	NC	3.90	MI	3.20	AL	4.20
10	GA	3.60	NC	3.00	NJ	3.90
11	VA	3.60	LA	2.90	SC	3.80
12	MI	3.30	TN	2.90	WI	3.30
13	SC	3.30	WI	2.60	TN	2.80
14	PA	3.00	AR	2.50	NY	2.70
15	MS	2.90	GA	2.20	GA	1.90
16	KY	2.60	IA	1.80	KY	1.80
17	MO	2.50	KY	1.70	LA	1.70
18	FL	2.40	NY	1.60	WV	1.70
19	CA	2.30	UT	1.60	AR	1.50
20	WI	1.90	NJ	1.50	IA	1.20
21	AR	1.90	AZ	1.50	NC	1.20
22	IA	1.80	OR	1.40	MA	1.10
23	NY	1.80	MA	1.30	AZ	1.10
24	WA	1.60	MS	1.30	CO	1.10
25	KS	1.50	CA	1.20	VA	1.00
26	OK	1.40	KS	1.10	KS	0.90
27	OR	1.30	MT	1.00	MS	0.80
28	MN	1.30	VA	1.00	WA	0.80
29	WV	1.10	FL	1.00	OR	0.80
30	NJ	0.70	WV	0.90	FL	0.80
31	AZ	0.70	NM	0.90	MT	0.70
32	MD	0.60	OK	0.80	OK	0.70
33	NE	0.50	WA	0.80	NE	0.60
34	PR	0.50	MN	0.70	CT	0.60
35	ME	0.50	NE	0.60	MN	0.50
36	MA	0.40	MD	0.60	NH	0.50
37	CT	0.40	CO	0.50	UT	0.40
38	ID	0.40	ME	0.50	DE	0.40
39	MT	0.30	DE	0.40	MD	0.30
40	AK	0.30	NH	0.40	NV	0.20
41	CO	0.30	CT	0.30	NM	0.10
42	DE	0.20	NV	0.20	ME	0.10
43	NM	0.20	ID	0.20	PR	0.10
44	WY	0.20	WY	0.10	ID	0.10
45	SD	0.20	SD	0.10	RI	0.10
46	NH	0.20	PR	0.00	WY	0.00
47	ND	0.10	RI	0.00	SD	0.00
48	RI	0.10	ND	0.00	ND	0.00
49	NV	0.10	AK	0.00	HI	0.00
50	VI	0.10	VT	0.00	VT	0.00
51	HI	0.00	VI	0.00	AK	0.00
52	VT	0.00	HI	0.00	VI	0.00
53	DC	0.00	DC	0.00	DC	0.00

[a]No air releases were reported for Guam (GU) in 1997. Although there were air releases reported for American Samoa (AS) in 1997, no population data have yet been incorporated into the RSEI model for AS and GU. Therefore, these two U.S. Territories are not included in these results. In addition to the 50 states, data are presented here for Washington, D.C. (DC), Puerto Rico (PR), and the U.S. Virgin Islands (VI).

chemicals' toxicity weights; and the resulting risks to human health, incorporating exposure and the size of the receptor population. The hazard-based and
risk-related perspectives realign the state rankings considerably. Utah, for
example, ranks 5th in the United States in sheer pounds of airborne releases,
19th from a hazard-based perspective, and only 37th from a risk-related
perspective, with the sparse population in much of the state driving down the
last ranking. A single facility in Utah had the highest quantity of air releases of
TRI chemicals in the country, but because no one lives within 30 kilometers
of that facility, these releases had minimal risk-related impact on human
health. Pennsylvania, on the other hand, ranks 14th in terms of sheer pounds
released but 5th in terms of hazard and 3rd in terms of risk.

The EPA's Risk-Screening Environmental Indicators Project

The EPA's RSEI model incorporates information about chemical toxicity,
exposure ("dose"), and the size of the exposed general population.[2] This
model was used to calculate the state-level rankings reported in Table 6.1; it
can similarly generate risk indicators on the basis of specific chemicals, facilities,
geographic areas, and release media (air and water).

Most studies of toxic releases have skirted the question of risk, generally
treating all chemical releases as equally dangerous (Brajer and Hall 1992;
Glickman and Hersh 1995; Kriesel et al. 1996; Perlin et al. 1995; Riley et al.
1993; Stockwell et al. 1993). Although some researchers have begun to weight
emissions for toxicity (Arora and Cason 1999; Bowen et al. 1995; Brooks and
Sethi 1997; Horvath et al. 1995), they generally have not extended the concern with risk to the issue of dispersion of chemicals from their sources to the
receptor populations. Instead, most researchers use a single threshold distance
to measure risk.[3] As Arora and Cason (1999) concede, most researchers "do not
attempt to analyze exposures as it would entail very elaborate mappings using
the census tract and a geographical information system." Yet practitioners
analyzing risk in specific towns and local regions consider information on
chemical dispersion to be essential. The crude approach of most researchers to
this question has often led to a discounting of their results by the scientific and
regulatory community.

Full-scale risk assessment is complicated and can require data that are not
always available. However, risk can be analyzed with varying levels of
completeness. Risk-screening approaches consider some or all of the factors
associated with formal risk assessment, without attempting to address every
detail that would be needed for a complete picture. In the case of the TRI data,
such approaches fall along a continuum ranging from the simplest depiction of
risk, in terms of pounds of chemicals released to the environment, to the most

sophisticated characterization offered by a formal risk assessment. The hazard-based perspective, which considers only the pounds of chemicals released and their toxicity, is one step along this continuum. To evaluate the degree to which people are exposed to the chemical (that is, the dose at a given location and the size of the population exposed), several models have used surrogate information, such as proximity to a facility discharging chemicals to the air. This approach does not account for such important factors as stack height, wind patterns, a chemical's decay rate in air, or pathway-specific toxicity.

The RSEI includes substantial site-specific information, placing it closer to the formal risk assessment end of the continuum.[4] To estimate the relative risks to chronic human health posed by toxic chemical releases in the United States, the model integrates toxicity weights for individual chemicals and exposure estimates, based upon pathway-specific reporting of releases to air, water, and land and the size of the residential population potentially exposed. The result is not a full-scale, quantitative risk assessment, but it does provide a screening-level, risk-related perspective for relative comparisons of chemical releases.

The toxicity weights are assigned separately for the oral and inhalation exposure pathways and include both cancer and noncancer effects. Chemical release data from TRI and pathway-specific fate and transport models, accounting for such factors as wind patterns and stream flow, are used to calculate the doses to which people may be exposed. For example, the Industrial Source Complex Long-Term model estimates concentrations for air releases in each square kilometer within a 101-kilometer by 101-kilometer grid in which a facility is centered. For this purpose, the entire country is divided into an array of 1-kilometer-square cells, with each facility assigned to one cell. Populations are also assigned to these grid cells, based upon relevant latitude and longitude coordinates. The model uses block-level 1990 census data (the finest resolution of population) updated using annual county-level data. The summed, risk-related value for all the cells in the 101-kilometer by 101-kilometer grid surrounding a facility is referred to as an "indicator element" for that facility. Indicator elements are calculated for each combination of facility, chemical, and release pathway (air and water).

The RSEI model allows indicator elements to be rapidly combined by chemical, release pathway, geographic area (national, EPA region, state, county, city, or zip code), industrial sector (2-, 3- or 4-digit Standard Industrial Classification code levels), or facility, or by combinations of these and other variables. The indicator values that correspond to these combined indicator elements (for example, for all the chemicals released to the air by a given facility in a given year) are unitless numbers designed to be used for comparative purposes. The output is presented not only from the full risk-related perspective but also from the pounds-based and hazard-based perspectives. This approach allows users to assess which factors are contributing most to potential risk-related impacts.

Unlike formal risk assessments, which require weeks, months, or even years of technical and scientific staff time to perform, RSEI can answer many crucial questions in a matter of hours. It can be used first to evaluate and compare the potential impacts of toxic chemicals. The results can (and should) then be supplemented by additional analyses if necessary. By allowing follow-up studies to focus, from the beginning, on initiatives that have the greatest risk-reduction potential, RSEI can substantially improve efficiency.

Providing Information to Citizens and Communities

Citizens and communities must have access to risk-related information if they are to assess the risks they face and take action to reduce toxics in their communities. In the course of its development, the RSEI project has been presented to diverse interested parties from the public and private sectors. After receiving Freedom of Information Act requests for the RSEI model from the Environmental Defense Fund (EDF) and the Bureau of Environmental News of the Bureau of National Affairs, Inc., the EPA decided to make the model publicly available. Since July 1999, approximately 1500 copies of the RSEI CD-ROM have been distributed to EPA offices and regions,[5] TRI regional and state coordinators, members of Congress, other federal and state agencies, environmental organizations, public interest groups, industry, law firms, educational institutions, the press, and citizens at large.

The RSEI model is designed to be user-friendly. The EPA facilitates its application by providing a user's manual, extensive context-sensitive help screens built into the software, an Internet home page, and direct help to users via e-mail or telephone. To promote proper interpretation of the model's results, extensive documentation of its strengths and limitations is provided. The EPA has also developed a training program for its headquarters and regional staff and interested state personnel. As the audience requesting the model widens, additional options for training, including Internet-based "distance learning," are being explored.[6]

National Environmental Justice Analysis Using RSEI

The primary focus of environmental justice research has been investigations of whether there are disparate impacts of toxic substance exposures along demographic lines, such as race, ethnicity, and income. The data generated by the RSEI are well-suited to analyze this issue. Earlier disparate impact analyses have been hampered by the lack of risk-related information available at a level of resolution that can be correlated with relevant demographic characteristics of the exposed population. In this section, we evaluate nationwide TRI on-site air releases using data from the RSEI model.[7] This national perspective can serve as a model for regional or local analyses to help identify hot spots of potential environmental justice concern.

Methodology

For the purpose of this analysis, we generated a separate RSEI database representing the *aggregated* risk-related impacts of all nearby facilities on a cell-by-cell basis.[8] To study the relationship between relative risk and community profiles, we matched these "cell scores" with census data pertinent to poverty and environmental justice concerns.[9] Our research question is whether risk from airborne chemical emissions is associated with race, Hispanic origin, or socioeconomic class[10]: that is, are some groups disproportionately predominant in areas with large exposures to chemical emissions?

To answer this question, we must consider how best to factor in the overall density of people living in an area. The risk-related score for each cell is based not only on the amount and toxicity of TRI air releases to which people residing in that cell are exposed but also on the number of people living there: all else being equal, cells with a higher population density will have a higher risk-related score. Difference-of-means comparisons based on those scores provide an accurate indication of how remedial policies based on the RSEI model would impact environmental justice concerns. However, the apparent differences among demographic groups could be due, in part, to the fact that some groups tend to live in more densely populated areas. To assess the extent to which this factor affects our results, we also present a difference-of-means analysis from a non-population-weighted risk-related perspective, in which population density does not affect the cell scores.[11]

We explore the expectation that racial and ethnic minorities will be found in higher proportions in higher-risk areas, as a result of choices that facilities make about emission processes or siting or choices that potential residents make about neighborhood selection, or some combination of the two.[12] We also examine differences in socioeconomic class, by including median per capita income (in $1,000 units), the percentage of people below the poverty line, and the proportion of the workforce that is unemployed. There are two potential and contrasting expectations regarding the association between income and risk. On the one hand, higher incomes in a community could lead to direct or indirect pressure on nearby facilities to decrease pollution or shift emissions to other facilities, resulting in a negative correlation. On the other hand, a larger manufacturing base could lead to higher incomes as well as higher emissions and higher populations, resulting in a positive correlation.

We also examine the differences in the percentages of adults with college-level education and those not completing high school. The expectation from an environmental justice perspective is that those with lower educational achievement may be located in greater proportions in areas with higher risk-related cell scores. Finally, we explore whether certain age groups are disproportionately represented in places exposed to high levels of airborne emissions. Because older residents and children may show particular sensitivities to airborne hazards, we examine the proportions above age 64 and below age 18.

To allow easier interpretation of the RSEI risk-related scores used in our analysis, the score for each grid cell is divided by the mean score for all cells, so that the new mean score is 1. These "centered" risk-related scores therefore are defined relative to the average for all cells impacted by TRI-reporting manufacturing facilities. A notable feature of the resulting scores is their extreme skewness. The vast majority of the centered risk-related scores for individual grid cells fall between 0 and 1, but a small number of grid cells have risk-related scores up to thousands of times higher than the average. The average relative risk score in the top decile of cells is 320 times that found in the rest of the sample. Because of these extreme variations, we focus below on the demographic differences between the areas of highest risk and the other areas.

Difference-of-Means from a Population-Weighted Risk-Related Perspective

Here, we report an analysis of the difference in means between the top risk-related decile and the rest of the sample. The difference-of-means analysis provides an indication of the association between risk-related scores and each of the racial, ethnic, and socioeconomic groups considered, without controlling for the independent effects of each other factor.[13] The results are displayed in Table 6.2. The first column reports the mean values of our demographic variables for the top risk-related cell score decile, and the second column reports the mean values for the remaining 9 deciles. The third column indicates the absolute difference between the means for the top decile and the other deciles, and its statistical significance. Column four presents the overall mean for all 10 deciles, and column five shows the difference as a percentage of the overall mean.[14]

The differences in these mean values suggest that there are grounds for concern about disparate risk-related impacts. The proportion of non–Hispanic whites living in cells in the highest risk-related score decile is significantly lower than in the lower-risk deciles; whereas the percentages of blacks, Asians, and persons of Hispanic origin are significantly higher. Asian populations show the greatest proportionate differences, but as we will see when we discuss the non-population-weighted risk-related perspective, this result is related strongly to their concentration in cells with high population densities. The percentages

Table 6.2. Difference-of-Means for Top Impact Decile versus Others, from a Population-Weighted Risk-Related Perspective[a]

Demographic Characteristic (by percentage)	Top Risk Decile	Other Deciles	Absolute Difference[b]	Overall Sample Mean	Difference as Percentage of Overall Sample Mean
White	83.0	92.3	−9.4	91.4	−10
Black	12.4	5.4	+6.9	6.1	+114
Asian and Pacific Islander	1.8	0.6	+1.2	0.7	+166
Native American	0.5	0.7	−0.2	0.7	−25
Hispanic origin	5.4	2.5	+2.9	2.8	+106
Below poverty	12.0	12.1	−0.1	12.1	−1
Unemployed	6.4	5.8	+0.5	5.9	+9
Median income (thousands of dollars)	32.7	30.5	+2.2	30.7	+7
Over 64 years old	12.9	13.7	−0.8	13.7	−6
Under 18 years old	25.5	24.9	+0.7	25.0	+3
Grade-school education or less	25.4	27.6	−2.2	27.4	−8
College educated	18.0	14.7	+3.3	15.1	+22

[a]$N = 77,307$ for top decile; 695,761 for rest of sample.

[b]In all cases, the difference is statistically significant ($p < .01$) using two-sample t-test with unequal population variance and using two-sided hypothesis tests.

of blacks and Hispanics also are more than twice as high in the top-risk decile as in the rest of the cells. These results support the concerns of environmental justice advocates. Also in line with environmental justice concerns, the percentage of the unemployed and the proportion of young people are higher in the top-risk decile.

The risk picture is not entirely unbalanced in favor of "advantaged" groups, however. Native Americans, who are less likely to live in highly industrialized areas, represent a smaller proportion of the population in the highest-risk neighborhoods than in the rest of the sample. Similarly, the proportion of those with college educations is larger in the highest risk-score decile, and the proportion of those with no more than a grade-school education is smaller. These results suggest that, at the national level, the propensity for personal income and education to rise with manufacturing production (and its potential risk-related impacts) is stronger than the countervailing pressure from higher-income or better-educated communities to reduce risk from chemical emissions.[15] In addition, the percentage of those people living below the poverty line and the proportion of elderly residents are lower in the highest risk-related cells than in the rest of the sample.

Difference-of-Means from a Non-Population-Weighted Risk-Related Perspective

To examine the extent to which the differences in risk reported above arise from differences in population density, we perform a similar analysis from a non-population-weighted risk-related perspective. That is, we exclude the population-weighting factor of the RSEI model and estimate the risk-related potential present in a cell regardless of population. For this purpose, the cell scores are calculated only from the aggregated chemical concentrations adjusted by toxicity and exposure considerations, without considering the number of people residing in a cell. The results are presented in Table 6.3.

In general, this non-population-weighted perspective shows somewhat smaller differences in the proportion of minorities in the top risk-score decile than did the population-weighted risk-related perspective. Nevertheless, the percentages of blacks, Hispanics, and Asians in the top-risk-potential neighborhoods remain significantly higher than in the rest of the areas. The difference-

Table 6.3. Difference-of-Means for Top Impact Decile versus Others, from a Non-Population-Weighted Risk-Related Perspective[a]

Demographic Characteristic (by percentage)	Top Risk Decile	Other Deciles	Absolute Difference	Overall Sample Mean	Difference as Percentage of Overall Sample Mean
White	87.9	91.8	−3.9[b]	91.4	−4
Black	9.4	5.7	+3.7[b]	6.1	+54
Asian and Pacific Islander	0.8	0.7	+0.1[b]	0.7	+7
Native American	0.6	0.7	−0.1[b]	0.7	−16
Hispanic origin	3.0	2.7	+0.3[b]	2.8	+8
Below poverty	12.7	12.0	+0.7[b]	12.1	+5
Unemployed	6.4	5.8	+0.5[b]	5.9	+9
Median income (thousands of dollars)	30	31	−1[b]	31	−3
Over 64 years old	13.7	13.7	−0.0	13.7	−0
Under 18 years old	24.9	25.0	−0.1	25.0	−0
Grade-school education or less	27.8	27.4	+0.4[b]	27.4	+1
College educated	14.2	15.1	−0.9[b]	15.1	−6
Population density (persons/square kilometer)	480	237	+244[b]	261	+93

[a]$N = 77,307$ for top decile; 695,761 for rest of sample.

[b]Difference is statistically significant ($p < .01$) using two-sample t-test with unequal population variance and using two-sided hypothesis tests.

of-means is particularly striking for blacks, suggesting that the disproportionate impacts to which African-Americans are exposed are not associated only with their residence in high-population-density locations.

RSEI as a Tool for Change

The preceding analysis uses a nationwide database generated by the RSEI model to assess environmental justice concerns with respect to TRI air releases. Such national-level analyses can help to identify disproportionate impacts on specific groups, but to take this information and act upon it will require additional investigation focusing on specific geographic areas. Properly identifying those sources of releases that present the greatest risk to the general public, or a disparate risk to specific population subgroups, is a particularly important challenge—one that the RSEI model can help to meet. Presently, decisions regarding policy and enforcement priorities are made either with inappropriate data (for example, pounds of emissions) or with expensive and time-consuming risk assessments typically conducted on an ad hoc basis. RSEI helps resolve these issues by providing a fast and inexpensive risk-screening tool for targeting purposes.

As described previously, the indicator elements generated by the RSEI model can be combined in a variety of ways to provide additional analytical capabilities. For example, drawing upon the findings described in the disparate impact analysis, RSEI could be used to provide relative rankings of all zip codes within the counties or cities of a particular region, such as southern California. Furthermore, the model can be used to identify the facilities, air exposure pathways, and chemicals of greatest concern. By comparing the changes in each year's indicator values, starting with the base year of 1988, one can also use RSEI to obtain a risk-related perspective on trends in environmental well-being, which can then be related to policies, socioeconomic variables, and human health. The flexibility of the model provides analysts with the opportunity to prioritize facilities or chemicals for strategic planning, risk-related targeting, and community-based environmental protection.

Since RSEI is a screening-level tool, additional investigation is required to ascertain whether high rankings are associated, for example, with significant health effects. Such investigation will be complicated by the fact that TRI emissions are only one component of the chemicals to which individuals are exposed. Other major sources of exposure include mobile sources, such as motor vehicles and indoor air emissions. TRI exposure levels that appear to be significant may require additional investigation of the chemicals and/or facilities identified as "drivers" of the relative rankings.[16] In cases where uncertainties exist, it is necessary to engage the relevant facilities in a dialogue to determine the nature of their emissions and whether remedial action is indeed warranted.

Conclusion

This chapter has described an approach to generate and disseminate information to those interested in environmental justice issues in a relatively sophisticated, quick, and inexpensive fashion. We also have presented the results of a nationwide analysis to assess environmental justice concerns with respect to TRI air releases. Overall, the RSEI risk-related scores reveal patterns of inequity of concern to environmental justice advocates: higher risks for blacks and Asians relative to whites and for Hispanics relative to non-Hispanics. They also reveal that higher unemployment is associated with higher risk. Other demographic characteristics reveal weaker patterns of inequity or relationships reversed from those that might be expected on environmental justice grounds.

The RSEI model can make important contributions to the analysis of environmental justice issues. It can be used in a two-step fashion. First, it can be used to generate a national database that provides estimates of risk-related impacts associated with TRI air releases for each square kilometer of the United States and its territories. The format of these data is compatible with census and proposed Geographic Information System (GIS) databases. When these data are coupled with census information as demonstrated here, it is possible to examine the relationship between these risk-related impacts and such demographic variables as race, income, and age.

In the second step, the RSEI model (incorporating components to evaluate impacts at various geographic scales) can be used to perform queries, based on the findings from step one, to identify geographic areas, chemicals, and facilities of particular concern. The results can be used to inform and empower citizen groups to help bring about environmental improvements and to correct disparate impacts. These results will aid decision makers, too, by helping to channel scarce resources to initiatives that have the greatest risk-reduction potential. The unique capabilities of this risk-screening tool will undoubtedly open other new research opportunities that can improve the health of communities across the United States.[17]

Notes

1. Specifically, a facility must report the pounds of its releases and transfers of any of the 604 chemicals and chemical categories that are currently on the TRI list if it (1) has 10 or more full-time employees, and (2) "manufactures" or "processes" more than 25,000 pounds, or "otherwise uses" more than 10,000 pounds, of any listed chemical during the reporting year. In May 1997, the EPA added several new industry sectors to those required to report releases: metal mining, coal mining, electric utilities, commercial hazardous waste treatment, wholesale chemicals and allied products, petroleum bulk terminals and plants, and solvent recovery services.

2. The RSEI project has been ongoing since 1991. During that time, a substantial amount of documentation of the model has been generated. For further details, see Bouwes and Hassur (1997a, 1997b) and the EPA RSEI web site at http://www.epa.gov/oppt/rsei/. Currently, TRI is the primary source of chemical release data used in the RSEI model. Although TRI reporting does not cover all toxic chemicals or sources of chemical emissions, it represents one of the better and more complete databases maintained by the EPA. A future version of the model will allow use of alternative databases (for example, release information for non-TRI facilities and monitoring data for non-TRI chemicals).

3. Pollock and Vittas (1995) use a logarithmic functional form but without any reference to chemical-specific dispersion and transportation. An exception to this pattern is Hamilton (1999), who uses a commercially available program that generates risk-related measures from TRI data. The price of such a program is out of reach for most community groups and researchers, and its assumptions (for example, nationally uniform stack heights of 10 meters) leave room for improvement.

4. The model does not provide estimates of actual risk to individuals as is done in a formal risk assessment, which incorporates all relevant toxicity information, exposure factors, and activity patterns.

5. The EPA structure can be loosely described as comprising headquarters and its regional offices. Headquarters is primarily responsible for policy and regulation development, and the regional offices perform the role of intermediary between the agency and states and the public. Following the release of RSEI, regional offices requested training for themselves and their state-based constituents in the use of RSEI to ensure the correct use of the model.

6. Background information, technical documents, guidance on the use of this tool, new developments, and model updates can be found on the EPA RSEI web site (http://www.epa.gov/opptintr/rsei/). The RSEI model is designed to run on a personal computer (PC) using the Microsoft Windows 3.1 or 95/98/NT operating systems. It can be obtained from the Toxic Substances Control Act Assistance Information Service by calling (202) 554-1404 or writing to tsca-hotline@epa.gov.

7. Version 1.02 of RSEI generated the data for the analysis presented here. Version 1.02 is similar to subsequent versions but has several differences: risk-related impacts are generated for the air pathway only; cell-by-cell impacts are estimated for a 21-kilometer by 21-kilometer grid; and population adjustments are made by interpolating between 1988 and 1990 and between 1990 and 1997, using annual U.S. Census Bureau county data (for years other than 1990) and the decennial U.S. census (for 1990 data).

8. The indicator elements generated by RSEI make use of information based on a 1-kilometer by 1-kilometer spatial resolution. This degree of resolution is particularly useful for disparate impact analyses, because grid cells of this size can be aggregated to any level in order to analyze the geographic area of interest (for example, census block or block group, census tract, zip code). Approximately 10 million grid cells represent the United States and its territories. In 1996, approximately 773,000 of these grid cells were impacted by on-site TRI air releases; that is, these cells had both an estimated dose and people living within the cell.

9. The race and income data used in the analysis below are drawn from the approximately 7 million census blocks and 230,000 census block groups delineated by
   the 1990 census. Blocks and block groups represent the smallest geographic units
   for which census information is available. The demographic variables are measured at the block level, with the exception of median income and unemployment,
   which are available only at the block-group level.
10. We follow the convention of using the U.S. Census Bureau–defined terms *black*
    and *white* to describe those racial groups in this paper. Hispanic origin is a sepa-
    rate category from race on census forms. Therefore, people who identify as
    Hispanic are included among various racial categories. The Hispanic-origin cate-
    gory is most highly correlated with the racial categories "white" and "other."
11. A drawback of exclusive reliance on a non-population-weighted risk-related
    perspective is that the results could be unduly influenced by the presence or
    absence of minorities in sparsely populated areas. For example, a cell inhabited by
    one person who happened to be African-American (making the cell 100 percent
    black) would receive equal weight with a cell inhabited by 1,000 people, of whom
    50 percent were African-American.
12. For a discussion of discriminatory siting versus minority move-in, see Chapter 4.
13. We also performed a multivariate analysis, holding constant the effect of correlated
    characteristics such as level of education. The results were consistent with the
    picture emerging from the difference-of-means analysis reported here. For a full
    report of the multivariate results, see Bouwes et al. (2001). Also see Shapiro (2000).
14. Note that the overall means represent the average cell, not the share of each group
    in all cells taken together. For example, blacks represent only 6.1 percent of the
    population in the average cell but a considerably larger percentage of the total
    impacted population, by virtue of the fact that they tend to live in more densely
    populated cells.
15. A cross-sectional (rather than time-series) test is not ideal for discriminating
    among complicated interactions such as these. The results here therefore are merely
    suggestive as to which underlying interactions might predominate.
16. For example, due to insufficient reporting information regarding chemical com-
    pounds (such as the precise chemicals in a chemical category) and the valence
    states (oxidation states) of certain metals and metal compounds, a priori assump-
    tions are sometimes made for modeling purposes. TRI reporters are required to
    estimate only the number of pounds of the parent metal for a metals category
    listing and are not required to specify the valence of these chemicals. In these
    instances, the EPA assigns the toxicity weight associated with the parent metal
    to metal compounds and assumes the valence state of the metal with the highest
    toxicity weight. This assumption is consistent with risk assessment practices at
    the EPA, which maintains a conservative position in the absence of sufficient
    information, preferring to err on the side of caution than to place the public at
    possible risk.
17. The usefulness of the RSEI model will expand with experience and with further
    improvements to the model, including the ability to examine non-TRI chemicals
    and reporters. In an effort to provide the most useful model possible, the EPA
    encourages users to share their research efforts and suggestions for model

improvements through the comments section of the RSEI web site at http://www.epa.gov/opptintr/rsei/ or by contacting the EPA authors of this paper directly.

References

Arora, Seema, and Timothy N. Cason. 1999. "Do Community Characteristics Influence Environmental Outcomes? Evidence from the Toxics Release Inventory." *Southern Economic Journal* 65(4): 691–716.

Bouwes, Nicolaas W., and Steven M. Hassur. 1997a. *Toxics Release Inventory Relative Risk-Based Environmental Indicators: Interim Toxicity Weighting Summary Document.* Washington, D.C.: EPA Office of Pollution Prevention and Toxics.

———. 1997b. *Toxics Release Inventory Relative Risk-Based Environmental Indicators Methodology.* Washington, D.C.: EPA Office of Pollution Prevention and Toxics.

Bouwes, Nicolaas W., Steven M. Hassur, and Marc D. Shapiro. 2001. "Empowerment Through Risk-Related Information: EPA's Risk-Screening Environmental Indicators Project." Working Paper No. DPE-01-06. February. Amherst, Mass.: Political Economy Research Institute.

Bowen, William M., Mark J. Salling, Kingsley E. Haynes, and Hellen J. Cyran. 1995. "Toward Environmental Justice: Spatial Equity in Ohio and Cleveland." *Annals of the Association of American Geographers* 85(4): 641–63.

Brajer, V., and J. V. Hall. 1992. "Recent Evidence on the Distribution of Air Pollution Effects." *Contemporary Policy Issues* 10:63–71.

Brooks, Nancy, and Rajiv Sethi. 1997. "The Distribution of Pollution: Community Characteristics and Exposure to Air Toxics." *Journal of Environmental Economics and Management* 32:233–50.

Glickman, Theodore S., Dominic Golding, and Robert Hersh. 1995. "GIS-Based Environmental Equity Analysis: A Case Study of TRI Facilities in the Pittsburgh Area." In *Computer Supported Risk Management,* edited by G. E. G. Beroggi and W. A. Wallace. 95–114. Boston: Kluwer Academic Publishers.

Hamilton, James T., 1999. "Exercising Property Rights to Pollute: Do Cancer Risks and Politics Affect Plant Emission Reductions?" *Journal of Risk and Uncertainty* 18(2): 105–24.

Horvath, Arpad, Chris T. Hendrickson, Lester B. Lave, Francis C. McMichael, and Tse-Sung Wu. 1995. "Toxic Emissions Indices for Green Design and Inventory." *Environmental Science & Technology* 29(2): 86A–90A.

Kriesel, Warren, Terence J. Centner, and Andrew G. Keeler. 1996. "Neighborhood Exposure to Toxic Releases: Are There Racial Inequities?" *Growth and Change* 27:479–99.

Lavelle, Marianne. 1993. "Environment Vise: Law, Compliance." *The National Law Journal* (30 August): S1–S9.

Lynn, Frances M., Jack D. Kartez, and Cheryl Connelly. 1992. *The Toxics Release Inventory: Environmental Democracy in Action.* EPA 700-F-92-001. January. Washington, D.C.: U.S. EPA, Office of Pollution Prevention and Toxics.

MacLean, Alair. 1993. "Bigotry and Poison." *Progressive* 57(1): 14–19.

Orum, Paul. 1994. "Reports Using Toxics Release Inventory (TRI) Data." *Working Notes on Community Right-To-Know* (July–August): 1–11.

Perlin, Susan A., R. Woodrow Setzer, John Creason, and Ken Sexton. 1995. "Distribution of Industrial Air Emissions by Income and Race in the United States: An Approach Using the Toxic Release Inventory." *Environmental Science & Technology* 29:69–80.

Pollack, Philip H. III, and M. Elliot Vittas. 1995. "Who Bears the Burdens of Environmental Pollution? Race, Ethnicity, and Environmental Equity in Florida." *Social Science Quarterly* 76(2): 294–310.

Riley, Gwen J., John L. Warren, and Rachel D. Baker. 1993. *Assessment of Changes in Reported TRI Releases and Transfers Between 1989 and 1990.* May. Research Triangle Park, N.C.: Center for Economics Research, Research Triangle Institute.

Settina, Nita, and Paul Orum. 1990. *Making the Difference, Part 1: Using the Right to Know in the Fight Against Toxics.* Washington, D.C.: National Center for Policy Alternatives.

———. 1991. *Making the Difference, Part 2: More Uses of Right to Know in the Fight Against Toxics.* Washington, D.C.: Center for Policy Alternatives and Working Group on Community Right-to-Know.

Shapiro, Marc D. 2000. *The Impact of Community Characteristics and State Policy on Changes in Emissions and Risk from Toxic Airborne Chemicals.* Ph.D. diss., University of Rochester, Rochester, N.Y.

Stockwell, John R., Jerome W. Sorensen, James W. Eckert Jr., and Edward M. Carreras. 1993. "The U.S. EPA Geographic Information System for Mapping Environmental Releases of Toxic Chemical Release Inventory (TRI) Chemicals." *Risk Analysis* 13(2): 155–64.

CHAPTER 7

The Sky Trust: The Battle for Atmospheric Scarcity Rent

Peter Barnes and Marc Breslow

This chapter proposes a strategy to appropriate rights to a crucial open-access resource—the carbon storage capacity of the atmosphere—on an egalitarian basis. The "sky trust" we propose could be established as part of an international agreement to cut carbon emissions, on the basis of an agreed allocation of the global atmospheric commons among the countries of the world. Yet it could also be established by the United States or other countries acting unilaterally. Even in the absence of an international agreement, the sky trust is politically attractive because the majority of citizens would be net beneficiaries, receiving more dividends from the trust fund than what they pay into it via higher prices on fossil fuels. The sky trust thus has the potential to serve as a stepping stone toward an international agreement and offers a way to implement whatever global accord is ultimately reached.

The Earth's atmosphere acts as an environmental sink for the emissions of carbon dioxide generated by the burning of fossil fuels. Excessive use of these fuels has led to increases in the atmospheric concentration of carbon dioxide. This increase is the main cause of the "greenhouse effect" that scientists consider responsible for global warming.[1] In 1997, at a meeting in Kyoto, Japan, governments from around the world drafted an agreement to cut carbon emissions. This agreement called on the United States to cut its emissions to 93 percent of their 1990 levels by the period 2008–2012 and set similar targets for other industrialized countries.[2] To date, the U.S. government has refused to ratify the Kyoto accord, partly because it does not include binding limits on carbon emissions by the developing countries. In the coming years, however, it is likely that the United States and other countries will take significant steps to curb carbon emissions. They can do so by adopting policies to raise the price of fossil fuels—in effect, charging "atmospheric scarcity rent" for the sky's limited capacity to store carbon without overheating the planet—and thereby induce cutbacks in the use of coal, oil, and natural gas.

When this happens, who will receive the rent? One possibility is simply to let the oil, gas, and coal companies reap windfall profits. Another is to let the government reap the rent via energy taxes, using the proceeds to lower other taxes or increase public spending. The sky trust that we propose here is a third alternative, one that would distribute the rent equally to every person in the country. Individuals would pay into the sky trust fund according to their consumption of fossil fuels and would receive annual dividends from it according to the principle of equal ownership of the sky—or, more precisely, of its carbon storage capacity. Those who consume more fossil fuel would pay more into the trust than they receive back in annual dividends, whereas those who consume less would come out ahead.

Lower-income households generally would be net beneficiaries, because they consume less fossil fuel (and less of most other things) than upper-income households. With the carbon fees calibrated to cut emissions enough to meet the Kyoto target, we estimate that the net impact of the sky trust would be to raise the net income of the poorest 10 percent of U.S. households by roughly 5 percent, while lowering the net income of the richest 10 percent of households by slightly less than 1 percent.

The sky trust exemplifies the appropriation route to natural-asset building. By transforming skyborne carbon storage from an open-access resource into an asset owned equally by all, it would increase the natural-asset base of low-income individuals and communities. At the same time, by creating incentives to reduce carbon emissions, the sky trust would ameliorate the threat to human livelihoods and the environment now posed by global warming.

Atmospheric Scarcity Rent

Atmospheric scarcity rent is a new idea that reflects the sky's limited capacity to provide critical services to humans. For example, the air carries electromagnetic waves that are indispensable to broadcasters and telecommunications companies, but there are only so many usable frequencies that do not interfere with one another. In 1997, when Congress gave broadcasters a large chunk of the electromagnetic spectrum to use for digital broadcasting at no charge, opponents such as Senator John McCain called it a $70 billion giveaway (Common Cause 1997).

The kind of scarcity rent that concerns us in this chapter has to do with the sky's limited capacity to absorb carbon dioxide. Our demand for skyborne carbon storage is the flip side of our demand for fossil fuels. The more fuel we burn, the more carbon dioxide the sky must absorb. Until now, we have paid

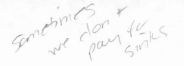

handsomely for oil dug from the ground, but we have paid nothing for air to hold combusted wastes. This disparity will soon disappear. The sky can safely handle only so much acid-brewing sulfur, ozone-eating chlorofluorocarbons, and heat-trapping carbon dioxide. We are now reaching those limits, if we have not already surpassed them. Governments have begun to recognize the problem of global warming. In 1997, 50 nations signed the Kyoto Protocol, an agreement to cut global carbon emissions by the year 2012. Notwithstanding the Bush administration's rejection of that agreement in spring 2001, it is almost certain that measures to reduce carbon emissions will be adopted in the coming decade. The question is, how will we implement the cuts? How will we fix the flaw in markets that so far has blinded us to the sky's limits?

Because there have not been any property laws for the sky, the air has been subject to what Garrett Hardin called the "tragedy of the commons."[3] Hardin envisioned an open pasture where herdsmen bring their cattle to graze. As long as there are not too many animals for the available land, each herdsman can take full advantage of the commons. But as the number of cattle increases, the land reaches the limit of its capacity. Seeking to maximize his own gain, each herdsman nevertheless adds more animals to his herd. Eventually the herdsmen ruin the land, the source of their own sustenance. Hardin applied this same parable to environmental sinks:

> In a reverse way, the tragedy of the commons reappears in problems of pollution. Here it is not a question of taking something out of the commons, but of putting something in. . . . The rational man finds that his share of the cost of the wastes he discharges into the commons is less than the cost of purifying his wastes before releasing them. Since this is true for everyone, we are locked into a system of "fouling our own nest." (Hardin 1968, 1245.)

One way to prevent this outcome is to set limits on overall pollution and then to issue permits allowing polluters to emit limited amounts. To promote flexibility and efficiency, companies can trade emission permits with other companies. Firms that find it easy to cut emissions can sell some of their permits to firms that find it more difficult, so that society obtains the same total reduction at the least cost. Such a cap-and-trade system was first put into place nationwide by the Clean Air Act amendments of 1990 in an effort to cut emissions of sulfur oxides, a health hazard and major cause of acid rain. The law has inspired many policy makers to propose a similar system to reduce domestic carbon emissions.[4] Therein lies both danger and opportunity.

The danger is that we could follow the model of the Clean Air Act too closely. That law included a grandfather clause for existing polluters: the government simply gave away permits to these companies, rather than charging for them. If we did the same for carbon permits, this would represent the biggest giveaway of public assets since the railroad land grants of the nine-teenth century—a giveaway of our once-spacious skies. In such a scenario, all future users of fossil fuels would pay atmospheric scarcity rent to a small number of corporate "skylords."

We have the opportunity, however, to capture the atmospheric scarcity rent on behalf of all citizens. To do this, we would auction annual permits to fossil fuel companies, at whatever price the market would bear. The revenue thus generated would flow into a trust whose beneficiaries would be all citizens, current and future. This sky trust would pay equal dividends to all. It would also be possible to earmark part of the proceeds for energy conservation programs, the development of renewable energy resources, and assistance to workers affected by the transition away from fossil fuels.

The beauty of this plan is that it would help to protect the environment and promote equality at the same time Conceptually, it is a rent-recycling machine, based on the principle: *from* all according to their use of the commons, *to* all according to their equal ownership of that commons. The equal distribution of dividends would have a progressive impact on income distribution in the United States, helping to narrow the yawning gap between rich and poor. A check of (for example) $1,500 per year would boost low incomes by a much larger percentage than it would high ones. Fuel prices would rise, but for the majority of people, the benefits would outweigh the costs, as we demonstrate below.

The Sky Trust

In 1998, the Corporation for Enterprise Development proposed the creation of a sky trust for the United States. One of the present authors was the archi-tect of that proposal (Barnes 1998). The following year, four economists at Resources for the Future (RFF) put forth a similar plan (Kopp et al. 1999). Under both proposals, companies selling fossil fuels in the U.S. economy would be required to purchase emission permits for the carbon content of these fuels. Efforts are now under way to enact these proposals into law.

Who Will Collect Rent?

One result has been a dialogue about who will collect atmospheric scarcity rent. The potential money at stake is substantial, far greater than in the case of sulfur emissions. After all, sulfur is just an impurity in coal, not the essence of coal itself. Carbon, on the other hand, is the irreducible pith of all fossil fuels. We Americans blow about 1.5 billion tons of it into the sky every year—about 6 tons each. At a price of $100 per ton, that would yield $150 billion of scarcity rent annually. By contrast, the value of the scarcity rent generated by the cap on sulfur emissions is estimated at less than $2 billion per year.[5]

The utilities that received free sulfur emission permits in 1990 were state-regulated entities at the time, and it was argued that any windfall they received would be passed through to ratepayers. The fossil fuel companies are different. Because their profits are mostly unregulated, free permits would send the benefits directly to shareholders. Since shareholding in energy corporations, as in the entire stock market, is highly skewed in favor of higher-income households, the result would be a regressive redistribution of income.[6] By contrast, the sky trust would have a progressive impact on income distribution, as documented in this chapter.

Who Will Own the Sky?

The question of who should "own" the economic value of the sky carries deep philosophic and religious overtones. Under the existing open-access regime, de facto ownership is appropriated by whomever emits carbon into the atmosphere. The creation of scarcity rents in response to the need to protect the atmospheric commons will compel us to establish de jure ownership rights, as a basis for the distribution of the proceeds. Practically speaking, there are three possible owners: private corporations, the federal government, or citizens through a trust.

The free granting of common assets to corporations has a long, if sordid, history in the United States, from the enormous land grants of the nineteenth century to the recent gift of the electromagnetic spectrum to broadcasters. The standard argument used to justify public largesse to private firms is that they deliver a public value in return. They build railroads, extract valuable minerals, or transmit sharper television images. The citizenry thus receives something in exchange for its generosity, making the deals at least arguably fair. Whether gifts of this sort really have been good deals for the public is, of course, debatable. But regardless of the merits of past grants, the gift of carbon absorption capacity would be in a class by itself. The public would get nothing in return, except perhaps cooperation from the energy companies in establishing a cap-and-trade system for carbon emissions. Indeed, such realpolitik is the only serious argument advanced for making such a grant today.

The case for government ownership of skyborne carbon absorption capacity is certainly stronger than the case for corporate ownership, in that the federal government is presumed to represent the public interest. But that presumption is debatable. If we look at the historical record, it is not clear that the government has consistently managed public assets to the public benefit. On the contrary, the government has all too often disposed of land, minerals, timber, and water at prices far below their market value. Even if the federal government were to receive market value for carbon absorption capacity, we must ask what it would do with the money. The odds that the proceeds would be distributed equitably are not terribly high.

When the Congressional Budget Office (2000) recently analyzed policies to curb carbon emissions, for example, it considered two alternative ways to distribute the revenues from selling carbon allowances. The first was a system of uniform lump-sum payments to all U.S. households, similar to our sky trust proposal.[7] The second was to cut corporate taxes by an amount equal to the carbon revenues.[8] The Congressional Budget Office concluded that the two policies would differ sharply in their distributional effects: the first policy would be progressive, with net costs borne primarily by upper-income households and net benefits for most lower- and middle-income households; the second policy would be regressive. Recent experience does not inspire confidence that the annual budget cycles of the federal government can be relied upon to yield progressive outcomes.[9]

The sky trust model represents an alternative to either corporate ownership or government ownership: citizen ownership, based on the principle of one person, one share. This idea builds on the model of a citizen trust along precisely these lines that has been in place for 25 years in the state of Alaska.

The Alaska Permanent Fund

Under the Alaska Constitution, the natural resources of the state belong to its people. After oil began flowing from Prudhoe Bay in large quantities, Alaskans realized that they were sitting on a bonanza, one that would not last forever. In 1976, they amended the state constitution to create a system for saving some of their oil wealth for the future. Since then, 25 percent of the state's oil revenue has been placed in an entity called the Alaska Permanent Fund.

The principal of the fund is managed as a trust for all current and future Alaska residents. The money is kept separately from the state treasury. It is invested in a diversified portfolio of stocks, bonds, and real estate, and the legislature cannot touch it. The annual income of the fund is divided into two roughly equal pots. About half is used for schools, highways, and other public capital investments, and the other half is paid in equal dividends to all Alaskans. In 1999, the individual dividend was $1,770.[10]

Like the Alaska Permanent Fund, a sky trust would be based on the premise that citizen ownership, if properly structured, is preferable to government ownership. From a purely technical perspective, implementing a sky trust is not difficult. Americans are the most ingenious creators of financial instruments the world has ever known. If we can invent 30-year mortgages, stock index mutual funds, and pork belly futures, we can surely design ways to structure common ownership of common assets. Compared to many other financial instruments, a sky trust would be relatively straightforward and highly transparent. Revenue would flow in from permit auctions, and dividends would flow out via annual checks or electronic funds transfers. As a percentage of the cash flow, administrative costs would be extremely low.

A sky trust would be the old commons in new clothes, a shared environmental resource transformed into an investment account. It would extend the political right of one person, one *vote,* to an economic right of one person, one *share* (of the commons). In so doing, it would create a new class of property owners whose membership would include every American. It would make every future baby a "trust-fund baby."

Narrowing the Income Gap

The sky trust would promote not only equality of ownership but also equality of income. The first benefit is fairly evident, but the second is less obvious. On the one hand, the payout from the trust would clearly have a progressive impact: all citizens would receive the same annual dividend, boosting the incomes of the poor by a larger percentage than the incomes of the rich. On the other hand, charging for emission rights could have a regressive impact: energy companies would face a rise in the cost of doing business, and they would try to pass on that cost to consumers by raising fuel prices. Businesses that use fuel in production would try to pass on their costs, too.[11] Higher fuel prices would take a bigger bite, in percentage terms, from low incomes than from high ones. So there are two opposing forces at work. Which is stronger?

In the end, the progressive effect of equal payouts outweighs the regressive effect of higher energy costs. That is, on average, low-income households would see a net gain in income, and upper-income households would see a slight loss. To arrive at this conclusion, we had to answer a number of questions. First, how much would fuel producers have to pay for carbon emission rights? Second, what percentage of that cost would be passed on to consumers in the form of higher prices? Third, how would these higher prices affect different income groups? Finally, what is the *net* gain or loss to each person, after the additional expense is subtracted from the dividend received from the sky trust? Although total payments into the sky trust would equal total payouts, some would receive more than they pay, and others would pay more than they receive.

The Price of Carbon

First we consider the price that energy companies would pay for carbon emission permits. Numerous studies by government agencies, academic researchers, and consulting firms have attempted to forecast the carbon price that would be needed to meet the Kyoto target of reducing average annual emissions during the period 2008–2012 to 93 percent of their 1990 level. Their estimates vary widely, partly because they use different methods and partly because they make different assumptions in dealing with the many unknowns. Some of the uncertainties are political, and some are economic. On the political side, we do not know, for example, how much international permit trading would be allowed. Some proposals would allow extensive international trading among firms, while others would limit trading to certain countries or allow only domestic trades. In general, the greater the opportunities for trading, the lower the carbon price that would be needed in the United States to meet the Kyoto target (Weyant and Hill 1999).

We also do not know how quickly the emissions cap would be phased in. If it were instituted abruptly, households and firms would have little time to respond to higher prices by switching to alternative technologies. Most studies assume that, once a cap is set, the carbon price would be driven entirely by the market. Resources for the Future, however, has proposed limiting the initial carbon price to as little as $25 per ton and then allowing the price to rise by 7 percent per year (in real terms) over the next 5 years, arguing that the low initial price would help to avoid a shock to the economy (Kopp et al. 1999). The RFF plan would also set aside some of the permit revenue in the first 10 years to assist workers and communities hurt by the shift to a lower-carbon economy. Under such a plan, the sky trust would collect less scarcity rent at the outset.

A key economic unknown is how consumers would respond to higher energy prices. If they were strongly resistant to cutting fuel consumption, then prices for emission permits would be bid up greatly. If, on the other hand, demand were quite elastic, so that consumers responded to higher fossil fuel prices by cutting back sharply in consumption, then permit prices and the scarcity rent would be lower.[12] Consumers could reduce their use of fossil fuels in at least three ways. They could do less of certain activities—cut back on driving, for instance. Or they could do the same things more efficiently—switch to more fuel-efficient cars, for example. Another option is to convert to a less polluting fuel—such as heating with natural gas instead of oil. In particular, switching from coal to other fuels can cut emissions without reducing total energy use, because petroleum and natural gas have less carbon per unit of energy.[13]

Taking these various possibilities into account, many researchers have attempted to forecast the carbon price needed to curb consumption enough to meet the Kyoto target.[14] In 11 such studies collected in a special issue of the *Energy Journal*, the estimated carbon price ranges from about $20 to more than $400 per ton (Weyant and Hill 1999). To assess the impact of the sky trust on income distribution, we examined three alternative scenarios presented in the *Energy Journal*. One study projects a relatively low carbon price of $83 per ton,

Table 7.1. Projected Scarcity Rent at Alternative Carbon Prices, Year 2010 (1999 dollars)

	Low	*Middle*	*High*
Carbon price (dollars per ton)	83.0	191.0	296.0
Total emissions (millions of tons)	1,249.0	1,249.0	1,243.0
Total revenue (billions of dollars)	103.7	238.7	367.7
Average revenue per household (dollars)	1,027.0	2,363.0	3,639.0
Revenue per person (dollars)	397.0	915.0	1,409.0

the second a moderate price of $191 per ton, and the third a relatively high price of $296 per ton (all figures are converted to 1999 dollars). Our base case, the middle scenario of $191 per ton, comes from the Pacific Northwest National Laboratory, operated by the Battelle Institute for the U.S. Department of Energy. Its model assumes no international trading of emission permits (MacCracken et al. 1999). These prices translate into total scarcity rents in 2010 of $104 billion, $239 billion, and $368 billion, respectively (see Table 7.1).

Cost and Benefit to Households

We assume that as energy companies incur higher costs, by virtue of having to purchase carbon-emission allowances at these prices, they will pass these costs on to consumers in the form of higher prices for oil, gas, and coal. In addition, we assume that firms that use fossil fuels to produce goods and services, and therefore incur higher expenses, will raise their prices to consumers as well. In our base case, we estimate that households would spend an additional $1,158 to $4,119 annually, depending on their income level, with the poorest households spending the least and the richest households the most (see Table 7.2).

To derive these estimates, we drew on an analysis by Gilbert Metcalf of Tufts University (1998) based on data from the 1994 Consumer Expenditure Survey. Metcalf did not analyze the effects of carbon emissions permits per se but rather the effects of a package of environmental taxes, dividing households into deciles, or tenths, of the population based on their income levels.[15] We used only the carbon tax portion of Metcalf's package in estimating the distribution of costs among deciles. Because Metcalf's carbon tax is smaller than the projected carbon price needed to meet the Kyoto targets, we then scaled his results upward accordingly.

In our proposal, the sky trust would collect revenues from the auctioning of carbon emission permits and then distribute the proceeds to households, with each individual receiving the same annual payout. Because households in the higher income deciles consist, on average, of a larger number of persons, the

Table 7.2. Costs and Benefits to Households across the Income Spectrum[a]

Income Decile	Mean Household Income (dollars)	Costs from Higher Prices (dollars)	Benefits from Sky Trust (dollars)	Net Effect (dollars)	Net Effect as Percentage of Income
1	6,884	1,158	1,512	+354	+5.1
2	13,127	1,418	1,777	+359	+2.7
3	20,453	1,800	2,034	+234	+1.1
4	28,107	2,085	2,358	+272	+1.0
5	35,900	2,089	2,393	+304	+0.8
6	44,406	2,303	2,429	+126	+0.3
7	53,613	2,719	2,549	−170	−0.3
8	66,179	2,800	2,902	+102	+0.2
9	87,480	3,144	2,916	−228	−0.3
10	161,801	4,119	2,740	−1,378	−0.9

[a]Based on a carbon price of $191 per ton (1999 dollars). Income figures are pretax but include transfers such as Social Security payments.

dividends per household are greater as one moves up the income distribution, ranging from $1,512 at the bottom to $2,740 at the top.[16] High-income households consume far more than low-income households, however, so their added expenses due to the higher fossil fuel prices rise more, too. The combined result of higher carbon costs and sky trust dividends is a net gain to households at the bottom of the income spectrum and a net loss to households at the top. The average household in the bottom decile would gain $354 per year, while the average household in the top decile would lose $1,378. Across the entire income spectrum, seven of the deciles—including the bottom six —would gain (see Table 7.2 and Figure 7.1). In percentage terms, households at the low end would enjoy the most significant gains, ranging from 5.1 percent of income for the first decile to 1.1 percent for the third. The top decile would see the largest loss, with income declining by 0.9 percent.[17]

As the price of carbon varies, so does the impact on household incomes, but the pattern in all cases is the same: poorer households see a net benefit, and richer households bear a net loss. Table 7.3 reports the net gains and losses under all three carbon-price scenarios.[18] It is clear, then, that a system based on the principle "from all according to their use of the atmosphere, to all according to their equal ownership of the atmosphere" would help to reduce the disparity between rich and poor in the United States.

Conclusion: A New Model for a New Millennium

The sky trust would be a historic breakthrough, a contribution to the twenty-first century possibly as great as the contribution of social insurance to the

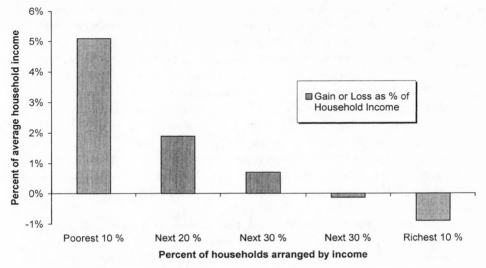

Figure 7.1. Effects of the Sky Trust on the Distribution of Income.

Table 7.3. Three Scenarios of Costs and Benefits Per Household in 2010 (1999 dollars)

Income Decile	Cost			Benefit			Net Effect		
	Low	Middle	High	Low	Middle	High	Low	Middle	High
1	503	1,158	1,792	657	1,512	2,340	+154	+354	+547
2	616	1,418	2,194	772	1,777	2,750	+156	+359	+556
3	782	1,800	2,786	884	2,034	3,149	+102	+234	+362
4	906	2,085	3,227	1,024	2,358	3,649	+118	+272	+421
5	908	2,089	3,234	1,040	2,393	3,704	+132	+304	+471
6	1,001	2,303	3,564	1,056	2,429	3,760	+55	+126	+196
7	1,182	2,719	4,208	1,108	2,549	3,945	−74	−170	−263
8	1,217	2,800	4,334	1,261	2,902	4,491	+44	+102	+157
9	1,366	3,144	4,865	1,267	2,916	4,512	−99	−228	−353
10	1,790	4,119	6,374	1,191	2,740	4,241	−599	−1,378	−2,133

twentieth century. Social insurance is an ingenious system for sharing risk and for protecting people from loss of income due to age, disability, or temporary unemployment. The sky trust is a further step in this direction. Social insurance provides a safety net; the sky trust provides a ladder. Social insurance draws from all according to their income and gives to all according to their longevity, disability, or economic need. The sky trust would draw from all according to their use of the atmosphere's carbon storage capacity and give to all on the basis of their equal ownership. One of the oldest principles of markets is that people should pay for what they use. The sky trust simply extends that principle to assets that previously were priced at zero. Similarly, it is a basic tenet of market economies that dividends should flow to property owners: what is novel here is the notion of *equal* and *universal* ownership.

How else could any country's share of ownership of the sky be divided? One might argue that the unequal distribution of human-made assets helps to encourage individual effort. But who can argue that sky ownership should be unequally divided or that unequal sky ownership—the de facto result of the current open-access regime—serves any social purpose? After all, no person lifted a finger to create it. The atmosphere is purely an inherited asset, bestowed not by anyone's parents but by the common creation.

In sum, a sky trust would marry two systems to meet two important goals. The cap-and-trade system would serve to limit our use of the atmospheric commons so as to sustain it, while the trust would serve to preserve common ownership. This solution would thereby remedy not only Hardin's *ecological* tragedy of the commons but also the oft-forgotten *economic* tragedy: the loss of the commons by the commoners, a loss that typically occurs just when a commons becomes commercially valuable. The sky trust is equitable as well as ecological, efficient as well as effective. By relying on property rights and market pricing, it allows the market economy to stay dynamic, while adjusting to scarcities created by its own success. And by putting into practice the democratic principle of equal rights to the natural assets that are humankind's common heritage, it reduces poverty and inequality.

Notes

1. The Intergovernmental Panel on Climate Change (2001) forecasts that global mean temperatures will rise by 5°F to 11°F over the next century.
2. The agreement calls on the United States to achieve an average carbon dioxide emissions level of 93 percent of 1990 levels during the "commitment period" of 2008–2012.
3. As James Boyce observes in Chapter 1, this is more accurately termed the "tragedy of open access."
4. For an account of the sulfur trading system, see Ellerman et al. 2000.
5. Based on 9 million tons of sulfur allowances and allowance prices in the range of $200 per ton during 1999. See http://www.epa.gov/airmarkets/arp/.
6. According to a recent study, the financial wealth of the top 1 percent of households exceeds the combined wealth of the bottom 95 percent (Wolff 1998, 37).
7. The main differences are that (1) we propose equal payments *per person* rather than *per household,* and (2) we propose that the revenues flow through a trust fund rather than relying on the annual budgetary process.

8. Although the tax cuts in Metcalf's analysis have a progressive impact, this is not enough to overcome the regressive effects of higher consumer prices. Because spending on fuel costs, both directly and indirectly, is a much higher fraction of income at lower income levels, it takes the more highly egalitarian effect of the sky trust to yield net benefits for lower income groups. For a comparison between the sky trust and an alternative set of tax reductions along the lines examined by Metcalf (1999), see Barnes and Breslow (2001).

9. Of course, federal legislation is needed to assign property rights to a sky trust. But winning a one-time battle to set up a sky trust is one thing; winning repeated battles over taxing and spending is quite another.

10. See the Alaska Permanent Fund web site at http://www.apfc.org.

11. Insofar as firms absorb the cost of carbon allowances internally, rather than passing them on to consumers, the resulting decline in profits would reduce the income of shareholders, who tend to belong to the upper income classes. In the analysis that follows, we assume the worst-case scenario, from a distributional standpoint, in which all the cost is borne by consumers.

12. Studies of the demand for fossil fuels indicate that the price elasticity of demand is rather low (less than 1); that is, a 10 percent increase in the price diminishes the quantity demanded by less than 10 percent (Espey 1998). For this reason, there is no need to worry that the sky trust would create an incentive for the majority of citizens (who are net beneficiaries) to encourage greater use of fossil fuels to maximize revenues and dividends. On the contrary, the higher the price charged for atmospheric scarcity rent, the greater the sky trust's total revenue, implying that if there were any such "incentive effect" on public policy, it would take the form of public pressure for even sharper cuts in carbon emissions.

13. Petroleum has about four-fifths the carbon content of coal per British thermal unit of energy, and natural gas has three-fifths.

14. Studies have been done, for example, by the U.S. Energy Information Administration (1998, 1999), DRI/McGraw Hill (Probyn and Goetz 1996), Pacific Northwest National Laboratory (MacCracken et al. 1999), and the National Institute for Environmental Studies at Kyoto University in Japan (Kurosawa et al. 1999).

15. Metcalf combines a carbon tax, an air pollution tax, and a motor fuels excise tax. He uses input-output data to trace the impacts of these taxes on various industries and assumes that the costs are passed on entirely to consumers. He then uses data from the Consumer Expenditure Survey to identify consumption patterns for each income decile of U.S. households.

16. As is usual in consumer expenditure surveys, the deciles are ordered by income per household. Average household size rises with income, from 1.65 persons per household for the poorest decile to 3.18 for the ninth decile and 2.99 for the tenth (richest) decile. This suggests an area for future research. Ranking households in terms of income per person arguably would yield a more accurate reflection of how households really compare in their ability to meet their living costs. Such a revised ranking would be likely to narrow the differences in the average family size across deciles; if so, the sky trust dividend per household would be

more equal across deciles, possibly making its estimated net effect even more strongly progressive.

17. The percentage reported for the richest 10 percent of households is likely to be an overestimate, however, because federal statistics do not report the incomes within the top decile above a few hundred thousand dollars per household, thus understating average income in the decile as a whole.

18. The low estimate also comes from the model devised by the Pacific Northwest National Laboratory (MacCracken et al. 1999), based on the assumption that trading would be allowed among the relatively wealthy industrial countries that are parties to the Kyoto Protocol (the so-called Annex I countries). The high figure comes from a model devised by a research group from Stanford University and the Electric Power Research Institute (Manne and Richels 1999).

References

Barnes, Peter. 1998. *Annual Report*. San Francisco: Corporation for Enterprise Development.

Barnes, Peter, and Marc Breslow. 2001. "Pie in the Sky? The Battle for Atmospheric Scarcity Rent." PERI Working Paper No. DPE-01-05. Amherst, Mass.: Political Economy Research Institute.

Common Cause. 1997. *Channeling Influence: The Broadcast Lobby and the $70 Billion Free Ride*. Available at http://www.commoncause.org/publications/040297_rpt.htm. April 2.

Congressional Budget Office. 2000. *Who Gains and Who Pays under Carbon-Allowance Trading? The Distributional Effects of Alternative Policy Designs*. June. Washington, D.C.: U.S. Congress, Congressional Budget Office.

Ellerman, A. Denny, Paul L. Joskow, Richard Schmalensee, Juan-Pablo Montero, and Elizabeth M. Bailey. 2000. *Markets for Clean Air: The U.S. Acid Rain Program*. New York: Cambridge University Press.

Espey, Molly. 1998. "Gasoline Demand Revisited: An International Meta-analysis of Elasticities." *Energy Economics* 20:273–95.

Hardin, Garrett. 1968. "The Tragedy of the Commons." *Science* 162:1243–48.

Intergovernmental Panel for Climate Change. 2001. *Climate Change 2001: Impacts, Adaptation, and Vulnerability: Summary for Policymakers*. Document approved by IPCC Working Group II in Geneva, 13–16 February. Available at http://www.ipcc.ch/.

Kopp, Raymond, Richard Morgenstern, William Pizer, and Michael Toman. 1999. *A Proposal for Credible Early Action in U.S. Climate Policy*. Washington, D.C.: Resources for the Future. Available at http://www.weathervane.rff.org/features/feature060.html.

Kurosawa, Atsushi, Hiroshi Yagita, Zhou Weisheng, Koji Tokimatsu, and Yukio Yanagisawa. 1999. "Analysis of Carbon Emission Stabilization Targets and Adaptation by Integrated Assessment Model." *Energy Journal*. Special Issue: The Costs of the Kyoto Protocol: A Multi-Model Evaluation: 157–76.

MacCracken, Christopher N., James A. Edmonds, Son H. Kim and Ronald D. Sands.

1999. "The Economics of the Kyoto Protocol." *Energy Journal*. Special Issue: The Costs of the Kyoto Protocol: A Multi-Model Evaluation: 25–71.

Manne, Alan S., and Richard Richels. 1999. "The Kyoto Protocol: A Cost-Effective Strategy for Meeting Environmental Objectives?" *Energy Journal*. Special Issue: The Costs of the Kyoto Protocol: A Multi-Model Evaluation: 1–24.

Metcalf, Gilbert E. 1999. "A Distributional Analysis of an Environmental Tax Shift." *National Tax Journal* 52(4): 655–81.

Probyn, Christopher, and Will Goetz. 1996. "Macroeconomic Impacts of Greenhouse Gas Control Policies." Paper presented to the Climate Change Analysis Workshop. 6 June. DRI/McGraw Hill.

U.S. Energy Information Administration. 1998. *Impacts of the Kyoto Protocol on U.S. Energy Markets and Economic Activity*. SR/OIAF/98-03. Available at http://www.eia.doe.gov/oiaf/kyoto/kyotorpt.html.

U.S. Energy Information Administration. 1999. *Analysis of the Impacts of an Early Start for Compliance with the Kyoto Protocol*. SR/OIAF/99-02. Available at http://www.eia.doe.gov/oiaf/kyoto3/kyoto3rpt.html.

Weyant, John P., and Jennifer N. Hill. 1999. "Introduction and Overview." *Energy Journal*. Special Issue: The Costs of the Kyoto Protocol: A Multi-Model Evaluation: viii–xliv.

Wolff, Edward N. 1998. "Recent Trends in Wealth Ownership." Paper presented at Conference on Benefits and Mechanisms for Spreading Asset Ownership in the United States, 10–12 December, New York University, New York.

PART III

CULTIVATING NATURAL CAPITAL

Interactions between humans and nature are not a one-way street in which humans monotonically deplete natural resources and degrade the environment, the only question being whether their negative impacts can be held within nature's capacity for recuperation. Humans can have positive impacts on the environment, too, not only by reducing pollution and replenishing stocks of renewable natural resources but also by engaging in the coevolutionary processes of our biosphere. Both sorts of activity represent what economists term "investment in natural capital" and others might term "nurturing the planet."

It is often assumed that all previous human technological achievements pale in comparison to the industrial and information revolutions of the past two centuries. This conceit is belied, however, whenever we sit down to a meal, for the foods we eat are a legacy of the technological advances made over thousands of years of human investment in natural capital. Without this cultivated natural capital, the fewer people alive today would be surviving on roots, berries, and wild game.

The chapters in Part 3 help to restore this sense of historical perspective. Winona LaDuke recalls the land-use practices of Native Americans and the origins of contemporary rights to land and natural resources in the United States—rights often founded on the dispossession of Native Americans by force and deceit. Her account echoes Gerald Friedman's point in Chapter 2 that property rights in the United States have been far from sacrosanct. Throughout the nation's history, property has been redefined and reallocated in response to society's changing goals—goals that are always articulated through the distribution of power. Yet as LaDuke's call for the "recovery of homelands" suggests, the social character of property rights opens the possibility of moves to redress past injustices.

Devon Peña describes the ecological services provided by the gravity-fed acequia irrigation systems that were built by some of the earliest European settlers in North America—Spanish farmers who arrived in the upper reaches of the Rio Grande decades before the Mayflower set anchor off the shore of New England. Today the descendants of these settlers maintain the anthropogenic wetlands created by the acequias, irrigating their fields from the earthen channels and supporting a host of valuable ecological services, including water regulation, the preservation of habitats and riparian corridors for wildlife, and the conservation of heirloom crop varieties. This unique reservoir of natural capital is now threatened, however, as poverty impels young people to abandon the land and as logging and real estate development in the river's upland headwaters disrupt water supplies.

Stephen Brush discusses the need to maintain one of humankind's most important investments in natural capital: agricultural biodiversity. This diversity provides the foundation for long-term world food security, permitting adaptations to new crop pests, plant diseases, and environmental conditions. Yet the farmers who sustain this biodiversity—including Native American corn farmers in Mexico and the southwestern United States, indigenous potato growers in the Andes, and peasant rice farmers in South and Southeast Asia—are often desperately poor. As ever wider areas of world agriculture are integrated into the global market economy, many traditional crop varieties are endangered. Policies to reward farmers for cultivating biodiversity could help to reduce rural poverty while protecting this vital biological heritage.

All four routes for natural-asset building are treated in the next three chapters. *Investment* in natural capital through the careful stewardship of land, water, and plants is shown to be not merely an abstract possibility but a historical reality. The need for *redistribution* of land and water resources to promote sustainable agriculture and social justice is an underlying theme. The *internalization* of benefits from ecological services such as watershed management and the conservation of agricultural biodiversity would raise the incomes of small farmers and protect natural capital. Finally, the questionable antecedents of some property rights in natural resources introduce the possibility of *reappropriation* of natural assets to advance the goals of social justice and sustainable use of resources.

CHAPTER 8

White Earth: Recovering a Homeland

Winona LaDuke

The last 150 years have seen a great holocaust. There have been more species lost in that 150 years than in the previous millennia since the Ice Age (U.S. Department of the Interior 1991). During the same period, indigenous peoples, too, have been disappearing from the face of the Earth. More than a thousand nations of indigenous peoples have gone extinct in the Western Hemisphere, and one nation disappears from the Amazon rain forest every year (Columbia Electronic Encyclopedia 2000; Clay 1992).

There is a direct relationship between the loss of cultural diversity and the loss of biodiversity. Wherever indigenous peoples still remain, there is a corresponding enclave of biodiversity. Trickles of rivers still running in the Northwest are home to the salmon that Native people still sing back. The last few Florida panthers remain in the presence of traditional Seminoles, hidden away in the great cypress swamps of the Everglades. Some of the largest patches of remaining prairie grasses sway on reservation lands. Half of all reservation land in the United States is still forested, much of it with old-growth trees. Remnant pristine forest ecosystems, from the northern boreal forests to the Everglades, largely overlap with Native territories.

There are more than 700 Native nations on the North American continent. Today, in the United States, Native America covers 4 percent of the land, with over 500 federally recognized tribes. More than 1,200 Native American reserves dot Canada. The Inuit homeland, Nunavut, formerly one-half of the Northwest Territories, is an area of land and water, including Baffin Island, five times the size of Texas—the size of the entire Indian subcontinent. Eighty-five percent of its population is Native.

This chapter is excerpted and adapted with permission from Winona LaDuke, *All Our Relations: Native Struggles for Land and Life* (Boston: South End Press, 1999).

Although Native peoples have fought and have been massacred, cheated, and robbed of their historical lands, today their lands are subject to some of the most invasive industrial interventions imaginable. Reservations have been targeted as sites for 16 proposed nuclear waste dumps. More than a hundred proposals have been floated in recent years to dump toxic waste in Indian communities (Seventh Generation Fund 1995). Seventy-seven sacred sites have been disturbed or desecrated by resource extraction and development activities (Peters 1994). The federal government is proposing to use Yucca Mountain, sacred to the Shoshone, as a dump site for the nation's high-level nuclear waste.

More than a thousand slag piles and tailings from abandoned uranium mines sit on Diné land, leaking radioactivity into the air and water. Nearby is the largest coal strip mine in the world, and some groups of Diné teenagers have a cancer rate 17 times the national average. According to Tom Goldtooth, executive director of the Indigenous Environmental Network,

> Most indigenous governments are over 22 years behind the states in environmental infrastructure development. The EPA has consistently failed to fund tribes on an equitable basis compared with the states. The EPA has a statutory responsibility to allocate financial resources that will provide an equitable allocation between tribal governments and states. (Akwesasne Task Force on the Environment 1997, 4.)

White Earth

I live on an Anishinaabeg reservation called White Earth in northern Minnesota, where I work on land, culture, and environmental issues locally through an organization called the White Earth Land Recovery Project and nationally through a Native foundation called Honor the Earth. We, the Anishinaabeg, are a forest culture. Our creation stories, culture, and way of life are entirely based on the forest, the source of our medicinal plants and food, forest animals, and birch-bark baskets.

Virtually my entire reservation was clear-cut at the turn of the century. In 1874, Anishinaabe leader Wabunoquod said, "I cried and prayed that our trees would not be taken from us, for they are as much ours as is this reservation" (Keller 1976, 14). Our trees provided the foundation for major lumber companies, including Weyerhauser, and their destruction continued for 10 decades.

In 1889 and 1890, Minnesota had the second largest lumber industry in the country, and the state's northwest region was the leading source of timber (Davis 1964). Two decades later, 90 percent of White Earth land was controlled by non-Indians, and our people were riddled with diseases. Many became refugees in nearby cities. Today, three-fourths of all tribal members live off the reservation. Ninety percent of our land is still controlled by non-Indians.

There is a direct link in our community between the loss of biodiversity—the loss of animal and plant life—and the loss of the material and cultural wealth of the White Earth people. But we have resisted and we are restoring. Today, we are in litigation against logging expansion, and the White Earth Land Recovery Project works to replant the forests, recover the land, and restore our traditional forest culture. Our experience of survival and resistance is shared with many others. But it is not only about Native people.

In the end, the survival of Native America is fundamentally about the collective survival of all human beings. The question of who gets to determine the destiny of the land, and of the people who live on it—those with the money or those who pray on the land—is alive throughout society.

On the White Earth reservation's 1,300 square miles, prairie, maple-bass-wood forest, and boreal pine forest intersect. The headspeople chose this land for this very reason and named it "White Earth," or *Gahwahbahbahnikag,* for the white clay that underlies part of it. In wintertime, or *biiboon,* below deep snow and layers of ice, the reservation's 47 big lakes teem with life. The remains of an indigenous prairie and its attendant grasses slumber through the dormant season, preparing for the spring, *ziigwan,* and new life. This wealthy, diverse ecosystem has been called the Medicine Chest of the Ojibwe. It is the well-spring of a traditional way of life, one that has nurtured biodiversity for thousands of years. The small camps, villages, and bands in the area would plan their hunts by dream and memory and would fill their birch-bark baskets with wild rice, maple sugar, berries, dried corn, and squash. By snowshoe, canoe, or dog team, they moved through the woods, rivers, and lakes. This life was not circumscribed by a clock, fence, or road. But there was a law just the same: natural law, Creator's law.

There is no way to set a price on this way of life. That simple truth more than anything else encapsulates the Anishinaabeg people's struggle with the federal government, the miners, and the logging companies. For the past hundred years, Native people have been saying that their way of life, their land, their trees, and their very future cannot be quantified and are not for sale. And for that same amount of time, government and industry accountants have been picking away, trying to come up with a formula to compensate Indians for the theft of their lands and livelihoods. So long as both sides remain steadfast, there appears to be little hope for a meeting of minds in the next generations.

The Appropriation of a Homeland

Land has always been a source of wealth and power, and the issue of land rights and ownership is a central point of contention between settler and indigenous governments. Between 1784 and 1894, the U.S. government signed 371 treaties with Native peoples and made some 720 related land seizures on Native territory. For what today would be about $800 million, the United States "bought" more than 95 percent of its present continental territory from Native peoples (Cohen 1947). In most cases, the federal government continues to exercise "trust responsibility" and "plenary power" over the Native peoples and remaining Native-held lands within U.S. borders. Legally this means that the government, as the "trustee" of the Native estate, is mandated to protect Native interests. As this chapter illustrates, however, this responsibility is often unfulfilled. Instead, the government has frequently moved into the realm of takings, plenary power, and acquiescence to the greed of economic interests.

Beginning at Fort McIntosh in 1785 and ending at Georgian Bay in 1923, the United States, England, and Canada entered into more than 40 treaties with the Anishinaabeg, laying the basis for some of the largest land transactions in world history. Original Anishinaabeg landholdings included millions of acres around the Great Lakes; today, the Anishinaabeg traditional homelands consist of close to 10 million acres in 100 reserves and reservations in the lakes region, and a sprinkling in the great prairies, spanning the northern part of five American states and the southern part of four Canadian provinces.

The U.S. government never claimed to hold or control Anishinaabeg land "by right of conquest." Rather, it claims to have legally acquired Anishinaabeg and other Native lands by mutual agreement. Some of the first incursions onto Anishinaabeg land were to secure access to iron and copper deposits. By 1800, representatives of both the Queen of England and the emerging United States had "discovered" a 2,500-pound boulder of naturally occurring copper called the Ontonogan Boulder resting on the south shore of Lake Superior in Anishinaabeg territory, in what is now known as the Keweenaw Peninsula. By the 1820s, the federal government had decided to do a comprehensive study of "mineral assets" of the Lake Superior area and a study of Indian title to the land therein. Within a very short period, four treaties were signed by the United States, each providing for access to and mining in Anishinaabeg territory. These treaties covered both the Keweenaw Peninsula and the Mesaba "Sleeping Giant" iron-ore belt in northern Minnesota. By mid-century, more than a hundred copper companies had been incorporated in the Minnesota, Wisconsin, and Michigan Territories. As early as 1849, copper production at Keweenaw Peninsula—"ceded" by the Anishinaabeg in the treaty of 1842—led the world. Similarly, beginning in 1890 and continuing for nearly 50 years, mining at Mesaba accounted for 75 percent of all U.S. iron ore production. Many of today's U.S.-based transnational mining corporations were founded on the exploitation of these natural resources (Keller 1976, 14).

In the summer of 1837, Governor Dodge of the Wisconsin Territory signed a treaty with the Anishinaabeg to acquire the pine lands in the St. Croix Valley. With that treaty, lumber interests secured the last outpost of the great white pine forests that once extended from Maine to Minnesota. The White Earth reservation was created in 1867, reserving for the Anishinaabeg some 36 townships of land—land of natural wealth and beauty, over two-thirds of which was covered with huge white pines and beautiful maples. In 1889, the Nelson Act opened up the White Earth reservation to allotment and annexed the four townships with the most white pines for the state of Minnesota. In that year, Minnesota ranked second in the country in logging, with the northwestern portion of the state leading the state's production. In 1889–1890, 11 million board feet of timber were taken from the White Earth reservation. In the next year, 15 million board feet were cut, followed by another 18 million in the 1891–1892 season.

Some are made rich and some are made poor. In 1895, White Earth "neighbor" Frederick Weyerhauser owned more acres of timber than anyone else in the world. The self-made German was considered "the richest and brainiest" of the lumber millionaire kings. His logging company sawed enough lumber in one season "to six times encircle the globe if it were cut up into inch strips, to build a baseball fence from here to San Francisco, or to construct two or three cities the size of Little Falls," enthused the local newspaper (McLeod 1997, 2, 7, 8). Weyerhauser's Pine Tree Lumber Company, the *Little Falls Daily Transcript* reported,

> is eating a big hole in the forests of northern Minnesota, as it runs steadily, rarely meeting an accident. . . . The Weyerhausers have secured a monopoly of the Mississippi River so far as the driving of logs is concerned, but if they carry out their present plans, it will work good to both the millmen and lumbermen, great and small. (*Little Falls Daily Transcript* 1893, in McLeod 1997, 11.).

In 1893, Weyerhauser and other lumber interests secured funding from public and other sources to build a railroad from Little Falls into Leech Lake reservation, where Weyerhauser had access to 800,000 board feet of standing timber (McLeod 1997, 9). But in October 1898, the Anishinaabeg people on Leech Lake reservation resisted the further encroachment. The military came to the defense of the lumber companies, and the uprising was staved off.

Not content to take just the great pines, the lumber companies and land speculators set their eyes upon the land itself. Mechanisms were put in place to pry land from children at boarding school, from blind women living in overcrowded housing, from soldiers at war and veterans, and from those who could not read or write English. A common saying, describing what happened, sprang up in nearby Detroit Lakes: "Fleec[ing] the Indian" (Folwell 1930, 263–64). A quarter of a million acres of White Earth land were taken by the state of Minnesota as tax payments. In other cases, minors were illegally persuaded to sell their land.

Some land transfers were facilitated by a miracle of "blood quantum transformation" that occurred largely at the hands of Dr. Ales Hrdlicka, a physical anthropologist from the Smithsonian, who measured heads, nose bridges, and chests to determine the "Indian-ness" of the Indians. Hrdlicka developed a "full-blood" physical standard against which he could measure the Anishinaabeg. In his work, families were often divided into different "blood quantums," conferring "mixed blood" status to many, who were then considered "competent" to sell their land. In some cases, full-blood children were attributed to mixed-blood parents and vice versa (Meyer 1994, 168–70).

Through almost every conceivable mechanism, the land changed hands. As one Anishinaabe elder, Fred Weaver, recalls,

> We used to have a lot of them lands here around Pine Point. We had eight 80s [80-acre allotments]. Them land speculators came and tricked us out of them lands. My mother had an 80 on Many Point Lake. They tricked her out of that for $50. Now that's a Boy Scout Camp. And my father-in-law, Jim Jugg, he had land, too. The County says it owns them lands, too. All of them. We lived poor a long time, and we should've had all of them lands. (Weaver 1981.)

By 1914, just 14 percent of the original White Earth land was still in Indian hands.

The newly acquired land was a bonanza to the border towns and the timber industry. Land companies emerged overnight, fly-by-night mortgage outfits held deeds for thousands of acres of lands, and timber companies closed leases to clear-cut almost a third of the reservation. "There is a myth, which was created at that time," Bob Shimek, a local Native harvester turned forest activist, reminds me. "It was this Paul Bunyan myth, Paul and Babe, and their ability to change the landscape. That myth is in the center of America, and that myth is what we are dealing with today" (Shimek 1998).

The stripping of the great forests of White Earth began a process that would devastate the Anishinaabeg forest culture. Great maple trees and maple sugar bushes moved horizontally toward logging mills, clear-cuts replaced biodiverse groves of medicinal plants and trees, basket makers searched for materials, and birch-bark canoe makers couldn't find the huge trees for the great Anishinaabeg canoes. The Anishinaabeg had become "painfully aware of the mortality of wealth which nature bestows and imperialism appropriates," as Latin American scholar Eduardo Galeano wrote in 1973 (Galeano 1973, 13).

"There was quite a forest when I left, before the war started," recalls Bill Gagnon, a White Earth elder, "and when I came back on furlough, there was just a desert—there was no timber left" (Gagnon 1983). Another elder notes how

> the clear-cut logging just hurts everything. . . . I have a place I like to pick strong woods medicines. The medicine I pick in the jack-pine forest, it's a lifesaver. The jackpines, they've been butchered. Where they've been butchered, the medicine's gone. (Oppegard 1997.)

In the beginning, the Anishinaabeg people simply crowded together in the remaining houses, as one family was pushed off the land into another family's house. This adaptation was not without consequences, as the recently trauma-tized refugee population was susceptible to illness. From 1910 to 1920, epidemics of trachoma and tuberculosis swept through the villages on White Earth. Every family was affected, and some families disappeared altogether. As Minnesota historian William Folwell (1930, 283) reports,

> The principal conditions of the Indians at White Earth the inspec-tors found to be "very bad." Fully 60 percent of the people were infected with tuberculosis, from 30 to 35 percent with trachoma, and from 15 to 20 percent with syphilis; and the diseases were on the increase.

After a few years, the federal government came to view the social experiment of White Earth as a failure and sought to relocate the White Earth people to urban areas. This plan was perceived as the final assimilation and the end of a long road for the White Earth people. By 1930, of the total enrolled popu-lation of 8,584 persons, only 4,628 remained on the reservation. In the mid-1930s, more White Earth land was annexed to form the northern half of the Tamarac National Wildlife Refuge, which ostensibly became a hunting area for non-Indians from the south. By 1934, only 7,890 acres, or less than 10 percent, of the reservation was in tribal trust, and Indians were being arrested for traditional harvesting on White Earth land that was now considered "private property" requiring permits. In a harvesting economy that had existed for eons, this was a strange transformation (LaDuke 1988).

Removals continued under the so-called Relocation Act of the 1950s, under which tribal members (and Native people across the country) were offered one-way bus tickets to major urban areas.

The Land Struggle Continues

In 1966, as a result of mounting criticism of its management of the estate of Native peoples, the "wards of the federal government," Congress decided to look at the problem of loss of land and other assets in Native America. It had become clear to the public that despite the supposedly vast Native landholdings, Indian people were not doing very well. Every economic, social, and health indicator showed Native people at the bottom. Title VIII of the U.S. Code, section 2415, mandated a federal investigation into land and trespass issues since the turn of the century on some 40 reservations in the United States. It wasn't until 1978 that what became known as the "2415 investigation" came to White Earth, and it was 1981 before federal investigators began to interview elders on the reservation, who had firsthand knowledge of how the land had been pried away, stolen, or taken.

The investigation revealed the tangled mess that each title to Anishinaabeg land had become. For over 60 years, the Bureau of Indian Affairs hadn't properly recorded the many complex transactions that had occurred during the great transfer of land from Indian to non-Indian hands. Ultimately, it was revealed that the state of Minnesota's claim to White Earth lands and their subsequent sales and transfers of those lands were, in fact, illegal. Further damning the state's Native land transactions, the Minnesota Supreme Court had ruled in the 1977 case *State of Minnesota v. Zah Zah* that the tax forfeitures that removed the Indians from the lands in the late 1800s were also illegal. According to the court, "The removal of the U.S. government's trust responsibility under the 1889 Nelson Act should not have occurred unless the allottee applied for such removal" (Meyer 1994, 230).

In 1982, with less than one-third of its research complete, the 2415 investigation team published a preliminary list of several hundred land parcels with questionable title transactions. The title to such parcels was "clouded," they wrote, and thus these parcels could not be legally sold or transferred until the title was cleared. This meant that thousands of acres of Minnesota's land, much of which was owned by farmers, could not be used by their erstwhile owners as collateral to secure mortgages or other loans.

It was at the same time that the northern rural farm economy was beginning its cycle of failure, primarily as a result of bad government policies and, some would say, corporate subsidies. Although some farms were not affected by the initial federal title determinations, others were implicated with clouded title on all or parts of their land, further deepening those farmers' already precarious financial situations.

There has always been an anti-Indian sentiment in America. Over time, and with awareness and the arrival of new immigrants to serve as scapegoats, those sentiments have waned in segments of the population. In areas adjacent to and within Native communities, however, anti-Indian racism has often remained and at times flourished. A 1995 paper by Rudolph C. Rÿser of the Center for World Indigenous Studies in Olympia, Washington, chronicles the growth of the anti-Indian movement, from vigilante groups in the

1980s to white-supremacist and "wise-use" groups in the 1990s. According to Rÿser (1995, 10),

> Since the 1970s, resident and absentee non-Indian landholders and businesses objected to the growing exercise of general governmental powers by tribal governments. This is . . . true in the areas of taxation, zoning, construction and land use ordinances. . . . When tribal governments began to exercise the will of tribal members, tribal officials used governmental powers to restrain the actions of persons who depended on reservation land and resources for their personal wealth, but were not willing to share with other members of the tribe.

The few court cases decided in favor of Native people fanned the anti-Indian sentiment. In the 1974 *Boldt* decision in Washington State, Native peoples' right to fish was recognized. For some non-Indian people in the region, this was perceived as a "gift" to Indians at the expense of personal property rights (Rÿser 1995, 15). Anti-Indian organizations such as the Interstate Congress for Equal Rights and Responsibilities, Protect American Rights and Resources, Stop Treaty Abuse, and Totally Equal Americans were formed.

A decade later, the *Voigt* decision in Wisconsin escalated the movement. This time, the controversy was over the court's affirmation of the Anishinaabeg right to harvest a multitude of natural resources including walleyes—the preferred fish of sports fishermen in Wisconsin and Minnesota. The court held that Anishinaabeg did not relinquish their reserved rights to harvest when permanent reservations were established.

The sports-fishing and hunting industries were some of the most vocal proponents of anti-Indian sentiments. Bumper stickers that read "Save a Deer, Shoot an Indian; Save a Walleye, Spear an Indian" began appearing on cars. Paul Mullaly from Wisconsin, founder of the 31,000-member anti-Indian organization Equal Rights for Everyone, claimed that the *Voigt* decision "discriminates against white people in the area and is not the kind of thing that should occur in a democracy" (Rÿser 1995, 29). The racial slurs, intimidation, and threats Native people experienced led the FBI to investigate the potential for violence. Resort owners were investigated to determine if they might be implicated in threats to "kill Indians if they came on certain lakes" (*Milwaukee Journal* 1994, cited in Rÿser 1995, 29).

Many of these groups moved to White Earth or surfaced on the reservation as the land issue became more visible. United Townships Association emerged, and chapters of Totally Equal Americans and Protect American Rights and Resources opened. These groups were concerned with the protection of their "private property," including both land and natural resources, on the reservation.

A number of these groups eventually coalesced with the national "wise-use" movement, in coalition with county governments that sought to abrogate Indian treaties and with the far-right and white-supremacist groups (Rÿser 1995, 41).

In 1982, the 2415 investigation at White Earth was suspended "indefinitely," with only one-third of the titles researched (Meyer 1994, 230). It was in this climate that Arlan Stangeland, a Republican representative from Minnesota, moved to terminate Anishinaabeg rights to land on the reservation. In 1983, Stangeland forwarded a bill calling for Congress to "clear title" to White Earth lands retroactively, by compensating Indian people for the land and confirming the titles of non-Indian landholders. His bill, the White Earth Land Settlement Act (WELSA), proposed to pay the White Earth people $3 million. "The Indians will get the land back when hell freezes over," he flippantly noted to the press on more than one occasion (Meyer 1994, 230). By couching the idea of returning land documented as stolen or otherwise illegally taken from Native people as a "misbegotten" effort to render "after-the-fact justice," Stangeland was able to attract some support for his proposal (Meyer 1994, 229–30; see also LaDuke 1988).

Stangeland entreated the White Earth Tribal Council to settle. The council, influenced by Stangeland's threats and by his political power as a multiterm Republican representative, initially agreed—until approximately 500 tribal members, and then hundreds more, demanded that the offer be rejected. By 1985, the federal government's proposed offer had risen to $17 million. But it was rejected again by community people who maintained that the "land is not for sale." For the Anishinaabeg, it had been clear for centuries that "cash payments for land mean little if a tribe has no political power," as Wabunoquod, headsman of the Mississippi band, had put it in 1874, "and consequently no control over the money paid for the land" (see Keller 1976).

The intensity of community resistance to the settlement grew, but in 1986 tribal chairman Darrell Wadena—who was later ousted on corruption charges—overrode his community, flew to Washington, D.C., and secured passage of the bill. It was passed in an unusual move known as "suspension of the rules," by a voice vote with only 12 members of Congress present. The final bill offered approximately $17 million—the 1910 value of titles, without interest or damages—paltry compensation for 10,000 acres of land.

WELSA was a slap in the face to the people of White Earth. It left our people with little choice. In June 1986, an organization dedicated to the White Earth land struggle, Anishinaabe Akiing, supported 44 plaintiffs in a class-action suit, *Manypenny v. United States,* challenging the legality of reservation land takings. In 1987 another suit was filed, *Little Wolf v. United States,* which argued that WELSA violated the Fifth Amendment guarantees of just compensation, due process, and equal protection under the law—rights that

Stangeland would apply to some citizens but not to Native people. A third suit, *Fineday v. United States,* was filed on the same grounds as *Manypenny.*

The federal circuit courts ruled against the Anishinaabeg. In *Little Wolf* the court decided that since Native people had the right to sue, they also had an option not to accept WELSA; in other words, they had redress if they felt their constitutional rights were violated. In *Manypenny* and *Fineday,* the courts decided that the statute of limitations on the titles in question had expired. So Congress's policies of land seizure and paltry compensation remained standing, and the land tenure crisis on White Earth continued.

In 1990, U.S. census data indicated that the unemployment rate for non-Indian people on the White Earth reservation was 12.6 percent, whereas the unemployment rate for Indian people on the reservation was almost 50 percent. Poverty rates for Indian people on the reservation were one-third higher than those for non-Indian people, and the overall social and physical health of the community was in decline.

Most of the white population on White Earth are landed farmers, whereas the majority of Indians live in government housing projects. Most of the lake shore is owned by absentee landlords, as are some of the larger landholdings—including the 5,000-acre Oxley Cattle Ranch, whose corporate headquarters are located in Tulsa, Oklahoma. But while the landed white farmers age, retire, and emigrate out of the area, the landless Indians get younger and more numerous. The average age for a non-Indian farmer on the reservation is 57 years; the average age of a Native person is 18 years. The Native birth rate is three times the non-Native rate. These trends—fewer non-Indian residents; more absentee owners; and a growing, mostly landless Indian community—are projected to continue over the next decades. The crisis between who lives on the land and who owns it will continue.

Non-Indians dominate hunting and fishing on reservation lands. Non-Indians on the White Earth reservation harvest roughly twice as many deer as do the Indian people. Inside the Tamarac National Wildlife Refuge, white deer hunters took nine times more deer than tribal members. Fishing is not much different. The White Earth Reservation Biology Department reported, for instance, that tribal members took just 3.3 percent of the walleye catch at one major reservation fishing lake; the remaining walleyes were taken by non-Indian fishers. Yet even though the Anishinaabeg take of the harvest is relatively small, many of the hunters and fishers who dominate the lands have opposed Anishinaabeg attempts to discuss recovery of land, exercise of jurisdiction, or traditional harvesting. These non-Indian sports-hunters and fishers seem to assume entitlement to the reservation lands, believing that the reservation lands should continue to be their hunting and recreation area.

In the past two decades, U.S. courts have recognized the "extra-territorial treaty rights" of Anishinaabeg people in the region. Most notably, the 1987

Voigt and 1997 *Mille Lacs* decisions upheld Anishinaabeg rights to harvest fish, animals, or whatever else they deem appropriate from lands in the northern third of Wisconsin and Minnesota (Whaley 1994, 23, 27). The five-to-four decision by the Supreme Court in the *Mille Lacs* decision ended a pitched battle between the state and the 1,200-member Mille Lacs band. The court recognized a continuation of Anishinaabeg harvesting rights to hunt and fish on 13 million acres of "ceded land" in east-central Minnesota and western Wisconsin, as had been upheld in the *Voigt* decision. The Mille Lacs band is allocated some 40,000 pounds of walleye on Mille Lacs Lake, for instance, one of the most plentiful walleye fishing lakes in Minnesota. In 1998, non-Indian sports-fishers harvested over 355,000 pounds of fish from the lake, while the Mille Lacs tribal members took some 38,000 pounds (Melmer 1999).

White Earth Land Recovery Project

In 1989, to address the crisis of land tenure on White Earth, we founded the White Earth Land Recovery Project (WELRP) with the proceeds of a Reebok Human Rights Award. WELRP works to return White Earth land to the Anishinaabeg by supporting the transfer of public lands back to the White Earth tribal government, buying land from willing sellers, and other mechanisms. To date, we have purchased over 1,300 acres of land—primarily maple sugar bush, the most endangered ecosystem on the reservation—which is held in a conservation land trust. The project also seeks to preserve White Earth land even when it is held by others, including Native cemeteries, forests, and other endangered ecosystems. The project works aggressively to preserve Native languages and culture, restore traditional seed stocks, and reinstate self-determination and self-reliance. WELRP is the largest independent reservation nonprofit organization in the state of Minnesota and one of the four largest nationally.

In 1993, WELRP launched its Sustainable Communities initiative. Its goal is to meld the useful and meaningful aspects of both traditional Anishinaabeg and Euro-American culture into a truly sustainable way of living for willing Anishinaabeg people. The four areas on which we focus are forestry, energy, agriculture, and culture. These are interrelated. The struggle to preserve the trees of White Earth, for example, is not solely about forest preservation and biodiversity. It is also about cultural transformation, for the Anishinaabeg forest culture cannot exist without the forest.

Non-Indians, the federal government, the state, the county, and tribal members all own lands adjoining the reservation. This puzzle of land ownership means that while one landowner may limit logging on his or her land to some 20-acre or 40-acre slot, clear-cuts (or "patch cuts" or "contour cuts" as they are also called) may well adjoin another clear-cut on someone else's land, increasing the ecological damage to the region. For instance, high winds exacerbated by the clear-cuts flattened over 100,000 acres of trees on the reservation in July 1995.

When the high winds hit the reservation, the press called it a "natural disaster." But when lumber companies similarly vanquish the trees, it is called "progress." All across the region, lumber companies are expanding—a result, many Anishinaabeg say, of heightened resistance to logging elsewhere in the country. The Minnesota lumber industry cuts 4.1 million cords of wood every year. This industry has turned its attention to the boreal forest that still covers most of northern Minnesota, Wisconsin, and Michigan and much of the Canadian provinces of Ontario, Manitoba, and Quebec. This land is largely Anishinaabeg Akiing, Ojibwe country.

Federally managed lands are equally problematic. President Bill Clinton, early in his administration, talked about providing economic opportunity for Indian tribes by "bringing backlogged Indian timber to market" (Clinton et al. 1993)—something Native forest activists have referred to as "equal opportunity clear-cutting." Federal officials prioritized logging and cultivation of aspen in the Tamarac National Wildlife Refuge, which spans some 21,000 acres of the reservation. Between 1982 and 1992, 97,970 cords of wood were taken from refuge lands, 83 percent of it "popple," or aspen. The vast majority of the harvest was taken from the areas of the refuge that fall within the reservation borders. Sixty-six percent of the total harvest was designated for the lumber company Potlatch (a descendant of Frederick Weyerhauser's empire) and other paper mills in the region.

Forest preservation work at WELRP is multifaceted, involving both litigation and organizing to preserve the forests of the north and to show that our forests are worth more as standing trees than as timber. In the summer of 1994, Potlatch attempted to cross WELRP land and roads to access adjacent forests for clear-cutting. After the county refused to stop the trespassing, community members and WELRP staff blockaded the road the loggers had used—which, as it turned out, was the WELRP driveway—only to be undercut by the tribal council, which allowed the company access across tribal land.

We have seen another way. The Menominee reservation in Wisconsin successfully fought to keep their forests, which today stand as a testimony to what could be. According to their booklet on sustainable forest development,

> To many, our forest may seem pristine and untouched. In reality, it is one of the most intensely managed tracts of forest in the lake states. During the past 140 years, we have harvested more than two and one-half billion board-feet of lumber from our land. That is the equivalent of cutting all the standing timber on the reservation almost twice over. Yet, the saw timber volume now standing is greater than that which was here in 1854 when the Wolf River

Treaty defined the reservation. (Menominee Tribal Enterprises 1997, 2.)

As with the Menominee and our other Algonkin relatives, determination and dignity motivate the people of White Earth, ensuring that our way of life continues.

In the 1990s, the Minnesota Department of Health and the Clean Water Action Project found that the area lakes were contaminated with mercury, heavy metals, and polychlorinated biphenyls (PCBs). The primary sources of the contamination are coal-fired power plants and incinerators often located hundreds of miles away. The entire food chain is exposed to the mercury; people are exposed primarily by consuming contaminated fish. The effects of mercury poisoning include nerve and kidney damage, muscle tremors, and fetal abnormalities.

Annually since 1993, Minnesota's Department of Health has advised a consumption limit of just one walleye per week for seasonal fish consumers and one walleye per month for year-round fish consumers at many lakes on or near the White Earth, Red Lake, Leech Lake, and Mille Lacs Lake reservations, which are extensively fished by indigenous people. Surveys and tribal data indicate that while non-Indians take more fish from White Earth than Indians do, most White Earth Anishinaabeg consume more fish per capita than do non-Indians. In response, a cooperative program between the WELRP, Indigenous Environmental Network, and Clean Water Action Project has been established to increase awareness of the link between the power plants and the mercury poisoning in the lakes and, in the case of White Earth, to counter it directly with an alternative source of energy: wind power.

Other WELRP programs have focused on restoring traditional farming. The Anishinaabeg people are traditionally strong agriculturalists. But traditional agricultural practices on the reservation have diminished, as non-Indians and corporate interests have controlled more and more reservation land. Over one-third of the reservation is under increasingly industrialized and chemical-intensive agricultural development, with devastating consequences. Since 1858, some 50 percent of the reservation's wetlands have been lost, largely due to ill-founded agricultural practices. Between 1987 and 1992, over 1,800 tons of fertilizer and over 110,000 gallons of pesticides and herbicides were applied to White Earth lands every year. More than 12,000 acres of reservation land are held by the largest corporate potato grower in the world, which has contaminated the groundwater with herbicides and fungicides. As more and more small farmers leave the reservation lands or fall into economic hardship, corporate interests become increasingly dominant.

In the face of globalization, we have moved toward recovery of local self-reliance. In the mid-1990s, WELRP began restoring the traditional hominy crop and purchased an organic raspberry farm. The project also began Native Harvest, a community development project, to restore traditional foods and capture a fair market price for traditionally and organically grown foods. Along with hominy corn and organic raspberries, Native Harvest sells wild rice, maple candy, buffalo sausage, and maple syrup.

There is nothing quite like walking through a small field of hominy corn, corn you know your ancestors planted on the same land a thousand years ago. Corn is in the recipes and memories of elders. That inherited memory is the essence of cultural restoration and the force that grows with each step on the path, or "the lifeway" as some of the Anishinaabeg call it.

Finally, at the center of WELRP's cultural work is language. While most North American indigenous languages are expected to be extinct by the year 2050, the Anishinaabeg language is one of approximately five expected to survive. Since 1995, WELRP has worked on a range of language restoration projects. WELRP's Wadiswaan Project is an early-childhood language-revitalization program in one of the tribal schools. WELRP also organizes adult and family language-immersion retreats and takes children out of school and into the woods, the sugar bush, the corn fields, and the heart of cultural practice. All this is a slow process, but in the WELRP philosophy it is thought that these children will be leading our community in 20 or 30 years and so we need to ensure that they know something about who they are, why we are here, and how we talk to the Creator. Renewal is a central part of each generation's responsibility.

WELRP is only a small part of the White Earth community. Even though all the white man's laws have made it difficult to be Anishinaabeg, this community, like many others along the trail of migration laid by long-ago ancestors, is maintaining its way of life. Surveys conducted in the late 1980s, supported by interviews in more recent years, show that at least 65 percent of the people on White Earth hunt for deer and for small game. Forty-five percent harvest wild rice, with somewhat fewer engaged in subsistence fishing. Most of those who do not themselves harvest traditional foods trade with others who do. Despite all the laws, all the time, and all the clear-cutting, the land is still here, and the land is still good.

References

Akwesasne Task Force on the Environment. 1997. "Superfund Clean Up of Akwesasne: Case Study in Environmental Injustice." *International Journal of Contemporary Sociology* 25(97): 267–90.

Clay, Jason. 1992. "Why Rainforest Crunch?" *Cultural Survival Quarterly* 16(2): 31–40.

Clinton, William, Al Gore, Bruce Babbitt, Mike Espy, Ron Brown, and Carol Browner. 1993. "Remarks by the President, the Vice President, Secretary of Interior Bruce Babbitt, Secretary of Agriculture Mike Espy, Secretary of Commerce Ron Brown,

EPA Administrator Carol Browner." In *Forest Announcement*. Washington, D.C.: Office of the Press Secretary.

Cohen, Felix S. 1947. "Original Indian Title." *Minnesota Law Review* 32:28–59.

Columbia Electronic Encyclopedia. 2000. "Native American Languages." Available at http://www.encyclopedia.com/html/N/NatvA1mlang.asp.

Davis, C. M. 1964. *Readings in the Geography of Michigan*. Ann Arbor, Mich.: Ann Arbor Publishers.

Folwell, William Watts. 1930. *A History of Minnesota*. St. Paul: Minnesota Historical Society.

Gagnon, Bill. 1983. Personal interview. June.

Galeano, Eduardo H. 1973. *Open Veins of Latin America*. New York: Monthly Review Press.

Keller, Robert H. 1976. "An Economic History of Indian Treaties of the Great Lakes Region." *American Indian Journal* 2:14.

LaDuke, Winona. 1988. "The White Earth Anishinaabeg: From Self-Reliance to Dependency and Back Again." Masters thesis, Antioch University.

Little Falls Daily Transcript. 1893. May 11. In McLeod, n.d. 11.

McLeod, Laura. 1997. Interview with Sunfish Oppegard. In *Harvester Study*, White Earth Land Recovery Project. Ponsford, Minn.: White Earth Land Recovery Project.

————. n.d. "Timber Barons in Central Minnesota: 1880s to 1910s." Unpublished paper.

Melmer, David. 1999. "Ojibwe Upheld: All Indian Country Eyeing Treaty Ruling." *Indian Country Today* (5–12 April): A-I.

Menominee Tribal Enterprises. 1997. *The Menominee Forest Based Sustainable Development Tradition*. Neopit, Wis.: Menominee Tribal Enterprises.

Meyer, Melissa L. 1994. *The White Earth Tragedy Ethnicity and Dispossession at a Minnesota Anishinaabe Reservation, 1889–1920*. Lincoln: University of Nebraska Press.

Milwaukee Journal. 1994. 7 December. In Rÿser 1995, 29).

Peters, Chris. 1994. Personal interview. 4 May.

Rÿser, Rudolph C. 1995. "Anti-Indian Movement on the Tribal Frontier." Occasional Paper #16-3. Olympia, Wash.: Center for World Indigenous Studies.

Seventh Generation Fund. 1995. *1995 Funding Proposal for Environment Program*. Arcata, Calif.: Seventh Generation Fund.

Shimek, Robert. 1998. Personal interview. 15 March.

U.S. Department of the Interior. 1991. *Why Save Endangered Species?* Arlington, Va.: U.S. Fish and Wildlife Service.

Weaver, Fred (Windigoowub). 1981. Personal interview. 10 August.

Whaley, Rick. 1994. *An Effective Alliance Against Racism and for the Earth*. Philadelphia: New Society Publishers.

White Earth Land Recovery Project. 1994. *Forestry Proposal*. Ponsford, Minn.: White Earth Land Recovery Project.

White Earth Land Recovery Project. 1998. *Language and Culture Funding Proposal*. Ponsford, Minn.: White Earth Land Recovery Project.

CHAPTER 9

The Watershed Commonwealth of the Upper Rio Grande

Devon G. Peña

The Upper Rio Grande, or Rio Arriba, bioregion presents some intriguing examples of local institutions that manage the ecological commons sustainably and equitably. Sense of place, defined here as local knowledge of the ecosystem, can be a crucial source of social capital for land-based communities. The multigenerational acequia farming families of the seven-county Upper Rio Grande watershed have developed a landscape mosaic that extends native wild and domesticated biodiversity.[1] Their vast body of ethnoecological knowledge is an important asset for local livelihoods and helps to sustain the community's natural assets.

The bioregion's unique acequias—earthen-work, snow-fed, gravity-driven, and cooperatively maintained irrigation ditches—are key components of the environment within the watershed. The clustering of farm fields, orchards, and wildlife habitats; the extensive networks of riparian corridors produced by the acequias; and the hydrological connection between the farming system and the montane headwater zones are important aspects of a vastly undervalued complex of natural assets, the acequia–riparian long-lot agroecological landscape mosaic (the acequia landscape mosaic, for short).

Conservation biologists have recently observed that humans can act as a keystone species—a species so central to the health of the ecosystem that without it many other species could not survive (Noss 1994, 33–40).[2] Human activity in the acequia landscape mosaic creates habitat niches and biological movement corridors that are vital to the survival of many native species of flora and fauna. In this sense, the acequia farmers can be considered a keystone community whose agroecological practices underpin the ecosystem (Peña 1998a, 14–15; Peña 1998b, 241–65; see also Rivera 1999, 192–94).

In this chapter, I am especially concerned with the role of local knowledge as a form of social capital that produces natural assets. I analyze the strategies that local acequia communities are using to democratize environmental ownership in the Rio Arriba bioregion through redistribution of rights and the internalization of benefits flowing from those assets. To succeed, these strategies will require public land and water use policies designed to protect the valuable ecological services that the acequia landscape mosaic provides to the regional ecosystem and economy.

The Culture-Ecology Nexus

From 1994 to 1999, a group of 43 people worked together as members of an interdisciplinary research team for a study entitled "Upper Rio Grande Hispano Farms: A Cultural and Environmental History of Land Ethics in Transition, 1598–1998."[3] Twelve of the team members were farmers; the rest were scholars with diverse specialties ranging from ethnobotany to hydrology and from cultural anthropology to geography and sociology. The group conducted research on eight historic acequia family farms and their respective watersheds within the Upper Rio Grande Basin, from San Juan Pueblo–Alcalde in northern New Mexico to San Luis in south-central Colorado, including Guadalupe, Mora, Taos, Rio Arriba, and San Miguel counties in New Mexico and Costilla and Conejos counties in Colorado.

These acequia farms represent more than 400 years of agricultural evolution and adaptation. The oldest farming family participating in the study is the Montoya family of Chicano and San Juan Pueblo Indian background. Mae Montoya's side of the family has been farming the same land since well before the first entry by an explorer, the 1598 Oñate *entrada* (Peña and Martínez 2000). The youngest farms in our study were founded in the 1860s in Colorado's San Luis Valley. The acequias not only provide the material basis of these farms but also serve as civic institutions to administer water rights, a form of local democratic self-governance once described by John Wesley Powell as a "watershed commonwealth" (Worster 1994, 1–20; also see Peña 1998a, 1998b; Rivera 1999; Rivera and Peña 1997; Hicks and Peña 2003).

Hispano traditional environmental knowledge has long played a crucial economic and ecological role in the bioregion. Once destroyed, this knowledge and its material basis, the acequia landscape mosaic, cannot be replaced.[4] As José Rivera notes in a recent study of acequias in New Mexico and Colorado (1999, 190–91):

> The *acequia* communities already form a part of the economic-development infrastructure of the Upper Rio Grande region in

terms of the huge tourism industry that showcases the quaint
village architecture, the farmers' markets in Santa Fe and other
nearby cities, the greenbelts that define the landscapes of the river
valleys, and very importantly, the cultural production renowned
and marketed as "New Mexico village arts and crafts": the *santos,*
retablos, wood furniture, and other hand-carved wood-craft pieces;
the folk art, tinworks, jewelry, hand-woven rugs, and other New
Mexican products marketed worldwide. . . . The crafts industries
of the [bioregion] thrive in large part due to the setting in which
objects and other handmade goods are produced by local artisans.
Without water, these villages literally would dry up, as would the arts and
crafts industry vital to the economic development goals of the [bioregion]
[emphasis added].

Our research supports this notion of an essential connection among a healthy
ecosystem, a robust material culture, and a prosperous and equitable local and
regional economy.[5] This nexus of interdependent relationships between natural
and cultural systems is the basis for social capital and for the production and
management of natural assets such as land and water. Given these links, and the
persistence of rural poverty in this region, the preservation of the acequia
communities is particularly urgent.

The Spanish–Mexican land allocation and settlement system was a defining
feature in the creation of acequia communities. Under this system, a
community grant (*merced*) allocated private long-lots to the settlers but
reserved the montane headwaters as common lands (*ejidos*) to be shared and
managed by the settlers collectively. Individual commercial exploitation of
the headwaters zone was strictly prohibited by customary law and practice
(see Rock 1976, Van Ness 1987, and Ebright 1994). The customary rights of
the acequia communities to the headwaters zone were eroded in the decades
after the Treaty of Guadalupe Hidalgo (1848), by which Mexico ceded this
territory to the United States. By the early 1900s, over 8 million acres
of these common lands had been lost to enclosure by private property or
conversion to the public domain. Nevertheless, more than 250 Spanish and
Mexican land-grant communities still assert claims to at least partial control
over these historic common properties, and the contested status of these
lands is a source of ongoing social conflict in the Rio Arriba watershed.
Movements for environmental justice and social equity in the bioregion
seek to reassert the legitimacy of the land-grant commons and respect for
the customary law of the acequia (see Ebright 1994, Peña 1998a, Peña and
Mondragon Valdez 1998, and Peña and Martinez 2000; Hicks and Peña
2003).

Economic and Ecological Benefits of the Acequia Landscape Mosaic

To quantify the value of Hispano land and water use practices, our research team developed an ecological services model of the acequia agroecosystem. We identified three major ways that acequia systems contribute to the bioregion:

- First, the acequia system generates agricultural income in goods and services sold in markets as well as through informal barter. In addition to being productive agricultural systems in their own right, the acequia agroecosystems are storehouses of native wild plant and landrace crop genetic diversity. The value of heirloom landraces and traditional knowledge to local plant breeders includes annual savings from reduced seed purchases, reduced agrochemical inputs, and reduced losses to pests and other pathogens. These heirloom landraces have additional value as a "firewall" protecting agricultural and food security from threats posed by the erosion of genetic agrobiodiversity (see Chapter 10).
- Second, the raw materials, open spaces, wildlife habitat, vernacular architecture, and built environments generated by the acequia system produce significant artisan, subsistence, and amenity values. Artisan production includes handcrafted wood products (furniture, wooden saints in the form of *retablos* and *bultos,* and other art objects); building and shelter materials (*vigas, latillas,* fence posts, lumber); hand-woven rugs, blankets, vests, and coats; hand-made artifacts; and tools for home and ranch. Subsistence production includes crops harvested from family garden plots and orchards; vegetables and fruits canned for storage, barter, or sale; medicinal and edible plants wildcrafted for home use; hunting and fishing for the family table; and the gathering of firewood. Amenity production includes lodging, food, and other retail sales generated by the tourism industry.
- Third, the acequia system provides additional ecosystem services in the form of soil formation and water regulation for the seven-county bioregion. For example, the anthropogenic wetlands created by acequias produce higher water quality, which in turn reduces the cost of water treatment for downstream users.

In total, we estimated that the historic acequia agroecosystem biome in the seven-county Rio Arriba bioregion annually produces an average of $350 million in agricultural, open space, wildlife habitat, water quality, forest conservation, and other environmental and economic values. The basis for this estimate is discussed briefly in the next section.[6]

The acequia landscape mosaic—including croplands, meadows, anthropogenic wetlands and woodlots, and riparian corridors—consists of a landscape pattern and a set of complementary agroecological practices. For example, the

Table 9.1. Economic and Ecological Services of the Acequia Landscape Mosaic

Service	Example	Benefits
Agrobiodiversity	Seed-saving of heirloom varieties preserves crop genetic diversity in situ and continually improves productivity and pest resistance	Agricultural sales
Food production	Riparian corridors and anthropogenic wetlands create habitat for medicinal and edible wild plants for home use or sale	Artisan, subsistence, agricultural sales
Raw materials	Woodlots and orchards provide materials for food, firewood, tools, and handicrafts	Artisan, subsistence, agricultural sales
Natural controls	Intercropping, allelopathic plants, and companion planting controls weeds and insect pests without chemical inputs, preserving trophic webs in agroecosystem	Subsistence, agricultural sales, ecological value
Soil conservation	Riparian corridors act as shield against wind erosion of soil	Agricultural sales, ecological value
Soil formation	Acequia flood irrigation and land management practices create soil	Agricultural sales, ecological value
Nutrient cycling	Perennial polycultures and companion planting add nutrients to the soil	Agricultural sales, ecological value
Water supply	Ditch networks and anthropogenic wetlands store and retain water	Ecological value
Water regulation	Riparian corridors and anthropogenic wetlands control and buffer water flow through local hydrological system	Ecological value
Water treatment	Anthropogenic wetlands absorb and filter pollutants and runoff and provide pH buffering	Ecological value
Microclimatic regulation	Riparian corridors are populated by phreataphytes that contribute to local hydrological cycle through evapotranspiration	Ecological value
Wildlife habitat	Riparian corridors and anthropogenic wetlands create habitat, food sources, and movement corridors for wildlife	Ecological value, amenity
Recreation	Cultural and ecological landscapes provide opportunities for recreation and tourism	Amenity
Cultural ecological	Local self-management of the acequia system encourages the inter-generational reproduction of land ethics	Groundwork for future benefit flows

trees and vegetation that grow in the riparian corridors, a landscape feature created by water seepage from earthen ditches, act as a shield against wind erosion. The farmers' preference for unlined earthen ditches also stems from a desire to produce such ecological services as habitat for edible and medicinal wild plants. Their preference for rotational intercropping (an agricultural practice) conserves soil and replenishes soil nutrients (an ecological service). The choice of landrace cultivars is further informed by local adaptations to climatic and other ecological limits. The mosaic thus extends biological diversity, blending native and domesticated landscapes to create a watershed-wide stock of natural assets.[7] Table 9.1 provides a synopsis of the types of economic and ecological benefits the mosaic provides.

Calculating Benefits: The Culebra Watershed

This section explains the calculation of benefits of the acequia system, using the Culebra watershed of southern Costilla County, Colorado, as a case study. Approximately 273 families in the Culebra watershed use acequias to irrigate 23,000 acres of privately owned croplands and pastures. These are the heart of the local agricultural economy. An additional 10,000 acres of anthropogenic wetlands are produced by subirrigation from acequias. We estimated the annual output of crops for cash sale from the Culebra Basin acequias at $9.4 million. This includes the substantial savings provided by the ecological services of the landscape mosaic, in the form of reduced outlays for agricultural production inputs. For example, in this region of Colorado, industrial-style farms spend considerable sums on herbicides and chemical fertilizers. Generally, the Hispano acequia farms of the Culebra watershed do not use these agrochemical inputs: they have always been "organic," relying on natural controls, principally crop diversity and rotation, to protect crops from pests and to maintain soil fertility. Additional savings are reaped from the local practice of heirloom seed saving, which means that the acequia farmers do not need to purchase seed commercially.

Artisan, subsistence, and amenity values contribute an additional $4.7 million in goods and services. Much of this sum represents income derived from tourism. According to the New Mexico Office of Cultural Affairs, the "unique cultural landscapes" of northern New Mexico and southern Colorado account for at least two-thirds of the tourism in the region. In Costilla County, the hunting and fishing component of the tourism economy is particularly important, and here the acequia farms play a crucial role. Most of the county's "blue-ribbon" trout fisheries are located on stretches of the local creeks that course through the heart of the acequia bottomlands. Also included in this estimate are the contributions of the so-called informal economy. Interviews revealed that most acequia farmers engage in a substantial amount of barter of goods and services. It is common, for example, for farmers to trade services (such as plowing) for a portion of the crops harvested. In a sample of 22 farmers, the average value given to this barter by the respondents was $3,000 a year (Peña 1997). From this average, we calculate that the annual value of informal barter among the 273 acequia farming families in Costilla County is about $800,000.

Taken together, the estimated annual economic impact of the acequia farms in Costilla County from agricultural production and artisan, amenity, and subsistence values is $14.1 million. This amount represents roughly 40 percent of total personal income in the county—including income from jobs in other sectors such as retail sales, government, and county services. Costilla County is an economically distressed region with high unemployment and poverty, so the impact of the acequia farms is especially important to the local economy.

The ecological services that the landscape mosaic in Costilla County provides also include substantial annual investments in the form of soil conservation and soil formation. Hydrologist Robert Curry, the director of the Institute for Watershed Science at California State University at Monterey Bay, views the acequias as "soil banks" that not only reduce erosion but actually create soil because the combination of irrigation practices, perennial polycultures, and crop rotations adds depth and organic materials to the soil horizon (Curry 1996). In contrast to many agricultural lands in the United States, the acequia landscape is actually gaining topsoil rather than losing it. We estimate that the acequias yield at least $1 million a year via soil formation and protection in the Culebra watershed. A further important ecological service the mosaic provides is the protection of water quality, thanks to the presence of anthropogenic wetlands and riparian corridors. In addition to underpinning the benefits derived from the protection of fish habitat, the water quality services the mosaic provides reduce the costs of water treatment by an estimated $5.5 million a year.[8] Taken together, the annual value of the ecological services of soil building and water quality is approximately $6.5 million.

Using similar procedures, the research team developed estimates for each of the seven counties in the Rio Arriba bioregion. These are presented in Table 9.2. As in the case of southern Costilla County, the data indicate that the mosaic contributes critically to the regional economy. An estimated 1,126 acequia systems in the seven-county bioregion irrigate roughly half a million acres of farmland. The acequia irrigation system creates an additional half-million acres of wetlands and riparian corridors, with their associated ecosystem and economic benefits. The estimated value of acequia-related agricultural income, sales, and services for the seven-county bioregion exceeds $90 million;[9] the estimated value of the artisan, subsistence, and amenity economies is $156 million. In addition, we estimate that the mosaic provides ecosystem services worth approximately $53 million.

Table 9.2. Estimated Value of the Acequia Mosaic, Seven-County Rio Arriba Bioregion (million dollars per year)

County	Agricultural Income, Sales/Services	Artisan, Subsistence, and Amenity Values	Soil and Water Conservation	County Totals
Costilla	9.4	4.7	6.5	20.6
Conejos	13.3	4.9	6.6	24.8
Guadalupe	17.7	17.0	7.8	42.5
Mora	13.2	2.2	7.1	22.5
Rio Arriba	14.1	23.3	7.5	44.9
San Miguel	18.5	17.8	7.7	44.0
Taos	3.9	86.5	9.8	100.2
Seven-county totals	90.1	156.3	53.0	299.4

Defending the Acequia Commonwealth

Uncertainty clouds the future of the acequia landscape mosaic. The land and water rights of the historic acequia communities have long been threatened by the ecological and economic impacts of enclosure and by the mining, logging, and livestock operations that followed the loss of common lands. Since the 1980s, speculative real estate development and the tourism industry have posed new threats by generating enormous pressures on farmland. Increasingly, acequia farmland is being lost to make way for high-end subdivisions and resort developments to accommodate growing numbers of newcomers who want to enjoy the region's natural and cultural landscapes. Acequia water rights are also under attack as industry, cities, and governments compete for access to new water resources (see Hicks and Peña 2003). All four of the strategies for natural-asset building James Boyce outlines in Chapter 1—investment, redistribution, internalization, and appropriation—can play a role in defending the acequia commonwealth from these threats.

Investment

Hispano farmers have long invested in the land and water resources of the bioregion, creating an enormously valuable stock of natural assets in the form of open space, wildlife habitat, wetlands, subirrigated meadows, greenbelts, and aquifer recharge zones. What remains to be seen is whether support for this investment can become a matter of positive public policy. Unfortunately, the tendency among the official state bureaucracies that administer water quality and water rights has been to view the acequias as primitive, wasteful, and inefficient (Peña 1998a, 1998b). Public policies have tended to favor the treatment of water as a commodity and have failed to consider cultural and ecological values of water resources (see Brown and Ingram 1987 and Rivera 1999). These policies also overlook the role of the acequia landscape mosaic in underpinning the substantial recreational, tourism, and amenity markets that are now thundering through the region and devouring acequia farmland at an alarming rate.

Although the acequia farmers have been adept at investing in natural capital, state policies and administrative regimes have not recognized or valued this contribution. The lack of federal responsiveness in many areas of public policy—ranging from agricultural research and extension to management of the public domain and water resources—means that the acequia farming communities have had limited success in defending and protecting their self-built natural assets. Mining, logging, and subdividing increasingly threaten the integrity of the watershed and the mosaic. For an investment strategy to succeed, public policy must acknowledge and support the cultural, ecological, and economic value of traditional land and water use practices.

Redistribution and Reappropriation

The case of the Hispano acequia farming communities in the San Luis Valley in Costilla County clearly illustrates the need for redistributional policies. Since 1979, through litigation for land rights in *Rael v. Taylor,* the local community has sought to restore access to the enclosed commons in the mountains of the Sangre de Cristo Land Grant (for discussion, see Peña and Mondragon Valdez 1996). The case centers on the historic use rights of the land-grant settlers and their heirs to the 77,000-acre commons of the Sangre de Cristo Land Grant, which the Taylor family surreptitiously acquired and enclosed in 1960—ending more than a century of local use and access under customary law and edict (see Peña 1998a, Peña and Mondragon Valdez 1998, and Peña 2001). The legal system has been generally unresponsive to the land rights claims of the plaintiffs. Refusing to acknowledge their legal standing, despite historical settlement, occupation, and use of the land grant, the court has repeatedly ruled against the efforts to restore usufruct rights to the common lands. The case is currently on appeal to the federal circuit court in Denver. Any future legal judgments will be complicated by the recent sale of the Taylor Ranch to Lou Pai, the billionaire chief executive officer of Enron Energy Services, a subsidiary of the now-defunct Enron Corporation, the Houston-based multinational corporation involved in large-scale energy and water development projects. In 1998, the Taylor family sold the southern third of the ranch, 23,000 acres, to Pai, and in 1999 Pai acquired the remaining 54,000 acres. The total cost of this transaction was reported as $21 million to $23 million (see Peña 2003, 2004).[10]

As has been the case in many other land-grant lawsuits, the efforts of local communities to restore historic common-use rights have been rebuffed by a legal system that sometimes characterizes Hispano claimants in racially charged language. Early in the history of *Rael v. Taylor,* one state district court judge, ruling against the plaintiffs, stated that it was "time to bring these Mexicans into the twentieth century" (see Peña and Mondragon Valdéz 1998).

The redistribution of natural assets in this context would involve restoration of historic use rights to the common lands granted to the Hispano settlers in the 1860s under the original U.S. government land-grant decrees. These rights were ignored when the Taylor family enclosed the uplands, in effect treating the land not as subject to community claims but rather as an open-access resource, which it proceeded to appropriate. The legal efforts of the acequia farmers in the protracted *Taylor* litigation can thus be described as an effort to reappropriate the commons.[11] By the mid-1990s, however, it had become apparent to many acequia farmers and social justice activists in the area that the lawsuit was unlikely to succeed and that, in any event, it could not restore community ownership of the land grant. Moreover, many in the community felt that the lawsuit could not go far enough to protect the headwaters zone and watershed: even if use rights were restored, the Taylor family partnership would retain the right to log, mine, or subdivide the common lands.

In response to these problems, community members established La Sierra Foundation of San Luis (LSF), with funding from the Ford Foundation, Great Outdoors Colorado, and other private nonprofit sources. Between 1994 and 1998, LSF worked with local and state governmental and nongovernmental agencies to arrange to purchase the Taylor Ranch and establish a new comanagement regime. One plan called for a 500-acre state park, with the remainder of the land to be comanaged as a state wildlife management area, with restoration of the historic use rights including grazing, hunting, fishing, wood gathering, and wildcrafting. But in 1998 the Taylor family rejected a final offer by the state and the LSF to purchase the land for $18 million (for further discussion see Peña 2002, 2003).

Between 1995 and 2000, the Taylor Ranch was subject to massive industrial-scale logging of the relatively undisturbed subalpine and montane forests. The logging, which involves more than 210 million board feet on the 34,000 acres of the land with merchantable timber, may prove to be the largest cut on a contiguous area of private land in the history of Colorado. The timber operations have been met by an intense local antilogging campaign that was characterized by the *New York Times* as "the hottest environmental dispute in the southern Rockies" (Brooke 1997; also see Peña and Mondragon Valdéz 1998 and Peña 1998a).

By the late 1990s, the local community had begun to pursue new strategies to protect the watershed, based on Colorado constitutional statutes establishing the primacy of county-level rule for land-use planning and zoning. The county government worked with a coalition of local groups, including People's Alternative Energy Sources, La Sierra Foundation, San Luis People's Ditch, Costilla County Conservancy District, and the Culebra Coalition.[12] In 1998, after a three-year, sometimes heated process of public review and commentary, the county adopted land-use regulations to protect a newly established "Watershed Overlay Protection District" that included the 77,000-acre Taylor Ranch. Key sections of the land-use code regulated mining activities and timber extraction, to protect the natural assets of the acequia farming communities from damage. Requirements included public hearings and the preparation of an environmental impact statement for major activities such as logging. The Taylor Ranch refused to abide by these regulations, however. In February 1999, the Costilla County Board of Commissioners sued in federal district court alleging that the Taylor Ranch was violating the law. The case was to be tried in June 1999, but the lawsuit was thrown into limbo when the Taylor Ranch was sold to Pai.[13]

Even if successful, the regulatory approach will not restore the historic use rights of the land-grant heirs. At best it may slow the destruction of the acequia community's natural assets. Frustrated by these failures, in 1999 the acequias organized the Colorado Acequia Association (CAA) to pursue other strategies for the redistribution of natural assets and environmental protection. One approach, which involves considerable scientific research, likely will result in yet another lawsuit against Taylor and the present owner of the land. The scientific research, under way since 1994, examines the cumulative impacts on the watershed of logging, road construction, and skid trails. The lawsuit is likely to argue that Taylor engaged in a "taking" or "inverse condemnation" by limiting and damaging the private property rights of downstream water users, the acequia farmers whose irrigated bottomlands are being adversely impacted by the effects of the logging activities on the enclosed common lands.[14]

These efforts were complicated by the sale of the Taylor Ranch to Enron executive Lou Pai. Shortly after purchasing the southern parcel in 1998, Pai initiated natural gas exploration. The search for natural gas was unsuccessful, but it raised concern among the Culebra residents that new extractive industries would be forthcoming. Pai has been secretive about his plans for the Taylor Ranch; however, members of his security staff have suggested that development plans may include a ski resort, subdivisions for high-end vacation homes, and recreational lodging. Pai has impounded water into ponds, an action that provoked an immediate protest by the CAA, but the Colorado wildlife division and water resources agency deemed the impoundment to be within the limits of the law. In fact, the state agency supports these actions as beneficial, because Pai is said to be promoting rehabilitation of damaged fisheries.

The acequia farmers, on the other hand, maintain that this constitutes an illegal impoundment of decreed water rights.

In an extraordinary and unprecedented move, Pai also sought to acquire long-lots with acequia water rights. Although numerous land speculators have staked claims to the upland commons since the late 1800s, never before have they ventured to acquire the acequia-irrigated farms in the valley bottom-lands. Given the tensions that mark the customary law of the acequia and the doctrine of prior appropriation, the CAA anticipates it will have to fight Pai to prevent the transfer of water rights that accompany ownership of long-lots from agricultural to nonagricultural uses. One such battle has already begun over one of the acequias in the southern tributaries. The acequias have so far prevailed in this case, and Pai has been prohibited from transferring the water out of the acequia system, but further battles over acequia water rights seem inevitable.

Internalization

Finally, the acequia farmers of the Culebra watershed and elsewhere could benefit from measures to reward them for the ecological services they provide to others via watershed management, habitat protection, and the in situ conservation of crop genetic diversity. Our model of the ecological and economic-base services of the acequia landscape mosaic illustrates the scope of such "positive externalities." If these could be internalized, both farm livelihoods and incentives for continued ecological stewardship would be strengthened.

To a limited extent, there may be some scope for internalization by tapping market demand from "green" and socially conscious consumers. Hispano acequia farmers are renowned for their unique native landraces of such crops as white maize, *bolita* beans, *calabacita,* and chile—all adapted by generations of farmers to drought, high altitude, and the short growing season (see Peña 1998a, 1998b). In recent years, farmers have organized cooperatives to tap emerging markets for specialty organic heirloom crops such as white corn roasted for *chicos.* Other mechanisms, involving public policies, will be needed to reward the acequia farmers for the creation and maintenance of the regional watershed. The hydrological services provided by the infrastructure of the mosaic are crucial to many economic activities in the bioregion. Whether the acequia farmers can be expected to provide these services without compensation is a critical question for public policy in the years ahead.

Conclusion

For many years, the acequia communities of the Culebra watershed and else-where have sought to protect and defend their land and water rights. They have relied on a variety of organizational and legal resources to maintain the water rights for the acequia farmlands, and more recently they have fought to protect the condition of the headwaters zone.

The case of the Taylor Ranch enclosure of the Sangre de Cristo Land Grant commons resulted not just in the loss of access for the rural poor but in a severe and accelerating rate of abuse of natural resources through logging, mining, and subdividing. The local community is now pursuing legal efforts to redistribute (or reappropriate) the enclosed common lands, hoping both to redress injustice and to protect the natural capital in which they and their ancestors have invested. Pending lawsuits over inverse condemnation may prove more successful than the other routes tried so far. This hope derives from an observation made by the legal theorist William H. Rodgers, who notes that

> assaults against the long-run productivity of [land], by loss of top-soil, destruction of watercourses, and elimination of vegetation, have been forbidden in waste litigation. A standard of "good hus-bandry" is often invoked, sometimes even to forbid changes in land use. . . . The waste cases support recognition of a universal "good husbandry" use restriction on all natural resources. (Rodgers 1982, 249.)

Such an effort would focus attention on the need for organizational forms and strategies that integrate good legal theory (and legal counsel) with watershed science, a commitment to "good husbandry" and the communities that sustain it, and the political mobilization needed to carry these demands to the public policy discourse (see Hicks and Peña 2003).

The acequia communities in the Rio Arriba bioregion are also seeking to establish farmer-to-farmer agricultural land trusts. The land trusts not only will work to acquire historic farmlands and sensitive watershed areas but also will support the struggle to reclaim the land-grant commons. In the current vision, this strategy will require the support of private foundations and charitable organizations to establish a "social venture capital" fund to seed permanent endowments for community land and water trusts in the region. Given the new pressures by investors such as Pai to acquire acequia long-lots and convert water rights to nonagricultural uses, there is an urgent need for new institutions to protect these natural assets.

The acequia landscape mosaic provides hundreds of millions of dollars in economic and ecological services to the bioregion. The protection of these natural assets and their continued control by the acequia commonwealth can be secured only if these communities can defend their access to water, earn sufficient income to sustain their livelihoods, and compete successfully with the burgeoning real estate market. Success in all these interrelated efforts is needed if the historic acequia communities are to preserve the watershed commonwealth's living legacy as a cornerstone of ecological democracy, social equity, and sustainable development.

Notes

1. The term *acequia* derives from the Arabic word *as-Saquiya,* which translates as "the one that bears water" or the "barmaid." For further discussion of the acequias see Peña (1998a, 1998b), Peña and Mondragon Valdéz (1998), Rivera (1999), and Peña and Martínez (2000).

2. Ecologists consider keystone species as the foundations of ecological communities because their activities create habitat important to other species in an area. For example, beavers are a keystone species because their disturbances (dams and ponds) extend riparian life zones and thus provide habitat for a greater diversity of flora and fauna. When anthropogenic disturbances add to the biodiversity of a locality, we can say that humans are serving as a keystone community. For further discussion, see Rivera (1999) and Peña (1998a, 1998b, 2002).

3. For further details, see Peña (1998a, 1998b) and Peña and Martinez (2000).

4. For further discussion of the significance of traditional environmental knowledge, see Nazarea (1999) and Hunn (1999).

5. Of course, the growth of tourism in the region is associated with other types of threats to the historic acequia communities. For example, tourism has been associated with highly speculative real estate development (resorts, condos, second homes, and so forth) that can displace local people from the land and result in the blacktopping of precious farmland. See Rodriguez (1987) and Peña (1998a, 1998b, 2002).

6. For the formal estimation models, data sources, and conceptual elaboration, see Peña and Van Hoy (2000). See also Rivera and Peña (1997) and Rivera (1999). For other approaches to the study of the economic values associated with biodiversity and ecosystem services, see, for example, Baskin (1997) and Pearce and Moran (1995).

7. For further elaboration of the biological and cultural principles underlying this approach, see Peña (1998a, 2002) and Kane (1994). Also see Grumbine (1992).

8. Estimate provided by the Costilla County Water and Sewage Department (in personal communication to the author, October 1999, San Luis, Colorado).

9. This figure is based on volume of agricultural sales. Its ecological components include annual savings from reduced costs for agrochemical inputs, estimated at $25 million, and reduced losses from pests due to the cultivation of pest-resistant heirloom varieties, estimated at $37 million.

10. After the Enron collapse, Pai achieved some notoriety as the largest single beneficiary of the company's stock options (Bernstein 2002).

11. In June 2002, in a landmark decision in the case of *Lobato v. Taylor,* the Colorado Supreme Court upheld local grazing and wood-gathering rights on the Taylor ranch (Noel 2002).

12. The Costilla County Conservancy District (CCCD), a local water rights and

conservation organization, serves as the umbrella organization for the area acequias and has played a vital role in local environmental struggles since its founding in the mid-1970s. The CCCD recently established the Colorado Acequia Association to promote the self-organization and cooperative development of the 73 acequias under its jurisdiction. For details, see Peña (1998a, 1998b) and Peña and Mondragon Valdéz (1998).

13. Ironically, when Lou Pai first bought the southern one-third of the Taylor Ranch in 1998, he sued Taylor over the remaining logging contracts. This private lawsuit proceeded through the courts without delay until an undisclosed out-of-court settlement was reached. The judge in *Jaroso Creek Ranch (Pai) v. Taylor Ranch* acknowledged that 300-year-old "beauty" trees were "worth protecting."

14. See Rodgers (1982) for elaboration of the legal theory of waste and nuisance litigation, on which this approach is based.

References

Baskin, Y. 1997. *The Work of Nature: How Diversity of Life Sustains Us.* Washington, D.C.: Island Press.

Bernstein, A. 2002. "Luck of the Draw: Divorce forced quiet ex-Enron exec Lou Pai to dump stocks, making him a very rich man, and a target in many lawsuits." *Houston Chronicle* (3 March).

Brooke, J. 1997. "In a Colorado Valley: Hispanic Farmers Battle a Timber Baron." *New York Times* (24 March).

Brown, F. L., and H. Ingram. 1987. *Water and Poverty in the Southwest.* Tucson: University of Arizona Press.

Curry, Robert. 1996. Personal communication. June.

Ebright, Malcolm. 1994. *Land Grants and Lawsuits in Northern New Mexico.* Albuquerque: University of New Mexico Press.

Grumbine, R. E. 1992. *Ghost Bears: Exploring the Biodiversity Crisis.* Washington, D.C.: Island Press.

Hicks, G. A. and D. G. Peña. 2003. "Community Acequias in Colorado's Culebra Watershed: A Customary Commons in the Domain of Prior Appropriation." University of Colorado Law Review 74: 2 (in press, March).

Hunn, E. S. 1999. "The Value of Subsistence for the Future of the World." In *Ethnoecology: Situated Knowledge/Located Lives,* edited by V. Nazarea. Tucson: University of Arizona Press.

Kane, G. S. 1994. "Restoration or Preservation? Reflections on a Clash of Environmental Philosophies." In *Beyond Preservation: Restoring and Inventing Landscapes,* edited by A. D. Baldwin Jr., J. DeLuce, and C. Pletsch. 69–84. Minneapolis: University of Minnesota Press.

Nazarea, V., ed. 1999. *Ethnoecology: Situated Knowledge, Located Lives.* Tucson: University of Arizona Press.

Noel, T. 2002. "Old Is New Again in Valley: High Court Returns Use of Taylor Ranch to Costilla Residents." *Rocky Mountains News* (13 July).

Noss, R. F. 1994. "A Sustainable Forest Is a Diverse and Natural Forest." In *Clearcut: The Tragedy of Industrial Forestry*, edited by B. Devall. San Francisco: Sierra Club Books.

Pearce, D., and D. Moran. 1995. *The Economic Value of Biodiversity*. London: Earthscan.

Peña, D. G. 1997. "The Ecological Services Provided by the Acequia-Riparian Long-Lot Agroecological Landscape Mosaic in the Seven-County Rio Arriba Bioregion: A Preliminary Model and Conceptual Discussion." Field research report series no. 8. Colorado Springs, Colo.: Upper Rio Grande Hispano Farms Study, Rio Grande Bioregions Project, Colorado College.

————. 1998a. *Chicano Culture, Ecology, Politics: Subversive Kin*. Tucson: University of Arizona Press.

————. 1998b. "Cultural Landscapes and Biodiversity: The Ethnoecology of a Watershed Commons." In *La Gente: Hispano History and Life in Colorado*, edited by V. C. de Baca. Denver: Colorado Historical Society.

————. 2002. "Endangered Landscapes and Disappearing Peoples? Identity, Place, and Community in Ecological Politics." In *The Environmental Justice Reader: Politics, Poetics, Pedagogy*, J. Adamson, M. M. Evans, and R. Stein, editors. Tucson: University of Arizona Press, pp. 58–81.

————. 2003. "Identity, Place, and Communities of Resistance." In *Just Sustainabilities: Development in an Unequal World*, J. Agyeman, R. D. Bullard, and B. Evans, editors. London: Earthscan.

————. 2004. *Gaia in Aztlan: The Politics of Place in the Rio Arriba*. Tucson: University of Arizona Press, forthcoming.

Peña, D. G., and M. Mondragon Valdéz. 1998. "The 'Brown' and The 'Green': Chicanos and Environmental Politics in the Upper Rio Grande." In *The Struggle for Ecological Democracy: Environmental Justice Movements in the United States*, edited by D. Faber. New York: Guilford Press.

Peña, D. G., and R. O. Martínez. 2000. "Final Report. Upper Rio Grande Hispano Farms: A Cultural and Environmental History of Land Ethics in Transition, 1598–1998." Submitted to the National Endowment for the Humanities and the Ford Foundation. Rio Grande Bioregions Project, San Luis, Colorado, and Seattle, Washington. January.

Peña, D. G., and B. Van Hoy. 2000. "The Ecological Services of the Acequia/Riparian Long-Lot Agroecological Landscape Mosaic: A Regional Analysis of Natural Assets." Unpublished research report. Department of Anthropology, University of Washington, Seattle. March.

Rivera, J. A. 1999. *Acequia Culture: Water, Land, and Community in the Southwest*. Albuquerque: University of New Mexico Press.

Rivera, J. A., and D. G. Peña. 1997. "Historic Acequia Communities in the Upper Rio Grande: Policy for Cultural and Ecological Protection in an Arid Uplands Environment." Report presented to the Rural Latino Studies Working Group, Albuquerque, New Mexico. April.

Rock, M. 1976. "The Change in Tenure New Mexico Supreme Court Decisions Have Effected upon the Common Lands of Community Land Grants in New Mexico." *The Social Science Journal* 13:13.

Rodgers, W. H. 1982. "Bringing People Back: Toward a Comprehensive Theory of Taking in Natural Resources Law." *Ecology Law Quarterly* 10(2): 205–52.

Van Ness, J. R. 1987. "Hispanic Land Grants: Ecology and Subsistence in the Uplands of Northern New Mexico and Southern Colorado." In *Land, Water, and Culture: New Perspectives on Hispanic Land Grants,* edited by C. H. Briggs and J. R. Van Ness. Albuquerque: University of New Mexico Press.

Worster, D. 1994. "The Legacy of John Wesley Powell." In *An Unsettled Country: Changing Landscapes of the American West.* Albuquerque: University of New Mexico Press.

CHAPTER 10

The Lighthouse and the Potato: Internalizing the Value of Crop Genetic Diversity

Stephen B. Brush

The incongruous juxtaposition of my title refers to two public goods of incalculable value: safe navigation and crop genetic resources. Neither lighthouse keepers nor the farmers who cultivate genetic diversity in potatoes and other crops provide their respective benefits to humankind without cost. The costs of lighthouses are relatively easy to measure: construction of the tower, fuel for the light, wages for the keeper. The costs of sustaining crop genetic resources are less evident but can be viewed as the income forgone by not switching to new varieties, new crops, or other economic pursuits. This forgone income is the functional equivalent of the cost of building and operating a lighthouse to provide the public good of safe navigation. The increasing availability of more profitable alternatives to growing traditional crops means that society must find ways to sustain diverse crop genetic resources and the environments where they are created and maintained: the small farms of poor farmers. We have long recognized that we cannot simply depend on the goodwill of coastal dwellers to maintain lighthouses for ships at sea (Coase 1974; van Zandt 1993). Gradually, we are becoming aware that we cannot depend on the goodwill of farmers to conserve crop genetic resources.

Crop genetic resources are a natural asset comprising the genes of domesticated plants, together with the dynamic human and ecological contexts that are indispensable to a crop's evolutionary system. The abundance and diversity of these resources are concentrated in locations where crops were originally domesticated or long evolved under heterogeneous conditions. These locations are known as Vavilov Centers in honor of the great Russian botanist Nikolai Vavilov, who pioneered the study of crop origins in the early twentieth century. Today, the primary stewards of crop genetic resources in these centers of diversity, which continue to provide the foundation for agricultural development around the world, are poor farmers. This natural asset is increasingly threatened, however, by the economic marginalization of poor farmers and by the competitive disadvantage of traditional crops compared to modern industrial agriculture. Genetic erosion—the loss of biological diversity and resources—is being caused by the replacement of local varieties with improved ones or with different crops altogether and by the exodus of farmers to non-farm employment.

The farmers who historically have provided crop genetic resources as a public good receive no direct reward for doing so. Developing a system to reward them for stewardship of this public good—an example of the internalization route to natural-asset building—would advance the goals of both poverty reduction and environmental protection. This chapter argues that neither a state-centered régime nor the privatization of crop genetic resources is likely to succeed in stemming the loss of crop genetic resources. Instead, I propose that crop genetic resources be preserved as a public good managed in common by farmers, and that farmers who maintain genetic resources be supported by public investment in community-based agricultural development.

Crop Genetic Resources

The Vavilov Centers are located, virtually without exception, in developing countries, and within them crop genetic resources are concentrated on the poorest farms. Several large gene pools of crop genetic resources are found in the Americas. These include food crops—the maize, bean, and squash complex of Meso-America; potatoes in the Andes Mountains; and manioc in the Amazon Basin—and high-value, specialty, and industrial crops, notably cacao, tomato, chile pepper, tobacco, and peanut. Prehistoric migration and crop diffusion established the principal crops of Meso-America throughout much of the continental United States, where they evolved into distinct and diverse regional crop populations.

Crop genetic resources are conventionally divided into two broad groups: wild and weedy relatives of domesticated plants, and landraces or "primitive crop varieties" from farmers' fields. The landraces have been inherited from previous generations and undergo continuous natural and artificial (that is, conscious) selection (Harlan 1975). Landraces are the most important crop genetic resource for agricultural science in terms of their historic value in crop breeding, the proportion of material collected and stored in conservation facilities, and their relevance to political conflicts. For most crops, landraces are counted in the thousands; for some, in the tens of thousands. This diversity embodies the collected wisdom and experience of the hundreds of generations of farmers who have selected and managed crop populations since the Neolithic Revolution, some 5,000 to 8,000 years ago.

Landraces form the backbone of the modern crop breeding industry. For instance, two farmer-selected varieties, Reid and Lancaster, dominate the inbred lines used in Corn Belt hybrid maize in the United States (Wallace and Brown 1988). In the American wheat crop, the variety Norin 10—which confers short stature to modern varieties and can be traced to landraces from Japan, Pennsylvania, and Turkey (Brush 1996a)—is common in pedigrees of all wheat classes (Cox 1991). Currently, landraces represent 60 percent of the 1,300 collections and 6.1 million accessions in more than 120 national and international gene banks; the remainder are in selected and bred varieties, breeding lines, and wild and weedy relatives (Food and Agricultural Organization 1996).

Although the social value of landraces has been demonstrated time and again in modern plant breeding programs (Evenson et al. 1998), their private value to the farmers who maintain them is increasingly jeopardized. The availability of purchased inputs such as fertilizer and pesticides; the existence of improved crop varieties; and the opportunities to increase income by changing crops, land uses, or employment all diminish the incentives for farmers to grow landraces. In addition, low grain prices from industrialized agriculture are transmitted via international trade, such as U.S. maize exports to Mexico (Boyce 1996), often to the detriment of the small-farm sector that maintains traditional crop varieties.

Despite the immense value of landraces and the importance of conserving them, their genetic structure and their relationship to farming groups is poorly understood. Although crop population biology is an active field of research, the task of describing the biological and social ecology of these dynamic species is daunting. Considerable effort has gone into understanding the evolutionary history of modern crops, in particular their relationship to wild and weedy relatives. Far less effort has been devoted to mapping the distribution of crop diversity across the agricultural landscape and its relationship to social and cultural diversity.

In the past, philanthropic institutions such as the Ford and Rockefeller foundations supported pioneering efforts to collect and study resources in Asia and Meso-America (for example, Wellhausen et al. 1952). Today these institutions could provide crucial support for understanding the ecology of crop diversity and designing conservation programs that involve farmers. One example of such philanthropic support is the McKnight Foundation's MILPA project in Mexico (Genetic Resources Conservation Program 2000).

Crop diversity is distributed within and across localities. In theory, it is conceivable that each individual locality hosts a genetically distinct population of the crop. At the other extreme, different regions may be sown with the same crop population—that is, the same mix of varieties. In the former case, where diversity is found entirely between localities, genetic resources are easily connected to particular people and places. In the latter case, no single site can be identified with specific genetic resources because they are shared across many localities. The distribution of diversity is crucial to claims of ownership or rights to private benefit from genetic diversity.

Several factors favor the distribution of diversity between rather than within localities and hence favor a tendency toward a situation in which each farming region is genetically distinct. Most important is local adaptation in agricultural systems that offer few other management tools to contend with such risks as drought, insect attack, and disease outbreaks. Harlan's (1975) classic definition of landraces stresses that these crop populations are in balance with their local environments. Adaptation to different microenvironments could be the major reason there is so much diversity. Another factor favoring a high proportion of diversity between rather than within localities is the physical and social isolation of farming communities: mountainous terrain, cultural and linguistic heterogeneity, and the lack of integrating mechanisms, such as markets, pose barriers that help to protect local varieties.

On the other hand, countervailing factors encourage the flow of genetic material between communities, fostering diversity within rather than between localities. As "pioneer species" that compete well in newly cleared land, crops by nature are able to exploit diverse habitats and often are broadly rather than narrowly adapted. Historically, broad adaptation allowed very rapid diffusion of species domesticated in one place to other places around the world. Moreover, farmers have long sought to increase returns to land and labor through experimentation and the exchange of knowledge and seeds. Seed exchange between farming communities is also necessitated by the loss of seed and by seed degeneration and can be accelerated by changes in diet and taste. Seed-exchange networks and markets quickly diffuse local varieties found to possess such valuable characteristics as disease resistance, drought tolerance, and special culinary qualities. Even a small amount of exchange between communities each year can result in thorough mixing of crop populations over time. Seed exchanges have resulted in the wide distribution of particular farmed varieties even in the most "traditional" agricultural communities (Brush et al. 1995; Louette et al. 1997; Zeven 1999).

Factors that encourage a close correspondence between social group and an inventory of crop genetic resources include (1) the propensity for local adaptation by crop varieties, (2) environmental heterogeneity and isolation of specific farming communities or cultural groups, (3) equivalence between the territory of a social group and a unique agricultural environment, (4) a lack of markets for seed or other agricultural inputs, and (5) selection for local tastes and uses. Factors that weaken a correspondence between social group and crop genetic resources include (1) sharing of a single agricultural environment by two or more social groups, (2) migration by social groups between agricultural environments, (3) markets or other exchange mechanisms that cut across social groups, and (4) crop introduction and improvement programs that use crop germ plasm from different sources. Both sets of factors are found in virtually every farming system, whether in traditional small-farm sectors or in modern industrial farms. Therefore, a close correspondence between a social group and a particular inventory of crop genetic resources cannot be assumed a priori. As discussed below, this issue weighs heavily in the question of whether genetic resources should or could be privatized.

Alternative Ways to Confront Genetic Erosion

Crop genetic resources in farmers' fields have historically been treated as assets that generate positive externalities whose only cost is that of collection and for whose loss no one bears liability. The issue today is whether, and if so how, to change this treatment of crop genetic resources so that the costs and benefits of producing and maintaining them are acknowledged and internalized into the international agricultural system.

For individual farmers and communities, the declining variability in crop populations is a by-product of the quest for higher productivity. The originally diverse crop inventories of North America were almost entirely eliminated in the development of modern American agriculture. For instance, as a result of the diffusion of hybrid maize, remnants of the original North American maize varieties are found only in isolated islands of traditional agriculture, notably in the southwestern United States among Native Americans (Nabhan 1985; Soleri and Cleveland 1993) and the acequia communities described by Devon Peña in Chapter 9. Farther south, in the Meso-American, Andean, and Amazonian Vavilov Centers, crop genetic resources retain some of the integrity of premodern agriculture, albeit under increasing threat of genetic erosion. These crop genetic resources are concentrated in the poorest farm sectors, among small farmers and indigenous producers: Hopi maize farmers in Arizona, Otomi and Maya maize farmers in Mexico, Quechua and Aymara potato farmers in the highlands of Peru and Bolivia, Amuesha manioc farmers in the Peruvian Amazon. In these very poor sectors, the pressures to augment food production and incomes are great, driving a wedge between the private value of traditional crops to farmers and their social value to crop breeders and consumers worldwide. These sectors offer the greatest potential benefits from reconciling economic incentives with the world's need to maintain these unique seed stocks.

Reconciling private and social values across national boundaries, and across highly contrasting social and economic groups, is central to international efforts to staunch the loss of biological diversity. Such reconciliation is an aim of the Convention on Biological Diversity (CBD), an international agreement initialed in 1992 that recognized national sovereignty over genetic resources and thereby foreshadowed a property system over them. The CBD represents a step toward a negotiated settlement between parties who manage genetic resources and parties interested in their conservation. Such a settlement represents an application of the Coase (1960) theorem, which suggests that bargaining between parties can bring an externality to a socially optimal balance between private and social costs, as long as one party is assigned property rights relative to the externality.

Three alternative ways to confront genetic erosion can be distinguished: (1) a state-centered approach, in which governments assume responsibility for conservation; (2) a privatization approach, in which farmers assume this responsibility; and (3) a community-based approach, in which a partnership between public and private interests provides for joint responsibility. Today the state-centered approach is dominant, relying on off-site (*ex situ*) maintenance of genetic resources and providing no recognition of farmers' interests or rights. The CBD's emphasis on sovereign control of biological resources also suggests a state-centered approach, in which it remains unclear whether and how states will negotiate with farmers to reduce genetic erosion. Privatization would circumvent direct state negotiation, shifting ownership rights of genetic resources to the farmers who produce them and involving direct negotiation with the farmers about conservation. The third avenue represents an intermediate path between the state-centered and privatization alternatives, one that would maintain crop genetic resources as part of the public domain but would establish community-based mechanisms to conserve crop genetic resources.

Common Heritage and the State-Centered Approach

Two characteristics—centralized institutions for the conservation of crop genetic resources and the conceptualization of these resources as the "common heritage" of humankind—define the state-centered approach. Crop genetic resources, such as maize germ plasm from Meso-America and potato germ plasm from the Andes, historically have been provided as a public good in an open-access regime known as common heritage. The principle of common heritage holds that genetic resources, whether found in farmers' fields or in gene banks, belong in the public domain. At their point of origin, access to genetic resources is implicitly mediated only by the willingness of the farmer to provide a sample of his or her crop. Likewise, the custom of crop collectors, conservators, and breeders has been to provide free access to crop genetic resources, mediated only by the credentials of the user who requests samples and by the availability of seeds. Once crop resources have been brought into the public-sector national and international systems of conservation and use, they are treated explicitly as open-access goods available to all bona fide crop breeders and other scientists. In addition to insisting that genetic resources remain in the public domain, this common heritage approach makes their conservation a public responsibility by vesting it in government and international agencies. Traditionally, the costs of genetic resource conservation under this scheme were only the costs of collection, storage, and distribution from publicly owned gene banks. These costs were borne by government and international agencies, without compensation to farmers, collectors, or conservators who provided the genetic resources.

Common heritage, however, does not exclude all private ownership of genetic traits. Once traits have been isolated and used to create new crop varieties, the gene sequence or the variety can be privatized as intellectual property. The contradiction between open access to plants in the farmer's field and privatization of plants in the seed company's test plots is consistent with the usual logic of intellectual property, whereby goods from the public domain can be drawn upon to create private goods. Nevertheless, this contradiction is politically flammable when it is applied across boundaries defined by nationality, economic class, and cultural group (Shiva 1997; Fowler and Mooney 1990). It is not surprising that poor nations, peasant farmers, and indigenous people often interpret common heritage as a facade for the appropriation of biological assets.

In recent years, the historic principles of common heritage and state-centered conservation have begun to break down. The assault on common heritage, which culminated in the CDB's assertion of ownership of biological resources by sovereign states, was presaged on the one hand by the creation of intellectual property in crop varieties and other biological materials and on the other by an international dialogue about the need to compensate traditional farmers, indigenous people, and other social groups that have conspicuously contributed to the world's store of biological resources (see, for example, Fowler and Mooney 1990). The emergence of the concept of biopiracy, defined as the "unidirectional and uncompensated appropriation" of plant genetic resources from developing countries (Odek 1994, 145), signals the close of the era of uncritical acceptance of the principle of common heritage. The image of theft is now widespread despite the fact that successful reciprocal relationships between providers and collectors of genetic resources can be demonstrated under the common heritage regime (Brush 1996a). Nevertheless, the principle of common heritage persists in the steadfast adherence to open access and public ownership of genetic resources by major institutions around the world, including the U.S. National Germ Plasm System and international collections of the world's most important crops, jointly managed by the Food and Agriculture Organization (FAO) of the United Nations and the Consultative Group for International Agricultural Research (CGIAR).

At the same time as the legitimacy of the common heritage model is under attack, there is growing recognition of the inadequacy of the state-centered management of genetic resources via centralized conservation in gene banks. Gene banks are a primary means for conserving genetic resources, but genetic erosion can be countered only partially by collecting and preserving landraces and other resources in off-site facilities. Crop scientists and conservators have become increasingly convinced of the need to maintain at least some portions of the agricultural environments that originally generated crop genetic resources. One reason is that gene banks simply cannot maintain the vast variability of crop genes. A second reason is that crop evolution in the field continues to generate a flow of new genetic material, whereas collections can at best maintain existing stocks. Third, the possibility of failure of *ex situ* conservation makes it prudent to maintain a backup system. Finally, gene banks are effective for conserving the "hardware component" of crop genetic resources (for example, alleles) but not the accompanying "software" (for example, local knowledge and farmer selection practices). The fiction of the adequacy of gene banks allows states either to overlook the poverty and marginalization that threaten farmers who produce and maintain genetic resources or to promote misguided economic development schemes that result in the destruction of those resources as a side effect. In sum, gene banks can be seen as the equivalent of zoos for the conservation of biological resources. They do not represent a comprehensive solution to conserving natural assets.

Were it not for the inadequacy of the centralized, gene-bank approach to conserving genetic resources, the sovereignty clause of the CBD might appear to resolve the issue of balancing the private and social values of genetic resources by multilateral negotiation among states. Conservationists of genetic resources now recognize, however, that some form of on-farm (*in situ*) conservation is necessary to complement *ex situ* conservation. *In situ* conservation requires that farmers continue to practice active seed selection, exchange, and maintenance, sustaining local crop populations as a dynamic and evolving component of the agricultural environment. The challenge is to find a way to raise the private value of these natural assets to match their high social value more closely.

The CBD continues the state-centered approach in that it retains the public good and public domain aspects of genetic resources for farmers within the nation, while making state institutions the direct beneficiaries of negotiated international access. A multilateral variant of the state-centered approach is the Farmers' Rights proposal at the FAO, intended to create an international mechanism to accumulate funds from industrial countries that import genetic resources and to disburse funds to developing countries that export genetic resources (Brush 1992; Esquinas Alcazar 1998). The funds are meant to assist farmers and farming communities, especially in the areas of origin and diversity of plant genetic resources (Esquinas Alcazar 1998, 209). This proposal remains state-centered, however, in its emphasis on keeping national rights over genetic resources and its assumption of the primacy of national institutions.

An inherent flaw in any state-centered approach is that the state interest in providing inexpensive food to urban populations has historically biased state policies against farmers who produce genetic resources—farmers who are often ethnic minorities on small farms in marginal agricultural zones. This bias helps to explain the failure of national institutions in gene-rich countries to articulate a farmer-based plan to conserve genetic resources. The Farmers' Rights proposal has been stymied so far by the reluctance of some industrial countries to agree to a poorly defined expansion of rights over genetic resources, by the lack of agreement on how to finance the international fund, and by the proposal's failure to stipulate exactly how funds would be used. Meanwhile, some major exporters of genetic resources have been reluctant to sign a multilateral agreement when potentially more lucrative bilateral agreements are possible.

Privatization and Bio-Prospecting

Accepting that the era of undisputed common heritage has passed, we can envision a continuum of mechanisms to provide access to genetic resources and benefit sharing for their producers and stewards. At one extreme are the state-centered approaches discussed above. At the other is privatization of genetic resources by individual farmers or small groups of farmers. This extreme is exemplified by "bio-prospecting" contracts between communities and pharmaceutical or seed companies, in which the companies receive exclusive access to genetic resources in exchange for short- and long-term financial returns.

The problem of genetic erosion appears to offer a promising situation for such "Coasian" bargaining solutions. The loss of crop genetic diversity is an externality for which state regulation is not a feasible option, because the governments in the Vavilov Centers have neither the incentive nor the means to mandate farmers to plant diverse traditional crop varieties. On the contrary, governments are actively involved in promoting agricultural development to increase food production, farm incomes, and food availability; and the replacement of local crop varieties with improved varieties is a proven method for reaching these development goals. If regulation cannot reduce the externality of genetic erosion, then bargaining between the producers and users of crop genetic resources would seem to offer a logical solution.

This approach is epitomized by the bio-prospecting contracts signed by ShamanBotanicals.com (née Shaman Pharmaceuticals) and indigenous communities in the Amazon (King et al. 1996). Contracts are logical ways to structure the relationship between the CBD's categories of "sources" and "users" of genetic resources (Gollin and Laird 1996; Cleveland and Murray 1997). Contracts provide short-term benefits—cash, materials, or services—to individuals and communities that allow collection of biological samples and provide local knowledge about those samples. Bio-prospecting contracts may also provide for long-term benefits in the form of a share of royalties, normally less than 5 percent, on inventions that use the material collected. In theory, bio-prospecting contracts offer a simple and direct way to increase the private value of crop germ plasm and thereby to reward stewardship, promote conservation, and provide for reciprocity from groups that benefit from genetic resources (Sedjo 1992; Vogel 1994).

According to the tenets of the Coase theorem, two conditions must hold if bio-prospecting contracts are to be effective in resolving the negative externality of genetic erosion: property rights must be well-defined, and transaction costs must be small enough to permit a mutually beneficial bargain. On one side of the contract, companies investing in bio-prospecting expect an intellectual property framework to protect the results of that investment (Gollin and Laird 1996). An array of intellectual property mechanisms is already available to protect improved crop varieties—including plant variety protection, utility patents, and trade secrets (Baeziger et al. 1993). The Global Agreement on Trade and Tariffs (GATT) and its attendant agreement on Trade-Related Aspects of Intellectual Property Rights (TRIPS) protect intellectual property in biological materials across national boundaries (Lesser 1998).

Implicit ownership by the gene providers is the other side of the bio-prospecting contract. Indigenous peoples' and human rights organizations have asserted the natural right to intellectual property over biological resources (see, for example, Shiva 1997 and Posey and Dutfield 1996). For instance, the 1993 Mataatua Declaration, drafted at the First International Conference on the Cultural and Intellectual Property Rights of Indigenous Peoples held in New Zealand, proclaims that intellectual property is a right implied in the right of self-determination: "We declare that Indigenous Peoples of the world have the right to self determination, and in exercise of that right must be recognized as the exclusive owners of their cultural and intellectual property" (Posey and Dutfield 1996, 205). This declaration reaffirmed assertions of earlier assemblies, notably Agenda 21 of the UN Conference on Environment and Development (Robinson 1993), the Kari-Oca Declaration and the Indigenous Peoples' Earth Charter, and the Charter of the Indigenous-Tribal Peoples of the Tropical Forests (Posey and Dutfield 1996). The unratified UN Draft Declaration on the Rights of Indigenous People (Part IV.29) similarly affirmed in 1993 that "indigenous peoples are entitled to the recognition of the full ownership, control, and protection of their cultural and intellectual property" (Posey and Dutfield 1996, 186).

These claims are largely rhetorical, and nation-states in countries with genetic resources seem unlikely to grant intellectual property rights over diffuse "indigenous knowledge" to indigenous peoples. The difficulty of defining "indigenous," the relatively small populations of people so defined, and their economic and political marginality do not favor state policies to establish indigenous intellectual property. Nevertheless, the government of the Philippines has created a precedent for such policies in Republic Act 8371, signed in 1997, which recognizes the rights of indigenous cultural communities and indigenous peoples "to special measures to control, develop and protect their sciences, technologies and cultural manifestations, including human and other genetic resources, seeds, derivatives of these resources, traditional medicines and health practices, vital medicinal plants, animals and minerals, indigenous knowledge systems and practices, knowledge of the properties of fauna and flora, oral traditions, literature, designs, and visual and performing arts" (Republic of the Philippines 1997).

Coupling this precedent with the recognition of intellectual property for improved crop varieties, the property rights preconditions for Coasian bargaining solutions may be emerging. Nevertheless, bio-prospecting contracts confront another substantial problem in the form of transaction costs. Critical reviews of the Coase theorem, including one by Coase himself (1988), stress that the zero-transaction-cost condition assumed in the theorem does not hold in real-world situations. In negotiations to reduce genetic erosion, transaction costs are pertinent in two ways. First, the costs of bargaining may exceed the value of the genetic resources, blocking any deal. Second, the transaction costs may affect the equity of the outcome, especially if they are higher for one party.

Two generic transaction costs described by Arrow (1969) are particularly relevant in the case of genetic resources: exclusion costs and the costs of communication and information. Exclusion refers to the "free-rider" problem, where persons can benefit from a bargained solution without incurring its costs. In the case of contracts between producers and users of crop genetic resources, the costs of exclusion would presumably be extremely high due to the wide diffusion of crop genes in farming communities that are not parties to the contract (Brush et al. 1995). This diffusion weakens ownership claims. The collector who pays for access to a community's genetic resources would logically wish to see that other collectors who do not pay are denied access, but the population structure of landraces and the ubiquity of seed exchange make it reasonable to expect that similar or identical genetic resources exist in other communities that are not included in the contract. On the other side, a community that negotiates a contract might want to increase its value by excluding other communities from negotiating similar, competitive contracts. Such exclusion, however, would incur the cost of determining the distribution of the genetic resource prior to the contract and the cost of establishing one community's rights vis-à-vis the others. Furthermore, a legacy of the common heritage principle is the existence of sizable national and international collections of crop genetic resources that are chartered to provide germ plasm openly to bona fide scientists. Another legacy is the research exemption in many plant variety protection systems, which allows crop breeders to use material developed by another without paying a royalty. Both legacies pose legal barriers to exclusion.

The costs of communication and information are also likely to be high in bargaining between producers and users of genetic resources. Uncertainty about future benefits poses extremely high information costs to firms; this uncertainty is likely to lower the amount a firm will invest in a bio-prospecting contract. For the seller, information about the value of genetic resources is made costly by social and economic inequality and by the paucity of communication between the farmers and the industrial scientific sector. This circumstance is exacerbated by the fact that few seed companies are active in collecting genetic resources, so that farmers often face a bargaining situation of monopsony, in which they have only one potential buyer of their resource.

These transaction costs not only threaten the efficiency of a bargaining solution to genetic erosion but also are likely to lead to inequities. A bio-prospecting contract between one community and a seed company may deny an equal opportunity to other communities with similar biological assets (Brush 1998). The costs of exclusion are almost certainly proportionately higher for farmers than for seed companies. The problem of monopsony in seed acquisition has already been mentioned. In addition, seed companies have alternative options: they can obtain genetic resources from public gene banks and, with the rise of biotechnology, can incorporate germ plasm from other organisms. Farmers lack such fallback options. As a result, most of the bargaining power is in the hands of the seed company, so that for the farmers, bio-prospecting is less a bargain than a take-it-or-leave-it proposition.

Community-Based In Situ Conservation

Both the state-centered and privatization approaches are problematic for addressing the welfare and environmental goals in the conservation of crop genetic resources. States have historical biases against on-farm conservation of crop genetic resources. Privatization through bio-prospecting is inequitable in allocating ownership of public goods to specific communities, and it is unlikely to be effective as a conservation tool because of high transaction costs.

Nevertheless, both approaches have some positive attributes. The state-centered principle of maintaining genetic resources as public goods in the public domain is valuable as a way to avoid the inequities of privatization. The decentralized aspect of privatization is valuable as a way to avoid the biases of the state-centered approach.

An alternative that combines the advantages of public domain and decentralization is needed to support *in situ* conservation of crop genetic resources. In the past decade, *in situ* conservation has emerged as a new strategy for maintaining crop genetic resources (Brush 1999; Wood and Lenné 1997). Although this strategy is still in its formative stages, future programs are likely to incorporate three components: (1) research, (2) participatory plant breeding, and (3) community development. The research component will draw on the biological and social sciences to study the status and dynamics of genetic diversity and to identify the appropriate areas and mechanisms for conservation. Research in Mexico (Perales et al. 1998) and Turkey (Meng et al. 1998) has demonstrated how interdisciplinary collaboration between social and biological sciences can identify target areas for *in situ* conservation, areas where the risk of genetic erosion is high and where conservation might be accomplished by incrementally increasing the value of landraces to farmers.

Participatory plant breeding can improve the value of local crop populations and make them more competitive in increasing food productivity and farmer incomes (Witcombe et al. 1996). This technique involves farmers and scientists in the identification of outstanding local crop populations, improved seed selection and management, recovery of "lost" varieties, improved information and seed exchange among farmers, and farmer selection of breeding material developed by scientists. In pilot projects, these mutual efforts have been shown to increase productivity (Sperling and Loevinsohn 1997). Participatory plant breeding has yet to be extensively adopted, however. National crop improvement programs have limited capacity to work at the community level, and nongovernmental organizations (NGOs) with greater access to farm communities typically are limited in the scientific capacity needed to manage the population biology and long-duration aspects of plant breeding. Partnerships between national programs and NGOs are needed to promote participatory plant breeding and *in situ* conservation.

The community development component of *in situ* conservation includes both market and nonmarket strategies. Marketing linked to environmental and social causes has scored successes in such high-value commodities as coffee, botanical food supplements, and cosmetics (Wasik 1996). Urban markets in many countries have specialized in relatively high value niches for local crops and produce. Certification systems for origin and quality exist in many countries and could be expanded to certify the status of local varieties that conserve genetic resources. Investment in market research, development, and insurance could help to widen these markets. Nonmarket strategies for promoting knowledge and interest in traditional crops include the "diversity fair"—a regional exposition of local crop varieties where farmers exchange seed and information and where public prizes, such as school supplies for a village, are used to stimulate participation. Another strategy is the promotion of seed-saver and seed-exchange networks, whose activities can include multiplying and distributing seeds of heirloom varieties that have been lost in farming communities but survive in gene banks (Tesemma and Bechere 1998).

Most of the institutions—international, governmental, and nongovernmental—involved in genetic resource conservation now accept the need to undertake both *ex situ* and *in situ* conservation as complementary strategies. Progress in this direction will require neither new organizations nor centralized management, but rather a way to stimulate partnerships among organizations with complementary skills. A key stumbling block is financial support for on-farm conservation. So far, such support has been provided on a partial and ad hoc basis through the work of NGOs and multilateral agencies such as the Global Environmental Facility, the UN Development Program, and CGIAR centers working in collaboration with national agricultural research programs. However, there is no dedicated, stable funding mechanism.

The Genetic Resources Trust

A Genetic Resources Trust, established with funding from private, foundation, and public sources, would create a financial mechanism for *in situ* conservation. The aim of the Genetic Resources Trust would be to enhance the private value of crop genetic resources to promote conservation, by involving public institutions operating in the public domain to support decentralized, community-based efforts. The challenge is to devise mechanisms to reward stewardship without recourse to privatization. The partners in the Genetic Resources Trust would include farm communities in Vavilov Centers of crop diversity; national and international research organizations focused on crop conservation and development; NGOs specializing in community development and conservation; and organizations and groups that benefit from open access to genetic resources, including seed companies, industrialized countries, and the modernized farm sectors of developing countries.

The Genetic Resources Trust concept builds on the model of the Genetic Resource Recognition Fund (GRRF) at the University of California, Davis (UC Davis). UC Davis faculty established the GRRF following the cloning and patenting of a gene that confers resistance to a bacterial rice disease, *Xanthomonas oryzae pv. oryzae* ("Xoo"). The resistance gene was found in a wild rice from Mali, *Oryza longistaminata*. The Central Rice Research Institute in Cuttack, India, obtained a sample of the Malian wild rice and found it to be resistant to multiple strains of the bacterium. In 1977, scientists at the International Rice Research Institute (IRRI) in Los Baños, Philippines, obtained and regenerated the sample, multiplied the clone, and found it to be resistant to all six known races of bacterial blight in the Philippines. From 1978 to 1990, Dr. G. S. Khush at IRRI conducted an intensive breeding program, crossing and backcrossing *O. longistaminata* with the widely used rice variety IR24, which was susceptible to rice blight. Eventually, Dr. Khush succeeded in transferring the *O. longistaminata* genetic material that coded for blight resistance, dubbed "Xa21," to IR24. Dr. Khush gave the new, resistant lines of IR24 to Professor Pamela Ronald, a plant pathologist at UC Davis, who isolated and cloned the Xa21 gene at UC Davis in 1995 (Ronald 1997). UC Davis then patented Xa21 for licensing to commercial companies. At the same time, UC Davis agreed to provide the Xa21 gene to IRRI and breeders in developing countries for free. Because most of the rice breeding in the world is done in the public sector and rice seed can be planted by farmers from year to year, the value of the Xa21 gene to commercial companies is likely to come from transference to crop species other than rice, where private-sector breeding and synthetic hybrids are more prevalent.

Contributions to the UC Davis GRRF will come from three sources: licensee companies, the university, and the inventors. The option agreements contain a clause that triggers a licensing agreement in the event that the company "commercializes" a product containing Xa21, requiring them to make payments into the GRRF. In addition, Professor Ronald and her fellow inventors will voluntarily contribute to the GRRF some of the royalties they receive from the companies in the event of commercialization. The university will use the revenues to support fellowships for graduate or postdoctoral students from designated countries in various disciplines of agriculture. Although the GRRF is a pilot program and still requires additional design to stipulate how GRRF funds are to be used to aid conservation or to benefit farmers, it provides a novel alternative to the state-centered and privatization approaches discussed earlier. The exchange of benefits between users and suppliers in the GRRF concept does not involve payments per se; instead, one public good (education, knowledge) is reciprocated for another (genetic resources). Other reciprocal mechanisms could include support for community development or participatory plant breeding programs that improve local welfare or raise the productivity and income of farmers. A similar mechanism could help *in situ* conservation efforts in centers of crop genetic diversity. In so doing, it could build on the work of an increasing number of NGOs and public institutions that are initiating *in situ* conservation projects around the world (Brush 1999), thus offering opportunities to support public rather than private solutions to benefit-sharing.

A Genetic Resources Trust cannot rely solely on benefit-sharing tied to commercial exploitation. Genetic resources remain public domain goods, and as such they require continued support from public sources. Consequently, the creation of the Genetic Resources Trust will also depend on the acceptance by public-sector donors of both the trust idea and of its program for *in situ* conservation. Previous support for the consortium of international agricultural research centers of the CGIAR provides a useful precedent. The Genetic Resources Trust might replace the existing funding mechanism for *ex situ* crop genetic resource conservation, augmented with the addition of *in situ* conservation. Alternatively, the existing funding mechanism for gene banks might remain in place, and the Genetic Resources Trust might be dedicated exclusively to on-farm approaches. In either case, the establishment of the trust could be greatly aided by private foundation leadership and support, as was demonstrated in an earlier era by the creation of international agricultural research centers such as IRRI and the International Maize and Wheat Improvement Center (CIMMYT). For instance, private foundations might demarcate high-priority regions for *in situ* conservation, identify private and public agencies to collaborate in implementing new conservation programs, and help negotiate long-term support from private and public interests that benefit from open access to genetic resources.

Conclusion

In situ conservation will be sustainable only if the private value of genetic resources to farmers is increased to the point that sufficient numbers of them continue to maintain diverse crop populations and agricultural ecosystems that generate new flows of diversity. The public approach to genetic erosion proposed in this chapter does not rely on the private mechanisms of bioprospecting nor the state-centered arrangements of the Convention on Biological Diversity. Rather, it seeks to enlist support from state agencies as partners in a broad consortium of governmental and nongovernmental organizations. In spirit, this approach returns to the common heritage principle but grafts onto it a more direct and formal system to achieve mutually reinforcing welfare and environmental protection goals through *in situ* conservation.

This solution, which builds on both the institutional practices of public-sector agricultural research and the cultural practices of farmers in keeping genetic resources in the public domain, is not without cost. Funding can build on existing public expenditures, by adding a new component designated for on-farm efforts, the Genetic Resources Trust. But accomplishing both *in situ* and *ex situ* conservation will require a higher level of investment than do current conservation programs (National Research Council 1993).

In terms of this chapter's original metaphors of the lighthouse and potato, the provisioning of crop genetic resources need not pass through the privatization experiment that proved to be short-lived in the case of lighthouses (Coase 1974). The compelling issue today is not how to privatize genetic resources to benefit a few farmers but how to augment public investment to protect this essential natural asset's flow of benefits to the public domain. *In situ* conservation, backed by the funding mechanism of a Genetic Resources Trust, can provide a public means to increase the private value of landraces and crop genetic resources. For poor farmers, the benefits from this community-based solution will arguably be more broadly distributed and longer lasting than those from either state-centered or private approaches.

Acknowledgments

I wish to thank James Boyce and Barry Shelley for suggestions and comments on an earlier draft. Research for this paper has been supported in part by the National Science Foundation and the University of California. My appreciation goes to the Ford Foundation for supporting the Natural Assets Project conference.

References

Arrow, K. J. 1969. "The Organization of Economic Activity: Issues Pertinent to the Choice of Market Versus Non-Market Allocation." Joint Economic Committee, 91st Congress of the United States, 1st Session, *The Analysis and Evaluation of Public Expenditures: The PPB System*. Vol 1. 47–64. Washington, D.C.: U.S. Government Printing Office.

Baenziger, P. S., R. A. Kleese, and R. F. Barnes, eds. 1993. *Intellectual Property Rights: Protection of Plant Materials*. Madison, Wis.: Crop Science Society of America.

Boyce, J. K. 1996. "Ecological Distribution, Agricultural Trade Liberalization, and In Situ Genetic Diversity." *Journal of Income Distribution* 6:265–86.

Brush, S. B. 1992. "Farmers' Rights and Genetic Conservation in Traditional Farming Systems." *World Development* 20(11): 1617–30.

————1996. "Is Common Heritage Outmoded?" In *Valuing Local Knowledge: Indigenous People and Intellectual Property Rights,* edited by S. Brush and D. Stabinsky. Washington, D.C.: Island Press.

————. 1998. "Bio-Cooperation and the Benefits of Crop Genetic Resources: The Case of Mexican Maize." *World Development* 26:755–66.

Brush, S. B., ed. 1999. *Genes in the Field: On-Farm Conservation of Plant Genetic Resources*. Boca Raton, Fla.: Lewis Publishers.

Brush, S. B., R. Kesseli, R. Ortega, P. Cisneros, K. S. Zimmerer, and C. Quiros. 1995. "Potato Diversity in the Andean Center of Crop Domestication." *Conservation Biology* 9:1189–98.

Cleveland, D. A., and S. C. Murray. 1997. "The World's Crop Genetic Resources and the Rights of Indigenous Farmers." *Current Anthropology* 38:477–515.

Coase, R. H. 1960. "The Problem of Social Cost." *Journal of Law and Economics* 3:1–44.

————. 1974. "The Lighthouse in Economics." *Journal of Law and Economics* 17:357–76.

————. 1988. "Notes on the Problem of Social Cost." *The Firm, The Market and the Law.* Chicago: University of Chicago Press.

Cox, T. S. 1991. "The Contribution of Introduced Germplasm to the Development of U.S. Wheat Cultivars." In *Use of Plant Introductions in Cultivar Development: Part 1,* edited by H. L. Shands and L. E. Wiesner. Madison, Wis.: Crop Science Society of America.

Esquinas Alcazar, J. 1998. "Farmers' Rights." In *Agricultural Values of Plant Genetic Resources,* edited by R. E. Evenson, D. Gollin, and V. Santaniello. Wallingford, England: CBI Publishing.

Evenson, R. E., D. Gollin, and V. Santaniello, eds. 1998. *Agricultural Values of Plant Genetic Resources.* Wallingford, England: CBI Publishing.

Fowler, Cary, and P. R. Mooney. 1990. *Shattering: Food, Politics, and the Loss of Genetic Diversity.* Tucson: University of Arizona Press.

Genetic Resources Conservation Program. 2000. "McKnight Foundation–MILPA Project: McKnight Integrated Landrace Preservation Activity: A Farmer-Based Approach to *In Situ* Conservation." University of California, Division of Agriculture and Natural Resources. Available at http://www.grcp.ucdavis.edu/milpa/mil-main.htm.

Gollin, M. A., and S. A. Laird. 1996. "Global Politics, Local Actions: The Role of National Legislation in Sustainable Biodiversity Prospecting." *Boston University Journal of Science and Technology Law.* Available from Lexis: 2 B. U. J. Sci. and Tech. L. 16.

Harlan, J. R. 1975. "Our Vanishing Genetic Resources." *Science* 188:618–21.

King, S. R., T. J. Carlson and K. Moran. 1996. "Biological Diversity, Indigenous Knowledge, Drug Discovery, and Intellectual Property Rights." In *Valuing Local Knowledge: Indigenous People and Intellectual Property Rights,* edited by S. Brush and D. Stabinsky. Washington, D.C.: Island Press.

Lesser, W. 1998. *Sustainable Use of Genetic Resources under the Convention on Biological Diversity: Exploring Access and Benefit Sharing Issues.* Wallingford, England: CAB International.

Louette, D., A. Charrier, and J. Berthaud. 1997. "In Situ Conservation of Maize in Mexico, Genetic Diversity and Maize Seed Management in a Traditional Community." *Economic Botany* 51:20–39.

Meng, E., J. E. Taylor, and S. B. Brush. 1998. "Implications for the Conservation of Wheat Landraces in Turkey from a Household Model of Varietal Choice." In *Farmers, Gene Banks and Crop Breeding: Economic Analyses of Diversity in Wheat, Maize, and Rice,* edited by M. Smale. Boston: Kluwer Academic Publishers.

Nabhan, G. P. 1985. "Native Crop Diversity in Aridoamerica: Conservation of Regional Gene Pools." *Economic Botany* 39:387–99.

National Research Council. 1993. *Managing Global Genetic Resources: Agricultural Crop Issues and Policies.* Washington, D.C.: National Academy Press.

Odek, James O. 1994. "Bio-Piracy: Creating Proprietary Rights in Plant Genetic Resources." *Journal of Intellectual Property Law* 2:141–81.

Perales, H., S. B. Brush, and C. O. Qualset. 1998. "Agronomic and Economic

Competitiveness of Maize Landraces and In Situ Conservation in Mexico." In *Farmers, Gene Banks and Crop Breeding: Economic Analyses of Diversity in Wheat, Maize, and Rice,* edited by M. Smale. Boston: Kluwer Academic Publishers.

Posey, D. A., and G. Dutfield. 1996. *Beyond Intellectual Property: Toward Traditional Resource Rights for Indigenous Peoples and Local Communities.* Ottawa: International Development Research Centre.

Republic of the Philippines. 1997. "Bicameral Conference Committee Report on Senate Bill 1728 and House Bill No. 9125." Congress of the Philippines. Tenth Congress, Third Regular Session.

Robinson, Nicholas A., ed. 1993. *Agenda 21: Earth's Action Plan.* New York: Oceana Publications.

Ronald, P. C. 1997. "Making Rice Disease Resistant." *Scientific American* 227(5): 68–73.

Sedjo, R. A. 1992. "Property Rights, Genetic Resources, and Biotechnological Change." *Journal of Law and Economics* 35:199–213.

Shiva, V. 1997. *Biopiracy: The Plunder of Nature and Knowledge.* Boston: South End Press.

Sperling, L., and M. Loevinsohn, eds. 1997. *Using Diversity: Enhancing and Maintaining Genetic Resources On-Farm.* Ottawa and New Delhi: International Development Research Centre.

Soleri, D., and D. A. Cleveland. 1993. "Hopi Crop Diversity and Change." *Journal of Ethnobiology* 13:203–31.

Tesemma, T., and E. Bechere. 1998. "Developing Elite Durum Wheat Landrace Selections (Composites) for Ethiopian Peasant Farm Use: Raising Productivity while Keeping Diversity Alive." *Euphytica* 102:323–28.

UN Food and Agriculture Organization. 1996. *Report on the State of the World's Plant Genetic Resources.* Rome: UN Food and Agriculture Organization.

van Zandt, D. E. 1993. "The Lessons of the Lighthouse: 'Government' or 'Private' Provision of Goods." *Journal of Legal Studies* 22:47–72.

Vogel, J. H. 1994. *Genes for Sale: Privatization as a Conservation Policy.* New York: Oxford University Press.

Wallace, H. A., and W. L. Brown. 1988. *Corn and its Early Fathers.* Ames: Iowa State University Press.

Wasik, J. F. 1996. *Green Marketing and Management: A Global Perspective.* Cambridge, Mass.: Blackwell Business.

Wellhausen, E. J., L. M. Roberts, and E. Hernandez X. 1952. *Races of Maize in Mexico: Their Origin, Characteristics, and Distribution.* Cambridge: The Bussey Institution, Harvard University.

Witcombe, J. R., A. Johsi, K. D. Johsi, and B. R. Sthapit. 1996. "Farmer Participatory Crop Improvement. I: Varietal Selection and Breeding Methods and their Impact on Biodiversity." *Experimental Agriculture* 32:445–60.

Wood, D., and J. M. Lenné. 1997. "The Conservation of Agrobiodiversity On-Farm: Questioning the Emerging Paradigm." *Biodiversity and Conservation* 6:109–29.

Zeven, A. C. 1999. "The Traditional Inexplicable Replacement of Seed and Seed Ware of Landraces and Cultivars; Review." *Euphytica* 110:181–91.

PART IV

OUT OF THE WOODS

Part 4 explores the scope for natural-asset-building strategies in forest-dependent communities. The central role of forests in providing ecological services—including regulation of the quantity and quality of waterflows, the provision of wildlife habitat, and the sequestration of atmospheric carbon—is now increasingly recognized by policy makers and the public. In recent years, this recognition has prompted shifts in federal and state government forestry policies, away from a narrow focus on timber production toward a broader vision of ecosystem management.

Investment in the natural capital of forests is a key element in this new forestry philosophy. This investment can take many forms: reforestation, soil conservation, the selective thinning of vegetation to limit forest fire threats, and the adoption of low-impact timber harvesting practices. Given the social value of forest ecosystem benefits, these are sound investments. Yet as Constance Best explains, market values remain poorly aligned with ecosystem values. On private lands, which account for more than half the forest acreage in the United States, timber production and real estate development continue to dominate land valuation and land-use incentives. Even on the publicly owned lands that are managed by the U.S. Forest Service and other government agencies, adequate funding for ecosystem management is not ensured.

Policies to promote the *internalization* of benefits from forest stewardship could help to augment the resources and the incentives for investment. The authors offer several innovative suggestions for how such policies could be achieved. Constance Best discusses the possibilities for developing markets for such ecological services as water provision and carbon sequestration and for adopting policies to promote new forms of private forest ownership that foster long-term stewardship. Deborah Brighton notes that substantial public resources have long gone into subsidizing private timber production and proposes that these resources should be reoriented to advance the public interest in forest ecosystem management. In the case of public forests, Cecilia Danks cites the recent Forest Service moves to recycle revenues from recreational fees and observes that policies to internalize the value of the water supplied by public forestlands could generate substantial resources for investment.

A key question is whether such policies will be coupled with strategies to reduce the widespread poverty in forest-dependent communities. The "jobs-versus-environment" tradeoff has figured prominently in recent forestry debates in the United States. In the controversy over protection of the spotted owl in the Pacific Northwest, for example, the threat of unemployment among loggers and sawmill workers was a central issue. Yet forest ecosystem management also can be labor-intensive, and it is less subject to boom-and-bust cycles, resource depletion, and international competition than is timber production.

The chapters that follow suggest that *redistribution* of forest assets and forest-based income streams is fully compatible with ecosystem management. Even if forestry policy posed short-run tradeoffs between distributional and environmental objectives, a strong case could be made for the importance of poverty reduction both as an end in itself and to secure public support for the transition to ecosystem management. The authors point to further complementarities between these goals. Citing Wendell Berry, Brighton maintains that forests and farmlands should be "used by people who know them best and care the most about them." Similarly, Danks points out that the employment of local labor to work on public forestlands offers cost savings via lower transportation costs and access to local knowledge. Brighton and Best both outline strategies to combat private forestland fragmentation, by dispersing the rights to some "sticks" in the property-rights bundle while retaining unified rights in those dimensions where integrated management is crucial.

The question of employment access also suggests a role for a variant of the *appropriation* route to natural-asset building. Today, Danks observes, work opportunities on public forestlands are open-access resources, in principle available to all. As in the case of open-access natural resources, however, often some people turn out to enjoy greater access than others. From its inception, the legislation that established the national forest system acknowledged the right of local communities to share in the benefits of forest resources, mandating that a percentage of all timber revenues be remitted to county governments. More recently, the Northwest Forest Plan developed to protect old-growth forests and the spotted owl has incorporated special provisions to address the economic needs of local communities. Building on these precedents, policies to encourage hiring local labor for forest stewardship—in effect, an appropriation of employment rights for local communities—could be one element of building natural assets in the woods.

CHAPTER 11

Values, Markets, and Rights: Rebuilding Forest Ecosystem Assets

Constance Best

Forests supply a wide array of goods and services of immense importance to human welfare, yet their economic valuation usually is limited to wood products and the real estate value of the land. This misalignment between the social and ecological value of forests and their market value is a key reason for the decline of forest natural capital, as complex forests are simplified, degraded, and liquidated to maximize wood production or real estate values. The current situation is not inevitable, nor is it irreversible. Promising strategies are being developed to align market and ecosystem values better so as to sustain forests. At the same time, these strategies can help to address the widespread poverty in forest-dependent communities. This chapter provides an overview of the present state of U.S. forests and explores some of these alternative approaches to forest ownership and management.

Forest Ecosystem Assets and Their Decline

Forests are dynamic natural systems that provide a variety of goods and services. In addition to diverse wood products, valuable forest ecosystem services include habitat for myriad species; watershed regulation services; the sequestration of atmospheric carbon dioxide and other climate regulation; and soil formation. Compared to the managed forests that dominate the U.S. landscape today, older and more complex natural forests have higher ecosystem asset value, thanks to their more productive and stable soils, greater carbon storage, and greater range of species and habitats from the forest floor to the high canopy.

Most forest ecosystem assets other than the production of wood for timber, pulp, and fuel are poorly understood and poorly quantified, and they typically are overlooked in conventional economic valuations. Commercial markets are well-developed only for wood products and for the conversion of forestlands to agricultural, residential, or other nonforest uses. The prevailing financial values therefore do not capture the suite of natural forest assets of value to society. The health of forest ecosystems depends on the decisions of forest landowners and forest communities. Because economic returns are almost exclusively driven by wood production or by the real estate market, forest ecosystem capital has been increasingly depleted by intensive timber harvesting and forest conversion.

Since European settlement began, the United States has lost at least one-third of its former forest cover. Most of that loss came in the nineteenth century. On average, between 1850 and 1920, some 13.6 square miles of forest was cleared every day (Powell et al. 1994). Today U.S. forests face continued losses. It is true that when the regeneration of former agricultural lands is taken into account, net forest loss declined significantly in the latter part of the twentieth century. For example, there was an apparently substantial net gain of 3.6 million acres in forest cover between 1982 and 1997 due to the shift of millions of acres of abandoned crop and pastureland to forest. However, during the same time period almost 10 million acres of forest was lost to development, with more forest acres converted than any other land type. This is a forest area twice the size of the state of Massachusetts turned into roads, residential construction and other infrastructure.[1] Further, the national data mask serious ongoing net forest losses in major timber producing states, including California, North Carolina, and Georgia. The annual rate of forest loss to development increased by 70 percent in the last five years of the data period over the previous decade, running at about 950,000 acres per year. So although net acreage of privately-owned U.S. forests has grown recently, losses in key regions have accelerated (U.S. Department of Agriculture 1999). These calculations also mask important changes in the character of forestlands. The quality and ecological value of many of the forests now being lost are often far superior to those of the new forest cover on former agricultural land. Moreover, although forestland that is converted to agricultural use can be reforested later, conversion to developed use is less reversible.

Forests that are not converted to "higher and better uses" are often being maintained in a simplified and fragmented state, with degraded ecological functioning compared to primary forests. Simplification refers to the reduction in the diversity of trees and other species and of the forest's horizontal and vertical structures including downed logs, understory, standing dead trees, older trees, and multilayer canopy. A natural forest typically contains a constellation of tree species, whereas secondary managed forests are increasingly plantations of one or two commercial species—species that may be non-native or genetically modified. Natural forests contain a variety of age classes intermingled in the landscape, but commercially managed forests tend to be of uniform age. Because of the economic pressure to capture the wood value more quickly, most U.S. timberland is never allowed to mature biologically. Yet older forests, with their larger trees and more complex structures, provide unique ecological and social values, including habitat for many threatened and endangered species and sometimes immense carbon sequestration. Younger, simplified forests provide habitat for fewer species. With less biomass and greater soil disturbance, managed younger forests can actually be net producers of carbon instead of acting as carbon sinks (Harmon and Ferrell 1990). Simplification of forest structure also alters nutrient cycling and hydrologic regimes, as soil "banks" of nutrients and organic matter are drawn down by frequent harvests and as soil structure and organisms are damaged by compaction.

Fragmentation also leads to the degradation of forest ecosystem functions. Fragmentation occurs via the division of larger single-owner forest tracts into smaller parcels under diverse owners, many of whom then develop their parcels. Increased isolation among forest "patches" due to timber harvest patterns; the expansion of road systems; and clearing for agricultural, residential, and other uses also lead to fragmentation (Birch 1996). The fragmentation of forests and other habitats has been characterized as one of the greatest threats to biodiversity worldwide (Burgess and Sharpe 1981; Noss 1983, 1987; Harris 1984; National Research Council 1998).

On average, between 1978 and 1994, almost 2 million acres of forestland— an area about the size of Yellowstone National Park—were broken up each year into parcels smaller than 100 acres (Best and Wayburn 2000). Nationally, over 32 million acres—an estimated 8 percent of total private forest area—are now held in parcels smaller than 20 acres. Although still counted for statistical purposes as "forest," parcels smaller than 10 acres usually are residential lots and have been converted de facto from functional forest ecosystems. As forest areas urbanize, the capacity of the remaining forest to maintain its functions— whether as wildlife habitat or a source of timber—is diminished.

Private Ownership of Forest Capital

More than half of the forestlands in the United States are privately owned (see Figure 11.1).[2] Industrial owners, defined as entities that own wood-processing facilities, account for roughly 10 percent of total U.S. forest area and nonindustrial private forest (NIPF) owners for another 48 percent. Of the nearly 10 million forest owners in the United States, larger owners hold the greatest forest area. Some 27,000 owners, representing just 0.3 percent of all owners, control 39 percent of the private forestlands (see Table 11.1). These holdings include most of the 13,300 industrial forest ownerships; the expanding class of NIPF financial and institutional ownerships; and other large holdings

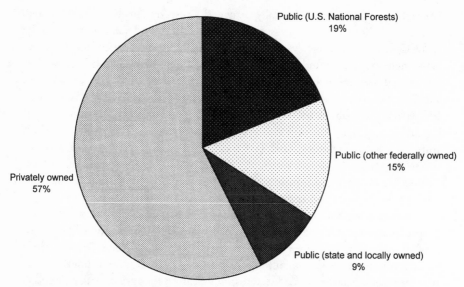

Figure 11.1. Distribution of U.S. Forestlands by Ownership Type.

Table 11.1. Profile of U.S. Private Forestland Ownership

Size Class	Number of Landowners	Percentage of Total Owners	Forest Acres (million)	Percentage of Total Acres
1–9 acres	5,795,000	58.5	16.6	4.2
10–99 acres	3,480,000	35.1	107.6	27.4
100–499 acres	559,000	5.6	91.6	23.3
500–999 acres	41,000	0.4	24.5	6.2
1000+ acres	27,000	0.3	153.0	38.9
TOTAL	9,902,000	100.0	393.3	100.0

Source: Birch (1996).

controlled by utilities, other industrial companies, families, and other private entities. Fewer than 7 percent of owners hold title to 68.4 percent of forestlands. Although there are many nominal forest owners in the United States, the decisions of a rather small class of owners have a huge impact on the condition of the nation's forest ecosystem assets.

Motivations and Management Practices

Generally, the overriding motivation of larger landowners, including forest product companies and institutional owners, is competitive financial return through wood production. These owners seek to maximize near-term profits and cash flow from their forest properties and to reduce the period during which their financial capital is tied up in standing timber inventories. Compared with smaller owners, they harvest their forests more intensively and use more inputs, including genetically manipulated plantings, fertilizers, and herbicides. Plantations have increasingly replaced natural forests in these holdings.

Forests managed in this industrial style are typically composed of young, fast-growing softwoods. Standing inventories are typically well below the biological carrying capacity of these forests, as indicated by the historical inventories of mature forests. Harvest levels have exceeded growth for the last 50 years—the period for which the U.S. Forest Service has data (Haynes et al. 1995)—leading to the current "unprecedented" shortages in the merchantable supply of softwoods (Haynes 1990). The need of industrial owners to cycle their capital as rapidly as possible within the biological constraints of the forest ecosystem has resulted in a shorter "rotation" or harvest cycle, with forests often cut at a fraction of their biological maturity and timber yield capacity.[3]

Nonindustrial owners—especially the smaller individual owners who make up 68 percent of owners and hold 34 percent of the private forest area—typically have multiple motives for forest ownership. They often place wildlife habitat, recreation, natural or scenic preservation, and other noneconomic values at the top of their lists of reasons for ownership (Birch 1996; Hodge and Southard 1992; Brunson et al. 1996; Bliss et al. 1994, 1997). These owners tend to have longer-term financial goals and to harvest timber more intermittently and in a fashion more consistent with noneconomic goals. For example, they tend to use uneven-age silviculture and to maintain higher timber inventories than many industrial owners (Newman and Wear 1993).

Although ownership goals clearly affect the condition of forest ecosystem assets, it would be overly simplistic to say that industrial ownership invariably depletes natural capital and nonindustrial ownership invariably builds it. Forest capital is often depleted in both industrial and NIPF forestlands in the United States. Moreover, industrial owners tend to have a stronger ongoing stake in maintaining their most productive forestlands in a healthy and vigorous state, so as to enhance wood production. Although certain qualities of these forests may be simplified and certain ecological functions degraded, these core industrial forest holdings are usually well-forested.

In addition, industrial ownerships tend to be more stable than NIPF properties, which are the primary source of increasing fragmentation and conversion. The midsized NIPF ownerships of between 100 and 999 acres are most at risk of fragmentation (Best and Wayburn 2000). Although the character of NIPF ownerships is exceptionally diverse, and therefore it is dangerous to generalize, the data suggest that many older rural residents, likely to be land-rich and cash-poor, are selling for subdivision to meet their retirement or other financial needs. Estate settlements also drive forest fragmentation.

Industrial owners tend to be more sensitive to the regulatory environment. Increasingly, they have invested in staff and planning for nontimber management to comply with regulatory requirements. To mitigate environmental risks to their ability to operate, they are incorporating higher standards for protection of forest ecosystem assets than was historically the case. Furthermore, they have the cash flows to be able to invest in the restoration of ecological assets. Within the constraints set by their commodity-production goals, the potential therefore exists to engage industrial owners in efforts to rebuild forest ecosystem wealth.

Despite their stronger noneconomic ties to the forests, nonindustrial owners generally have shown an unwillingness—or inability—to invest in their forest assets. This circumstance results from a combination of factors, including a lack of information and technical assistance, a lack of time, cash demands, and the illiquidity of forest investments. Furthermore, timber harvesting on individual NIPF ownerships is often poorly planned and implemented. NIPF lands are often "high-graded" by loggers, leaving behind a forest stand of poor quality and stocking. Compared to industrial forest management, logging practices and the nonforest development of buildings and roads on NIPF lands are subject to less regulatory oversight and thus are less constrained in their potential negative impacts on ecosystem values.

The Nature of Forest Property Rights

Forest property rights can be as complex, interconnected, and chaotic as the forest ecosystem itself. The image of a "bundle of sticks" is often used to represent the variety of rights that accrue with ownership. There can be many sticks in a forest property, often held by different persons, firms, organizations, or other entities. In addition to the land title and timber harvest rights, private forest ownership can include riparian and other water development rights; mineral rights; subdivision rights; and a host of building rights for roads, utilities, and other structures. Rights for timber and mineral extraction can be separated from the fee title to the property and are often held by others. Because they relate to production of commodities with established markets, these rights have strong legal foundations. Ironically, the rights most highly valued in commercial terms—logging, mining, and building—are those whose exercise can most disturb the forest ecosystem.

The public, too, has certain rights with respect to private property. The manner in which private owners use their lands is subject to local, state, and federal regulations that are meant to protect forest ecosystem services, such as water quality and wildlife habitat, and to protect community health and safety by regulating road use and logging operations and by organizing fire prevention. These public rights are founded on the recognition that the unregulated exercise of private property rights could seriously infringe on the rights of workers, neighbors, local communities, or the public at large. The provision of such ecosystem services as wildlife habitat, biodiversity, and water quality is of immense social value, yet insofar as these services affect private forest property values at all, they do so negatively, reflecting the degree to which public regulation constrains timber harvest, mining, and other commercially valued development.

Forested counties often are among the poorest rural areas in the United States. Some low-income residents—especially those whose families have lived in an area for generations—own forestland, but as owners of small properties where timber harvest is infrequent, they often lack liquid resources. Many other low-income residents do not own any forestland but are employed in forest-based enterprises, and many supplement their earnings by gathering grasses or mushrooms and by hunting in the forests. Yet the owners of forest properties are not obligated to take community expectations and traditional uses into consideration in their management decisions. The conversion of older natural forests to younger, simplified plantations, or the development of forest properties as second homes for affluent professionals, can drastically curtail opportunities for local people to use the woods for hunting, gathering, or recreation. Furthermore, the local benefits from timber production tend to be volatile. Periods of overharvest are often followed by divestiture of mills and lands by absentee owners. Absentee owners can move their operations elsewhere, but local communities are left to readjust their economy and lives, often at great cost.

The goals of rebuilding forest ecosystem assets and reducing poverty are not typically pursued together. In fact, efforts to achieve one of these goals sometimes inadvertently undermines achievement of the other. For instance, a program that assists the poor to gain property titles may increase forest fragmentation if it helps to fund new developments carved from larger tracts. Similarly, efforts to marshal greater private and public investment in forest conservation may perpetuate the ownership of forests—and the realization of their financial benefits—by the wealthy. The following sections consider ways in which the two goals can complement each other.

Stewardship Forestry

Stewardship forestry refers to forest management practices that work with natural forest composition, structure, and processes to produce not only timber but also the wider array of goods and services that a healthy forest ecosystem can provide. This approach takes a long-run view, emphasizing total returns and asset appreciation over current income. It encourages ongoing reinvestment to produce a range of forest goods and services, and in so doing it maintains market options, hedges risk, builds economic and ecological resilience, and enhances ecosystem productivity.

Given the financial attractions of the more narrowly focused conventional forestry business model, a variety of new incentives are needed to support economically viable stewardship forestry alternatives. Catalytic investment by philanthropic, public, and private capital sources is also necessary (Best and Jenkins 1999). These investments and incentives can be structured to give preference to those forest owners with the greatest financial needs, encouraging lower-income forest owners to invest in rebuilding natural assets. In this section, I briefly discuss five components of such a strategy.

Conservation Easements

Conservation easements are permanent deed restrictions that prevent nonforest development and can guide forest management to restore ecosystem wealth. Such easements effectively reallocate some sticks in the bundle of ownership rights, placing them in trust with an agency that ensures they are not exercised. The public gains the permanent protection of the forest and, possibly, access for purposes such as hunting and recreation, while the landowner can continue productive use of the forest consistent with the easement terms. The conservation value protected by the easement can be appraised as the opportunity cost of the restrictions on marketable rights.

Funding for conservation easements comes primarily from state and federal appropriations and general revenue bonds. Philanthropies have also contributed funds to conservation transactions. In addition, landowners are eligible for income and estate tax deductions through the charitable donation of conservation easements, a provision that is especially useful for families who would otherwise lack the liquidity to pay estate taxes without overharvesting the forest or selling the land. In principle, it would be possible to target cash purchases of easements, and tax benefits, to lower-income forestland owners.

The Science of Ecologically Grounded Silviculture

Many forest owners are constrained by a lack of scientific knowledge about the impact of silviculture and timber harvests on forest ecosystems. Research on forest management has tended to focus narrowly on enhancing timber yield. Ecologically grounded silviculture that seeks to conserve and restore other forest values is not well developed. Further research is needed to document the contributions of managed forests to carbon storage, water supplies, and other ecosystem services; to develop and test low-impact systems for the harvest of timber and other forest products; and to establish and disseminate knowledge of the sustainable harvest levels of nontimber products such as understory plants, mushrooms, roots, lichens, and mosses.

Access to Harvesting and Processing Technology

Timber harvest systems have improved substantially in recent years, becoming more capital-intensive in the process. For instance, newer equipment can minimize soil compaction in thinning operations that enhance growth and restore structural diversity to young, overstocked stands. This equipment can be very expensive, but community-development loan funds can help to finance its purchase. Investment in low-impact forestry technology need not be limited to equipment acquisition. There is a new generation of skilled manual jobs in stewardship forestry, including precommercial thinning, pruning, nonchemical control of competing vegetation, habitat enhancement, and the gathering of special forest products. Job training programs can help low-income forest community residents to fulfill the demand for skilled stewardship labor.

Significant technological advances have also occurred at the processing stage. In particular, newer industrial softwood processors use the trees harvested more fully. Smaller sawmills often lack access to the knowledge and capital required to upgrade their technology to yield greater value per unit of wood processed. The processing of nontimber forest products tends to be more centralized, and communities could capture significantly more of the value from these products if primary sorting, cleaning, and bundling facilities were located closer to the forests.

Developing New Markets for Forest Goods and Services

Market-making is crucial to the development of ecosystem services as a viable revenue source for forest stewardship. These services must be identified, quantified, and sold in a marketplace quite different from that for wood products. Consider, for example, the ecological service of carbon sequestration. Whereas timber harvest and land conversion generate carbon dioxide emissions,[4] sustainably managed forests are net sinks of atmospheric carbon dioxide. Net forest carbon stores can be increased by preventing forests from being converted by development, protecting old-growth forests from removal, growing managed forests to older ages, reforesting previously cleared forest areas, and altering harvest and replanting to reduce impacts on the soil carbon.

The market for carbon sequestration services is still in a very early phase, because national policies and international agreements to reduce carbon emissions are yet to be resolved. Moreover, there is a risk that the system eventually established will not create incentives for restoring ecosystem wealth but instead will subsidize business-as-usual practices such as the expansion of short-rotation plantations. Strategic philanthropic investment can provide resources for public policy formulation and for the implementation of model forest-based carbon transactions that meet credible scientific standards, with transparent accounting and third-party monitoring. An example is the forest carbon banking mechanism currently being organized by the Pacific Forest Trust to facilitate the acquisition and remarketing of carbon credits secured by conservation easements on forests in the Pacific Northwest.

New Financial and Fiscal Tools

Forests and humans often have clashing time frames. Forests reach biological maturity well after the most economically advantageous time to harvest. Even though forests are being harvested young, with short intervals between harvests, this practice is considered a long-term activity compared to other investments and hence carries added financial risk. A variety of new financial and fiscal tools can be developed to improve liquidity, reduce risk, and lower the costs of restoring forest ecosystem wealth.[5]

Liquidity can be improved by initiating a market for timber futures, allowing landowners to receive income against future harvests at risk-adjusted prices, and by developing long-term, low-interest lending facilities to allow owners to borrow against future harvests. Such facilities could be publicly funded and managed through private commercial banks, similar to existing government programs for small business loans. Publicly supported programs of this sort could give preference to low-income forest owners and to the owners of small properties.

Forest management expenses and carrying costs can be reduced by improving their tax treatment. Currently, smaller forest landowners who rarely or never harvest timber cannot deduct many of the costs related to forest stewardship and restoration, even when the owner qualifies as a business under the tax code. Furthermore, investments intended to enhance habitat or water quality may never qualify as tax deductions, because the Internal Revenue Service does not regard these investments as being based on the profit motive. Tax code revisions are needed to recognize the public benefit of stewardship investments and to allow taxpayers to deduct such expenses against income from any source. Again, such fiscal tools would allow preferential treatment for low-income individuals, in accordance with the principle of progressive taxation. Reducing capital gains taxes for long-term forest investments would also remove a disincentive against growing older forests. If the capital gains tax rate were indexed for inflation for timber held more than 10 years, then only its true appreciation in value would be taxed. Similarly, capital gains taxation could exclude a portion of the income from the sale of forest property or conservation easements to government agencies or land trusts.[6]

Markets for Nontimber Forest Products

Although wood production is likely to remain the main source of revenue for most forest landowners, nontimber revenues are increasingly available to those who enhance forest biodiversity and ecological restoration. Potential nontimber revenue sources include special forest products such as edibles, herbs, and decorative florals; fee-based hunting, recreation, and ecotourism; payments for ecosystem services such as carbon sequestration and watershed protection; and conservation real estate transactions. Ecologically sound development of these nontimber revenue streams can benefit forest landowners, local communities, and the public at large.

Special Forest Products

Special forest products have considerable economic value. In 1989, for example, the wholesale value of floral greens harvested in the Pacific Northwest— including boughs, cones, grasses, ferns, mosses, and ornamental plants—was $128 million; and in 1992, wild mushrooms harvested in Washington, Oregon, and Idaho were valued at $40 million (Schlosser and Blatner 1994). Private forest owners who lease access rights to special product harvesters usually receive 10 percent of the value of the harvest, typically reaping a return of $5 to $15 per acre, and if the landowner directly engages in gathering, sorting, and bundling the plants, the per-acre returns increase (Pacific Forest Trust 1997). Special forest products can therefore provide regular annual revenues to smaller landowners.

Recreation and Ecotourism

Fee-based forest recreation is a growing revenue source for public and private forests in the United States. Although the popularity of hunting is decreasing somewhat, nature-based ecotourism is on the rise, with a worldwide economic value estimated at $83 billion (Fillion et al. 1992). In the United States, publicly owned parks and forest reserves are the major destinations for nature-based tourism and recreation. Visits to national parks generate direct and indirect revenues of more than $14 billion, supporting roughly 300,000 jobs (Cordell et al. 1990). As public lands become more crowded, however, demand for outdoor recreation is spilling onto private forestland. The U.S. Forest Service estimates that 8 percent of private nonindustrial forestland is leased for recreational use and predicts that this figure will rise in coming years. Fee-based hunting is the most established commercial recreational use of private forests in the United States. Fees typically range from $2 to $15 per acre per season, but on high-quality bird-hunting properties in the southeastern United States, where public land is relatively scarce, lease rates can be two to three times higher.

Payments for Ecosystem Services

In a ground-breaking study, Costanza et al. (1997) valued the global contribution of all ecosystem services—defined as "flows of materials, energy, and information from natural capital stocks which combine with manufactured and human capital services to produce human welfare"—at $33 trillion per year, of which $4.7 trillion was attributable to forests. Key forest services include the provision of water for human consumption and power generation, carbon sequestration for climate stabilization, pollination and bio-controls for agriculture, and flood protection. Although these services are crucial to human welfare, mechanisms to compensate forest landowners and communities for providing such services have not existed until very recently.

As noted above, markets for enhanced forest-based carbon sequestration are now beginning to emerge. The potential size of the global market for carbon emissions offset credits is difficult to predict, but the World Bank estimates that if the Kyoto accord were implemented, world demand could amount to 500 million tons annually during the first compliance period (2008–2012), at prices ranging from $5 to $30 per ton. Because the best forest carbon sinks are mature timber stands, this market could promote the restoration of older forests. A recent analysis of industrial forests in British Columbia found that over a 10-year period, at a price of $10 per ton of additional carbon stored, carbon reduction credits would yield more than the estimated forgone timber harvest income (Pacific Forest Trust 1999). At $20 per ton, forest owners in the Pacific Northwest could earn $250 to $750 per acre, thanks to the tremendous carbon storage capacity of the coastal temperate rain forests (Pacific Forest Trust 1998).

Markets are also now emerging for waterflow services provided by forests. Water is often supplied to metropolitan regions and irrigated agriculture from upland forest catchments. The nature of forest management can positively or negatively affect the quantity and quality of water supplies, in particular the degree of siltation and the periodicity of flows. As water use rises and the need for watershed protection increases, the market for forest-based water provision is growing. In general, this trend has been driven by public investment. For example, when faced with having to spend an estimated $12 billion for a new water filtration facility, New York City adopted a watershed protection program that is expected to cost one-tenth that amount. This alternative approach includes the purchase of conservation easements on privately owned watershed lands to reduce sedimentation and improve water quality, as well as programs to reward farmers and woodlot owners for adopting management practices designed to safeguard water supplies. Such watershed conservation programs can be targeted to benefit low-income forestland owners in a variety of ways. For instance, they could be focused on watersheds with greater numbers of smaller owners, or they could preferentially fund acquisitions of conservation easements from low-income owners. A combination of increased watershed protection regulation for larger owners and financial incentives for smaller owners could be the most equitable strategy.

Conservation Real Estate

Conservation value refers to forest services that do not, and may never, have a market value and yet may have profound intrinsic value. A market value can be obtained, however, through the opportunity costs of conservation. For instance, the market value of wildlife habitat or biodiversity can be appraised in terms of the value of forgone alternative land uses, such as timber harvest or development. That value can be fully or partially monetized through the sale or tax-deductible gift of a conservation easement to a government or nonprofit agency. This incremental difference in return is often enough to make stewardship forestry competitive in the marketplace. As with water services, the market for conservation is driven primarily by the public sector, with funding from government appropriations, bond issues, and tax surcharges, and indirect public funding through tax deductions and sometimes tax credits.

Aligning Forest Ownership with Forest Ecosystems

Many current forest ownership structures in the United States are not well aligned with either the biological time frames of forests or with the complexity of their asset values. The frequent turnover in forest ownership means that titles are bought and sold in less time than it takes the forest to mature. Because the goals of forest ownership often vary with each new proprietor, frequent title transfer results in inconsistent forest management, overharvesting, and increased road-building and other construction. Industrial ownership can be more durable and intergenerational than individual ownership, but after a decade of poor performance in the face of increasing competition from low-cost producers in Asia and South America, the U.S. forest products industry is today seeking to generate greater shareholder returns. The result has been a wave of mergers, acquisitions, and land sales.

Theoretically, ownership by financial investors in general, and by tax-exempt institutions in particular, could be more stable. Pension funds and other institutional investors have long time horizons. However, institutionally owned forestlands are generally managed by third-party "timber investment management organizations" (TIMOs) as a portfolio of assets, akin to stocks or bonds. Forest acquisition, management, and disposition decisions are based on internal rate-of-return goals against which TIMOs are evaluated by their institutional clients. Using sophisticated economic models to maximize returns, these organizations move in and out of ownership of specific forest types, regions, and countries, providing no greater (and possibly less) stability in decision-making for the corresponding forest properties.

Several alternative forms of forest ownership are considered below. These may offer better prospects for aligning financial, natural, and social values within the context of U.S. laws and traditions. Their common aim is to secure consistent long-term stewardship for the forest. A further attraction is that these new ownership structures are compatible with expanded forest ownership by low-income individuals and forest-dependent communities.

Forest Investment Management Organizations

One alternative, especially relevant for larger properties, is the creation of forest investment management organizations (FIMOs), a variant of the existing institutional management by TIMOs. Practicing a stewardship forestry business model rather than a conventional timber-centered model, FIMOs would organize and manage funds for investors to provide competitive, risk-adjusted returns through the acquisition, conservation, and management of forestland. In the acquisition process, the FIMO would establish conservation easements and then seek to capitalize on the suite of ecological goods and services produced by its forest properties. Although FIMOs might sell properties at some future date, the easement would continue to protect the forest asset values under the new owners.

Low-income people could gain ownership of forestland through FIMOs in two ways: First, community development corporations (CDCs) or other nonprofit organizations could, with philanthropic funding, acquire FIMO investment units. These could be repackaged into subunits and resold, perhaps with subsidies, to low-income investors. Second, a CDC could buy outright title to a forest property from a FIMO, and again the ownership could be repackaged into investment units available to low-income people. In either case, the price of ownership would be reduced by the earlier monetization of the conservation value through the easement.

Forest Stewardship Communities

Another promising private ownership form, especially in rural areas experiencing growing residential demands, is the forest stewardship community. In this arrangement, a conservation-minded developer acquires an appropriate forest tract and then clusters residential development in a small portion of the land, allowing for efficient infrastructure and service delivery, while the major portion is protected by a conservation easement and managed for long-term ecological values. Residential property owners are vested with an undivided interest in the forest, enjoying its uses subject to the terms established by the easement and the community. Forest stewardship communities can be organized by for-profit conservation-minded developers or by nonprofit agencies such as CDCs or Resource Conservation and Development Districts (RCDDs). By accessing low-cost funds available for financing affordable home ownership by low-income people, some units can be reserved for purchase by low-income residents.

Forest Landowner Cooperatives

The creation of forest landowner cooperatives that "reassemble" forest tracts to facilitate common, longer-term stewardship is a growing movement in the Midwest and New England. A cooperative can be structured as a legal partnership among previously separate owners or as a federation of owners who agree to common management but retain individual land titles. Members share expenses and revenues. For small owners, there are multiple advantages to joining a forest cooperative: economies of scale in management and product merchandising; a pooled revenue stream that smooths cash flows to individual owners; and collective investment and information-sharing, making stewardship forestry practices more accessible.

Nonprofit Forest Conservation Ownerships

Nonprofit conservation organizations have acquired forestlands to protect them as quasi-public preserves. In recent years, such organizations have begun to engage in timber harvesting and other productive uses compatible with the protection of ecological assets. In the northeastern United States, for example, some 500,000 acres of private timberland have been acquired by the Vermont Land Trust, The Nature Conservancy, and the Conservation Fund. Portions of these acquisitions have been transferred into public ownership, with the remaining forestlands being managed as demonstration forests or resold to private landowners subject to conservation easements. Land trusts that retain ownership hope to provide working models of stewardship forestry for other private forest owners and to generate revenues to be used in the protection of more forestlands. Land trusts can also partner with conservation-minded developers, CDCs, RCDDs, and others to resell acquired forest properties as forest stewardship communities, with the objective of expanding forest ownership opportunities for low-income families.

A variation on these traditional nonprofit acquisitions is the Forest Bank recently established by The Nature Conservancy in the Clinch River watershed of Tennessee and Virginia. The bank acquires the timber rights of woodland owners in return for a consistent annual dividend. By collecting these "deposited" rights, the bank assembles a critical mass of forest properties that can be managed for long-term values, to serve as a buffer to the Conservancy's adjacent protected areas. The landowners gain consistency in revenue and an assurance that their forests will be well managed. The Forest Bank model could be especially beneficial to low-income forest owners, whose ability to invest independently in rebuilding ecosystem assets is limited.

Conclusion

Forests and people can sustain each other. There are many opportunities to create markets and ownership structures that could help to rebuild forest ecosystem assets and secure a more equitable distribution of their benefits. Catalytic investments and creative strategies are needed from philanthropies, public agencies, and the private sector to break through the inertia of business as usual. Hybrid investment strategies, combining capital pools and new instruments, have the potential to develop the stewardship forestry model to a stage where it can attract conventional capital flows and become economically self-sustaining. By better aligning the private and social values of forests through new institutional arrangements, we can rebuild these natural assets and sustain their vital contributions to human well-being.

Notes

1. Primary drivers of accelerating forest conversion are increasing populations, greater numbers of older people, increasing personal income, decreasing family size, growing numbers of smaller households, sprawling development patterns, and increasing migration to rural areas and warmer regions (Alig 1986). These trends are projected to drive the conversion and development of at least an additional 20 million acres by 2020 (National Research Council 1998).
2. The data presented here on private forest ownerships are drawn primarily from Birch (1996). Unfortunately, data are not available to correlate ownership with information on income.
3. Douglas fir trees, for example, reach their point of maximum annual growth somewhere between 80 and 120 years of age, yet in the Pacific Northwest the Douglas fir currently is harvested at an average age of 40 years.

4. Worldwide, forests are the second-greatest emissions sector after energy production, yielding 17 percent of carbon dioxide globally (Dixon et al. 1994).
5. For further details, see Johnson (1995).
6. Another mechanism for reducing the cost of certain forest capital investments is the creation of tax-exempt bonding authority for 501(c)(3) nonprofit organizations that acquire forestland and manage it subject to a conservation easement. Access to the tax-exempt bond market would reduce capital costs of such acquisitions.

References

Best, Constance, and Michael Jenkins. 1999. *Opportunities for Investment: Capital Markets and Sustainable Forestry.* Boonville, Calif.: Pacific Forest Trust. Chicago: John D. and Catherine T. MacArthur Foundation.

Best, Constance, and Laurie A. Wayburn. 2000. *Accelerating Effective Conservation of U.S. Forests.* Boonville, Calif.: Pacific Forest Trust. San Francisco: Consultative Group on Biological Diversity.

Birch, Thomas W. 1996. "Private Forest-land Owners of the United States, 1994." Resource Bulletin NE-134. Radnor, Pa.: U.S. Department of Agriculture, Forest Service, Northeastern Forest and Experiment Station.

Bliss, John C., Sunil K. Nepal, Robert T. Brooks Jr., and Max D. Larsen. 1994. "Forestry Community or Granfalloon: Do Forest Owners Share the Public's Views?" *Journal of Forestry* 92(9): 6–10.

———. 1997. "In the Mainstream: Environmental Attitudes of Mid-South Forest Owners." *Southern Journal of Applied Forestry* 21(1): 1–7.

Brunson, Mark W., Deborah T. Yarrow, Scott D. Roberts, David C. Guynn Jr., and Michael R. Kuhns. 1996. "Nonindustrial Private Forest Owners and Ecosystem Management: Can They Work Together?" *Journal of Forestry* 94(6): 14–21.

Burgess, R. L., and D. M. Sharpe, eds. 1981. *Forest Island Dynamics in Man-Dominated Landscapes.* New York: Springer-Verlag.

Costanza, Robert, Ralph d'Arge, Rudolf de Groot, Stephen Farber, Monica Grasso, Bruce Hannon, Karin Limburg, Shahid Naeem, Robert V. O'Neill, Jose Paruelo, Robert G. Raskin, Paul Sutton, and Marjan van den Belt. 1997. "The Value of the World's Ecosystem Services and Natural Capital." *Nature* 387(6630): 253–60.

Cordell, H. Ken, John C. Bergstrom, Lawrence A. Hartmann, and Donald B. K. English. 1990. "An Analysis of the Outdoor Recreation and Wilderness Situation in the United States: 1989–2040." General Technical Report RM-189. Fort Collins, Colo.: U.S. Department of Agriculture, Forest Service, Rocky Mountain Forest and Range Experiment Station.

Dixon, R. K., S. Brown, R. A. Houghton, A. M. Solomon, M. C. Trexler, and J. Wisniewski. 1994. "Carbon Pools and Flux of the Global Forest Ecosystems." *Science* 263:185–90.

Fillion, Fern L., James P. Foley, and Andre J. Jacquemot. 1992. "The Economics of Global Ecotourism." Paper presented at the Fourth World Congress on National Parks and Protected Areas. Caracas, Venezuela. 10–21 February.

Harris, L. D. 1984. *The Fragmented Forest: Island Biogeography Theory and the Preservation of Biotic Diversity.* Chicago: University of Chicago Press.

Haynes, Richard W. 1990. "An Analysis of the Timber Situation in the United States: 1989-2040. A Technical Document Supporting the 1989 USDA Forest Service RPA Assessment." General Technical Report RM-199. Fort Collins, Colo: U.S. Department of Agriculture, Forest Service.

Haynes, Richard W., Darius M. Adams, and John R. Mills. 1995. "The 1993 RPA Timber Assessment Update." General Technical Report RM-259. Fort Collins, Colo.: U.S. Department of Agriculture, Forest Service, Rocky Mountain Forest and Range Experiment Station.

Harmon, M. E., and W. K. Ferrell. 1990. "Effects on Carbon Storage of Conversion of Old-Growth Forests to Young Forests." *Science* 247: 699.

Hodge, Sandra S., and L. Southard. 1992. "A Profile of Virginia NIPF Landowners: Results of a 1991 Survey." *Virginia Forests* 47(4): 7–9, 11.

Johnson, Kirk. 1995. "Building Forest Wealth: Incentives For Biodiversity, Landowner Profitability, and Value Added Manufacturing." Seattle: University of Washington, Northwest Policy Center.

National Research Council. 1998. "Forested Landscapes in Perspective: Prospects and Opportunities for Sustainable Management of America's Nonfederal Forests." Committee on Prospects and Opportunities for Sustainable Management of America's Nonfederal Forests. Board on Agriculture. Washington D.C.: National Academy Press.

Newman, David H., and David N. Wear. 1993. "Production Economics of Private Forestry: A Comparison of Industrial and Nonindustrial Forest Owners." *American Journal of Agricultural Economics* 75(3): 674–84.

Noss, Reed F. 1983. "A Regional Landscape Approach to Maintain Diversity." *BioScience* 33(11): 700–706.

Noss, Reed F. 1987. "Protecting Natural Areas in Fragmented Landscapes." *Natural Areas Journal* 7:2–13.

Pacific Forest Trust. 1997. "Cascadia Forest Stewardship Investments: Special Forest Products Business Planning Research." Unpublished report.

Pacific Forest Trust. 1998. "Analysis of Potential Carbon Stores in Pacific Northwest Forests." Unpublished report.

Pacific Forest Trust. 1999. "Changes in On-Site Stores Resulting from Transitions in Silviculture on Forests Managed by Macmillan Bloedel: A Report for the World Resources Institute." On file with the Pacific Forest Trust, Santa Rosa, Calif.

Powell, Douglas S., Joanne L. Faulkner, David R. Darr, Zhiliang Zhu, and Douglas W. MacCleery. 1994. "Forest Resources of the United States, 1992." General Technical Report RM-234 (Revised). Fort Collins, Colo.: U.S. Department of Agriculture, Forest Service, Rocky Mountain Forest and Range Experiment Station.

Schlosser, William E., and Keith A. Blatner. 1994. "Special Forest Products: An Eastside Perspective." Manuscript for the Interior Columbia Basin Ecosystem Management Project. On file with Social and Economic Values Research Program, Pacific Northwest Research Station, Forestry Sciences Laboratory, Portland, Ore.

U.S. Department of Agriculture. 1999. *1997 National Resources Inventory* (Revised 2000). Washington, D.C.: National Resources Conservation Service. Available at http://nhq.nrcs.usda.gov/NRI.1997/.

CHAPTER 12

Land and Livelihoods in the Northern Forest

Deborah Brighton

Until recently, the large areas of unbroken forest in the northern portions of Maine, New Hampshire, Vermont, and New York were not much in the news. The small towns remained small, and the surrounding forest—mostly owned and managed by timber, pulp, and paper companies—remained intact. When large tracts held by Atlas Timber Company, Diamond International Corporation, and Champion International, Inc., went on the market beginning in the 1980s, Northern Forest residents were jolted by the realization that the last remaining large, undeveloped forest areas in the northeastern United States could be suburbanized: subdivided and developed, as in southern New England. Whether one is concerned about future supplies of timber, the health of local forest-based economies, wildlife habitat, outdoor recreation, clean water, or maintaining the region's way of life, the prospect of dividing this land into small lots for development poses a serious threat.

Yet it is still possible to avoid the kind of subdivision that has occurred elsewhere, by separating and redistributing rights to use the land in ways that meet social goals and permit continued management of the forest as a single large tract. An unprecedented collaboration of nonprofit groups, private investors, and government agencies is advancing innovative proposals that call for purchasing large tracts of land, assigning certain rights to public agencies or nonprofit organizations, and then reselling the acreage to private investors at a price based on the remaining subset of rights. To date, such efforts have focused mainly on protecting the land from development, but other social goals can be incorporated as well. In particular, shares in the land can be resold to people who live and work in Northern Forest communities, to provide assets and income to the residents whose median incomes fall well below those elsewhere

227

in the Northeast. To succeed, such a strategy would require a combination of public, private, and philanthropic support. Both timber production and land conservation have long received a great deal of backing from these sources. The main change would be in redirecting this support to promote a restructured ownership of forest assets designed to protect both the forests and the livelihoods of forest-dependent communities.

The Setting

The Northern Forest is a sparsely populated area stretching across northern New York, Vermont, New Hampshire, and Maine. The forest has shaped the character of the rural communities, and it remains integral to the way local residents make ends meet and spend their time. Logging and wood processing pay the bills for many residents of the area, and some of the bills are paid to other people in the community. When fewer trees are cut, not only the loggers but also the shopkeepers, the gas-station owners, and the barbers have fewer dollars in their pockets. Many generations have grown up hunting, fishing, and trapping in the woods, and nearly everyone uses the forest for recreation (U.S. Department of Agriculture 1991). The forest also provides diverse ecological services, as Constance Best discusses in Chapter 11, including clean air, clean water, and wildlife habitat. These benefits extend well beyond the forest's boundaries. Likewise, the conflicts over timber management practices that threaten these ecological services have involved some individuals who have never set foot in the Northern Forest.

Beginning in the 1980s, many forest parcels owned by industry were put on the market. The reasons were various. The first massive land sale resulted from a hostile takeover of a timber company by a foreign firm that had no particular interest in forests. Corporate restructurings brought a new emphasis on short-run timber profitability. This led to land sales because some Northern Forest land was not expected to produce marketable timber for many years, as a result of recent heavy timber cuts in response to good market prices for pulp or to outbreaks of spruce budworm. Other factors that were cited as contributing to lower anticipated returns from forestland included the rising cost of workers' compensation, unfavorable capital gains treatment of timber, high property taxes, environmentalists' opposition to logging and the use of herbicides, and regulatory instability (Whitney 1989; Dobbs and Ober 1995, 124–25).

The land sales alarmed conservationists and loggers alike. They shared a nightmare of southern New England creeping northward and of the land being divided into small parcels to be bought by flatlanders who prefer the bright fall colors of red maples to the sturdy but less flamboyant sugar maples that yield syrup, high-quality lumber, and fuelwood. A federal study echoed these concerns:

> The demand by millions of people living within hours of the Northern Forest to possess a piece of the northern landscape is insatiable. This will insure that eventually every piece of unprotected lakeshore, river frontage and land adjacent to mountain areas will be subdivided, bought and built upon. One only need look to the changes in southern New England over the last 20 years for evidence of these trends. (U.S. Department of Agriculture 1990, 80.)

Many local residents feared that these new owners would "post" the land, barring public access to long-time favorite hunting and fishing spots. Nearly everyone saw drawbacks to the division of land into small parcels with many owners, since such division would make it difficult to guarantee a sustained flow of wood to local mills, to maintain long recreation trails, and to protect the ecosystem.

In 1990, the four state governments created the Northern Forest Lands Council to study the situation and to recommend actions to protect natural resources, local economies, and the quality of life. The council's report, which was four years in the making and was reviewed by more than 3,000 people, concluded:

> The conditions which up to now have conserved the Northern Forest can no longer insure its perpetuation. In our discussions time and again we faced a fundamental conflict—between market-driven efficiency that encourages maximum consumption of resources with the least amount of effort in the shortest time, and society's responsibility to provide future generations with the same benefits we enjoy today.
>
> We believe that until the roots of this conflict are addressed and the economic rules changed so that markets reward long-term sustainability and recognize the worth of well-functioning natural systems, existing market forces will continue to encourage shorter-term exploitation instead of long-term conservation of the Northern Forest. . . .
>
> We believe that to ignore what the Council has discovered about the forces for undesirable change and take no action would be to guarantee an uncertain future for the Northern Forest, one that could lead to break-up of large undeveloped tracts of forest land, a steadily weakening economy, and continuing pressure on finite natural resources. (Northern Forest Lands Council 1994, 11–12.)

A strategy to protect large tracts of land from what the council called the "forces for undesirable change" was developed in a collaboration among federal and state agencies, nonprofit conservation organizations, private foundations, and private investors. When Champion International, Inc., sold 132,000 acres of forest in Vermont in 1999, these groups moved to secure the land. The Conservation Fund, a nonprofit organization, purchased the land. A portion of this land determined by a team of biologists to be especially important for purposes of wildlife habitat, ecological protection, and recreation was then transferred to public ownership: 26,000 acres to the Silvio O. Conte National Wildlife Refuge and 22,000 acres to Vermont's Agency of Natural Resources. On the remaining 84,000 acres, property rights were "unbundled." Using both state and private funds, the Vermont Housing and Conservation Board, the Vermont Land Trust, and The Nature Conservancy acquired easements that protect the land from development, guide its management, and safeguard public access. The Conservation Fund then sold the land with its remaining rights to private investors, who will manage the forest for timber production. All 84,000 acres will remain in one unbroken tract, and the easements will ensure sustainable harvesting practices and the protection of key biological attributes. The price of the resold land was, of course, lower than it would have been had all the property rights remained bundled together. Even so, the pool of potential buyers was limited to those investors with large amounts of "patient" capital. The parcel was big, and because of past harvesting it would not yield substantial timber revenues for quite some time. The Essex Timber Company, which bought the land, considered this purchase an "exceptional opportunity," given its ability to wait for long-term returns (Vermont Land Trust 1999).

Although this transaction ensures that the land will be managed responsibly and will not be developed, it is possible to envision a different pattern of ownership that would serve the needs of forest-dependent communities even better. Rather than reselling land in large parcels to new absentee owners, some forestland could instead be sold to local residents, those who work in the woods and are most directly affected by its management. To avoid the problems of fragmentation, the land could be managed as one large tract, with ownership vested in one or more communities, a local nonprofit organization, or a cooperative. This approach would place covenanted forestland into the hands of people who now have few assets and whose lives are strongly connected to the Northern Forest. Local ownership would ensure that the forest would be managed by people who consider it more than just a financial investment. Such a strategy would further the goal of sustaining the traditional uses of the forest—a goal consistent with the recommendations of the Northern Forest Lands Council and the conservation efforts of state, local, and nonprofit groups—while advancing the additional goal of strengthening local communities and engaging them more directly in the long-term management of the forest.

Both public and private funding would be needed for such a strategy to work. Public funds and tax policies have long been used to support the management of the nation's private forestland, including smaller tracts owned by people who do not make their living from the land. These public subsidies typically have been based on the rationale that the market fails to encourage adequately the owners of these smaller forest tracts to invest in timber production, which is deemed to be a national need (Boyd and Hyde 1989). One result has been an increase in the value of the assets of nonindustrial private forest landowners, many of whom already tend to be relatively affluent. No comparable investment has been made to help lower-income individuals acquire forest assets.

Existing Forestry Subsidies

By the late 1800s, so much forestland in the United States had been cleared, with no expectation of reforestation, that a "timber famine" seemed likely. Because market forces appeared to offer inadequate incentives to undertake the long-term management necessary to avert this famine, Congress passed legislation to acquire National Forest land to "furnish a continuous supply of timber for the use and necessities of citizens of the United States" (16 U.S.C. 475, Organic Administration Act of 1897).

This same logic was used to justify public subsidies for the management of private forestland. In 1924, the Clarke-McNary Act directed the secretary of agriculture to help landowners "through advice, education, demonstrations and other similar means in establishing, renewing, protecting, and managing wood lots, shelter belts, windbreaks, and other valuable forest growth, and in harvesting, utilizing, and marketing the products thereof" (16 U.S.C. 568). This marked the beginning of the public cost-sharing programs that are still in effect today.

In the 1950s, the U.S. Forest Service undertook a fresh appraisal of the ability of the United States to meet its future need for timber and concluded that public support, especially of owners of small parcels, remained crucial:

> Tomorrow the Nation's need for timber will be strikingly greater than today or at any time in the past. We have the potential to meet that need if we fully apply our forestry knowledge and skills promptly, with vigor and determination. . . .
>
> Growth must be increased on industrial and public lands, but unquestionably the key to adequate future timber supplies lies mainly with the 3.4 million farm owners and the miscellaneous

group of 1.1 million "other" private ownerships. Although they own mainly very small tracts of forest land, and their principal interests usually are not timber growing, in the aggregate they control well over half of the Nation's commercial timberland and they must continue to supply a substantial portion of the raw materials for forest industry. . . .

Forestry is not a short-time proposition. Where this Nation stands in timber supply in the year 2000 will depend largely on actions taken during the next two decades. Recent encouraging forestry trends must continue. But this is not enough. Acceleration of these trends is vital, and to a degree that will startle many of us. There are no grounds for complacency. (U.S. Department of Agriculture 1958, ii, 107–9.)

There are several impediments to timber production on small tracts of individually owned forestland. The difficulty of earning a living from woodlots of, say, 50 acres, has made forest management a secondary activity for the owners. The parcels are too small to yield an economically viable harvest each year, so timber income is sporadic. In many cases, management costs incurred today will not produce economic returns until the current owner is long gone. Many owners of small tracts of forestland are more concerned about recreation, privacy, and the resale value of their property than they are about its long-term potential timber value (Birch 1996).

In southern New England, a high proportion of the forest has already been chopped into small parcels. In the mid-1970s, the U.S. Forest Service found that 78 percent of private commercial forestland in Massachusetts, Connecticut, and Rhode Island was owned by individuals and only 16 percent by industrial corporations (Kingsley 1976). About 35 percent of the forest was in parcels smaller than 50 acres, making it difficult to manage the land for timber or wildlife. According to the prevailing wisdom, this fragmentation made government intervention necessary to ensure adequate management.

The northern New England states, with their much larger tracts of forestland, present a different picture. A much smaller proportion of the Northern Forest has been subdivided into small parcels (see Figure 12.1). If the fragmentation of forests jeopardizes the provision of crucial national resources, making government intervention necessary, it may be wiser to redirect some public funds to prevent fragmentation in the first place. The Northern Forest is the only significant area in the Northeast where such redirection is still possible. At the same time, however, many people want to own land, and fragmentation may foster a more democratic pattern of ownership than the concentration of land in the hands of a few. An alternative solution would be to have large tracts of forestland managed as one but owned by many.

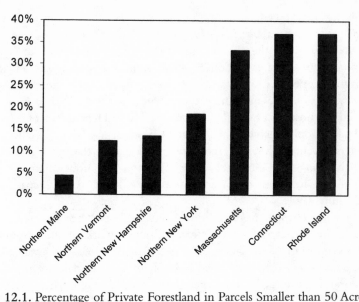

Figure 12.1. Percentage of Private Forestland in Parcels Smaller than 50 Acres.
Sources: Birch (1989) for New Hampshire; Widmann and Birch (1988) for Vermont; Birch
(1983) for New York; Birch (1986) for Maine; Kingsley (1976) for Massachusetts,
Connecticut, and Rhode Island.

Although perhaps falling short of the all-out effort recommended by the
Forest Service in the 1950s, federal and state governments have invested
substantial amounts of public money in private forestland. Over the years,
the emphasis of this involvement has shifted from averting the specter of a
timber famine to promoting sustainable forest stewardship. Government
policies have supported both investment in forest resources and the internalization of ecosystem values. To the extent that these efforts have been
successful, they have increased the value of private assets. Redistribution—
putting assets and income into the hands of lower-income citizens—generally
has not figured among the goals of government intervention in private-
sector forestry.

Government Intervention as Investment

Before the 1970s, the central aim of most public efforts was to protect and
improve the timber supply and enhance the efficiency of timber use. The
emphasis of government programs has shifted somewhat over the years, but
current law still declares that "it is in the national interest for the Secretary [of
Agriculture] to work through and in cooperation with State foresters, or
equivalent State officials, non-governmental organizations, and the private sector

in implementing Federal programs affecting non–Federal forest lands" (16 U.S.C. 2101, Cooperative Forestry Assistance Act of 1978).

One element of the government strategy for dealing with private forest landowners has been education. Federally funded extension foresters in every state give workshops, write and distribute information, conduct demonstrations, and visit landowners. In 1979, the Forest Service published 1,954 works, "including those of a how-to-do-it nature" (U.S. Department of Agriculture 1981a, 40). Topics include how to calculate stumpage values, how to conduct a timber inventory, how to recognize and deal with the spittlebug, chainsaw safety, building solar kilns, collecting soil water in porous ceramic cups, and fertilizing Christmas trees with sewage effluent (U.S. Department of Agriculture 1981b).

A second element has been direct technical assistance in forest management. State foresters, mostly federally funded, work on the ground with landowners. In the early days, these foresters marked trees and arranged timber sales. Since the 1970s, they have devoted more time to helping landowners understand what they own, what they could do, and where to turn for assistance.

A third element of the strategy has been to make timber production more profitable by reducing the income tax levied on the profits. From 1944 to 1986, income from timber harvesting was treated as a capital gain, with only 40 percent of its value taxed as income. The Government Accounting Office (GAO) estimated that in the fiscal years 1976–1980, the capital gains tax treatment of timber resulted in a benefit to the landowners amounting to $1.6 billion (U.S. Government Accounting Office 1981, 36).

A fourth element has been direct financial incentives and subsidies for forest management. For example, federal monies are available to match private funds in paying for timber stand improvement, reforestation, forest road building, and the construction of ponds. Some of the best cross-country skiing trails in New England wind their way along forest roads through plantations of red pine and Norway spruce, ending on the banks of a scenic pond—all cofinanced by the government's cost-sharing programs.

In the 1970s, government priorities began to shift. The public now seemed more concerned about environmental protection than about the prospect of a timber famine. Perhaps the most visible indication of this changing focus occurred on the day when the U.S. Forest Service mascot Smokey the Bear was joined by Woodsy Owl, "a fanciful owl, who wears slacks, a belt, and a Robin Hood style hat with a feather, and who furthers the slogan 'Give a Hoot, Don't Pollute'" (16 U.S.C. 580, Woodsy Owl–Smokey Bear Act of 1974). Although the focus of public programs on private land has been slow to change, in the Northeast there is clearly less emphasis now on timber and more on ecological conditions. A 1999 Forest Service brochure states that the mission of its programs on private land is "to ensure that landowners apply environmental and economic resource management principles to benefit themselves, future landowners, and society" (U.S. Department of Agriculture 1999, 2). Among the environmental objectives it lists are biodiversity and water quality.

The Forest Service pursues these objectives through two main programs that aid nonindustrial private forest landowners in the United States. The Forest Stewardship Program focuses on the preparation of management plans for private land. The complementary Stewardship Incentive Program offers cost-sharing for management activities prescribed by these plans. The landowner generally pays 25 percent of the cost and the government funds 75 percent. From fiscal years 1990 to 1999, the federal government allocated $15.6 million to nonindustrial private forestland owners for these two programs in the Northern Forest states, and the Stewardship Incentive Program received another $7 million in state funds.

Government Intervention for Internalization

As Woodsy Owl joined Smokey the Bear, development came to be seen as at least as big a threat to the future of U.S. forests as forest fires. Increased development threatened the future of the working forest in two ways: first, the land was worth more to developers than to timber growers; and second, the resulting increases in the market value of land led to higher property tax bills, making timber even less profitable.

New public programs have 'emerged in an effort to alter this financial picture and protect land from development. Most states have modified their property tax laws so that forestland meeting certain requirements is taxed on the value of its productive capacity, rather than on its market value. Maine, New Hampshire, and Vermont calculate the taxable value of forestland by capitalizing the annual income that can be derived from forest management, and New York simply assesses eligible land at a percentage of its market value.[1] All four states assess penalties on owners who develop land that receives preferential tax treatment. Although not explicitly designed as payments for the private production of public benefits, these tax programs do attempt to compensate landowners for forgoing development. In a sense, the public is thus renting some sticks in the bundle of private property rights.

Other federal, state, and nonprofit programs purchase development rights, permanently removing the right to develop the land. Land that is held or resold with perpetual conservation easements no longer can be subdivided into lots or clear-cut for quick cash. Society pays for this transformation from land as an unrestricted commodity to land as part of a forest system, by paying the landowner the difference in value. Since 1992, the federal Forest Legacy

Program has spent about $11 million in the Northern Forest to purchase development rights; conservation easements; or, in some cases, all rights to forestland. At the end of 1998, the program had protected about 60,000 acres within the Northern Forest. State and private efforts have provided matching funds and have purchased conservation easements on other parcels. Altogether, 130,000 acres have been conserved, and projects are under way to protect another 1.3 million acres (Northern Forest Alliance 1999).

Distributional Effects of Government Intervention

Government interventions often contain some provisions designed to ensure an equitable distribution of economic benefits. The federal Stewardship Investment Program, for example, does not offer cost-sharing support to people who own more than 1,000 acres, presumably attempting to direct its limited funds to owners who are less able to pay for improved management on their own.

In general, however, redistribution has not been a major aim of government interventions in private forestry. When the GAO reviewed the capital gains treatment of timber in 1981, it reiterated an earlier finding that the tax subsidy benefited industrial and large forest landowners much more than landowners with smaller holdings. "The tax subsidy program reverses the pattern of most direct subsidy programs," the GAO (1981, 14) concluded, "because it favors the large integrated timber company and gives almost nothing to the small woodlot farmer." In a more comprehensive study, Boyd and Hyde (1989, 278) analyzed the full range of government interventions in forestry in the United States and concluded that

> the distributive effects are the opposite of what US society gener-
> ally prefers. . . . Wealthier landowners, higher-wage employees,
> and Canadian producers gain from these interventions. Small
> private producers, lower-wage employees, US consumers, and the
> public treasury bear the burdens of these interventions.

In general, public programs investing money in forestry on private lands in the Northeast are biased toward higher-income individuals, mainly for the simple reason that forest landowners are wealthier than average citizens. In Vermont, for example, about 85 percent of nonindustrial private forestland owners have household incomes exceeding the state's median.[2] Similarly, when Esseks and Mouton (2000, 32) surveyed the private forestland owners nationwide who were participating in the Forest Stewardship Program in 1998–1999, they found that "while the Census Bureau estimated the median household income nationally for 1997 to be $37,303, the medians for the same year reported by our four samples of FSP participants were all in the range of $50,000 to $75,000."

As Northern Forest land is sold by timber companies, it is likely to be purchased by people who are wealthier than average, following the pattern of nonindustrial ownership of forestland elsewhere in New England. Moreover, there are indications that the difference between the incomes of forest landowners and of nonowners is widening. In a recent study of the ownership of forestland in the northern United States, Birch (1996, 5) found that "in general, the 'new' individual private forest-land owner is younger, better educated, and earns more than the owner of a decade ago," while at the same time, "there has been a substantial decrease in the percentage of owners in 'blue collar' occupations and in the proportion of acreage held by these owners." In the sparsely populated Northern Forest area, a substantial percentage of the potential future landowners are likely to be absentee. If present trends continue, much of the Northern Forest ultimately will be owned by the recreation industry or by nonresidents for investments or second homes, and only a small percentage of the owners will be year-round residents.

Protecting Forestlands and Livelihoods: Alternative Approaches

Ensuring an equitable distribution of land ownership was an important concern in the early history of this nation. Shocked by the extremes of wealth in France, Thomas Jefferson wrote to James Madison in 1785:

> The earth is given as a common stock for man to labour and live on. If, for the encouragement of industry, we allow it to be appropriated, we must take care that other employment be furnished to those excluded from the appropriation. If we do not the fundamental right to labour the earth returns to the unemployed. It is too soon yet in our country to say that every man who cannot find employment but who can find uncultivated land, shall be at liberty to cultivate it, paying a moderate rent. But it is not too soon to provide by every possible means that as few as possible shall be without a little portion of land. The small landholders are the most precious part of a state. (Jefferson 1950 [1785], 682.)

Whereas Jefferson saw private property as a cornerstone of democracy, today the term "private property rights" is often interpreted by conservationists as a code phrase for the presumption that the owner can abuse the land regardless of the effects on others or on the environment. Many recent conservation efforts have been directed at transferring land away from private owners and

into public ownership. Yet some conservationists, among them the author
Wendell Berry, have expressed hope that private ownership of land—
especially in the hands of local residents—can foster social and ecological
responsibility:

> To say that the right of private property has often been used to
> protect individuals and even global corporations in their greed is
> not to say that it cannot secure individuals in an appropriate eco-
> nomic share in their country and in a consequent economic and
> political independence, just as Thomas Jefferson thought it could.
> That is the political justification of the right of private property.
> There is also, I believe, an ecological justification. If landed prop-
> erties are democratically divided and properly scaled, and if family
> security in these properties can be preserved over a number of
> generations, then we will greatly increase the possibility of authentic
> cultural adaptation to local homelands. Not only will we make
> more apparent to successive generations the necessary identity
> between the health of human communities and the health of local
> ecosystems, but we will also give people the best motives for care-
> taking and we will call into service the necessary local intelligence
> and imagination. (Berry 1995, 49–50.)

In the Northern Forest, local ownership of forestland has several potential
benefits. Because local owners are likely to be more sensitive to the needs of
their neighbors and more invested in the well-being of their communities,
they could help to protect regional economies from the boom-and-bust cycles
characteristic of absentee ownership. Local ownership also could foster a forest
economy that is more diverse and profitable than the feed-the-mill economy.
Resident owners might be more willing and able to protect the forestland by
monitoring harvesting practices and recreational uses. Finally, local ownership
would produce income for residents and broaden their participation in the
local economy and ecology. At the same time, however, there are potential
drawbacks to local ownership. There is no guarantee that local owners will be
good managers. Fragmentation of land-use decisions would pose problems for
ecological integrity. And if local owners cannot obtain adequate returns from
careful timber harvesting, they too may be tempted or forced to overcut,
subdivide, or develop their forests.

An alternative approach would be to vest ownership of a large tract of land
in the hands of many people, under unified management. In principle, a
community or a cooperative could buy the tract with a loan and eventually
repay the loan with returns from the timber. If development rights to the land
have been removed via an easement, the purchase price for the land should be
commensurate with its value for long-term timber production.

Such an approach faces substantial obstacles at present. Some efforts are now under way to bring environmentally responsible investments to the Northern Forest, but little is being done to promote a democratic distribution of land ownership. There are no established financial models or mechanisms for such a strategy, and even if a suitable tract were to appear on the market, there are currently no organized groups prepared to take advantage of the opportunity. Moreover, low-income communities often lack the economic ability to undertake long-term investments, and projects such as these may not produce much income for many years.

Alternative Models of Management

A few innovative efforts are tackling some of these problems. As Constance Best mentions in Chapter 11, in rural Virginia and Tennessee, The Nature Conservancy, working with local landowners, set up the Clinch Valley Forest Bank with the aim of sustainable forest management. Landowners voluntarily "deposit," in perpetuity, the right to manage and harvest trees on their land, and the bank then manages all the land to ensure a predictable flow of wood to local mills. The bank pays the landowners annual dividends based on the value of their deposits. The landowner can choose to withdraw the cash value of the deposit—in effect, selling the land to the bank—but not the land itself (Clinch Valley Forest Bank 1998). By grouping small parcels together, this approach spreads risk, gets better prices, and feeds smoothly into the local economy. At the same time, unified management helps to maintain wildlife habitat, recreation trails, and ecological diversity across property boundary lines.

In Vermont, a nonprofit organization called Vermont Family Forests promotes the cultivation of family-owned forests for ecological, economic, and social benefits. The organization targets what Wendell Berry (1995, 57) identifies as the two great ruiners of private lands: ignorance and economic constraint. The organization undertakes a variety of programs to educate landowners and the general public about the value of sustainable forest management. Using the combined clout of its members, it secures a better timber-market position than they would have individually. To ensure that the organization's marketing success does not prompt overcutting, the management practices of all members must be certified. Unlike the Clinch Valley Forest Bank, the owners retain full ownership of their land and can remove it at any time.

Neither of these models can be easily transposed to the Northern Forest, where local residents do not currently own the forestland and lack the "patient" capital necessary to buy it. In addition, most parcels that come onto the market are too large for local residents to purchase. Both models, however, suggest useful mechanisms to aggregate smaller ownerships so as to promote economic viability and sustainable forest management.

The redistribution of forestland in the Northern Forest would require a significant package of funding and other support. Some philanthropic or public funding for initial purchase of the land and/or conservation easements is certainly necessary. Such lands will have to be reconfigured into parcels of appropriate size with modified property rights, to be sold at a lower price reflecting the value of the remaining rights. Community-based nonprofit organizations or cooperatives must be formed to coordinate the purchase of land and/or the distribution of shares. These organizations will need to be funded by deferred loans or partial grants until the land is capable of producing sufficient economic returns.

This approach draws on the land-banking model, in which land is purchased and then reconfigured and redistributed to serve social goals. In this model, some land is retained by state, federal, or private conservation organizations to be maintained as wilderness, wildlife habitat, or recreation areas; some is resold with all its rights intact; and some is resold with easements and management restrictions. This land-bank strategy could be adapted to resell at least some of the land to local residents, thereby serving not only ecological goals but social and equity goals as well. To do so, two key mechanisms would have to be grafted onto current practices: the creation of organizations to manage the process, and the provision of initial funding to help local residents who do not have "patient" capital to acquire the assets.

Conclusion

Over the years, considerable public monies have been invested in increasing the timber value of forest assets for wealthy landowners and, more recently, in promoting ecologically sound stewardship by these same private owners. Federal and state government investments in education, technical assistance, cost-sharing, and tax incentives have supported these goals. In the case of environmental objectives, these public investments have been complemented by considerable resources from philanthropic and nonprofit organizations. As the Northern Forest confronts the threat of fragmentation and development, a compelling case can be made for broadening these social objectives to embrace the ownership of forest assets by the residents of forest-dependent communities. In a nation founded on the vision of a democratic society, there is ample justification for deploying public and philanthropic resources to this dimension of natural-asset building, too.

Notes

1. This value generally exceeds the income-producing value in the southern part of the state, but land values are low enough in the Northern Forest that this method probably serves its intended purpose.

2. Based on Widmann and Birch (1988, 41) and information provided by the Vermont Department of Taxes.

References

Berry, Wendell. 1995. *Another Turn of the Crank*. Washington, D.C.: Counterpoint.

Birch, Thomas W. 1983. *The Forest-Land Owners of New York*. Resource Bulletin NE-78. Broomall, Pa.: U.S. Department of Agriculture, Forest Service, Northeastern Forest Experiment Station.

———. 1986. *The Forest-land Owners of Maine, 1982*. Resource Bulletin NE-90. Broomall, Pa.: U.S. Department of Agriculture, Forest Service, Northeastern Forest Experiment Station.

———. 1989. *The Forest-land Owners of New Hampshire, 1983*. Resource Bulletin NE-108. Broomall, Pa.: U.S. Department of Agriculture, Forest Service. Northeastern Forest Experiment Station.

———. 1996. *Private Forest-Land Owners of the United States, 1994*. Radnor, Pa.: U.S. Department of Agriculture, Forest Service. Northeastern Forest Experiment Station.

Boyd, Roy G., and William F. Hyde. 1989. *Forestry Sector Intervention: The Impacts of Public Regulation on Social Welfare*. Ames: Iowa State University Press.

Clinch Valley Forest Bank. 1998. *Virginia Chapter Fact Sheet*. Abingdon, Va.: The Nature Conservancy.

Dobbs, David, and Richard Ober. 1995. *The Northern Forest*. White River Junction, Vt.: Chelsea Green Publishing Company.

Esseks, J. Dixon, and Robert J. Mouton. 2000. *Evaluating the Forest Stewardship Program Through a National Survey of Participating Forest Land Owners*. DeKalb: The Center for Governmental Studies of Northern Illinois University.

Jefferson, Thomas. 1950 [1785]. *The Papers of Thomas Jefferson*. Vol. 8. Edited by Julian P. Boyd. Princeton: Princeton University Press.

Kingsley, Neal P. 1976. *The Forest-Land Owners of Southern New England*. Resource Bulletin NE-41. Upper Darby, Pa.: U.S. Department of Agriculture, Forest Service, Northeastern Forest Experiment Station.

Northern Forest Alliance. 1999. *Investing in the Northern Forest: Fiscal Year 2000 Appropriation Priorities*. Montpelier, Vt.: Northern Forest Alliance.

Northern Forest Lands Council. 1994. *Finding Common Ground: Conserving the Northern Forest*. Concord, N.H.: Northern Forest Lands Council.

U.S. Department of Agriculture. 1958. *Timber Resources for America's Future*. Forest Service. Forest Resource Report No. 14. Washington, D.C.: U.S. Government Printing Office.

U.S. Department of Agriculture. 1981a. *Report of the Forest Service, FY 1980*. Washington, D.C.: U.S. Forest Service.

U.S. Department of Agriculture. 1981b. *List of Publications, 1981*. St. Paul, Minn.: U.S. Forest Service, North Central Forest Experiment Station.

U.S. Department of Agriculture. 1986. *The Timber Industries of New Hampshire and Vermont: A Periodic Assessment of Timber Output*. Resource Bulletin NE-89. Broomall, Pa.: U.S. Forest Service, Northeastern Station.

U.S. Department of Agriculture. 1990. *Northern Forest Lands Study.* Rutland, Vt.: U.S. Forest Service.

U.S. Department of Agriculture. 1991. *Northern Forest Lands: Resident Attitudes and Resource Use.* Research Paper NE-653. Radnor, Pa.: U.S. Forest Service, Northeastern Forest Experiment Station.

U.S. Department of Agriculture. 1999. *Forest Stewardship Program: '99 Status Report.* Newton Square, Pa.: Northeastern Area State and Private Forestry.

U.S. Government Accounting Office. 1981. *New Means of Analysis Required for Policy Decisions Affecting Private Sector Forestry.* Gaithersburg, Md.: U.S. Government Accounting Office.

Vermont Land Trust. 1999. "Champion Lands Have New Owners." Press release. Montpelier, Vt.: Vermont Land Trust.

Whitney, Robert H. 1989. "Forces for Change in Forest Land Ownership and Use: The Large Landowners' Situation." In *Conserving the North Woods: Issues in Public and Private Ownership of Forested Lands in Northern New England and New York,* edited by Clark S. Binkley and Perry R. Hagenstein. New Haven: Yale School of Forestry and Environmental Studies.

Widmann, Richard H., and Thomas W. Birch. 1988. *Forest-Land Owners of Vermont.* Resource Bulletin NE-102. Broomall, Pa.: U.S. Department of Agriculture. U.S. Forest Service, Northeastern Forest Experiment Station.

CHAPTER 13

Community-Based Stewardship: Reinvesting in Public Forests and Forest Communities

Cecilia Danks

Forest communities—small rural communities tied economically and culturally to nearby forested landscapes—often have high rates of poverty despite the wealth in natural resources around them. Community-based forest stewardship initiatives offer the possibility of addressing both environmental degradation and local poverty by reconfiguring how work is structured and how forestry incomes are distributed. By creating new, higher-skilled jobs in forest communities, and by making them available to local businesses and residents, federal land management agencies can reduce both poverty and their own costs. The U.S. Forest Service's change in emphasis from timber production to ecosystem management creates new opportunities to move in this direction.

Public Forest Land and Forest Communities

The U.S. Forest Service manages the 187 million acres of forests nationwide, land that is publicly owned by the people of the United States.[1] These forest-lands are expected to produce a wide range of goods and services. The original purposes of the national forest reserves, as stated in the Organic Administration Act of 1897 (16 U.S.C. 475), were to preserve forests, maintain water flows, and provide a continuous supply of timber (Dana and Fairfax 1980, 62). Additional land uses, including grazing, recreation, and wildlife and fish conservation, have been authorized by subsequent legislation. The Forest Service is funded by annual Congressional appropriations. Revenues from timber sales, which amounted to $224 million in 1999 (U.S. Department of

Agriculture 1999), are remitted to the U.S. Treasury, as are most other Forest Service revenues.

Public forest management presents distinctive possibilities for reducing poverty through natural-asset building. Across the United States, forest counties tend to have higher poverty rates than nonforest counties.[2] In this respect the United States is similar to other countries, where forest resources are controlled by national governments or other powerful entities and only a small share of their benefits are captured in local forest communities (see, for example, Peluso 1992). A natural-asset-based approach to addressing poverty in such communities would strive to increase the share of forest benefits that flow to poor local residents.

At present, the two most significant benefits for forest communities are revenues to local governments from forest receipts and employment in the harvesting and processing of forest products. Additional benefits include income and employment from tourism and recreational concessions (such as ski areas) and the local multiplier effects of forest-related income. Apart from these economic benefits, national forests also supply a number of ecosystem services, including watershed protection, clean air, wildlife habitat, biological diversity, and scenic beauty, for which markets do not capture economic value (see Chapter 11).

As public assets, national forests are managed to produce revenues for the federal government and to provide public goods such as water, wildlife, and scenery for the benefit of the nation as a whole. Legally, the national public has as much say as do local citizens in shaping forest management decisions. Some rural counties have pushed for local control of federal lands, but suggestions that some groups should have more rights to national forests than others have generally met with strong opposition by competing claimants. Some of the proponents of greater local rights to national forests are associated with the wise-use movement in the West, under the guise of which industry and local elites have sought to obtain greater control of federal land to pursue conventional resource-extraction activities, especially grazing, mining, and timber harvesting. Rather than proposing to reassign the rights to national forest resources, it is more fruitful to talk about redistributing access to the benefits from national forests.

Under federal legislation, forest counties generally have received 25 percent of the gross revenues from national forests within their boundaries to support local schools, roads, and other county services (Dana and Fairfax 1980).[3] Based on the premise that local governments should be compensated for the fact that public forestlands are exempt from property taxes, federal law recognizes the right of forest counties to a special share in the flow of benefits from national forests. In 1999, the Forest Service disbursed $208 million to counties, with the Pacific Northwest states receiving the largest payments: Oregon, $81 million;

California, \$29 million; and Washington, \$26 million (U.S. Department of Agriculture 2000).[4] The importance of these funds to county budgets varies widely. In sparsely populated western counties with large, timbered national forests, these payments are often a substantial part of county budgets. For example, Trinity County, California, received \$4.6 million in national forest receipts in 1998, roughly one-seventh of the county's total budget of \$33.7 million.

In 1999, Congress considered ways to "decouple" forest receipts from the amount paid to counties. These efforts were supported by legislators and environmentalists who were concerned that the county payments generated political pressure for unsustainably high timber harvests. An opposing coalition of the timber industry, local governments, and school districts, backed by many western legislators, argued that decoupling would lead the Forest Service to abandon its commitment to forest communities. The Secure Rural Schools and Community Self-Determination Act (PL-106-393) was passed in 2000 to address both of these concerns. It stabilizes funding to forest counties while promoting forest restoration activities that are implemented in a way that benefits local communities.

In addition to county payments, forest communities benefit from employment opportunities in the forest and in the wood-processing industry. Because of the boom-and-bust cycles that have characterized timber harvesting, it has long been argued that national forests should contribute to the stability of local communities by supplying a steady flow of timber (Dana and Fairfax 1980, 332). Forest Service planners generally have assumed that timber sales automatically result in local jobs and thereby serve community needs. The connection between timber and local jobs, however, is no longer as strong as it once was. Several recent studies have shown little relationship between timber output and economic well-being in the Pacific Northwest (see, for example, Niemi et al. 1999). In California forest counties, the timber harvest is not significantly correlated with either employment or poverty rates (Hoffmann and Fortmann 1996). In some cases, this lack of correlation may reflect the economic diversity of many California forest counties, but even in a county composed exclusively of small forest communities, such as the one I discuss below, there has been little correlation between the timber harvest and employment or poverty rates since the mid-1980s (Danks and Jungwirth 1998).

In practice, then, simply selling timber from the national forests does not necessarily generate local jobs. Employment opportunities—whether in the woods, in processing industries, or in recreation—are mediated through the marketplace and also, in the case of public land management, through federal contracting rules. Current Forest Service contracting practices limit access to work in the woods, as illustrated in the case study below, resulting in unequal access to jobs in national forests. Recent changes in the wood products industry have exacerbated this problem: as sawmills modernize, they employ fewer workers per board foot of timber, and processing facilities are becoming increasingly centralized in towns outside of the forest areas (Stewart 1993).

The Shift from Timber Production to Ecosystem Management

The U.S. Forest Service is now in the process of changing its management emphasis from "commodity production" (that is, producing marketable outputs) to "ecosystem management" (Forest Ecosystem Management Assessment Team 1993; Committee of Scientists 1999). This shift provides an opportunity to change how work is structured and thus to address the employment needs of forest-dependent communities while improving environmental health. Although the Forest Service has had a mandate from its inception to manage national forests for multiple benefits, as noted above, timber production has been the primary goal in most western forests. Ecosystem management represents a very different philosophy: it seeks simultaneously to maintain the functional integrity of the ecosystem, to conserve biological diversity, and to integrate broader social goals. This approach requires not only extensive scientific information and monitoring but also—if it truly is to reflect social objectives—inclusive processes for decision-making.[5]

In ecosystem management, commodity outputs are regarded not as the overriding objective but rather as by-products of other management goals such as restoring forest structure and reducing fire risks. As a result, timber harvests typically are expected to be lower than with traditional timber-centered management and considerably lower than the historically high harvest levels of the 1980s. For example, in the spotted owl region of Washington, Oregon, and California, federal forests are expected to produce roughly 1.1 billion board feet of timber per year under the new ecosystem management strategy, compared to 2.4 billion board feet per year in the early 1990s and 4.6 billion board feet per year in the 1980s (Forest Ecosystem Management Assessment Team 1993).

The smaller timber harvests under ecosystem management have reduced revenues to county governments and led to losses in traditional timber industry jobs. Under the Northwest Forest Plan discussed below, timber industry employment was projected to drop from about 145,000 jobs in 1990 to 120,000 in 2003 (Forest Ecosystem Management Assessment Team 1993). The socioeconomic impacts fall unevenly throughout the region. Where there are alternative job opportunities, such as in larger towns with more diverse economies or in towns within commuting distance of expanding job markets, the decline in timber jobs has had little impact on overall employment rates.[6] But in areas with few alternative employment opportunities, the loss of timber jobs can hit not only unemployed workers and their families but also local stores, schools, and community organizations.

Depending on how it is implemented, the transition to ecosystem management could *increase* local employment despite the lower timber volumes and could improve conditions in both forests and forest-dependent communities. Ecosystem management activities require not only a light touch with heavy equipment but also skilled labor to work in data collection, mapping, watershed restoration, wildlife surveying, habitat enhancement, fuels reduction, and prescribed burning. Moreover, these new jobs could be more stable and better paid than traditional forestry occupations.

Because the emerging work opportunities in ecosystem management are so new, they have not yet been "allocated," and therefore there is an opportunity for them to be appropriated by and for low-income forest workers and residents of forest-dependent communities. The very fact that traditional forest employment is being reduced by the shift to ecosystem management gives displaced workers and forest communities a justifiable claim to these work opportunities and may help create the political impetus needed to ensure that they get a fair share of the new jobs. Access to job training and employment can thereby provide an avenue for access to the benefits of natural assets.

The Northwest Forest Plan: A Case Study of Trinity County, California

The Northwest Forest Plan, initiated in 1994, was an early effort to make the transition from commodity production to ecosystem management, while incorporating strong concern for the effects on community well-being. The plan was developed by the U.S. Forest Service and the Bureau of Land Management in response to lawsuits by environmentalists seeking to curtail the cutting of old-growth forests. Historically, heavy timber harvesting, road building, fire suppression, and the conversion of forestland to nonforest uses have dramatically altered forest ecosystems in the Pacific Northwest, putting a number of species at risk of extinction. In 1991, a federal court decision halted all timber sales on public land in the territory of the northern spotted owl, an animal considered an "indicator species" of the health of old-growth forests. The owl's territory included the forests of western Washington, western Oregon, and northwestern California. The decline of the spotted owl was seen as evidence that many species, and the integrity of the forest ecosystem as a whole, were in trouble. The court ordered the federal government to devise a comprehensive management plan that would protect all species, before the Forest Service could sell any more timber from these lands.

The Northwest Forest Plan was developed to meet the criteria for lifting the court injunction. The plan instituted "ecosystem management" not only to promote the survival of the spotted owl but also to protect the overall integrity of "late successional" or old-growth forests, while maintaining sustainable levels of timber production. Meeting these goals required a sharp decline in timber harvest. At the same time, the plan called for increased involvement of local communities and for special efforts to address their socioeconomic needs, especially in areas designated in the plan as Adaptive Management Areas (AMAs). These are described as places "to learn how to manage on an ecosystem basis in terms of both technical and social challenges," and "are intended to be prototypes of how forest communities might be sustained" (U.S. Department of Agriculture 1994, D-4).

As the site of the Hayfork AMA, Trinity County, California, has been a focus of these new policies. Trinity is one of the most timber-dependent counties in the region, with no large towns, cities, or major transportation corridors to add economic diversity. County-level data for Trinity County thus reflect the realities of many forest-dependent communities in the West.[7] In recent years, the county's economy has been deeply affected by the transition from commodity production to ecosystem management. Redistribution of employment and reinvestment in natural assets could affect Trinity County's low-income residents in measurable ways.

The Setting

Trinity County is sparsely populated, with about 13,200 people living in an area of approximately 3,000 square miles. Its three largest towns are Weaverville (population 3,200), Hayfork (population 2,600), and Lewiston (population 2,550); all other towns have fewer than 1,000 residents. After a moderate influx of new residents in the 1970s, the county's population has remained fairly constant, declining slightly in recent years. Trinity has higher poverty and unemployment rates than most other California counties. Statewide, 12.5 percent of residents were below the poverty line in 1989 (U.S. Department of Commerce 1992). Trinity County's poverty rate was 19 percent, and in the Hayfork community the rate was 30 percent. In the 1980s, the poverty rate in Trinity County rose by 62 percent, the largest increase in any California county (U.S. Department of Commerce 1993). Poverty in the county continued to increase in the 1990s, despite California's strong economic growth. One indicator of this trend is that participation in the free and reduced-cost school lunch program, a proxy for low-income families with children, steadily increased: more than half of the county's schoolchildren now qualify for the program.[8]

Trinity County was not always poor. In 1969 and 1979, the county's poverty rate was roughly comparable to the state and national rates (U.S. Department of Commerce 1983). Much of the increase in poverty since 1980 is attributable to a decline in timber jobs, exacerbated by the economic recession of the early 1980s and the lack of employment alternatives for local residents. The timber-market slump of the early 1980s caused widespread layoffs and mill closures throughout the region. Two of Trinity County's four industrial sawmills closed permanently in that decade, and a third shut down in 1996. Throughout the 1990s, unemployment rates in Trinity County have been about twice the California average. In 1998, for example, the county's unemployment rate was 13.0 percent, compared to 5.9 percent statewide (California Employment Development Department 1999). Monthly data show that unemployment is highly seasonal in Trinity County, with peaks in the winter months and rates closer to the statewide average in the summer (see Figure 13.1). Forest dependence, in both the timber and recreation industries, explains this strong seasonality.

The rich forest resources of Trinity County are concentrated in the hands of a few land managers. The federal government administers more than 70 percent of the county's land area, and approximately 99 percent of the private timberland in the county is held by nonresident owners (County Assessor Maps 1996).[9] Apart from local commerce and services (shops, schools, and government agencies), there is little economic activity, public or private, that is not directly related to national forest management. Agricultural and mining income is negligible, although these were important economic sectors before World War II. The timber industry accounted for more than 30 percent of

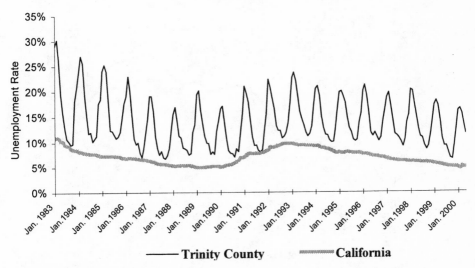

Figure 13.1. Monthly Unemployment Rates, Trinity County and California, January 1983 to January 2000.
Source: California Employment Development Division, Labor Market Information.

employment in the late 1980s, making Trinity one of the two most forest-dependent counties in the Pacific Northwest by this measure (Greber 1994).

Trinity's only remaining sawmill is in Weaverville, the county seat. The permanent closure of the Hayfork mill in 1996 was a particularly heavy blow, since it had been the largest employer in the county.[10] Even before the mill's closure, many of Hayfork's residents lived in poverty. In 1989, 30 percent of individuals and nearly 50 percent of children lived below the poverty line (U.S. Department of Commerce 1993). By 1999, 79 percent of Hayfork elementary school students were in the free and reduced-cost lunch program, up from 52 percent in 1989 (Trinity County Office of Education 1999).

Despite the high degree of economic dependence on the national forests, measures of local well-being in Trinity County have not closely tracked timber harvest levels in the past three decades. Poverty, as measured by the number of families receiving Aid to Families with Dependent Children (AFDC), generally increased in the 1970s and 1980s, despite fluctuations in the timber harvest (see Figure 13.2).[11] The number of manufacturing jobs fluctuated with the timber harvests from 1972 to 1982, but the correlation has been weaker since then, due in part to the increased mobility of logs in the timber industry. Simply cutting more timber no longer guaranteed that there would be more local jobs, as processing facilities have been centralized along major transportation corridors in nonforest communities (Stewart 1993). From 1991 to 1996, buyers headquartered outside of Trinity County purchased 93 percent of the timber sold from the Trinity National Forest. Although some local

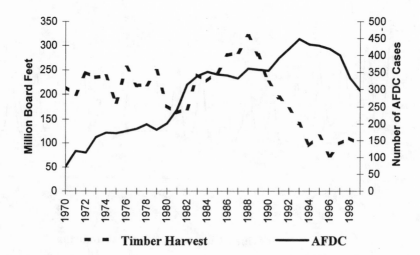

Figure 13.2. Timber harvest and AFDC Cases, Trinity County, 1970–1999.
Sources: California State Board of Equalization and California Department of Social Services.

contractors were hired to cut trees and some of the logs were milled within the county, the dominance of outside purchasers meant that decision-making resided elsewhere and that most of the profits left the county.

A similar pattern holds for service contracts. The Forest Service hires private firms to provide reforestation, wildlife surveys, inventories, road work, construction, and other services. From 1991 to 1996, Trinity County contractors received only 6 percent of the total value of all service contracts and only 3 percent of the value of reforestation and restoration contracts (McDermott and Danks 1997).

Access to Work Opportunities

Why did Trinity County firms receive such small percentages of both timber sales and service contracts? One reason is that local businesses are relatively small.[12] The contracts acquired by Trinity County bidders were generally much smaller than those acquired by out-of-county contractors. For example, the average size of timber harvests awarded to Trinity County bidders was 102,000 board feet, compared to 1,259,000 board feet for out-of-county bidders. The majority of Forest Service timber sales were packaged in contracts that exceeded the capacity of Trinity County bidders. A related barrier is the local firms' lack of access to the capital required to undertake larger projects. Crew size is also important. Local contractors tended to bid on work that was offered regularly and in small packages, creating a predictable and steady flow of work, or for contracts with long time windows that allowed them to use small crews to complete the work.

These limits on work opportunities in national forests are not determined solely by market forces. They are also the result of government procedures that package timber and service contracts in ways that effectively exclude local contractors. Only a small fraction of these contracts are now targeted for very small businesses[13]. In timber harvesting, local purchasers are most competitive in sales set aside for businesses with fewer than 25 employees through the "special salvage timber sales" program, but only 6 percent of the total volume was sold in this program. Local service contractors have bid most successfully on work offered as "Requests for Quotes," which had a maximum size of $25,000 in the early 1990s and simply required that the bidder submit a dollar quote. They have not been successful in bidding on work offered as "Requests for Proposals" (RFPs), which tend to be very large packages and require a detailed technical and price proposal, necessitating substantial office skills and up-front work for a proposal that might not succeed. Unfortunately for Trinity County contractors, service contracts increasingly are being offered in large packages as RFPs.

If local firms and residents have not been getting the work, who has? The majority of timber sold from the Trinity National Forest is purchased by sawmills that can capitalize large-scale operations. Increasingly, these mills are located in California's Central Valley, in towns and cities on major transportation corridors with substantial labor pools. Highly skilled service-contract work (for example, archeological studies, environmental impact assessments, and Geographic Information System mapping) generally has gone to consulting firms based in large urban centers. Low-skilled work such as tree planting, which currently makes up the vast majority of service-contract work, is generally provided by businesses from cities in the central valleys of Oregon and California, where contractors tap agricultural labor markets to recruit work crews that travel hundreds of miles to camp out in forest areas for a few weeks at a time. These large mobile crews enjoy a distinct advantage when the work is packaged in large contracts with short time frames for completion, when contract work is offered sporadically and spread across a large geographic area, and when contract specifications provide little room for applying local workers' special skills or local knowledge. The Forest Service has long depended on a mobile workforce to carry out field tasks from tree planting to fighting forest fires. Given the agency's declining budgets, and the associated consolidation of contracting authorities at the regional level, the trend in recent years has been toward large contracts offered in ways that make it increasingly difficult for small-scale contractors to compete.

Forest Stewardship: Redistributing Work Opportunities and Reinvesting in Communities

The case of Trinity County can be generalized for many forest communities across the United States, which are also faced with declining timber harvests, rising poverty, and high unemployment. National forests can provide more employment opportunities, but only if local forest businesses are specifically targeted as beneficiaries, rather than being excluded through complicated bidding procedures, large-scale projects, and irregular work offerings. The management and use of forest resources—whether in an asset-depleting or an asset-building manner—does not automatically result in income gains or poverty reduction in forest-dependent communities. The extent to which it does so depends on the institutional arrangements governing access to forest resources and to employment opportunities.

Different ways of packaging forest work, especially the tasks involved in ecosystem management, could realize administrative savings while improving the socioeconomic status of forest-dependent communities. An example is the Willamette Province Workforce Project in Oregon, which has combined a number of individual tasks on Forest Service, Bureau of Land Management, and some private lands into multidisciplinary contracts that offer steady, long-season work to small crews of five or six workers. In a similar fashion, the ecosystem management tasks for individual subwatersheds could be packaged into multiyear contracts that could be completed with a small crew. Spreading work sites across different elevations could extend the window for time-sensitive projects, such as tree planting.

A pilot project in Trinity County shows the promise of a forest stewardship approach that is sensitive to the needs of local communities. In early 1997, the winter after the Hayfork sawmill closed, local contractors, loggers, environmentalists, concerned citizens, and Forest Service employees met to discuss how to address local environmental and employment concerns. The group determined that a properly scaled, multiyear, multitask contract that addressed all the stewardship needs of a given tract could provide steady, long-season work that would improve both the biological health of the forest and the economic health of the community. As a pilot project they selected Grassy Flats, a subwatershed near the center of the county, where forest management needs included the creation of shaded fuel breaks[14] and the thinning of over-stocked stands to reduce the threat of catastrophic fire, as well as road maintenance and the decommissioning of old roads to reduce soil erosion.

The U.S. Forest Service supported the Grassy Flats Stewardship Project as part of the Hayfork AMA. The Northwest Forest Plan explicitly calls for collaboration among community groups and government agencies for the benefit of forest communities in the AMAs: "These areas should provide opportunities for land managing and regulatory agencies, other government entities, non-governmental organizations, local groups, landowners, communities, and citizens to work together to develop innovative management approaches" (U.S. Department of Agriculture 1994, D-4).

The 400,000-acre Hayfork AMA, which spreads across the middle of Trinity County and the Trinity National Forest into neighboring counties and the Six Rivers National Forest, is the largest AMA in the Pacific Northwest. Forest Service AMA coordinators saw the Grassy Flats Stewardship Project as an experiment in the kind of innovation needed to sustain forest communities, while saving on administrative costs and increasing the quality of forestry work performed.

After considerable effort, the Forest Service packaged a mixed timber sale and service contract together as an RFP, in which the value of the commercial timber to be thinned from the forest would help pay for other restoration work. Recognizing the difficulties local contractors have had in bidding on RFPs, the Forest Service held special training sessions for them, and a local nongovernmental organization offered to help contractors prepare proposals. The contract included a number of provisions friendly to local businesses: for example, preference was given to bidders who planned to hire locally and who planned to use, rather than burn, the small-diameter trees cut in the project.

The contract also called for the processing of small-diameter material in local facilities, to support additional local employment.

Such preferences are quite unusual in Forest Service contracting. The provisions for local hiring and wood use could be included because the contracting officer will award the contract on a "best value" basis—that is, to whomever provides the best value to the government (a combination of technical approach and price)—rather than simply to the lowest bidder.[15] In this case, the government's expressed interests include the desire to maintain a well-trained, local workforce engaged in ecosystem management and to support market development for small-diameter timber.

Although the Grassy Flats Project is open to all bidders regardless of location, local contractors will have natural advantages due to their proximity and local knowledge. Long-term stewardship contracts, which involve commitment to one place for long seasons over several years, enable local contractors to save on transportation and housing costs. When, as in this case, the contractor has latitude to choose the best practices and work schedule, knowledge of the terrain, weather conditions, and road systems can help local contractors to save time, cut costs, and increase efficiency.

Potential for a Stewardship Approach

If a steady flow of contracts like those in the Grassy Flats Project were made available, a local stewardship business sector could develop, providing long-season employment at decent wages, with career paths leading to better job opportunities for forestry workers. The anticipated social benefits of this approach include the greater social stability that could result from decreasing the need to work away from home. Forest workers who spend less time on the road can participate more fully in family and community life.

Simply moving toward ecosystem management will not necessarily generate work opportunities for poor forest communities. The Forest Service instead could continue to contract specific tasks out to mobile consultants and work crews. Alternatively, the Forest Service could contract all of a district's management needs to a private land management company. Depending on the practices of the company, such large-scale contracting could exclude the residents of small forest communities from decision-making, support services, and the development of a value-added industry, as well as from direct forest employment.

But as timber harvests decline and government agencies attempt to implement ecosystem management, there is a window of opportunity not only to change ecological conditions on the ground but also to change the structure of work to benefit forest communities. The diverse and site-specific work of ecosystem management can be carried out either in ways that promote community development or in ways that continue to benefit larger, nonlocal corporations. At least a portion of ecosystem management work can and should be allocated to stewardship-style contracts that aim to support forest communities. Attention must also be paid to low-income mobile workers who are displaced in the transition to ecosystem management. Efforts to improve working conditions and employment opportunities must be extended to all low-income forest workers, regardless of residency. Otherwise, poverty may be merely displaced from one area to another.

Ecosystem management requires investment in lands that have been degraded by resource extraction. Some forms of forest restoration can generate revenues, as in the removal of marketable trees to reduce fire hazard, and commercial logging can be compatible with ecosystem management if done in an ecologically appropriate and sustainable manner. In general, however, ecosystem management will require more money than timber revenues can produce. One way to fund stewardship initiatives would be to capture, or internalize, some of the value of nontimber forest ecosystem services. Such revenue could then be reinvested in the productivity of the ecosystem. For example, the Forest Service is currently experimenting with raising recreation fees in national forests and retaining the proceeds to fund recreation-related services and facilities, rather than passing the revenues to the U.S. Treasury and hoping for adequate appropriations.

One of the most valuable external benefits of forest ecosystems is the provision of clean and stable supplies of water. The value of water from the Sierra Nevada, for example, is estimated to be $1.35 billion per year, more than the value of timber, recreation, and grazing combined.[16] There are currently no mechanisms for capturing the value of water produced by national forests and returning it to the forests for investment in watershed management. Agricultural water users currently pay only a small percentage of what urban water users pay, and virtually none of that money reaches the watersheds of origin. In places like Trinity County, where as much as 90 percent of the flow of the Trinity River has been diverted out of the basin to support agricultural development, capturing even a fraction of the value of that water could provide substantial funding for stewardship contracting, helping to maintain the health of forests and forest communities and to safeguard water for downstream users.

Conclusion

Many forest communities in the United States have high rates of poverty and unemployment. These communities have rights to share in the benefits—both revenues and work opportunities—flowing from national forests. Yet they often receive a relatively small percentage of the forest-sector employment. The current transition in U.S. forestry policy from timber extraction to ecosystem management offers an opportunity to enhance both the stock of natural assets and the flow of benefits to poor forest areas. Reinvestment in forest resources is needed to produce a sustainable flow of benefits both to forest communities and to the national constituency. A redistribution of the flow of benefits, in particular by appropriating the supposedly "open access" work opportunities in national forests, can help to reduce poverty in forest communities. New institutional arrangements are required for this purpose. New mechanisms are also needed to capture more of the value of ecosystem services, for investment in the restoration and ecological management of forests in ways that benefit forest communities.

In conclusion, I offer several recommendations for natural-asset building in communities that are dependent on public forests: First, the Forest Service needs adequate federal funding and stronger incentives to support its mandate to address the needs of forest communities, particularly in the promotion of forest restoration and ecosystem management. New criteria, other than volume of timber sold, must be developed to help assess how Forest Service programs affect local communities and how their actions impact poverty.

Second, although not all ecosystem management needs to be implemented through stewardship contracts, a steady and predictable share of ecosystem management work is needed to test, realize, and promote the benefits of a stewardship approach.

Third, workforce development is needed to assist in the transition from timber production by mobile work crews to ecosystem management by local stewardship contractors. Training opportunities must be made available to enhance the skills of all forest workers, local and mobile, if stewardship contracting is to alleviate poverty and not merely redistribute it.

Fourth, nongovernmental organizations should be involved in stewardship approaches. Like the transition within federal agencies from timber production to ecosystem management, the transition within the private sector from a timber sales and services contracting capacity to a stewardship contracting capacity will take time, training, capital, and experimentation. Nongovernmental organizations can play an indispensable role in helping both the private sector and the public sector to make these transitions.

Finally, links with private forestland management and conservation should be explored.[17] Just as in the case of public lands, sustainable forestry on private lands requires the development of improved harvesting practices, value-added processing, and new product markets. Linking efforts on public and private lands will facilitate development of the commitment and technologies needed to sustain forest stewardship at a scale that can help to reduce poverty.

Acknowledgments

This research was supported in part by funds provided by the Pacific Southwest Research Station, Forest Service, U.S. Department of Agriculture. This paper draws on the work and experience of the staff of the Watershed Research and Training Center, Hayfork, California.

Notes

1. In addition, the Bureau of Land Management (BLM) manages 11 million acres of productive forestland, mostly in Alaska and Oregon. Forestland is a small fraction of the BLM's 264 million acres, most of which are grasslands, tundra, and desert.
2. See, for example, Fortmann and Kusel (1991) and Howze et al. (1994).
3. Congress first declared that forest counties would receive 10 percent of gross forest revenues in 1906, then raised the figure to 25 percent in 1908. For certain lands in the West managed by the BLM, 50 percent of revenues are given to counties.
4. A court injunction on timber sales in 1991 led to a sudden drop in revenue in the spotted owl counties in California, Oregon, and Washington. To ease the impact on county budgets, Section 13982 of the Omnibus Budget Reconciliation Act of 1993 tied payments in spotted owl counties to a gradually diminishing percentage of the five-year average timber harvest of 1986–1990. Because these were the highest timber-producing counties in the country, the overall national distribution to counties in recent years has exceeded 25 percent of timber revenues.
5. See Cortner and Moote (1999, 11–35) for a review of the roots of ecosystem management, including the changing social values that have led to its growing acceptance.
6. In Oregon and Washington, timber employment declined approximately 16 percent from 1990 to 1996 (calculated from Niemi et al. 1999, 22), similar to the 17 percent decline predicted by the Forest Ecosystem Management Assessment Team (1993). Total employment in the region, though not necessarily in forest communities, grew over the same time period, reflecting strong job growth in other sectors. See Niemi et al. (1999) for further discussion.
7. Normally the community—not the county—is the more appropriate unit to analyze forest dependence. Analysis at the community level is hampered, however, by the limited availability of socioeconomic and timber harvest data, which are more commonly reported at the county level. The absence of significant agricultural, industrial (other than timber), or urban sectors in Trinity County makes it statistically resemble a forest-dependent community more than an economically diverse California county.
8. Unlike the Aid to Families with Dependent Children (AFDC) program, eligibility for free and reduced-cost lunches was unchanged by welfare reform in the 1990s. It includes families with incomes up to 200 percent of the official poverty level.

9. The private timberland figure here is derived from enrollment in the "timberland production zone" (TPZ) property-tax category, which applies to private forest-land with some kind of timber management plan. In Trinity County, 250,000 acres are in TPZs, most of them owned by a single industrial timber corporation.

10. The owner of the Hayfork mill, the largest timber company in the state, had recently bought the land holdings and mills of a number of other companies. This made the Hayfork mill, with its 1948 headrig designed for old-growth timber, redundant—if not obsolete—since large-diameter (old-growth) trees are now scarce in the area, and many of those that remain are protected in late successional reserves. Hayfork's mill buildings were partially torn down, and its equipment was relocated to another mill site more than 200 miles away.

11. AFDC as a proxy for annual poverty rates is less useful after the mid-1990s, due to changes in welfare eligibility.

12. Two-thirds of Trinity County businesses that pay payroll taxes have fewer than 5 employees, and 85 percent have fewer than 10 employees (Porter 1999).

13. The federal government has a small business set-aside program that allocates a percentage of timber sales and service contracts to businesses with no more than 500 employees. Such "small" businesses are still extraordinarily large by rural com-munity standards, and therefore the standard small business set-asides do not help businesses from forest communities to access work. In contrast, an upper size limit for a "very small" business based in forest communities might be 25 employees, with most businesses having under 10 employees.

14. Shaded fuel breaks are strategically selected strips of forest in which much of the fuels (brush, small trees, dead woody matter, and low branches) are cleared in order to slow the spread of wildfires and to provide spaces from which to fight fires. The breaks generally retain 40 to 60 percent of the overstory canopy to sup-press regrowth of the understory.

15. The Secure Rural Schools and Community Self-Determination Act (PL-106-393) is one of several recent congressional acts and proposed legislation that include provisions to encourage the use of "best-value contracting" and a commitment to hiring "highly qualified workers and local residents." Although best-value contract-ing is already an existing authority and requires no further special authorization, congressional encouragement for the use of this tool is proving helpful for imple-menting stewardship projects in ways that benefit forest communities.

16. This represents the annual value of irrigation, municipal water, and hydropower. The annual value of recreation is $475 million, timber is $320 million, and graz-ing is $82 million (Stewart 1996).

17. For discussion, see the chapters by Constance Best (Chapter 11) and Deborah Brighton (Chapter 12).

References

California Department of Social Services. 2000. AFDC cases by county. Information obtained by phone contact.

California Employment Development Department. 1999. "Labor Force and Unemployment Data." Retrieved from http://www.calmis.cahwnet.gov/htmlfile/subject/ lftable.htm. 4 May.

California State Board of Equalization. 2000. "Timber Harvest Data by County. Retrieved from http://www.boe.ca.gov. June.

Committee of Scientists. 1999. *Sustaining the People's Lands: Recommendations for Stewardship of the National Forests and Grasslands into the Next Century.* Washington, D.C.: U.S. Department of Agriculture.

Cortner, Hanna J., and Margaret A. Moote. 1999. *The Politics of Ecosystem Management.* Washington, D.C.: Island Press.

Dana, Samuel Trask, and Sally K. Fairfax. 1980. *Forest and Range Policy.* New York: McGraw-Hill.

Danks, Cecilia, and Lynn Jungwirth. 1998. "Community-Based Socioeconomic Assessment and Monitoring of Activities Related to National Forest Management in California," *Journal of Environmental Science and Management* 1(2): 1–18.

Forest Ecosystem Management Assessment Team. 1993. *Forest Ecosystem Management: an Ecological, Economic, and Social Assessment: Report of the Forest Ecosystem Management Assessment Team.* Produced jointly by the U.S. Department of Agriculture, Forest Service; U.S. Department of Commerce, National Oceanic and Atmospheric Administration; U.S. Department of Commerce, National Marine Fisheries Service; U.S. Department of the Interior, Bureau of Land Management; U.S. Department of the Interior, Fish and Wildlife Service; U.S. Department of the Interior, National Park Service; and the Environmental Protection Agency. Washington, D.C.: U.S. Government Printing Office.

Fortmann, Louise, and Jonathan Kusel. 1991. *Well-Being in Forest Dependent Communities.* Sacramento: California Department of Forestry and Fire Protection.

Greber, Brian. 1994. "Economic Assessment of FEMAT Options." *Journal of Forestry* 92(4): 36–40.

Hoffmann, Sandra A., and Louise Fortmann. 1996. "Poverty in Forested Counties: An Analysis Based on Aid to Families with Dependent Children." In *Sierra Nevada Ecosystem Project Final Report to Congress.* Vol. 2. Davis: University of California, Centers of Water and Wildland Resources.

Howze, Glenn, Conner Bailey, and John Bliss. 1994. "The Development of Timber Dependency: An Analysis of Historical Changes in the Demographic, Social, Economic and Agricultural Profiles of Timber Dependent Counties in Alabama." Paper presented to the 57th Annual Meeting of the Rural Sociological Society. Portland, Ore. 11–14 August.

McDermott, Connie, and Cecilia Danks. 1997. "Socioeconomic Monitoring of Ecosystem Management Activities in the Trinity National Forest." A draft research report of the Watershed Research and Training Center, Hayfork, Calif.

Niemi, Ernie, Ed Whitelaw, and Andrew Johnston. 1999. *The Sky Did Not Fall: The Pacific Northwest's Response to Logging Reductions.* Eugene, Ore.: ECONorthwest.

Peluso, Nancy. 1992. *Rich Forests, Poor People: Resource Control and Resistance in Java.* Berkeley: University of California Press.

Porter, Kathy. 1999. "Trinity County." County data sheet of the California Employment Development Department. 7 June.

Stewart, William C. 1993. "Predicting Employment Impacts of Changing Forest Management in California." Ph.D. diss., University of California, Berkeley.

———. 1996. "Economic Assessment of the Ecosystem." *Sierra Nevada Ecosystem Project: Final Report to Congress*. Vol. III, Assessments, Commissioned Reports, and Background Information. Davis: University of California, Centers for Water and Wildland Resources.

Trinity County Assessor. 1996. "County Assessor Maps and Ownership Records: Trinity County." 1996. Napa, Calif.: CD-Data.

Trinity County Office of Education. 1999. "Enrollment in School Lunch Program." Printout of spreadsheet.

U.S. Bureau of the Census. 1983. *1980 Census of Population*. Vol. 1, Characteristics of the Population. Chapter C: "General Social and Economic Characteristics," Part 6: "California." PC80-1-C6. Washington, D.C.: U.S. Government Printing Office.

———. 1992. *1990 Census of Population and Housing: Summary Social, Economic, and Housing Characteristics: California*. 1990 CHP-5-6. Washington, D.C.: U.S. Government Printing Office.

———. 1993. *1990 Census of Population and Housing*. Summary Tape File 3B. Washington, D.C.: U.S. Government Printing Office.

U.S. Department of Agriculture. U.S. Forest Service. 1994. *Record of Decision for Amendments to Forest Service and Bureau of Land Management Planning Documents Within the Range of the Northern Spotted Owl*. Produced jointly by the U.S. Department of Agriculture, Forest Service, and U.S. Department of the Interior Bureau of Land Management. Washington, D.C.: U.S. Government Printing Office.

———. 1999. "Timber Sold on the National Forests." Retrieved from http://www.fs.fed.us/land/fm/s_h/99q4sold.htm. 10 December.

———. 2000. "Forest Service Final Payments to States." News release. Retrieved from http://www.fs.fed.us/news/20000216.htm. 25 April.

PART V

GREENING THE CITIES

Part 5 discusses strategies for building natural assets in cities. Environmentalists often think of urbanized areas as the antithesis of nature. Yet by virtue of the fact that the majority of Americans live in metropolitan areas, the lands, air, water, and living organisms of our cities constitute some of the most important—and potentially valuable—natural assets in the country.

Many of the key dimensions of urban environmental quality are public goods, including air quality, water quality, and open space. Public policies and investments therefore have been crucial in shaping the environment in our cities. Municipal water and sewer projects were among the earliest government-funded environmental investments, and the Rivers and Harbors Act of 1899, which regulated waste discharges into the nation's urban waterways, marked the beginning of federal efforts to control pollution. As the following chapters demonstrate, public policies and public resources remain crucial to the prospects for building natural assets in urban settings.

Investment in ecological restoration, the *redistribution* of control of urban lands (notably vacant lots), and the democratic *appropriation* of the right to clean air and clean water are among the routes to urban natural-asset building. The appropriation route was discussed extensively in Part 2, which deals with the reclamation of environmental sinks. The following chapters also consider possibilities for investment and redistribution.

Greg Watson surveys a range of investments that can contribute to the greening of our cities. The redevelopment of brownfields, the construction of bioshelters for urban agriculture, the restoration of riverfronts, and the creation of "brightfields" to generate solar energy are examples. These projects require substantial investments and in most cases will involve public resources as well as private capital. Yet financial capital is not the only requirement. As the chapters by Patricia Hynes and Raquel Pinderhughes document, social capital and human capital can be crucial for investments in urban natural capital. Social capital underpins comprehensive community initiatives for urban revitalization. Human capital—above all, the labor power of local residents—is a key ingredient in the success of the urban agriculture and other labor-intensive natural-asset-building projects.

Investment alone cannot ensure that the urban poor share fully in the benefits of urban environmental restoration. As in the case of conventional strategies for urban renewal, there is a danger that the poor will be displaced, as neighborhoods are made more attractive by virtue of investments in environmental quality. This makes redistribution a key element of urban natural-asset-building strategies. As documented in earlier chapters, asset redistribution has been an enduring feature of struggles over the definition and allocation of property rights. Today the assignment of rights and responsibilities for the vacant lots and brownfields that dot our cities is being negotiated among diverse actors including community-based organizations, private-sector owners and developers, and government agencies. These negotiations create possibilities to redistribute rights to low-income communities. Examples include the right to participate in planning and land-use decisions; the right to grow food on lands held by municipal governments or nonprofit trusts; the right to a share of the employment opportunities created by redevelopment; and even, as in the case of Boston's Dudley Street Neighborhood Initiative, the right to eminent domain over vacant lots.

A key to successful redistribution is the mobilization of communities both to tap the internal resources of their members and to forge alliances at the municipal level and beyond. The democratization of environmental ownership in our cities is not likely to come about as a result of top-down urban redevelopment strategies: it must be built patiently and systematically through bottom-up struggles.

CHAPTER 14

Can Natural Assets Help Address Urban Poverty?

Greg Watson

Efforts designed to revitalize poor urban areas have typically concentrated on issues related to the built environment and human resources, such as affordable housing, job creation, and welfare reform. For many neighborhoods in the ailing central cities, the only environmental issues that have generated much interest are those related to environmental injustices. Hazardous waste sites, contaminated brownfields, polluted air, and lead-laden soils are all too commonplace in these impoverished communities.

A relatively new approach to urban revitalization known as "comprehensive community initiatives" encourages residents to view their problems, opportunities, and planning efforts from a whole-systems perspective. Guided by this methodology, some communities are now reassessing what they are, and what they might be. In doing so, residents, activists, elected officials, and professional planners are coming to recognize the potential for infusing central cities with a new sense of vibrancy, by incorporating the natural assets of urban environments into the planning process.

In this chapter, I survey some of the principal natural assets in cities—vacant land, water, air, trees, and energy—and evaluate how community organizations have attempted to use these assets to manage their own development and reduce poverty. Although none of these initiatives has yet been entirely successful in addressing the overwhelming magnitude of urban poverty, they point to new directions for building sources of wealth and power for the poorest residents of our cities.

The Urban Challenge

Cities are becoming the main environments in which people throughout the world live and work. In their 1974 book, *Ecumenopolis: The Inevitable City of the Future,* J. G. Papaioannou and Constantin Doxiadis traced the history of human settlements from villages and small towns to cities and megalopolises, and concluded that we are headed toward the formation of a global city they termed "Ecumenopolis." Today the numbers suggest that we are indeed moving in that direction. In 1900, approximately 5 percent of the world's people lived in cities with populations over 100,000. A century later, an estimated 45 percent—more than 2.5 billion people—live in such urban centers. From 1950 to 1995, the number of cities in the industrialized countries with populations greater than 1 million more than doubled; in the same period, the number of million-plus cities in the developing countries increased sixfold. The United Nations forecasts that in the coming years, rural populations worldwide will remain virtually steady, while urban populations continue to grow, so that by the year 2025, 5 billion people—more than 60 percent of humanity—will be living in cities (Linden 1996).

In recent decades, urban growth in the United States has been accompanied by widening economic polarization. The poor are increasingly concentrated in our metropolitan cities, particularly in African-American communities (Wilson 1996). In 1996, 42 percent of the U.S. poor lived in cities, up from 30 percent in 1968 (Kelly 1996). Meanwhile, the urban wealthy and middle class are moving to suburbs, leaving the central cities to the poor. The exodus of middle- and upper-class residents, with subsequent erosion of investments and political influence, has led to impoverishment and degradation of the urban environment. Lacking political clout, poor communities become sites for a disproportionate number of junkyards, trash facilities, and other pollution-intensive businesses that pose threats to the quality of the environment and to the health of the nearby residents.

The Natural Assets of Urban Areas

Natural assets are not confined to bucolic rural landscapes or to wilderness areas—they are vital to the life of cities, too. Indeed, urban land, water, air, biota, and energy are among the most valuable of natural assets.

Land

From an environmental perspective, low-density urban areas are considered optimal for development. From an economic perspective, however, the costs of reclaiming and redeveloping low-density, low-income urban areas, with their abandoned lots and buildings, are formidable. As a result, major U.S. cities have substantial areas of unused land. Philadelphia's city limits, for example, contain 15,800 parcels of vacant land; New Orleans has 14,000 vacant lots; Chicago has approximately 70,000; and St. Louis has 13,000 tax-delinquent parcels of vacant land (Kaufman and Bailkey 1999). Across the country, city officials and community activists are seeking ways to transform their vacant land into performing assets. A frequent obstacle they face is the weakness of social capital in low-density areas. "More abandoned buildings mean more places for crack dens and criminal enterprises," observes Jargowsky (1997). "Lower density also makes it harder for a sense of community to develop, or for people to feel they can find safety in numbers." The high cost of cleaning up contaminated tracts of land also frightens off potential developers, who view new development of uncontaminated sites as a safer investment.

In a number of urban communities, past industrial activity and illegal dumping, often of hazardous materials, have contaminated a large proportion of the vacant lands. The U.S. Environmental Protection Agency (EPA) refers to these parcels as brownfields, defined as "abandoned, idled, or under-used industrial and commercial facilities where expansion or redevelopment is complicated by real or perceived environmental contamination" (U.S. Environmental Protection Agency 1998). Much more than eyesores, browfields may pose health risks to surrounding communities and act as deterrents to business investments.

The EPA views the cleanup and redevelopment of brownfields as one way to counteract the problem of urban sprawl. Mounting pressure to site new manufacturing and commercial establishments on suburban and rural greenfields has led the government to invest in resources and expertise to help communities develop strategies for returning brownfields to productive use. The EPA estimates that there are between 150,000 and 450,000 brownfields nationwide. In Massachusetts alone, the state's Department of Environmental Protection has identified over 7,000 contaminated sites. In communities such as Roxbury, Massachusetts, where illegal dumping occurred for years before residents organized against it, virtually every vacant lot is considered to be a brownfield.

Although often located in economically distressed areas with severe environmental problems, many sites include prime industrial properties, often with reusable buildings, existing infrastructure, and convenient access to railroads, airports, and highways. Federal and state brownfield laws encourage redevelopment of these blighted properties, providing grants for pilot projects and other financial incentives for brownfield reclamation. From a community development perspective, the most important and controversial provisions in these efforts are those that seek to reduce the risks of cleanup liability for new property owners and that take the final use of redeveloped property into consideration when defining environmental regulations. For example, if the final use will be industrial, the law may allow a lower standard of cleanup than if the site will be used for housing or a day care center. The EPA refers to such provisions as "special efforts toward removing regulatory barriers without sacrificing protectiveness," but some communities fear that this aspect of the legislation allows higher levels of contamination in urban neighborhoods (Dalton 1998). Although it is relatively easy to envision how brownfield redevelopment can rehabilitate derelict urban lands, the extent to which it reduces poverty clearly depends in large part on issues of ownership and control-issues that K. A. Dixon explores in Chapter 3.

Water

"All cities," observes Anne Whiston Spirn (1984), "even those in humid climates, must soon face the loss of their most precious resource—an abundant supply of uncontaminated water." She notes that U.S. cities import more water than all other goods and materials combined.

Boston, Massachusetts, for example, relies for its water on the Wachusett and Quabbin reservoirs, located 35 miles and 65 miles to the west, respectively. The Wachusett holds 65 billion gallons of water; the Quabbin, which covers a 39-square-mile surface area, holds 412 billion gallons. The construction of the Wachusett Reservoir during the first decade of the twentieth century displaced hundreds of residents from their homes in the towns of Boylston and West Boylston. The Quabbin, built in 1928 to address an impending water shortage in the city, displaced the entire populations of four rural Massachusetts communities. Similarly, New York City imports upward of 1.5 billion gallons of water each day, from as far away as 125 miles, through a system of 6,100 miles of pipelines. And the California water system has been described as one of "the most massive rearrangements of the natural environment that has ever been attempted" (Shaeffer and Stevens 1983).

Ensuring that there is enough water to support growing urban demands is only one aspect of the challenge that cities face. Poor water quality looms as another major concern, one that grows more serious as urban populations increase. Many freshwater supplies—including the five Great Lakes, which contain one-tenth of the total amount of fresh water in the world—have been badly polluted by urban activity. Point sources such as waste outlets and discharge pipes—as well as nonpoint sources such as runoff, air pollutant fall-out, and releases from contaminated sediments—have contributed to this problem. Yet many elected officials and planners still insist on treating the problems of flooding, storm drainage, water pollution, water use, and water supply separately (Spirn 1984).

Indeed, most cities treat water as if it were an inexhaustible resource. A notable exception is San Jose, California, where the city has established a tiered rate structure for residential customers that is designed to serve as an incentive for conserving water. The less water a household uses, the lower the rate it is charged per gallon.

Water is mostly invisible to city dwellers, buried beneath the ground within miles of hidden pipes. Like the food that mysteriously appears on supermarket shelves, water always flows with the turn of the tap, its origin obscure. Even those who are willing (and able) to pay a premium for bottled water often do not know the source of the water they drink.

Despite the crucial importance of water, it rarely emerges as a concern in urban design. Nancy Jack and John Todd (1984) suggest a new approach to ecological design, arguing that water should be allowed to resurface from the underground labyrinth of pipes, be exposed to solar energy, and be purified by living organisms, all within the communities where it is used. The Todds envision every city block with a fountain and every neighborhood with its own solar-powered aquatic sewage system, in which aquatic organisms purify water in long, thin structures resembling greenhouses. Christopher Alexander, another designer who integrates water into his urban environments, admonishes planners and residents alike to "preserve natural pools and streams and allow them to run through the city; make paths for people to walk along them and footbridges to cross them" (Alexander et al. 1977).

In recent years, some cities have taken significant steps to reintegrate their rivers and ponds into their overall urban designs and economies. More than 4,500 rowers from all over the world now come to Cambridge, Massachusetts, each year to compete in the Head of the Charles Regatta. The Providence River in Providence, Rhode Island, is home to a highly successful annual jazz festival. Baltimore's once blighted Inner Harbor is now the centerpiece of that city's revival. Cleveland's Cuyahoga River, formerly the brunt of jokes about its propensity to catch fire, now frames the revitalized "Flats"—one of the landmarks of that city's remarkable recovery—a strip of riverfront real estate that has emerged as a magnet for boaters, athletes, and tourists.

Although it is heartening that these and other urban centers are rebuilding their economies with water as a focal point, these actions can have adverse results for poorer communities. As a report of the Greater Boston Urban Resources Partnership (1999) cautions, "often as [urban] watersheds improve, real estate prices increase, long-time residents are forced to move, and gentrification sets in." In the case of water, as in the case of land, designs to improve blighted communities by harnessing their natural assets must also include plans to retain and empower their low-income residents—an issue that Patricia Hynes explores further in Chapter 15.

Air

Air quality directly impacts human health, and it varies dramatically from place to place depending on geographical and human-made factors. Because cities are densely populated and host a wide range of activities, they have long been plagued by serious air pollution problems.

In the past two decades, exposure to airborne lead, a particularly dangerous pollutant, has decreased markedly, thanks mainly to more stringent automobile emissions standards and the mandatory switch to unleaded gasoline. However, the list of air pollutants that continue to threaten public health remains formidable. It includes ozone (irritates and impairs breathing), carbon monoxide (reduces blood oxygen), nitrogen dioxide (impairs breathing), particulate matter (penetrates deep into the lungs, and reduces visibility), sulfur dioxide, volatile organic compounds, and asphalt fumes. Cities such as New York, Los Angeles, and Houston often fail to meet ambient air quality standards due to the excessive concentrations of one or more of these substances.

Poor air quality in cities translates into a greater incidence of pollution-related diseases for inner-city inhabitants. Although the long-term effects of exposure to air pollutants are not well understood, it is believed that they act individually or in concert to exacerbate respiratory diseases, particularly asthma (Gershwin 1999). According to a report issued by the city of Providence, Rhode Island, 10 to 20 percent of all summertime respiratory-related hospital visits in the northeastern United States are associated with ozone pollution. There has been a substantial increase over the past several decades in the morbidity and mortality from asthma in the United States. By 1996, asthma accounted for around 1.9 million visits to hospital emergency departments, according to annual survey data—up from about 1.4 million visits in 1990—with the greatest increase seen among inner-city African-Americans and Hispanics, especially children and young adults (Weiss 1998).

We know what it will take to improve our cities' air quality: we must reduce the harmful emissions generated by power plants, industries, and automobiles; reverse the decline of urban trees and vegetation; and find ways to hold accountable those who are responsible for loading the atmosphere with pollutants. In Chapter 7, Peter Barnes and Marc Breslow offer a provocative policy suggestion for reducing carbon emissions, one that could be extended to other air pollutants.

Biota

Cities harbor a surprising diversity of plants and animals. There are more than 100 species of animal wildlife in the city of Boston alone, and as many as 300 species of plants and trees on the grounds of an abandoned state hospital in Mattapan, one of the city's most densely populated neighborhoods. These species survive in urban environments despite a variety of stresses that include polluted air, contaminated land, and inadequate supplies of water.

Trees are among the most important and least appreciated natural assets in our cities. During the summer, when cities are transformed into heat islands, the shade provided by trees and the cooling effects of evapotranspiration help to provide welcome relief from heat and humidity. Trees also filter dust; sequester atmospheric carbon dioxide from the air and exchange it for oxygen; and remove some harmful pollutants, including sulfur dioxide and hydrogen fluoride. Landsat satellite images and Geographic Information System technology reveal that urban forests—stands of trees in city parks, along streets, and in backyards—are fast disappearing. Air pollution, plant diseases, insect infestations, and development have conspired to decimate many of the trees that have kept American cities cool and green over the years (Wong 1999). Trees growing in natural urban lands such as parks generally fare much better than those planted along city streets, because the latter are subjected to constant stress from lack of sunlight (blocked by tall buildings), compacted soils, lack of water (which runs off the compacted soils), and (in northern cities) poisoning from deicing salt. Restoring urban forests could improve the health and comfort of residents.

Energy

One new approach to brownfield development is called *brightfields*. The U.S. Department of Energy (DOE) describes brightfields as the conversion of contaminated lands into usable sites for the generation of pollution-free solar energy and for high-tech solar manufacturing jobs. Although appealing at first glance, the brightfield concept raises some fundamental questions about the best uses of vacant urban lands. To be economically feasible, solar-powered electricity requires large photovoltaic arrays occupying large tracts of land that might otherwise be used for housing, manufacturing, commercial development, or urban agriculture. DOE officials stress, however, that solar panels can be used flexibly, since they can be fairly easily dismantled and trucked to another site if a better use for the land is found.

The Spire Corporation is one of the first companies to take advantage of the brightfield initiative, with a plan to establish a photovoltaic factory in Chicago. The business will locally manufacture and install solar electric modules, in a partnership among Spire, the mayor's office (through the city's Department of Environment), Commonwealth Edison, and DOE. The production facility is intended to support a commitment by the city of Chicago to install environmentally friendly solar electric systems throughout the metropolitan area. Spire expects to create more than 100 new jobs in a distressed urban area. The solar energy systems to be installed in the city will produce more than 10 million kilowatt hours of electricity annually, in the process reducing carbon dioxide emissions by almost 25 million pounds.

The Chicago brightfields partnership may provide a blueprint for other urban communities. A key stumbling block, however, is that the cost of electricity generated by photovoltaics remains very high compared to the cost of power derived from conventional sources. For this reason, the city government will be the primary purchaser of the first panels to be manufactured at the Chicago facility. The cost problem could be alleviated by creating new incentives for the use of renewable energy. For example, a renewable energy set-aside could be funded as part of the "pollution dividend" proposed by Barnes and Breslow in Chapter 7. The set-aside would subsidize renewable energy purchases and could be phased out after a period of time or as the price of renewables becomes more competitive. Such provisions to encourage the consumption of renewable energy could stimulate new markets for solar technologies manufactured in urban neighborhoods.

The Promise of Urban Agriculture

Drawing on the various assets inventoried above—land, water, air, biota, and energy—urban agriculture affords opportunities both to enhance environmental quality and to improve the well-being of inner-city residents. In her groundbreaking book *The Economy of Cities,* Jane Jacobs (1969) chronicled the genesis of major agricultural revolutions over the past 10,000 years, arguing that all dramatic changes in farming originated in cities and spread outward to the countryside. The current movement to create a new ecological agriculture, capable of producing a diversity of foods in relatively small spaces, is no exception.

The goal of the new agriculture is to replace current dependence on fossil-fuel-intensive technologies with structural and living analogs of natural systems powered by renewable energy. One component of the new agriculture is the "bioshelter," a structure containing a miniaturized ecosystem that relies on the sun as its primary energy source.

> In the future urban agriculture will have many forms. Shade trees will be partially replaced by an urban orchardry of fruits and nuts. Sunlit walls will become architectural backdrops for espaliered fruits and vine crops. Shrubs, which purify air by removing auto exhaust, lead and zinc will be planted in raised beds between the streets and sidewalks. Community gardens and gardening will increase as participation grows. Agricultural bioshelters will fill vacant lots and ring parks. Floating bioshelters will line harbors and produce their fish, vegetables, flowers and herbs for sale. . . .

Rooftops will utilize bioshelter concepts for market gardens all year. One day towns and cities will add farming to their repertoire of functions. (Todd and Tukel 1981.)

As the 150-year trend to separate cities from their sources of nutrition draws to a close, urban neighborhoods can find themselves in the forefront of the new agricultural revolution. "As our cities grow larger they are producing a greater share of their food demand," observes Jac Smit, president of the Urban Agriculture Network. "And greater shares of their citizens are becoming active in food production" (Smit et al. 1996). As Raquel Pinderhughes explains in Chapter 16, urban agriculture has many attractions for urban communities seeking to rebuild their economies. Agriculture has the potential to create jobs at low capital investment, the acquisition of land being the biggest challenge. Insofar as low-income residents secure rights to the land, urban agriculture contributes directly to asset building. With the additional investments in such technologies as greenhouses, closed-loop aquaculture, and value-added processed foods, urban agriculture can be a powerful tool for sustainable economic development.

Some Examples

At this stage, examples of truly successful urban food production enterprises are still rare. However, there are a number of notable experiments under way:

- *Hartford Farms* in Hartford, Connecticut, established in 1983, has a 13,000-square-foot facility that houses a hydroponic lettuce operation. A group of nonprofit organizations purchased a vacant lot from the city for the nominal sum of $1 and constructed the greenhouse as a way to supplement existing community gardens, so as to produce more food and create more job opportunities than was possible through gardens alone. The greenhouse was financed with $300,000 in low-interest loans and $30,000 in grants.
- *Bioshelters, Inc.,* an integrated aquaculture-hydroponics growing system in Sunderland, Massachusetts, is located in a rural community, but it offers some important insights into the potential for growing food in the city. Modeled after the New Alchemy Institute bioshelter and constructed on nonagricultural land, this 40,000-square-foot facility produces about 1 million pounds of fish and 60,000 pounds of fresh basil annually. Bioshelters, Inc., uses highly sophisticated, innovative technologies financed by more than $10 million in venture capital funds. Its owners have discovered niche markets for their products including natural food stores, supermarkets, and restaurants in the Boston area. Nonetheless, after more than 13 years in operation, the company has yet to realize an operating profit.

- *Delftree Corporation* of North Adams, Massachusetts, has been growing shiitake mushrooms in an abandoned textile mill since 1982. The company employs about 25 workers and annually produces roughly 300,000 pounds of this specialty crop—approximately 5 percent of the national market.
- *AquaFuture, Inc.,* established in 1988 in Turners Falls, Massachusetts, is a pioneer in advanced aquaculture systems. Located in a rather ordinary looking corrugated metal building in the town's industrial park, it produces a continuous supply of high-quality striped bass for Northeast seafood markets. Its integrated technologies, which dramatically improve aquaculture productivity while minimizing environmental impacts, are well-suited to city environments.
- *Village Farms* in Buffalo, New York, may be the most successful urban agriculture venture in the country from a strict business perspective. Established in 1987, Village Farms is an 18-acre greenhouse constructed on a brownfield that was formerly the site of a steel mill. AgroPower Development, the largest greenhouse operator in the country, owns and operates the facility, producing about 8 million pounds of vine-ripened tomatoes per year. Employing nearly 100 people, Village Farms has achieved economies of scale that are currently out of reach of most inner-city entrepreneurs and investors.

"Take a Stand, Own the Land": The Dudley Street Neighborhood Initiative

A key issue for urban agriculture is access to land. Due to owner abandonment and lapsed tax payments, a large percentage of vacant urban land has been seized by city governments. The manner in which a particular city administration chooses to dispose of these holdings depends on its overall development strategy, its knowledge of the available options, and its commitment to building wealth in low-income communities. City officials can focus their efforts on attracting outside investors, or they can develop programs to encourage local communities and entrepreneurs to invest in vacant urban land.

The Dudley Street Neighborhood Initiative (DSNI), a nonprofit grassroots planning organization in Roxbury, Massachusetts, provides an example of community-based redevelopment of vacant lands, in which urban agriculture has been an important component. This multicultural neighborhood of African-Americans, Cape Verdeans, Latinos, and whites was afflicted in the 1960s and 1970s by disinvestment and redlining by banks, government neglect, and arson-for-profit by greedy speculators. In 1988, following a campaign built around the slogan, "Take a stand, own the land," DSNI became the first nonprofit community organization in the country to be granted the power of eminent domain (see Medoff and Sklar 1994, and Dixon in Chapter 3), giving residents the right and the power to determine how vacant parcels of land in their community would be developed.

The residents of the Dudley Street neighborhood created a land trust, Dudley Neighbors, Inc., to manage the land acquired by eminent domain. With funding from the EPA's Supplemental Environmental Fund, DSNI is constructing a 10,000-square-foot commercial solar greenhouse as part of a comprehensive urban agriculture program (Fulford 1997).

Residents will grow vegetables, herbs, and flowers for sale, including sales to markets outside the community. A percentage of the profits will be deposited in a Community Development Account for reinvestment in socially responsible businesses and to make grants and loans to community-based groups to support revitalization efforts.

DSNI's agricultural strategy also includes a network of community gardens, inspired not only by community demand for fresh produce but also by the vision of a vibrant urban village in which agriculture, linked to cultural traditions, helps to provide jobs, food security, and a healthy environment. In 1995, DSNI conducted a community-wide survey to determine the kinds of fresh produce residents wished were more available. The results showed that most residents spent between $200 and $600 monthly for food and that they spent a quarter of their food budget for produce, 80 percent of which was fresh. DSNI's urban agricultural system, based on the principles of sustainable agriculture, attempts to meet part of this demand.

The goal is not to become the primary source of food for residents but to enhance the availability of fresh produce to improve local economic and environmental conditions. This is also seen as an effective strategy for preserving open space in the face of strong pressures for development.

Challenges to Urban Agriculture

Urban agriculture faces many of the same problems as do farmers in rural communities, as well as some obstacles specific to city farming. Pressure from competing land uses, including demand for adequate affordable housing in central cities, coupled with rising city land values, makes it difficult for urban agricultural ventures to succeed on a strictly for-profit basis. A recent national study reached the sobering conclusion that, to date, few attempts to establish commercially viable urban agriculture have succeeded (Wohl 1999). The success of AgroPower Development, which operates large hydroponic greenhouses, suggests that economies of scale may be necessary for profitable urban agriculture, an idea that is in tension with the philosophy of most grassroots community initiatives. Yet agriculture has long been subsidized in the United

States, and it may be appropriate to shift some of those subsidies to urban communities wishing to promote their own food production and economic development.

A further obstacle arises from doubts about the quality and safety of food grown in sites on or near brownfields and near busy streets filled with traffic. This issue is being addressed creatively in a variety of ways. Many city farmers are creating compost, or importing it, from zoos and wholesale food markets to rebuild or replace soils. They are also using phytoremediation techniques, growing plants that remove, or decompose, pollutants to clean contaminated soils. If urban agriculture successfully meets these challenges, it can make an important contribution to the greening of our cities and the reduction of urban poverty.

Conclusion

The natural assets of cities represent considerable sources of wealth. Whether they can be used to combat urban poverty remains an open question. The answer will depend on the degree to which the poor are able to obtain a measure of control over those assets and on their ability to manage them sustainably. The issue of control is largely political. Residents of Roxbury's Dudley Street neighborhood have shown that grassroots community organizing can achieve significant political power to gain access to urban natural assets and use them to combat poverty.

Although politics and economics are significant factors in determining the extent to which urban natural assets can help address issues of urban poverty, cultural attitudes toward these assets may prove to be even more crucial. For example, a search of the documents of the Dudley Street Neighborhood Initiative reveals few references to *real estate*—but many to *land*. This reflects a view of wealth as a resource to be nurtured and passed along, as opposed to treating it as a commodity to be bought and sold. Urban redevelopment efforts guided by the conventional wisdom that drives Wall Street have failed miserably in their attempts to revitalize economically distressed neighborhoods. The Dudley experiment and a growing number of comprehensive community initiatives across the country are demonstrating that development strategies inspired by quality-of-life concerns are more likely to build natural assets and to empower residents.

References

Alexander, Christopher, Sara Ishikawa, and Murray Silverstein. 1977. *A Pattern Language: Towns, Buildings, Construction.* New York: Oxford University Press.
Dalton, Kathy L. 1998. *Reclaiming Lost Ground: A Resource Guide for Community Based Brownfields Development in Massachusetts.* Boston: Dudley Street Neighborhood

Initiative, Lincoln Filene Center, Tufts University.

Doxiadis, C. A., and J. G. Papaioannou. 1974. *Ecumenopolis: The Inevitable City of the Future.* New York: W. W. Norton.

Fulford, Bruce. 1997. *Options for Successfully Operating a 10,000 Square Foot Greenhouse in the Dudley Street Neighborhood.* Roxbury, Mass.: Dudley Street Neighborhood Initiative.

Gershwin, M. Eric. 1999. "Urban Asthma." *Allergy and Asthma Magazine* 8(1).

Greater Boston Urban Resources Partnership. 1999. "Piecemeal to Cohesion: Collaboration for Environmental Change." Discussion paper presented at a meeting of Greater Boston's Public and Private Environmental Grantmakers at the offices of the Boston Fund. 15 October.

Linden, Eugene. 1996. "The Exploding Cities of the Developing World." *Foreign Affairs* 75(1): 52–65.

Kelly, Chris. 1996. "In Search of New Life for Smaller Cities." *Land Lines* 8(2).

Jacobs, Jane. 1969. *The Economy of Cities.* New York: Random House.

Jargowsky, Paul. 1997. *Poverty and Place: Ghettos, Barrios, and the American City.* New York: Russell Sage Foundation.

Kaufman, Jerry, and Martin Bailkey. 1999. *Exploring Opportunities for Community Development Corporations Using Inner City Vacant Land for Urban Agriculture.* Madison: University of Wisconsin.

Medoff, Peter. and Holly Sklar. 1994. *Streets of Hope: The Fall and Rise of an Urban Neighborhood.* Boston: South End Press.

Shaeffer, John R., and Leonard A. Stevens. 1983. *Future Water.* New York: William Morrow and Company.

Smit, Jac, Annu Ratta, and Joe Nasr. 1996. *Urban Agriculture: Food, Jobs and Sustainable Cities.* New York: UN Development Program.

Spirn, Anne Whiston. 1984. *The Granite Garden.* New York: Basic Books.

Todd, Nancy Jack, and John Todd. 1984. *Bioshelters, Ocean Ark, City Farming: Ecology as the Basis for Design.* San Francisco: Sierra Club Books.

Todd, John, and George Tukel. 1981. *Reinhabiting Cities and Towns: Designing for Sustainability.* San Francisco: Planet Drum Foundation.

U.S. Environmental Protection Agency. 1998. *Road Map To Understanding Innovative Technology Options for Brownfields Investigation and Cleanup.* Cincinnati: National Service Center for Environmental Publications.

Weiss, Kevin. 1998. "Asthma in an Urban Environment: What Do We Know?" Address at the New York Academy of Medicine, New York. 4–5 May.

Wilson, William Julius. 1996. *When Work Disappears.* New York: Alfred A. Knopf.

Wohl, Hope. 1999. "Feasibility Analysis of For-Profit Agricultural Businesses Using Urban Vacant Land." Executive Summary prepared for the Pennsylvania Horticultural Society Philadelphia Green. Philadelphia. October.

Wong, Kathleen. 1999. "Satellite Images Reveal Startling Tree Loss in American Cities." *U.S. News and World Report* (July 19).

CHAPTER 15

The Chelsea River: Democratizing Access to Nature in a World of Cities

H. Patricia Hynes

Rivers and their floodplains sustained both indigenous peoples and the early settlers. Like interstate highways and flyways today, waterways carried people, raw materials, and finished goods to and from distant markets. Virtually every city of renown is built along the water and gains character, identity, and wealth from its waterbody. Yet by the early twentieth century, cities had segregated rivers from nearby neighborhoods by constructing flood-control dikes, wastewater treatment plants, railroads, highways, warehouses, and factories along riverfronts. In some cases, urban rivers were rerouted or buried (MacBroom 1999). In a natural-assets tradeoff of sorts, philanthropists who had built their industrial wealth on the banks of city rivers chose to preserve rivers elsewhere—wild and scenic rivers and upstream rural stretches of city rivers—for recreation, sport fishing, and tourism.

Now, in a provocative turnabout, cities are revisiting their riverfronts as catalysts for urban redevelopment and as destination points for tourism. For many an urban politician and planner, dingy and economically idle waterfronts have gained new currency as magnets and engines for center city revitalization. And for neighboring communities, a local river's edge is becoming a desirable place for recreation, boating, fishing, ecosystem restoration, and overall neighborhood betterment. The Providence River in downtown Providence, the Boston Harbor and the East Boston Greenway, Baltimore's Inner Harbor, the riverfront parks of Milwaukee and Cleveland, the Chattanooga Riverwalk, and Paseo del Rio of San Antonio all spring to mind.

The Chelsea River, also known as the Chelsea Creek, is the most recent of Boston's rivers to gain a constituency calling for riverfront restoration and recreational access. The Chelsea is a narrow industrial river whose depth and

277

protected inner harbor inspired the state of Massachusetts to zone virtually its entire waterfront as a marine industrial park for the port of Boston and the larger metropolitan economy. What has been a working marine industrial waterfront, however, is now a hodgepodge of fuel storage tanks, bulk material storage sites, a burgeoning number of parking lots for Boston's Logan Airport, and brownfields—idle lands contaminated by past industrial or commercial use. The river has been described by public regulatory agencies as the most polluted tributary of Boston Harbor. Yet it has also been dubbed "a river of dreams" for the waterfront city of Chelsea and the cross-river neighborhood of East Boston. In fact, it is East Boston's primary natural asset. Community activists have staged a series of public actions calling for environmental improvements along the waterfront and have created a handful of green spaces that symbolize their cause.

The most vocal advocates of access to the Chelsea River are racially diverse and working-class neighborhoods on both sides of the river. Framing their campaigns in terms of environmental justice, these community advocates seek both an improved quality of life and local housing and economic development for residents. Developers, working in varying degrees of partnership with municipalities, typically propose waterfront models that focus on attracting the disposable income of tourists and a new urban middle and upper middle class. This development model has so far failed to create economically and racially integrated communities and has displaced local lower-income people in the process of redevelopment. Moreover, the proximity of the Chelsea River to the port and airport of Boston, together with its unique marine industrial zoning, makes government planners reluctant to cede the waterfront to local communities for natural-assets development. Thus, community advocates, city planners, and developers bring a seemingly divergent set of claims, goals, and resources to the Chelsea River waterfront.

The communities of East Boston and Chelsea describe themselves as "rich in history and poor in resources." Yet in their struggles for a cleaner and more accessible river, they have amassed a demonstrable wealth of leadership, credibility, public attention, and financial and technical assistance from public and nonprofit agencies. The Chelsea Creek Action Group, a local coalition, has effectively employed public interest and environmental law, negotiation, and confrontation to achieve inclusive waterfront planning that integrates local public rights to the river with regional maritime interests.

This study of the Chelsea River is set in the context of urbanization, the plight of the poor who are concentrated in inner cities, and the recent upsurge of the environmental justice movement. These phenomena are reconfiguring the agenda and priorities of mainstream environmentalism, creating alliances among urban ecologists, urban planners, community organizers, and sympathetic governmental and nongovernmental organizations.

Environmental Justice

Environmental justice arose in the United States during the 1980s and 1990s as a new paradigm of environmental protection, informed by the experience of low-income and working-class people in both rural and urban communities and giving credence to the expertise of experiential knowledge. An early spur for this new framework was the successful protest of blue-collar housewives and mothers at Love Canal, New York, which resulted in government relocation of families from a neighborhood that had been built adjacent to a mile-long trench filled with industrial waste. The Love Canal protests, which began in the late 1970s, launched modern grass-roots environmentalism. This movement is based on "popular science" and citizen protest; makes links between human health and environmental pollution; and calls for cleaner products and production processes, waste reduction, and community awareness of and involvement in regional planning (Gibbs 1982).

In the early 1980s, an African-American community in Warren County, North Carolina, protested the plans of the U.S. Environmental Protection Agency (EPA) to site a national landfill for the disposal of polychlorinated biphenyls (PCBs) in their community. The action, which used the tactics and tradition of the civil rights movement, garnered national attention and sparked a sequence of studies of and protests against the disproportionate siting of waste facilities and "dirty" industry in poor communities of color, calling the practice *environmental racism*. People of color gathered in Washington, D.C., in 1991 for their first national conference on environmental justice to organize, strategize, and promulgate a set of principles. The government and major environmental organizations were publicly challenged to include people of color and to integrate issues of race and economic justice into their environmental analysis and decision-making (Bullard 1994; see also Chapters 4 and 6 in this volume).

Environmental justice introduces new dimensions to older environmental frameworks. The movement injects a consciousness of class, race, and gender into environmental analysis, research, remedial action, and resource allocation. Additionally, environmental justice brings a place-based and community-based focus to environmental protection. The central paradigms of the earlier environmental movement—"nature as wilderness remote from people" and "the environment as physical media threatened by pollution"—lack the historical connection of community environmental health to the environment where most people actually live. This environment includes the nexus of buildings, infrastructure, streets, social life, and human services, together with ambient air, water, soil, and urban open space: the environment as city people experience it.

The Urban Habitat

One of the major forces reshaping the world's environment is the massive migration of people to cities and the growth of metropolitan areas. Half of the world's 6 billion people live in urban locales, and almost two-thirds will be living in urban areas by 2030, according to estimates by the United Nations. In the United States, four-fifths of the people live in metropolitan areas.[1] Yet, although the urban habitat is increasingly the primary human environment, the majority of environmental research and policy has been decidedly nonurban in focus. As recently as 1992, the landmark UN Conference on Environment and Development, held in Rio de Janiero, Brazil, devoted only 1 of the 40 chapters in its official consensus document, *Agenda 21,* to cities (Platt et al. 1994).

The mainstream environmental movement draws on a long tradition that has conceived of nature as pristine wilderness without people. This image was extolled and idealized by preservationist John Muir and transcendentalist Henry David Thoreau in texts that were tinged with misanthropy and animus toward cities. The federal Wilderness Act of 1964 codified the definition of wilderness as "nature unaffected by humans." There is, however, a discernible shift in the modern understanding of the natural environment, away from nature as separate and distinct from humans and toward a view of humans and the rest of nature as inexorably linked in a common environment, both by our origins and by our current patterns of development.

In the United States, the poor, people of color, and immigrants are most highly concentrated in depressed center cities and extensive ghettos of pollution and poverty. This concentration of poor people and pollution stems largely from an earlier pattern of "white flight" from center cities to suburbs and the resulting disinvestment in central cities by corporations, financial institutions, and government (O'Hare 1996). The primary environmental health crises of urban children living in poverty—asthma, lead poisoning, and accidental injuries—correlate most closely with these children's physical and built environments; that is, local air, soil, and housing (Doc4Kids Project 1998). Urban children's daily and dominant experiences of nature are weedy, littered lots where housing once stood; industrial brownfields in and at the edges of their neighborhoods; and polluted bodies of water.

Vacant Land: An Inadvertent Asset

One outcome of the environmental justice movement is the reclaiming of natural assets at the neighborhood level, which is now occurring in numerous inner and center cities. Urban disinvestment has left vast amounts of vacant land. Chicago, for example, has 56,000 vacant lots. One of every eight lots in Central Harlem—the equivalent of 112 acres—was vacant in the early 1990s.

Philadelphia, the oldest industrial city in the United States, has 15,000 vacant housing lots and 21,000 abandoned houses. Abandoned lots that once were the footprints of houses, businesses, parks, and industries became local eyesores and sites of waste dumping and drug trafficking. Many such lots have been transformed into community gardens, as described by Raquel Pinderhughes in Chapter 16. A recent survey found growing interest in community gardens as job training sites for youth and as market gardens where plants can be grown for sale and for value-added products (American Community Gardening Association 1998). This incipient trend reflects a growing link between environmental justice and economic development.[2]

Linking Poverty and Pollution

Environmental justice embodies the goal of social and political empowerment for communities unjustly burdened by poverty and pollution. In the city of Boston, for example, the neighborhoods of Roxbury and North Dorchester have the highest indices of household poverty, ill health, childhood lead poisoning, asthma, mixed industrial and residential zoning, hazardous waste sites, vacant land, traffic, injury by weapons, and substance abuse. Simultaneously, these neighborhoods are increasingly recognized for their social assets: community-based groups that are organizing and rebuilding their debilitated and underserved urban neighborhoods with initiatives that promote affordable housing, community environmental health, development of local economic and human services, and restoration of local natural assets. Recent environmental justice campaigns, such as the defeat of an effort to site an asphalt plant at the boundary of Roxbury and South Boston, have served to create a common political cause—albeit issue-specific and fragile—among white and black working-class and poor communities historically divided by racial conflict.

Urban Revitalization

Another frontier of activism—one that particularly appeals to mainstream, middle-class environmentalists—is the movement to contain metropolitan sprawl by land-use planning, clustered building design, and center-city redevelopment. Metropolitan growth and development in the United States has been driven mainly by market forces for private gain and only minimally directed by regional planning for social and environmental well-being (Davis 1992; Kennedy 1992; Warner 1987). As a result, land development has far outpaced population growth since the mid-twentieth century, spilling and scattering onto farmland and open space adjacent to cities. Metropolitan Cleveland grew in area by 33 percent between 1970 and 1990 while the population fell by 11 percent; in the same years, Chicago's population grew by only 4 percent while developed land in the metropolitan region increased by 46 percent (Trails and Greenways Clearinghouse 1999). Some metropolises, such as the Philadelphia-Wilmington-Baltimore-Washington metro areas, are growing into one another. Virtually half of the large cities ranked as "most sprawl-threatened" by the Sierra Club in 1998 are ones with little population growth but large population dispersal into the city hinterlands (Stoehl 1999). With its typical pattern of new construction of utilities and low-density development, sprawl incurs personal, public, and environmental costs that have only begun to be calculated: time spent in travel, taxes for infrastructure development, and the loss of irreplaceable natural assets.

"Smart growth" initiatives aim to control sprawl and revitalize center cities. Smart-growth designs provide for clustered housing and easy pedestrian access to workplaces, shopping areas, and trails and greenways for recreation. The idea is to protect open space and to direct growth to where there is already supporting infrastructure. In November 1998, voters approved more than 100 antisprawl measures around the country (Stoehl 1999). Among the best-known examples of smart-growth initiatives are those in Austin, Texas, and Portland, Oregon—cities that have, nonetheless, maintained rapid economic growth. The principles of smart growth draw from the design maxims that have historically made city neighborhoods "work" for people: neighborhoods that integrate residential and commercial districts, increase pedestrian-friendly spaces and passages, and provide nearby natural amenities are neighborhoods that thrive (Jacobs 1961).[3]

Urban Rivers and Smart Growth

Smart-growth initiatives are drawing increasing attention to urban rivers. Urban rivers usually run through the historical heart of a city and beckon people to their edges—provided they can get to them. Although they rarely can be restored to the quasi-pristine conditions that permit safe fishing and swimming, urban rivers—with their scenic vistas, proximity to neighborhoods, opportunities for outdoor recreation, local ecology, and rich historical heritage—do invite uses and benefits that have made cities work in the past and that can make city neighborhoods live again.

The Trust for Public Land, a national land conservation organization, reports three outcomes enjoyed by select cities that have developed their urban waterfronts as open spaces and greenways. First, restored waterfronts retain and lure back the middle class to urban residential neighborhoods, shoring up the tax base. Second, waterfronts with shops, cafés, and various marketplaces promote tourism, which the National Park Service in 1999 forecast to become the largest economic sector in the United States in the near future. Third, waterfronts with greenways attract mobile business sectors, such as information, finance, and related service sectors, which can more easily relocate for quality of life factors and natural amenities (Lerner and Poole 1999).

Bringing middle-class people and their money back into cities, however, is too often seized upon as the only index of success in waterfront revitalization. Speaking at a November 1999 EPA conference on smart growth in Boston, landscape architect Shirley Kressel observed that "new urbanism," which aims to attract middle- and upper-middle-class people back to the city, is about "variety not diversity" and is revitalizing *places* rather than *people*. She characterized the new urban architecture and landscape as "suburbanizing from within" and faulted them for sorting by socioeconomic class as deliberately as has suburbanization.

The point is not that a return by the middle class to urban neighborhoods such as East Boston, Chelsea, or Roxbury would not be good for the neighborhoods. Rather, redeveloping for the middle class should not be done at the expense of the poor and working class, who so often have been driven out of their homes and neighborhoods by the regressive real estate impacts of urban renewal and gentrification. Community goals for an affordable and stable housing market must be at the center of an urban redevelopment policy based upon attracting the middle class.

Reclaiming the Chelsea River

In a new twist on the conventions of smart growth, activists in Chelsea are building a campaign to reclaim the Chelsea River premised on their own homegrown neighborhood model of waterfront revitalization. The most visible and vocal revitalization stewards of the creek are neither city officials working with consultant planners and developers nor a high-profile private-public partnership. Rather, the catalysts are local residents of diverse ethnic, racial, and economic backgrounds, supported by a set of nonprofit and public agencies. Many, if not most, of the leaders are women who want just what other successful riverfront communities enjoy: a heritage park, restored wetlands, greenways and esplanades for outdoor recreation, vistas of the city and the harbor, affordable housing, and businesses for local people (Bongiovanni 1999). Their accomplishments to date are a loosely strung set of site-by-site waterfront opportunities and gains, some they have initiated and others precipitated by a development or pollution event. The question then arises: how can a small set of strategic, but fragmented, gains grow into a realizable master plan and long-term program for restoring the river? How can communities turn a few nodes of green, linked by community will, into what Frederick Law Olmstead, describing his plans for a series of open spaces and water corridors for nineteenth-century Boston, called an "emerald necklace"?

The Setting

Like many older industrial cities, Chelsea evolved from early affluence to become a solid working-class city during the industrial revolution. Now it is a racially and ethnically diverse city, with about 21 percent of families below the poverty line (versus 6.7 percent for the state) and the highest unemployment in the region. Chelsea has been a gateway for all the successive waves of immigrants arriving since the nineteenth century: Today, at least 20 languages are spoken in the city. At its height, population rose to about 50,000, dropped to half that in the 1980s with white flight, and has climbed incrementally since then with immigration. Latinos now make up almost half the population.

For a city of its size, Chelsea has had incommensurate physical and political catastrophes, including two major fires and the construction of a regional highway that bisected the city and destroyed vital neighborhoods taken by eminent domain. In 1991, the city was placed into receivership (the first post-Depression municipal receivership) due to the dismally incompetent and corrupt state of municipal politics, and there was talk of annexing it to Boston.

The riverfront renaissance that has produced striking results in many cities has largely bypassed small and economically challenged cities like Chelsea. Only two of the seven rivers flowing into Boston Harbor and Massachusetts Bay—the Charles and the Neponset—were early targets for revitalization (see Figure 15.1). Chelsea Creek—the most intensively industrial, commercial, and polluted of the seven—has been neglected. In 1978, the state of Massachusetts zoned virtually its entire waterfront as a designated port area (DPA), prioritizing development for industrial uses. Thus, even as Boston Harbor elsewhere has enjoyed a renaissance, public access to the river and the inner harbor of Chelsea has been sacrificed.

More than half of Chelsea's land is zoned for industrial and commercial use, a larger percentage than in any other city in metropolitan Boston (Goody, Clancy and Associates and Connery Associates 1995). The fuel storage industry dominates the waterfront: The DPA has capacity for 40 percent of the petroleum used in Massachusetts, with additional capacity for New Hampshire and Vermont.[4] Past and present land uses have left a legacy of pollution and minimal green space. Residential neighborhoods bear a heavy burden from industrial and commercial truck traffic. Except for the marina of the Chelsea Yacht Club and one exclusive housing development outside the DPA, residents have no access to the riverfront.

Depending on the perspective of those interviewed for this study, the waterfront of Chelsea Creek was described as underemployed as a marine

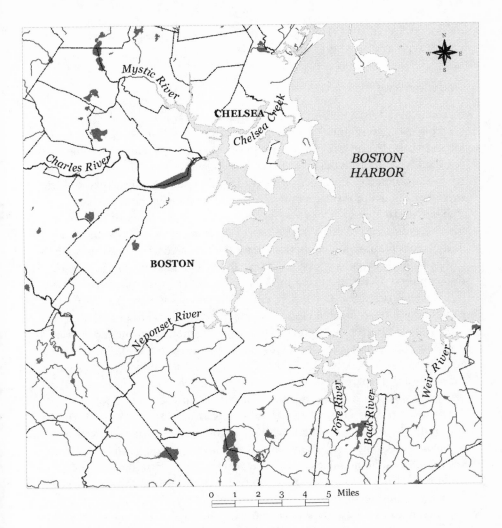

Figure 15.1. Chelsea and Boston Harbor.
Source: MassGIS.

industrial park; inappropriately (but lucratively) employed as commercial parking for Logan Airport; and underdeveloped as a natural asset for recreation, urban ecology, and nearby housing. As a natural asset, the river can be a composite of working, marine-related uses and a series of planned open spaces, which—like the Boston HarborWalk—would form a green and blue waterfront spine for public use. This vision poses a question to the growing constituency for public access to Chelsea Creek: how can local claims for access to the creek as a natural asset be combined with regional claims to the same natural asset for marine industrial uses? How, in other words, does a "designated port area" coexist with a "desired green space area"?

Pollution Profile

Since the mid-1990s, a coalition of nonprofit organizations and public agencies working with community groups has assembled a picture of the pollution burden borne by the city due to land and waterfront uses. The environmental status of the waterfront has been assessed through a review of historical industrial and commercial uses, interviews with local people, visual surveys, and an inventory of environmental reports, permits, and enforcement records.

The Massachusetts Toxics Campaign conducted an inventory of documented industrial pollution in the city of Chelsea between 1987 and 1994. The largest number of continuous large industrial chemical releases (the Toxics Release Inventory, or TRI, releases) and emergency spills (one-time, discontinuous events) occurred in the waterfront area. Over the years investigated, industries reported releasing nearly 700,000 pounds of volatile organic compounds into ambient air. Emergency spills, mostly gasoline or oil, were as large as 200,000 gallons. Numerous other smaller, nonemergency spills were scattered throughout the city. At the time of the study, in 1994, Chelsea contained 44 sites known as "21E" sites, a designation given by the Massachusetts Department of Environmental Protection to sites where a significant quantity of hazardous waste or petroleum waste—but not enough to classify the site as a federal Superfund site—has accumulated. The 21E sites are clustered along the waterfront and in other zones of industrial and commercial activity, but many are also scattered throughout residential neighborhoods. Four industries alone reported using 2.5 million pounds of chemicals that are known reproductive toxins (Massachusetts Toxics Campaign Fund 1996).

The environmental justice paradigm examines the justice dimensions of pollution and poverty by posing the question of whose neighborhoods bear the burden of pollution for the larger society. In that spirit, the Massachusetts Toxics Campaign overlaid the reported pollution sources in Chelsea onto a map of the city showing poverty status and racial and ethnic composition from the 1990 census (Figure 15.2). They found that poverty and pollution coincide: two of the three census tracts with the highest percentage of people living below the poverty level, tracts 1604 and 1605, contain the largest number of pollution facilities and spills in every category analyzed. Census tracts with the highest percentage of whites and the lowest percentage of people living below the poverty line, 1606 and 1603, had the smallest number of pollution sites. Census tract 1603, an enclave of white professionals, had no reported sites.

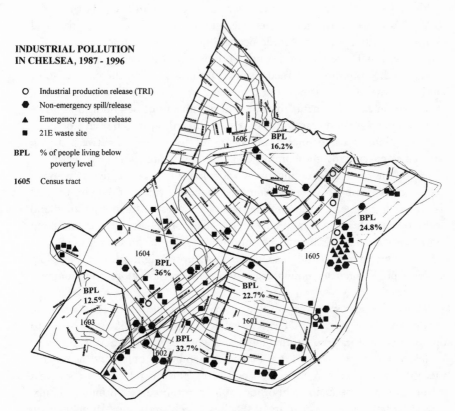

**INDUSTRIAL POLLUTION
IN CHELSEA, 1987 - 1996**

○   Industrial production release (TRI)
◆   Non-emergency spill/release
▲   Emergency response release
■   21E waste site

BPL   % of people living below
              poverty level

1605   Census tract

Figure 15.2. Industrial Pollution in Chelsea.
Source: Massachusetts Toxics Campaign Fund (1996).

The New Chelsea

The city of Chelsea emerged from receivership in 1995, following an intensely democratic process that involved citizens from all of the city's constituencies in developing a new city charter. Since then, it has risen like a phoenix. In 1998, Chelsea was one of 10 municipalities selected for the All-America City award, based on its success in promoting citizen participation in community improvement and its inclusion of a diverse population in all levels of community building. The award is a tribute to the rising tide of community pride, purpose, and initiative in facing major social challenges: poor schools and housing, crime and drugs, poverty, and environmental injustice. As a result of voter registration drives, the city now surpasses the statewide averages both in voting rates among minority groups and in people of color in office (City of Chelsea 1998).

The Chelsea Green Space and Recreation Committee was born in the mid-1990s out of a struggle to replace outdoor recreational space that had been lost in a tradeoff between desperately needed new schools and popular park space heavily used by local youth. Founded on principles of environmental justice, the committee marked a significant passage from the city's crisis of survival in the face of crime, drug trafficking, and fiscal decline to a growing concern about environmental hazards and the quality of neighborhood life.

Through direct advocacy and lobbying—including marches and demonstrations, strategic use of media, and sit-ins at city hall—and active planning with city government, the committee made rapid gains. The city declared a commitment to reconstructing parks and pledged to create five new open spaces. In the flush of success, committee members turned to environmental hazards facing the city, including the many toxic waste sites; the polluted and declining waterfront; and industrial bulk storage of oil, asphalt, and salt along the waterfront near residential neighborhoods. The various campaigns have attracted new members and created alliances across neighborhoods, including residents, public agencies, nonprofit environmental organizations, and municipal employees.

Within five years, the committee made remarkable progress in bringing regional attention to the Chelsea River. The committee took to the streets to oppose asphalt storage in existing tanks and worked with politicians to win its campaign in the state legislature. Likewise, members lobbied and negotiated successfully to have a cover placed on a 100,000-ton pile of rock salt that towers over a residential neighborhood. The committee's environmental fairs, walking tours, guided boat tours of Chelsea Creek, and canoe launchings on the upper reach of the creek have been reported in the local and metropolitan news media.

The committee has become the best-known forum and the most aggressive vehicle for Chelsea residents to address issues of health, environment, and quality of life, according to the city's All-American City application (City of Chelsea 1998). Ed Marakovitz, director of the Chelsea Human Services Collaborative, characterizes the committee's environmentalism admiringly as tough, uncompromising, and politicized, with a consciousness of injustice and racism (Marakovitz 1998). The committee has joined with an equally vocal cross-creek organization in East Boston to form the Chelsea Creek Action Group, an alliance that has elevated the campaign for waterfront access and cleanup to a regional issue.[5]

Activists in Chelsea have also drawn support from the Massachusetts Urban Riverways Program, created in 1996 by Maria Van Dusen, director of the Massachusetts Riverways Program, to redress the neglect of many urban rivers.[6] The Urban Riverways Program focuses on the benefits of rivers to their local communities, the restoration of degraded habitats and fish runs, and the power of organizing. This programmatic philosophy, especially the focus on residential communities and the value of community organizing, promotes an alternative model of waterfront revitalization—one that fits the Chelsea River communities more organically than the market model, with its trickle-down community benefits, promoted by waterfront developers as the economic engine for postindustrial cities.

The Urban Riverways Program is part of a network of like-minded public agencies and nonprofit organizations that supports the unique community activism on both sides of the Chelsea River. These organizations, which offer financial as well as technical assistance, are analogous to private-sector consultants, offering the Chelsea River activists some of the skills and resources that waterfront developers bring to municipal planners.

Democratizing Access to the River

In the early 1990s, an architectural and planning firm sketched a scenario for the designated port area (DPA) of Chelsea that incorporated zones for public access to the river, open space, housing, and commercial development (Dixon 1993). Chelsea was in receivership and was seeking economic development and community revitalization—including jobs, housing, and open space—compatible with its ethnic and economic diversity. The receiver saw Chelsea Creek as the city's most significant economic asset and sought a plan for new economic and housing development along the waterfront—one that would not, however, precipitate gentrification.

The consultant report viewed the Chelsea River waterfront as having three unique zones: a neighborhood zone, a general industrial use zone, and a port activity zone. Together, the report suggested, these zones could accommodate both the city's need to invigorate its local economy and community life and the region's need for industrial port capacity. The part of the DPA waterfront closest to the city's historic center, from the Tobin Bridge and the end of Broadway Street to Highland Street, was tagged a "neighborhood zone." This small section of the DPA was identified as the waterfront area that could offer both proximity to Chelsea's downtown residential and commercial life and vistas of Boston's Inner Harbor and downtown skyline. Capitalizing on its proximity to the waterfront would stabilize Chelsea's historic downtown area, the "heart" of the city, and strengthen the neighborhood's tenuous economic base. The study acknowledged that, in this scenario, the multistory salt pile and the oil storage tanks in Coastal Oil and Atlantic Fuels terminals would have to be relocated to more appropriate sites upriver within the DPA. Related truck traffic would be rerouted around the district.

The consultants concluded that open space, such as an esplanade or water-front park with water transportation, would require both public investment and cooperation from the private sector. The plan would necessitate negoti-ation and a memorandum of understanding between the city of Chelsea and two state agencies: the Office of Coastal Zone Management, which is responsible for the designated port area, and the Metropolitan District Commission, which is responsible for parks and recreation. Simultaneous agreements with the affected industries would also need to be negotiated—not a simple process.

Unfortunately, for reasons unknown (but probably related to the transition from receivership to an elected government), the study ended up on a shelf with no further realization. At this point, it serves as a heuristic device rather than as a blueprint for opening the waterfront to public access.

Community Activism versus City Planning

Many of the people interviewed for this study expressed the opinion that the new community activism focused on Chelsea Creek results from the fact that the river is the last environmental frontier in the city, which otherwise has a dense built environment and little open space. Unfortunately, the postreceiver-ship government has not made waterfront revitalization a priority. Ned Keefe, a city planner for Chelsea, asserts that planning for the city overall is more important to municipal officials than planning for the designated port area. He cites the former Amoco fuel storage site, now a commercial parking lot serving Logan Airport, as an example of an interim and lucrative use of the waterfront that the city welcomes until long-term economic uses are decided. Without an overall waterfront plan, the city will make site-specific decisions about land use as need and opportunity arise.

Asked about the relationship between the city and the community in regard to land-use planning along the waterfront, Keefe replied that there is no "formal environment for communicating planning to the community" and that "access to City Hall is difficult, but not closed." He noted that although individuals in city government and the community get along personally, the two "are institutionally remote" (Keefe 1999). The city planner's candid assess-ment of the political relationship between city hall and the Green Space and Recreation Committee suggests that, despite the democratic process employed in rewriting the city charter and despite the All-American City award, a participatory process in public decision-making is not a fait accompli of postreceivership government. A mixture of respect and wariness characterizes the local government's attitude toward its activist environmental organization.

Thus city government land-use decisions and community activism focusing on Chelsea Creek currently operate on separate tracks, with little transparency and considerable potential for fragmentation—except where both parties find common cause, as they have recently in the redevelopment of a shopping plaza in the upper tidal reach of the creek. Yet Chelsea Creek's future as a compatible mix of local and regional uses and as a restored urban natural asset for everyone hinges on transparency between the city government planning department and the environmental community. It also depends on a holistic and open planning process for the waterfront, with equal participation by citizens, city government, and relevant state agencies and private-sector stakeholders.

Weaving Public Access into Port Uses

A master-planning process involves defining a study corridor; preparing a base map; conducting an inventory and analysis of land use and natural resources; preparing a concept plan; and, finally, preparing a master plan. In the ideal scenario, the city of Chelsea, on behalf of the community, would initiate the public process (as the receiver did in the early 1990s) with the Office of Coastal Zone Management, the state agency responsible for the designated area, and create a planning committee composed of public-sector, private-sector, and community members with equal standing and resources. Future land-use decisions along the Chelsea River would then be integrated into an overall vision of a riverfront city.

One of the more holistic riverfront planning efforts—at least in theory—is the one conducted for the Mississippi Riverfront in the Minneapolis–St. Paul area. "From an urban design viewpoint," writes the Design Center for American Landscape (1994), "the river is both the imaginative heart and the historical foundation of a great metropolis, generating many opportunities for revitalizing its many surrounding communities." Working with public officials, citizens, experts, businesses, and other interest groups, the center proposes that "the river corridor become the backbone of a community-building network that extends . . . into the fabric of each nearby community, enhancing its character, bridging its diversity, and enriching its environment" (Design Center for American Urban Landscape 1994). In this vision, the river is a development framework for the urban communities near it.

It may seem presumptuous to apply metaphors and design principles for the Mississippi River at the Twin Cities to the Chelsea River; but Chelsea has risen singularly from municipal failure, with a civic spirit that has achieved national honor for its diverse and inclusive democracy. The same acclaimed civic process could be employed to build an inclusive framework for future development centered on the river. Without such a process, decisions about a new open space site or a new tenant for a waterfront parcel will continue to be isolated, opportunistic, and potentially antagonistic.

State regulations for the DPA are flexible enough to allow for fitting some green space, open space, and local commercial development into a master plan for the Chelsea Creek waterfront (Grob 1999; Keefe 1999; Lord 1999; Van Dusen 1999; Wiggin 1999). Elizabeth Grob (1999) of the Massachusetts Office of Coastal Zone Management says that although the state is vested in the deep-water port designation for Chelsea Creek, she can envision the "weaving of public access into port uses" within a city-initiated municipal waterfront master-planning process. By regulation, 25 percent of the DPA can be developed commercially to support maritime use and simultaneously attract public use. For example, restaurants and boat-related businesses could have public viewing points. The city could also apply to de-designate part of the DPA and set it aside for more appropriate uses.

If an agreed-upon goal of the master plan were, for example, a greenway corridor along the riverfront open to community access and recreation, then waterfront tenants would also be involved in negotiating easements, relocating industry where necessary, and cleaning up sites. Public-sector agencies would be responsible for implementing and financing waterfront recreation development. Nonprofit agencies and private foundations could support the goal of a democratic and inclusive waterfront plan by investing in the community's skills and in its capacity to participate as an equal partner with the city in the river-front planning process. Public and private funds could be used to hire technical and design consultants to work with the community group throughout the master-planning process.

Environmental Enforcement

Many opportunities for improving the environmental quality of the Chelsea River exist within environmental and natural resource law, including the Massachusetts Chapter 91 Waterways Regulations, the federal Clean Water Act, and hazardous waste statutes at the federal and state levels. Chapter 91 is based on public trust doctrine, which holds that the public has fundamental rights to natural resources and that the state has a duty to preserve and enhance those rights. In the case of the Chelsea River, Chapter 91 is being invoked to restore part of a salt-marsh ecosystem within an upriver section of filled tideland, a section outside the DPA. Within a DPA, however, Chapter 91 offers few public benefits and limits public access to the river's edge, according to Charlie Lord (1999), an environmental attorney and director of the Watershed Institute. Thus, the best chance for the community to gain better river access remains participation in the overall master-plan development process.

All the fuel storage sites on the river have been issued permits for their chemical discharges into the river that can be examined and monitored. The waterfront state hazardous waste sites (21E sites) are at various stages of study or cleanup. Public oversight of these mandated site cleanups and strategic use of applicable environmental statutes through enforcement and negotiation—as the federal EPA has done in other cases—is one of the avenues available for making the river safer for public access.

The Housatonic River in Pittsfield, Massachusetts, serves as an example of how certain rivers that have been essentially "sacrifice zones" for corporate and regional economic benefit can be restored by government environmental enforcement working in concert with citizen activism. From 1932 to 1977, the General Electric Company (GE) used PCBs—suspected carcinogens and endocrine-disrupting compounds—in its operation of a transformer plant in Pittsfield. During this period, GE discarded tens of thousands of pounds of PCBs onto local land and directly into the river. Oil containing PCBs contaminated groundwater as a result of leaks from underground storage tanks, and it flowed downgradient into the river. Contamination in the sediment and water column spread into the aquatic food web, most egregiously in the Pittsfield stretch of the river but also in distant downstream stretches in Connecticut. Health advisories were posted in Massachusetts and Connecticut to discourage fish consumption.

In September 1998, state and federal agencies reached an agreement with GE that required the company to make substantial investments in cleaning up the river and local contaminated land and in redeveloping brownfields in Pittsfield. GE was also required to provide compensation for damages to natural resources. The sweeping agreement concluded almost 20 years of enforcement actions that had languished in the file drawers of bureaucrats. The U.S. Environmental Protection Agency (1999) recently credited three community efforts with raising public awareness of the value of the river and reenergizing its enforcement action: the activism of local citizens who spurred community reconnection and stewardship through riverbank cleanups and the creation of urban river trails; the vigilant reporting of a local journalist; and the tenacity of the city government in negotiating with GE. The RiverWalk on the Housatonic River in Great Barrington, Massachusetts, was simultaneously honored by the federal agency as a model urban river trail.

The EPA, in support of the Chelsea Creek Action Group, has undertaken an ecological reconnaissance by boat along the Chelsea River to identify and map outfall pipes; to locate sites where the community could safely do river cleanups; to document nonpoint source pollution; and to identify industrial pollution where environmental enforcement or technical assistance is needed. The environmental reconnaissance findings could ultimately result in a master plan for environmental remediation of the Chelsea River much like the plan for the Housatonic River. Such a plan would be a framework that would parallel—and, ideally, link with—a master plan for redeveloping the Chelsea riverfront for combined public access and maritime industrial use.

Conclusion

At a recent Harvard University conference on Waterfronts in Post-Industrial Cities, Zheng Shiling of Tongji University, Shanghai, spoke of the determining spirit of rivers in urban development. In some Chinese traditions, water is connected with wisdom. Water, Zheng said, is the environment of the city, the identity of the city, and it offers historical meaning while it also directs future development. The waterfront of Shanghai embodies the center of city life and is vital to the city's future urbanization—which, he concluded, will be planned around the river (Zheng 1999). Speaking in tandem, a member of the development team for Baltimore's Inner Harbor and Boston's Faneuil Hall Marketplace claimed that waterfronts have a way of unlocking a new concept for a city and beginning a process of development that does not end. Both conference speakers captured a turning point in public attitude toward urban rivers in the United States.

The Chelsea community, working in concert with community organizations in East Boston, claims access to the creek as a heritage and natural asset. Public agencies, nonprofit organizations, and private foundations throughout the region have mobilized to offer legal and technical assistance in researching the pollution of natural resources and the applicability of environmental statutes. At the time of this writing, the Chelsea Creek Action Group was submitting a grant proposal to a state program for funding to plan and conduct a visioning and land-use planning charette for the upper reach of the Chelsea Creek known as Mill Creek. The charette would move them from working on isolated sites on the creek to creating a holistic, coherent plan that would increase the organizations' abilities to dialogue with industries on the creek, participate in an overall master-planning process, and leverage resources to revitalize the river.

The city of Chelsea has been nationally acclaimed for the strength of its community-based organizations, in particular for the Chelsea Green Space and Recreation Committee. Refusing to let the city recede into closed-door planning, the committee has set its agenda for the future of Chelsea Creek, as an equal voice with government and industry. The ingredients exist for an unprecedented model of riverfront planning and revitalization based both on local community health and development—the goal of environmental justice—and on regional development.

Notes

1. Metropolitan areas include a central city and satellite cities and towns that are linked by economy, transport, and ecology. Metropolitan areas in the United States have expanded outward with the centrifugal movement of the middle and upper

middle classes from center cities to suburbs and exurbs, whereas cities in the developing world tend to grow at the edges with the new urban settlements of the once-rural poor.

2. In addition to Chapter 16 of this volume, see Hynes (1996) for more detail on the history of community gardens and for case studies in U.S. inner cities. See Smit et al. (1996) for data on urban agriculture in developing and newly industrializing countries. Also, see Chapters 3 and 14 in this book for more detail about how communities have reclaimed the "inadvertent asset" of vacant land.

3. See *The Conservation Fund* (1993), a manual offering guidance in overall planning for and creation of a greenway. Topics include developing a master plan, organizing public-private partnerships, building public support, and obtaining funding. Also see *Massachusetts Coastal Zone Management* (1996). This is a practical handbook for reclaiming public access to coastal lands in Massachusetts. It does not cover coastal land within designated port areas, however.

4. The fuel storage industry has experienced a great deal of flux. A number of Chelsea's designated storage sites are vacant, and many remaining tanks are empty. Uncertainty in this market has stymied waterfront planning in the past, according to Jack Wiggin of the Urban Harbors Institute at the University of Massachusetts, Boston, who coordinated discussions between Chelsea administrators and state agencies in the early 1990s. He found that the oil firms either would not or could not forecast trends for their industry (Wiggin 1999).

5. East Boston has a long activist tradition of opposing Logan Airport expansion into the neighborhood, and on that basis built the current activism for green space and access to the water's edge.

6. Van Dusen could not interest the state government in funding the Urban Riverways Program, but she succeeded in setting up a state-sponsored program with funding from other sources, including the EPA; the U.S. Department of Agriculture; and the Urban Resources Partnership, a public-private consortium dedicated to investing in the urban environment of greater Boston (Van Dusen 1999).

References

American Community Gardening Association. 1998. *National Community Gardening Survey.* Philadelphia, Pa.: American Community Gardening Association.

Bongiovanni, Roseann. 1999. Series of interviews and discussions. Boston and Chelsea, Massachusetts. July–December.

Bullard, Robert. 1994. "Overcoming Racism in Environmental Decisionmaking." *Environment* 36(4): 10–20, 39–44.

City of Chelsea. 1998. *1998 All-America City Award Application.* Chelsea, Mass..

The Conservation Fund. 1993. *Greenways: A Guide to Planning, Design, and Development.* Washington, D.C.: Island Press.

Davis, Mike. 1992. *City of Quartz: Excavating the Future in Los Angeles.* New York: Vintage.

Design Center for American Urban Landscape. 1994. *Redefining the River Corridor as a River Community.* Minneapolis: University of Minnesota, College of Architecture and Landscape Architecture.

Dixon, David. 1993. Memorandum on DPA Strategy. Goody, Clancy and Associates. 31 March.

Doc4Kids Project. 1998. *Not Safe at Home: How America's Housing Crisis Threatens the Health of Its Children*. Boston: Boston Medical Center. Available online at http://www.bostonchildhealth.org/research/Research/Doc4Kids/docs4kids_report.pdf.

Gibbs, Lois. 1982. *Love Canal: My Story*. Albany: State University of New York.

Goody, Clancy and Associates, and Connery Associates. 1995. "Chelsea Zoning Study." Unpublished report prepared for the City of Chelsea, Mass.

Grob, Elizabeth. 1999. Interview at Massachusetts Coastal Zone Management office. Boston. 2 December.

Hynes, H. Patricia. 1996. *A Patch of Eden: America's Inner-City Gardens*. White River Junction, Vt.: Chelsea Green.

Jacobs, Jane. 1961. *The Death and Life of Great American Cities*. New York: Vintage.

Keefe, Ned. 1999. Interview at Chelsea city hall, Mass. 20 July.

Kennedy, Lawrence W. 1992. *Planning the City Upon a Hill: Boston Since 1630*. Amherst: University of Massachusetts Press.

Lerner, Steve, and William Poole. 1999. *The Economic Benefits of Parks and Open Space*. San Francisco: The Trust for Public Land.

Lord, Charlie. 1999. Interview at Watershed Institute office. Newton, Mass. 1 December.

MacBroom, James Grant. 1999. *The River Book*. Hartford: Connecticut Department of Environmental Protection.

Marakovitz, Ed. 1998. "Environmental Organizing in Chelsea: The Green Space and Recreation Committee." Unpublished report prepared for Chelsea Human Services Collaborative. Chelsea, Mass.

Massachusetts Coastal Zone Management. 1996. *Preserving Historic Rights of Way to the Sea*. Boston: Executive Office of Environmental Affairs. June.

Massachusetts Toxics Campaign Fund. 1996. "Industrial Pollution in Chelsea." Unpublished report prepared for the U.S. Environmental Protection Agency.

O'Hare, William P. 1996. "A New Look at Poverty in America." *Population Bulletin* 51(2): 1–48.

Platt, Rutherford, Rowan Rowntree, and Pamela Muick. 1994. *The Ecological City: Preserving and Restoring Urban Biodiversity*. Amherst: University of Massachusetts Press.

Smit, Jac, Annu Ratta, and Joe Nasr. 1996. *Urban Agriculture: Food, Jobs and Sustainable Cities*. New York: UN Development Program.

Stoehl, Thomas B., Jr. 1999. "Reining in Urban Sprawl." *Environment* 41(4): 6–11, 29–33.

Trails and Greenways Clearinghouse. 1999. *Trails and Greenways for Livable Communities*. 1–4. Washington, D.C.: Trails and Greenways Clearinghouse,

U.S. Environmental Protection Agency. 1999. *1999 State of the New England Environment*. Boston: U.S. Environmental Protection Agency.

Van Dusen, Maria. 1999. Interview. Massachusetts Riverways Program. Boston. 23 September.

Warner, Sam Bass, Jr. 1987. *The Private City: Philadelphia in Three Periods of Its Growth.*
    rev. ed. Philadelphia: University of Pennsylvania Press.
Wiggin, Jack. 1999. Interview. Urban Harbors Institute. Boston. 1 July.
Zheng, Shiling. 1999. Presentation at Waterfronts in Post-Industrial Cities Conference,
    7–8 October, at Harvard University Graduate School of Design, Cambridge.

CHAPTER 16

Poverty and the Environment: The Urban Agriculture Connection

Raquel Pinderhughes

In the spring of 1997, New York City Mayor Rudolph Giuliani announced that he would sell off city-owned properties that were home to more than 100 community gardens. The real estate market was surging, and the land was ripe for housing and commercial development. But the city's community gardeners, recognizing the multiple social and environmental benefits of urban gardening, had other ideas.

New York City's community gardening movement traces its history to 1973, when Liz Christy, founder of the Green Guerrillas, organized her neighbors on the Lower East Side to clean out a vacant lot and start planting. Local residents and institutions donated plants, seeds, vegetable clippings, time, and talent. In 1978, the Green Guerrillas helped to spark the city's Green Thumb program, which arranged year-to-year leases for community gardens on public land and supported growers in cleaning up properties, putting up fences, and bringing in topsoil. At the time, New York City had numerous empty lots concentrated in the poorest neighborhoods, and the land was viewed as worthless for other purposes. By the late 1990s, more than 700 community gardens, with thousands of participants, yielded nutritious food for the city's neighborhoods and provided donations to emergency food shelters. The gardens promoted cooperation across generations and ethnic groups and fostered youth development, leadership skills, environmental awareness, and community action (Green Guerrillas 1999). In many of New York's neighborhoods, they served as the closest thing to a public park.

So when Mayor Giuliani scheduled an auction for 113 gardens, the opposition moved quickly and forcefully. Thousands of city residents took to the streets. The city council passed a resolution opposing the sale and considered blocking it outright through an amendment to the city charter. State Senator John Sampson questioned whether the city could legally sell the gardens without approval from the state legislature. Other members of the state assembly proposed a bill to prevent a unilateral sale. Finally, two nonprofit organizations came forward with an offer to buy the properties at below-market prices and preserve them for gardening. Their proposals became quite attractive when lawsuits aiming to block the city's auction were filed. The city would not get full value for the land, but it would avoid a court battle and thus, at the very least, a delay of the sale, if not more dire consequences. So in the end, the city agreed to sell 63 gardens for $3 million to the Trust for Public Land and the other 50 gardens for $1.2 million to the New York Restoration Project.

Urban agriculture yields a wide variety of social and environmental benefits, from strengthening local food systems and providing green spaces to creating opportunities for youth programs, job training, and prisoner rehabilitation. The principal form of investment needed for this type of natural-asset building is labor. A precondition for this investment, however, is the redistribution of access to land for community gardens.

As in the case of the brownfield reclamation initiatives described by K. A. Dixon in Chapter 3 of this volume, communities have devised a variety of strategies to obtain rights to reclaim and make productive use of the vacant lots that dot our cities. These rights are often insecure. As the events in New York demonstrate, city officials can move swiftly to take back property when they perceive that it could be used more "productively." In many cases, the large sums of money needed for a rescue are hard to come by. To thrive over the long term, urban agriculture needs to mobilize both public and private support, founded on a recognition of its many benefits.

The Benefits of Urban Agriculture

In the United States, urban cultivation does much more than fill a simple need for food. In neighborhoods plagued by incinerators, leaded paint, hazardous waste facilities, inadequate housing and health care, and scarce open space, urban gardens and farms transform blighted areas into vibrant green ones, absorb organic urban waste, and reduce dependency on fossil fuels by decreasing the distance from field to table (Kass and McCarroll 1999). In neighborhoods that lack decent supermarkets, food cultivation reduces pressure on limited family budgets and increases the intake of much-needed fresh fruits and vegetables. Community gardening provides an excellent venue for education about nutrition and food preparation, creates a focus for community activity, empowers residents, and fosters neighborhood development.

Strengthening the Food System

Supermarkets have abandoned many low-income communities. The markets that remain tend to be relatively small, with a narrow selection of lower-quality goods and services, and they charge higher prices due to lack of competition and higher operating costs (Weinberg 1999). Residents without cars who want to shop outside the community often must choose between expensive taxi rides and making multiple bus transfers while laden with grocery bags (Ashman et. al. 1993). Low-income, inner-city residents across the United States find it particularly difficult to obtain fresh produce (Rinehart 1999a; Weinberg 1999). Poor access to affordable, nutritious food aggravates malnutrition and hunger and contributes to such health problems as diabetes, hypertension, obesity, and cancer. Despite the recent economic boom, the longest in U.S. history, more than 30 million people around the country still suffer from food insecurity and hunger (Center on Hunger and Poverty 2000). A Tufts University study found that poor children ages five and younger consume less than 70 percent of the recommended daily allowance of 10 out of 16 nutrients and consequently are at risk for impairments in growth, cognition, and immunity (Cook and Martin 1995).

In this context, urban gardens provide a crucial source of fresh, nutritious produce at relatively low cost. A study by the Philadelphia Urban Gardening Project found that most urban gardeners ate fresh produce from their gardens five months of the year (Rinehart 1999a). Sixty-two percent preserved some of the yield for off-season consumption, too. Most growers shared the harvest regularly with relatives and neighbors, and more than 40 percent of them donated food to a local church or community organization. For families dependent upon food banks and shelters, donations of local produce often provide their only access to fresh food. In Missoula, Montana, to cite another example, Garden City Harvest supplied the local food bank with 20,000 pounds of produce in 1999 and also gave to the city's emergency food programs.

Urban gardening and agriculture can be highly productive. Yields vary widely depending on inputs, resources, and know-how. But with intercropping and intensive farming techniques that maximize use of both horizontal and vertical space, urban agriculture can yield far more output per acre than conventional rural agriculture. The French *marais* method of gardening—characterized by double-dug, raised beds with heavy applications of manure and compost—can produce huge amounts of produce from a small space year-round in soil that is heated by decomposition of the organic fertilizers (Smit et al. 1996). To use vertical space, urban farmers can plant crops in containers and stack them in pyramids. Plants also can be grown on walls and trellises, providing shade as well as crops. The use of containers and walls can effectively triple the productive farm acreage. And greenhouses, through labor-intensive techniques, can produce 15 to 20 times more per acre than crops grown under normal field conditions (Lockeretz 1987).

Learning about Nutrition and Food Preparation

Urban gardens and farms offer opportunities for educating local residents about nutrition and the preparation of meals with fresh ingredients. The Sustainable Food Center in Austin, Texas, serves as a good example. As part of its program, the center sponsors farmers' markets in low-income communities, where people can buy fresh produce using coupons from the federal Women, Infants, and Children (WIC) program. WIC customers buy more than 85 percent of the produce sold. After staff learned that many residents, particularly young mothers, were using their WIC coupons to purchase only fruit, because they did not know how to prepare vegetables, the center began its cooking program. Free classes demonstrate how to grow, buy, and prepare healthful, inexpensive, and satisfying meals; topics include budgeting, shopping, hygiene, nutrition, child development and disease, and menu planning. The center incorporates local volunteer trainers to increase community skills and allow for low-cost expansion, and it also works with a local volunteer organization that assists residents in starting backyard gardens.

Youth Programs and Job Training

Urban gardens and farms offer an especially attractive arena for programs serving low-income youth. Here are a few examples:

- The All People's Garden, founded in 1978 in Manhattan, runs a program for juvenile first offenders, a teen drug prevention project, a Head Start program for 4- to-12-year-olds, and a program that connects youth with local artists.
- The cooperative extension service at Ohio State University runs an alternative sentencing program in conjunction with the Cuyahoga County Juvenile Court. Judges can send juvenile offenders to a youth garden to work off the hours they have to serve. The program is so successful that there are plans to expand the garden to cover a whole city block.
- Green Oasis, also in Manhattan, involves youth in community activities, promotes self-esteem and civic pride, and set up a junior board of directors to foster organizational and managerial skills.
- The Children's Aid Society in Cleveland, Ohio, runs a residential treatment center for children from abusive environments. Gardening has been integral to the program since the society was formed in 1832. In the beginning, the garden simply provided the kitchen with food; today, it also offers therapeutic activity for the children. The goal is to give each child an experience of

success, with each child's plot becoming his or her land to foster a sense of ownership, control, and responsibility (Ohio State University 1999).

- In communities with high rates of joblessness and underemployment, urban gardens and farms have proved excellent vehicles for job training. Berkeley Youth Alternatives (BYA) offers such training at its half-acre farm in West Berkeley, California. Youth raise and sell vegetables, herbs, and flowers. They also propagate nursery seedlings in two greenhouses. Most of the produce is sold at the weekly local farmers' market. In addition, flower bouquets are sold to local businesses and seedlings are sold to stores and landscapers. Teens earn $6 per hour, working 15 to 20 hours per week during the school year and 20 to 30 hours per week in the summer. All the teens come from low-income families; most give their paychecks to their parents. Participants must be in school to work in the garden, and tutoring is available year-round for those who need it.
- Re-Vision House, a home for teen mothers in Worcester, Massachusetts, runs a garden and a three-story greenhouse. In addition to growing food for themselves and their children, the young women sell produce at the farmers' market and seedlings to other urban gardeners. They also grow fish in an aquaculture project and hold fish fries for the community.
- The Sustainable Food Center in Austin, Texas, employs at-risk youth at its farmers' markets. The work provides young people with much-needed income while enhancing their skills in customer service, financial management, retailing, and food handling.
- The Green Guerrillas Youth Environmental Fellowship trains young people in community leadership skills and environmental education. It provides job opportunities for youth as they prepare for academic or professional careers related to the environment.

Prisoner Rehabilitation

Some job training programs are designed specifically for prisoners. One of the oldest is San Francisco's Garden Project, started in 1982 by Catherine Sneed and Sheriff Michael Hennessy. The project runs a farm on public land next to the San Francisco County jail, and a half-acre garden on a private parcel in Bayview Hunter's Point, a predominantly African-American neighborhood. Inmates learn farming and job skills and receive support in breaking drug and alcohol addictions. Upon release, they are offered the option of working at the smaller parcel in Bayview Hunter's Point. Some of the produce is sold to fine restaurants in the area; the rest is donated to Bayview Hunter's Point residents and area soup kitchens.

More than 10,000 prisoners have come through the San Francisco program. Despite their criminal records, many of these men and women have found jobs, after their release from prison, in the city's tree-maintenance program, in restaurants, and in other positions related to urban gardening. A 1992 study found that graduates had substantially lower recidivism rates than the general population at the county jail. Of 390 participants studied, only 6 percent were rearrested within four months of release, compared to 29 percent of their peers. Only 24 percent were rearrested within two years of release, compared to 55 percent of the general prison population (American Jails 1996).

Another initiative to rehabilitate prisoners is the Greenhouse Project, sponsored and funded by the Horticultural Society of New York. Located on a 1.5-acre parcel behind the Rose M. Singer jail for women in the Rikers jail complex, the project gives inmates a refuge from the pressures of prison life, where most are awaiting trial or serving sentences of less than a year. Staff teach the inmates self-discipline and organizational skills that will be useful for a wide range of jobs. Some participants have gone on to work with plants, several enrolling in the professional horticulture training program at the New York Botanical Garden (Gardiner 1999).

Reversing Blight

Throughout the United States, urban gardens and farms have taken over empty, debris-filled lots that had been neglected for years. Many of these lots were contaminated due to years of industrial use or illegal dumping. Growers have transformed these properties into vibrant green spaces. Waste and toxic soil have been removed or buried, and once-idle land has become productive as seeds and trees have been planted. In these areas, the gardens have promoted social networks and helped to revitalize neighborhoods.

In Manhattan, for example, Brises del Caribe created a garden out of an abandoned 90-foot by 24-foot lot on the Lower East Side, once strewn with refuse and inhabited by drug addicts and dealers. The plot, now covered with trees and plants, features a pool with goldfish and two wooden cabanas built from scavenged materials. Latino residents not only run the garden but also sponsor cultural, educational, and social programs for children in the local school. In Ohio, more than 3,000 community volunteers help to organize and manage 212 gardens, which have replaced 53 acres of vacant land and yield an annual harvest valued at $1.2 million (Ohio State University 1999).

Such green spaces offer a welcome and healing respite to urbanites overwhelmed by noise, movement, and visual stimulation. A study by a University of Michigan psychologist found that one of the primary benefits of gardening was tranquility; a study at the University of Illinois revealed that people shown urban scenes with vegetation recovered more quickly from stress; and a 1990 study concluded that cancer patients engaged in restorative activities, including gardening, recovered more quickly than those who were more passive (Malakoff 1994).

Environmental Protection

Urbanization has taken a heavy toll on the environment. In his article "Why Urban Agriculture?" William Rees (1997) describes how locally integrated ecological systems have been replaced by horizontally disintegrated throughput systems, disrupting the recycling of wastes into the farms and forestlands where they are needed. Urban agriculture can help to redress this imbalance by recycling organic matter and nutrients that would otherwise go to waste in landfills and/or pollute ground and surface waters. It can thereby reduce reliance on the fertilizers and pesticides typically used in industrial food production.

Before modern sanitation systems were developed in the late nineteenth century, urban agriculture was the principal method for treatment and disposal of urban wastes. By diverting organic waste from dumps and landfills and using it to make compost, urban agriculture can reduce stress on local and regional waste management systems. Compost enriches soil and increases its ability to hold and retain moisture. Because urban produce is sold close to the land where it is raised, transportation and storage costs are minimal, reducing the consumption of fossil fuels (Rodrigues and Lopez-Real 1999).

Urban gardening is one strategy for confronting the environmental injustice arising from the fact that low-income communities suffer from disproportionate levels of toxins and unwanted land uses. Various techniques are available to clean up vacant lots contaminated by previous industrial or commercial uses or by heavy traffic nearby. One method is simply to remove the toxic soil and replace it with clean soil; but this can be expensive, and sites to dispose of the contaminated soil are often hard to find. If all the tainted soil cannot be removed, growers may create a series of raised beds, built from clean soil, possibly with barriers to prevent root growth into the contaminated layers. Another technique is phytoremediation, a process that uses specially selected plants and trees to gradually detoxify soil by absorbing contaminants and neutralizing, containing, or releasing them into the atmosphere.

Community Development

Urban gardens promote community development in a variety of less tangible, but no less important, ways. They foster cohesion, local leadership, and pride of place (Payne and Fryman 1999). They build links between farmers and consumers (Gottlieb and Fisher 2000) and, in so doing, change their ideas about the environment and encourage a stronger sense of responsibility for their local ecosystem (Kirschenmann 1998). They offer a place to meet, play, and hold festivals and workshops. A member of New York's Jardin de Los Amigos says the garden serves as a combination day-care center and recreation hall, a place where people talk, play bingo, and hold baby showers.

Recent studies suggest that community gardens and farms help to reduce inner-city crime. A 1993 study for the Merck Family Fund found that after a Philadelphia police officer started a community garden, burglaries and thefts in the vicinity plummeted from about 40 incidents per month to 4. The Trust for Public Land reported a 28 percent drop in crime around a new garden in San Francisco's Mission District after its first year, as the garden led to the formation of a Neighborhood Watch group, and the place was no longer attractive to drug dealers (Harvest of Pride 1999).

Manhattan's Green Oasis was created in 1981 when community residents cleared five abandoned, crime-ridden lots on the Lower East Side. They replaced rubble and rusting cars with a playground, a picnic area with a pond, a barbecue pit, vegetable plots, honey-producing beehives, a grape arbor, and a gazebo. All these areas are wheelchair accessible, and raised beds are designed so that people with special needs can garden, too. Realizing from the beginning that gardening was not enough to create an alternative to the streets for neighborhood youth, the founders of Green Oasis went on to develop an arts and theater program. Members of the group now share their expertise with local schools and city programs, including the Manhattan Alternatives to Incarceration Program, City Volunteer Corps, New York Cares, Summer Youth of the Board of Education, United Cerebral Palsy, and community senior centers.

Recent research reveals that urban gardening and agriculture can enhance a neighborhood's political power. A study at Northwestern University reported that through gardening projects, low-income residents gain access to government and economic resources and get the chance to meet officials in public and private nonprofit agencies (Bjornson 1994). Building on the sense of power and enthusiasm generated when neighbors apply their talents and resources toward common goals, one community effort can lead to others. Recognizing this broader potential, the American Community Garden Association has developed a program to train low-income residents in community development. Its "From the Roots Up" program provides mentoring and technical assistance to city-wide gardening organizations and coalitions. Participants learn how to establish a board of directors, conduct grassroots fundraising and strategic planning, foster leadership skills, and launch programs in environmental education and entrepreneurship.

Making It Happen: Financial and Institutional Support

Urban gardens and farms rely on help from public and nonprofit organizations. Growers need access to land. They need material inputs: a water system, soil, compost, seeds, and tools. They need capital improvements and repairs: fences, toolsheds, and raised beds. They need management: office work, community outreach, and advocacy to sustain property and funding. They need a system of governance and a plan for distributing plots. They need training in horticulture and organizational leadership. Public and nonprofit agencies can provide support for all these tasks (Johnson 2000a).

Public-Sector Agencies

Federal assistance to urban gardens has waxed and waned over the years. The earliest aid dates from the 1890s, when the government sponsored gardening programs to alleviate poverty. The Victory Gardens of World War II gave a great boost to urban agriculture. After the war, however, public-sector support withered as competition for urban land increased and the government promoted commercially processed food in an effort to build the market economy.

A new wave of interest came in the late 1970s, when the U.S. Department of Agriculture set up an urban gardening program that initially targeted 6 of the nation's poorest cities and was later extended to 23 cities (Rinehart 1999b). The initiative met with great success, involving 150,000 growers, but eventually it was severely weakened when the total appropriation was cut and the money was spread among all the states, leaving the original programs without the bulk of their funds. More recently, Congress passed the Community Food Security Act in 1995, offering one-time infusions of capital for urban gardens and farms through 2002, in an effort to promote local solutions to hunger. In addition, Community Development Block Grants sometimes have been used to support urban gardening projects, especially by funding capital improvements.

Agricultural extension services based at public universities have provided strong support to some urban gardens. Their involvement has varied from state to state, with the federal government supporting extension services only if the state chooses to provide matching funds. The gardening program of the Ohio State University Extension (OSUE) is active in seven counties, particularly Cuyahoga County, which includes the city of Cleveland. Since the mid-1970s, OSUE has worked with the Cleveland Division of Neighborhood Services to provide city gardens with basic materials and technical advice. The extension service offers technical assistance and lends hydrant equipment and garden hose adapters. The city also contributes seeds, plants, fertilizer, soil amendments, rototilling, and a reduced rate for water supplies. In an interagency collaboration, the city, OSUE, and the Ohio National Guard work together to truck composted manure from the Cleveland Metroparks Zoo to the city's juvenile offenders' garden. The vast majority of the gardens are in the city's poorest enclaves, and most of them serve neighborhood residents. Others are at elementary schools and social service agencies, including the housing authority, the Children's Aid Society, and a nursing home. All told, according to urban agriculture extension officer Dennis Rinehart, in 1997 volunteers in Cleveland coordinated the planting of 184 sites covering more than 42 acres.

The cooperative extension service at the University of Georgia similarly has an active urban gardening program, working with more than 200 gardens in Fulton and De Kalb counties, including Atlanta. The gardens are located at centers for troubled youth, mental health facilities, public and private schools, preschools, senior centers, summer camps, churches, and public housing communities. Extension staff provide instruction and technical assistance in the areas of food production, meal preparation, household budgeting, environmental issues, recycling, leadership development, and entrepreneurship (Wilson 2000).

Access to Land

Finding and keeping land is one of the biggest challenges for urban growers. They often find small bits of open space to cultivate: side yards, balconies, rooftops, containers. But to grow crops on any scale, they have to compete for land with businesses, housing developers, and transportation planners. Needless to say, both markets and public officials usually judge these other uses to be of higher value (Mbiba 1995). As land becomes scarcer, gardeners can easily lose their plots.

In Cleveland, as elsewhere, many of the urban gardens use properties confiscated by the city because of delinquent taxes. In other cases, gardeners obtain permission from an individual owner to use a lot; they typically must renew their permit annually. Since owners of vacant lots are responsible for weed removal and general maintenance of their property, they risk a municipal fine if they fail to keep it up; thus, they have an incentive to allow the neighborhood to care for the land as a garden.

Perhaps the best way to secure land for the long term, however, is through land trusts. These are nonprofit organizations dedicated to acquiring and protecting land for community purposes, whether for scenic, recreational, natural, historic, residential, or productive value. Trusts can acquire land through purchases or donations. Owners who sell property to the trust at less than its full market value can receive tax benefits. In some cases, the owner will donate the land but continue to live on it (Land Trust Alliance 1999). In other instances, the land trust will not own the land outright but will purchase an easement, a legal agreement that restricts the use of the land to agreed purposes.

In New York City, the Trust for Public Land plans to transfer ownership of its 63 gardens to newly created borough land trusts, which will own the land permanently. The borough trusts are nonprofit corporations, with neighborhood gardeners filling the majority of seats on the boards of directors. Community gardeners will enter into use agreements with the borough land trusts, allowing them to cultivate the land as long as they meet certain standards.

Drinking alcohol on-site is prohibited, for example, and each garden must consult with the board of the borough trust before building any structure (Stone 2000).

Land trusts also have helped to protect urban gardens in Boston. In 1986, after losing one garden to a city housing initiative, growers got organized. Representatives from the South End and Lower Roxbury neighborhoods persuaded city officials to donate some land that the city had acquired for urban renewal through eminent domain. The neighborhoods set up a land trust that bought the property for the nominal sum of $1 per parcel. Following this lead, other nonprofit organizations around the city—including another neighborhood land trust and a community development corporation—moved to acquire property for gardens. In 1994 these organizations together owned nearly 60 gardens, and they came together to form the Garden Futures Collaborative (Johnson 2000b).

Where such ownership strategies are not feasible, an alternative strategy for community gardeners is to secure a lease to city property. Berkeley Youth Alternatives has this sort of arrangement, paying the city of Berkeley a nominal $1 per year to work the land along the right-of-way of the historic Santa Fe railroad. Leaseholders are vulnerable, however, and often need to mobilize politically to maintain their leases. In Berkeley, for example, the growers became concerned when the city sold off a parcel of the Santa Fe right-of-way to individual homeowners. After pressing the city council, Berkeley Partners for Parks and the Berkeley Community Gardening Collaborative won an agreement that the city would cease sales and maintain the right-of-way as open space. One way to make leases more secure is to place public land under the protection of the city department of parks and recreation. In New York City, for example, growers and local representatives successfully pressed the city to transfer about 55 community gardens to the parks department.

Another strategy is to use land owned by a private or public institution, such as a church, school, university, or business. A prominent Cleveland businessman donates use of his land for the alternative sentencing program at Cuyahoga County Juvenile Court. Similarly, the Garden Project sponsored by the San Francisco County jail uses a half-acre parcel donated by the owner of a well-known Bay Area bakery.

Drawing on Multiple Sources

For many urban farms, success requires that they draw on multiple sources of support and prove flexible enough to respond when conditions change. Garden City Harvest, in Missoula, Montana, is a good example. The program grew out of a city coalition representing federally funded nutrition programs such as WIC, food stamps, and emergency feeding. Mary Pittaway, WIC director for Missoula, says the group was interested in working with people who were tired of being on welfare and had dropped out of social services. The coalition saw community gardens as an alternative way to improve access to food. Beginning with an existing community garden, the coalition successfully attracted low-income families, and it now operates five gardens on land borrowed or rented from private and public parties, including the Salvation Army, the Catholic church, and a private bank that donated a piece of its lawn.

In addition, Garden City Harvest now has a farm founded on the model of community supported agriculture (CSA). CSA farms are based on the Japanese *teikei* concept, in which consumers buy food directly from a local farmer (Kneen 1995). Each year, members of the CSA farm purchase a share of the harvest, providing upfront capital to cover production costs, in return for which they receive a weekly supply of produce. They may also contribute some volunteer time. Shares in the Garden Harvest CSA are sold on an income-based sliding scale, from $180 to $350 per season. The CSA farm is located on land belonging to the University of Montana that was once part of the historic Fort Missoula.

For three years, Garden City Harvest relied on federal support through the Community Food Security Act. When this grant ended in 1999, the United Way stepped forward, and churches organized volunteers to work in the gardens devoted to the local food bank. There was no longer enough money to support an executive director, so the garden coordinator assumed a broader leadership role. Staff members are now working to make the project more self-sufficient. Using 12 acres of park land being made available by the county, Garden City Harvest will launch a commercial farm venture with the hope of generating enough income to sustain the rest of the organization.

Holcomb Farm, near Hartford, Connecticut, has also achieved some degree of self-sufficiency through the CSA model, with membership fees covering 85–90 percent of operating costs. The farm relies on grants and other donations to cover additional expenses, including administration, education, and capital improvements. The land is leased from the city of West Granby, which received the farmland in 1980 as a bequest from the Holcomb family. Holcomb Farm collaborates with the Hartford Food System Project, an antipoverty organization. Many of the shares in the farm are purchased by community organizations that combat hunger, agencies that might otherwise be paying comparable fees to a local food bank. The farm solicits donations to subsidize the cost of bulk shares for these institutional members. According to the farm's 1998 annual report, 216 households and 13 organizations partook of the harvest, and the agencies distributed produce to more than 1,500 low-income families in Hartford.

Conclusion: "Greenlining" for Community-Based Urban Development

Gardens and farms can make unique contributions to urban communities. With adequate support from government agencies and philanthropies, they can supply nutritious food at a low price, helping to reduce poverty and improve public health. They can help to restore and protect the environment. They can beautify neighborhoods and make them more livable. They can stimulate business development, reduce crime, and foster social connections and pride of place. Marti Ross Bjornson (1994) has coined the term *greenlining* to describe the synergistic benefits of community gardening, in contrast to redlining, the practice of discrimination in mortgage lending.

Without a partnership of public and private institutions, however, urban gardening will be continually under threat. In New York City, residents mobilized to press public officials to block the sale of gardens, and this mobilization in turn opened the door for private foundations and nonprofits to step forward to buy the land. With a similar combination of community mobilization, supportive public policy, and philanthropic backing, urban agriculture can continue to contribute both to the greening of our cities and the reduction of poverty.

Acknowledgments

Thanks to Danny Engelberg, George Hadley, Betsy Johnson, Karen Payne, Howard Pinderhughes, Ximena Naranjo, Anna Maria Signorelli, Andy Stone, Beebo Turnman, and Bobby Wilson for their assistance in preparing this chapter.

References

Ashman, L., J. de la Vega, M. Dohan, A. Fisher, R. Hippler, and B. Romain. 1993. *Seeds of Change: Strategies for Food Security in the Inner City*. Los Angeles: UCLA Urban Planning Program.

American Jails. 1996. Vol. 10, no. 4 (September/October).

Bjornson, Marti Ross. 1994. "Greenlining." Unpublished thesis, Northwestern University, Evanston, Illinois.

Gardiner, Beth. 1999. "Gardens Offer a Respite at Jail." Associated Press release. 8 March.

Gottlieb, Robert, and Andy Fisher. 2000. "Community Food Security and Environmental Justice." *Race, Poverty and the Environment* 8:2.

Green Guerrillas. 1999. *Vitis Vine* (Winter).

Harvest of Pride. 1999. *Benefits of Community Gardening*. Lafayette, Calif.: Center for Health Design.

Johnson, Betsy. 2000a. "Description of the Weaknesses and Strengths of Land Trust Options." Unpublished manuscript. February.

Johnson, Betsy. 2000b. Personal communication. March.

Kass, Stephen, and Jean McCarroll. 1999. "Environmental Justice and Community Gardens." *New York Law Journal* (27 August).

Kirschenmann, Frederick. 1998. "Expanding the Vision of Sustainable Agriculture." In *Community Food Systems in California,* edited by Gail Feenstra and Dave Campbell. Davis: University of California, Davis, Division of Agriculture and Natural Resources.

Kneen, Brewster. 1995. "CSA Roots in Japan." *In Context: A Quarterly of Humane Sustainable Culture* (Fall).

Lockeretz, William, ed. 1987. *Sustaining Agriculture Near Cities.* Ankeny, Iowa: Soil and Water Conservation Society.

Malakoff, David. 1994. "Final Harvest? How the Federal Government's Urban Gardening Program, Which Served 23 of America's Poorest Inner Cities, Flourished—Then Faltered." *Community Greening Review.*

Mbiba, Beacon. 1995. *Urban Agriculture in Zimbabwe.* Brookfield, Vt.: Avebury.

Payne, Karen, and Deborah Fryman. 1999. "Principles and Practices for Using Community Gardens as a Tool for Community Development in Low-Income Neighborhoods." Unpublished manuscript. American Community Garden Association.

Rinehart, Dennis. 1999a. "Harvest of Pride: A resource for community vegetable gardeners." *Common Ground,* vol. 5, no. 11 (November).

———. 1999b. Personal communication.

Rodrigues, M. S., and J. M. Lopez-Real. 1999. "Urban Organic Wastes, Urban Health and Sustainable Urban and Peri-Urban Agriculture: Linking Urban and Rural by Composting." Urban Agriculture Notes web site. Vancouver, B.C.: City Farmer, Canada's Office of Urban Agriculture. Available at http://www.cityfarmer.org/urbanwastes.html.

Smit, Jac, Annu Rattu, and Joe Nasr. 1996. *Urban Agriculture: Food, Jobs and Sustainable Cities.* Publication series for Habitat II, vol. 1. New York: UN Development Program Publications.

Stone, Andy. 2000. Personal communication. March.

Weinberg, Zy. 2000. "No Place to Shop: Food Access Lacking in the Inner City." *Race, Poverty and the Environment* 7 (Winter): 2.

Wilson, Bobby. 2000. "A Comprehensive Look at the Urban Gardening Program of the University of Georgia Cooperative Extension Program." Unpublished report.

About the Contributors

PETER BARNES is a writer and entrepreneur who has started and guided several socially responsible companies. Barnes's first business, The Solar Center, pioneered in providing solar-heated water to apartment buildings in the San Francisco Bay area. In 1983 he cofounded Working Assets Money Fund, one of the first socially screened investment funds, and in 1985 created the Working Assets Visa Card. Barnes is a founding member of the Social Venture Network and Businesses for Social Responsibility and serves on the boards of Greenpeace International, the Noise Pollution Clearinghouse, and TV-Free America. He is the author of *Who Owns the Sky? Our Common Assets and the Future of Capitalism* (Island Press, 2001) and *The People's Land: A Primer on Land Reform in the U.S.* (Rodale, 1974). At present, Barnes directs the Common Assets Project at the Corporation for Enterprise Development.

CONSTANCE BEST is managing director and cofounder of the Pacific Forest Trust (PFT), a nonprofit organization dedicated to conservation and steward-ship in private forests of the Pacific Northwest, with a focus on northern California, Oregon, and Washington. The author of numerous papers on the intersections of forest conservation and commerce, in the last five years she has helped PFT to conserve more than 15,000 acres of private forestland and to provide conservation advisory services to owners of more than 750,000 acres of forestland. In addition, Ms. Best led the company that created Soho Natural Soda, the first "alternative" soft drink in the United States. She serves on several boards, including the national Land Trust Alliance and the Investor's Circle, an association of socially responsible venture capitalists.

NICOLAAS W. BOUWES has been one of the principal investigators of the U.S. Environmental Protection Agency's Risk Screening Environmental Indicators Project since its inception in 1991. He is chief of the Economics and Environmental Assessments Branch in the EPA's Office of Water, prior to which he was a senior economist in the Office of Pollution Prevention and

Toxics. He has worked on a wide range of projects, including studies to develop methodologies for the estimation of socioeconomic impacts for regulatory impact analyses, environmental justice issues, and chemical market and use studies. Dr. Bouwes has also consulted for the World Bank and has taught at the University of Wisconsin, Northern Virginia Community College, and in Eastern Europe.

JAMES K. BOYCE is a professor of economics at the University of Massachusetts, Amherst, and director of the Program on Development, Peacebuilding, and the Environment at the Political Economy Research Institute. His books include *The Political Economy of the Environment* (Edward Elgar, 2002), *The Philippines: The Political Economy of Growth and Impoverishment in the Marcos Era* (Macmillan, 1993), *Agrarian Impasse in Bengal: Institutional Constraints to Technological Change* (Oxford University Press, 1987), and *A Quiet Violence: View from a Bangladesh Village* (coauthored with Betsy Hartmann, Zed Books, 1983).

MARC D. BRESLOW is research director at Northeast Action, in Boston, Massachusetts, and cochair of the Massachusetts Climate Action Network. Previously he was coeditor of *Dollars and Sense,* an economics magazine based in Somerville, Massachusetts. He has also been employed as a research associate by the Tellus Institute for Resource and Environmental Strategies and as a research analyst by the Philadelphia City Council. Breslow is the author of numerous studies on topics including federal and state fiscal policies, labor markets, environmental regulation, economic development, and the employment effects of environmental policies. He holds a Ph.D. in economics from the University of Massachusetts, Amherst.

DEBORAH BRIGHTON is a forester by education, but most of her work has been in public policy and economics. She has worked for the U.S. Forest Service and the Vermont Department of Forests and Parks as a systems analyst and has administered Vermont's program of preferential taxation for agricultural and forest land. She currently consults for the Vermont legislature on education funding reform and livable wage issues and for municipalities trying to find a balance between growth and conservation. She is chair of the Vermont Housing and Conservation Board, which receives money from a tax on land transfers and returns it to communities for affordable housing and land conservation.

STEPHEN B. BRUSH is a professor of human and community development at the University of California, Davis. He has worked in the field of international agricultural development for 30 years, beginning with service as a Peace

Corps volunteer in Peru (1965–1967). An anthropologist by training, his research focuses on the cultural ecology and resources of traditional agricultural systems. He has conducted long-term research in Peru, Mexico, and Turkey. He has studied the indigenous knowledge and maintenance of crop genetic diversity by potato farmers in the Andes of Peru, maize farmers in Mexico, and wheat farmers in Turkey. Brush was program director for anthropology at the National Science Foundation and senior scientist at the International Plant Genetic Resources Institute, where he helped to develop a worldwide program for on-farm conservation of genetic resources.

CECILIA DANKS is an assistant professor in the School of Natural Resources at the University of Vermont. From 1997 to 2001, she directed the Socioeconomic Monitoring and Assessment Program at the Watershed Research and Training Center in Hayfork, California. The Watershed Center is a nongovernmental organization that supports "healthy forests and healthy communities" through research, job training, and economic development. Dr. Danks is on the board of the Forest Stewardship Council-U.S. She has also worked on forestry issues in Latin America and Indonesia. She has a Ph.D. in Wildland Resource Science from the University of California, Berkeley.

K. A. DIXON is a project manager at the John J. Heldrich Center for Workforce Development at Rutgers University. Dixon coordinates the center's work on brownfields redevelopment, telework, and employment policies for people with disabilities. She is coauthor of the Heldrich Center's national study, *Turning Brownfields into Jobfields,* which focuses on the job-creating and community-building potential of brownfields redevelopment. Dixon received her master's degree in public policy from the Bloustein School at Rutgers, and she is currently pursuing a Ph.D. in public policy.

GERALD FRIEDMAN is a professor of economics at the University of Massachusetts, Amherst. He is the author of *State-Making and Labor Movements: France and the United States, 1876–1914* (Cornell University Press, 1999), as well as numerous articles on the economic and labor history of the United States and France. He is currently preparing a study of the origins of the social sciences in the United States, provisionally entitled *The Vanguard of the New: Richard Ely and John Bates Clark as Economists and Ideologists.*

STEVEN M. HASSUR has been a principal investigator of EPA's Risk-Screening Environmental Indicators Project since its inception in 1991. He is a senior chemist with the EPA's Office of Pollution Prevention and Toxics, where he has worked for 22 years on a wide variety of projects, including assessments under the Toxic Substances Control Act, pollution prevention activities, the development and application of "green chemistry," hazard communication guidelines, and environmental justice issues. Dr. Hassur developed the role of technical integrator for Emergency Planning and Community Right-to-Know Act, Section 313, Toxics Release Inventory Petitions, and conducted the first such reviews for the agency.

H. PATRICIA HYNES is a professor of public health at the Boston University School of Public Health and director of the Urban Environmental Health Initiative. An environmental engineer, she served as section chief in the Hazardous Waste Division of the U.S. Environmental Protection Agency and as chief of environmental management at the Massachusetts Port Authority. She won the Environmental Service Award of the Massachusetts Association of Conservation Commissions for her work in the EPA's Superfund program. As codirector of the Lead-Safe Yard Pilot Project, she received a Certificate of Merit from the U.S. Environmental Protection Agency. She is author of *The Recurring Silent Spring* (Pergamon, 1989), *EarthRight* (Prima, 1990), and *Taking Population out of the Equation: Reformulating I = PAT* (Institute on Women and Technology, 1993). Her latest book, *A Patch of Eden* (Chelsea Green, 1996), on community gardens in inner cities and their potential contribution to social justice and urban ecology, won the 1996 National Arbor Day Foundation Book Award.

WINONA LADUKE lives on the White Earth Reservation in Minnesota and is a member of the Mississippi Band of Anishinaabeg. She is the program director of the Honor the Earth Fund and the founding director of the White Earth Land Recovery Project. In 1988 she received the Reebok Human Rights Award. In 1994 she was named by *Time* magazine as one of America's most promising leaders under 40 years of age, and in 1997 she was named a "Woman of the Year" by *Ms.* magazine. She ran for vice president in the Green Party presidential campaigns of 1996 and 2000.

MANUEL PASTOR directs the Center for Justice, Tolerance, and Community at the University of California, Santa Cruz. His most recent book, *Regions That Work: How Cities and Suburbs Can Grow Together* (University of Minnesota Press, 2000), coauthored with Peter Dreier, Eugene Grigsby, and Marta Lopez-Garza, examines urban sprawl, poverty reduction, and environmental sustainability. He is currently working on environmental justice issues with support from the California Endowment and the California Policy Research Center, and he has published articles on this topic in *Social Science Quarterly, Economic Development Quarterly, The Journal of Urban Affairs,* and *Urban Affairs Review.*

DEVON G. PEÑA is a professor of anthropology, environmental studies, and Chicano studies at the University of Washington in Seattle. His books include

The Terror of the Machine: Technology, Work, Gender, and Ecology on the U.S.–Mexico Border (University of Texas, 1997) and *Chicano Culture, Ecology, Politics: Subversive Kin* (University of Arizona Press, 1998). Peña is the founder and research director of the Rio Grande Bioregions Project, an independent research network of social scientists, environmental scientists, farmers, and sustainable agriculture advocates dedicated to the study of native farming systems in the U.S. Southwest. He owns and manages a sustainable agriculture field research station in Colorado's San Luis Valley. Peña is currently completing a new book, *Gaia in Aztlan: The Politics of Place in the Rio Arriba* (forthcoming from the University of Arizona Press).

RAQUEL PINDERHUGHES is a professor and director of the Urban Studies Program at San Francisco State University. Her research focuses on community-level impacts of social inequality and poverty in the United States. Within this framework, her recent research has focused on the impact of race on environmental quality in residential communities; inequality in local food systems; and the role of urban agriculture in reducing poverty. She recently received a grant to compile case studies on existing urban sustainable development projects throughout the world.

MARC D. SHAPIRO works at ICF Consulting in the Environment, Transportation, and Emergency Management Division, specializing in environmental policy analysis and regulatory issues. In addition to working on environmental justice and the risk from toxic airborne chemical emissions, he has performed economic and econometric research on the costs of compliance with emission standards for off-road diesel engine vehicles and on the responsiveness of manufacturing facilities to enforcement activity under the Clean Air Act. Shapiro has played a central role in a research project analyzing air emission allowance allocation mechanisms in the utility industry, and he also has been involved in studies of the air quality effects of transit development.

BARRY G. SHELLEY is a Ph.D. candidate in the department of economics at the University of Massachusetts, Amherst. He previously studied theology and ethics at Harvard Divinity School. From 1988 to 1994, Shelley worked in El Salvador, primarily as coordinator for the Mennonite Central Committee, a faith-based organization that worked with Salvadoran communities to provide human rights monitoring, improve health and education services, and promote local initiatives for economic development.

PAUL TEMPLET is a professor of environmental studies at Louisiana State University and has been involved in environmental issues in Louisiana since 1969. He teaches environmental planning and management and conducts research on environmental management, risk assessment, energy analysis, and systems analysis of economic and environmental systems. He has developed and implemented coastal management programs in Louisiana and in American Samoa and served as Secretary of the Louisiana Department of Environmental Quality from 1988 to 1992.

GREG WATSON is the program director for the Massachusetts Renewable Energy Trust, which was created by a 1997 state law restructuring the electric utility industry, and is charged with accelerating the development of clean and renewable energy. From 1995 to 1999, Watson served as executive director of the Dudley Street Neighborhood Initiative, a community-based planning organization that was founded in 1984 in Roxbury, Massachusetts, to help revitalize the economically disenfranchised Dudley neighborhood. Watson previously served as Commissioner of the Massachusetts Department of Food and Agriculture; director of The Nature Conservancy's Eastern regional office; and executive director of the New Alchemy Institute, a nonprofit research and education center dedicated to developing environmentally sound approaches to agriculture. He serves on the boards of numerous organizations, including Ocean Arks International, the Henry A. Wallace Institute for Alternative Agriculture, and the E. F. Schumacher Society. Watson attended Tufts University, where he majored in civil engineering.

Index